LANGUAGE ENGINEERING AND TRANSLATION

AF770429

BENJAMINS TRANSLATION LIBRARY

The Benjamins Translation Library aims to stimulate academic research and training in translation studies, lexicography and terminology. The Library provides a forum for a variety of approaches (which may sometimes be conflicting) in a historical, theoretical, applied and pedagogical context. The Library includes scholarly works, reference books and post-graduate text books and readers in the English language.

ADVISORY BOARD

Jens Allwood (*Linguistics, University of Gothenburg*)
Mona Baker (*Universy of Birmingham and UMIST*)
Morton Benson (*Department of Slavic, University of Pennsylvania*)
Marilyn Gaddis Rose (*CRIT, Binghamton University*)
Yves Gambier (*Institute of Translation and Interpreting, Turku University*)
Daniel Gile (*ISIT, Paris*)
Ulrich Heid (*Computational Linguistics, University of Stuttgart*)
W. John Hutchins (*Library, University of East Anglia*)
José Lambert (*Catholic University of Louvain*)
Willy Martin (*Lexicography, Free University of Amsterdam*)
Alan Melby (*Linguistics, Brigham Young University*)
Makoto Nagao (*Electrical Engineering, Kyoto University*)
Roda Roberts (*School of Translation and Interpreting, University of Ottawa*)
Juan C. Sager (*Linguistics, UMIST, Manchester*)
María Julia Sainz (*Law School, Universidad de la República, Montevideo*)
Klaus Schubert (*Technical Translation, Fachhochschule Flensburg*)
Mary Snell-Hornby (*School of Translation & Interpreting, University of Vienna*)
Gideon Toury (*M. Bernstein Chair of Translation Theory, Tel Aviv University*)
Wolfram Wilss (*Linguistics, Translation and Interpreting, University of Saarland*)
Judith Woodsworth (*FIT Committee for the History of Translation, Concordia University, Montreal*)
Sue Ellen Wright (*Applied Linguistics, Kent State University*)

Volume 1

Juan C Sager

Language Engineering and Translation: Consequences of automation

LANGUAGE ENGINEERING AND TRANSLATION

CONSEQUENCES OF AUTOMATION

JUAN C. SAGER

JOHN BENJAMINS PUBLISHING COMPANY
AMSTERDAM/PHILADELPHIA

The paper used in this publication meets the minimum requirements of American National Standard for Information Sciences — Permanence of Paper for Printed Library Materials, ANSI Z39.48-1984.

Library of Congress Cataloging-in-Publication Data

Sager, Juan C.
Language engineering and translation : consequences of automation / Juan C. Sager.
p. cm. -- (Benjamins translation library ; v. 1)
Includes bibliographical references and indexes.
1. Translating and interpreting. 2. Computational linguistics. 3. Applied linguistics. 4. Communication. 5. Discourse analysis. I. Title. II. Series.
P306.2.S24 1993
418'.02--dc20 93-34837
ISBN 90 272 2139 1 (Eur.)/1-55619-476-5 (US) (Hb.; alk. paper) CIP
ISBN 90 272 2140 5 (Eur.)/1-55619-477-3 (US) (Pb.; alk. paper)

© Copyright 1994 - John Benjamins B.V.
No part of this book may be reproduced in any form, by print, photoprint, microfilm, or any other means, without written permission from the publisher.

John Benjamins Publishing Co. · P.O. Box 75577 · 1070 AN Amsterdam · The Netherlands
John Benjamins North America · 821 Bethlehem Pike · Philadelphia, PA 19118 · USA

Acknowledgements

This book is the outcome of my reflections about the essential elements for a translation theory capable of addressing the problems of the language industry. It seeks to bring together many traditional and several new ideas I consider necessary for the training of language engineers and mediators in courses which must combine computational linguistics and modern languages. My main purpose in writing this book stems from the dual recognition that potential translators need to be made aware of the technology available and likely to develop in future to support translation; and that potential language engineers and designers of machine translation systems need to acquire an understanding of what is involved in certain types of human translation.

A number of the themes and observations brought together here have appeared in tentative form in a number of my publications over several years and have been presented in lectures at Manchester and elsewhere.

I am indebted to the many students who have made a valuable contribution to my seminars on the various topics under discussion. A special word of gratitude must go to Peter F. McDonald of Salford University. Our joint research into communication theory and the nature of special languages forms the basis of chapter two. I am also grateful to several colleagues in my own department: to John McNaught for his advice regarding certain details of information technology and to Blaise Nkwenti-Azeh who read the manuscript and put my text and the figures into machine-readable form. Finally my heartfelt thanks to Wolfram Wilss whose writings on translation have proved a constant source of inspiration and who encouraged me at every stage of my exploration of the industrial aspects of translation.

Contents

CHAPTER TWO: COMMUNICATION THEORY FOR TRANSLATION

CHAPTER FIVE: THE AUTOMATED DIMENSION OF TRANSLATION

Abbreviations used:

AI	Artificial Intelligence
AL	Artificial Language
ASCII	American Standard Code for Information Interchange
BS	British Standards
CAD	Computer-Assisted Design
CALL	Computer-Assisted Language Learning
CALS	Computer-Aided Acquisition and Logistics Support Initiative
CAM	Computer-Assisted Manufacture
CB	Communicative Background
CD-ROM	Compact Disc with Read-Only Memory
CEC	Commission of the European Communities
CFE	Caterpillar Fundamental English
CL	Computational Linguistics
EAP	English for Academic Purposes
EC	European Communities
ECU	European Currency Unit
ESP	English for Specific Purposes
FAHQT	Fully Automatic High Quality Translation
FAX	Facsimile Transmission
FIT	International Federation of Translators
IEC	International Electrotechnical Commission
ILSAM	International Language for Service and Maintenance
INIST	Institut National pour l'Information Scientifique et Technique
IT	Information Technology
IUPAC	International Union for Pure and Applied Chemistry
ISO	International Organisation for Standardisation
KWIC	Key Word In Context
L	Language
MCE	Multinational Customized English
MT	Machine Translation
NL	Natural Language
NLP	Natural Language Processing
OCR	Optical Character Recognition
PACE	Perkins Approved Clear English
RL	Restricted Language
SGML	Standard Generalised Mark-up Language
SL	Source Language
TL	Target Language
UMIST	University of Manchester Institute of Science and Technology

Preface

Translation in an Industrial Setting

At a time when information technology has become a regular tool of technical translators in all aspects of their work, it is useful to place the activity of specialised translation into its appropriate environment and to describe it from the point of view of its role in the wider context of communication in which it occurs.

The main object of this book is therefore language in its confrontation with the environments in which it is used, the diverse uses to which languages are put and finally the industrial processes and products that can be associated with these uses of languages. While our concern with the phenomenon of language is as old as human memory, it is only the advancing sophistication of industrialisation at all other levels of our society that has forced us to take a functional view of languages which in its turn has prepared us for accepting languages as a suitable object for industrialisation.

Early approaches to languages were descriptive, with the exception of a few treatises on rhetoric. For many centuries the theoretical study of language and languages, namely linguistics, was then taken over by philosophers on the one hand and by the grammarians of prescriptive school primers on the other. In the 19th century two separate movements started to develop: one was the historical school of language description and reconstruction; the other was the natural science approach of minute observation, initially often based on historical evidence. With the growing importance given to the 'exact sciences' in the 20th century and under the influence of mathematics and philosophy a new concern with formal description of systems took root, regardless of their functions, which is reflected in current views of theoretical linguistics. On the other hand, the natural science approach led to the fragmentation of linguistics into its many applied branches of sociolinguistics, ethnolinguistics, psycholinguistics, lexicography, terminology, language acquisition etc., which have laid the foundations for an engineering view of language.

Once we believe that we have established not only the structure but also the functions of a natural phenomenon we can try to copy and reproduce it.

Language engineering started a little earlier than the even more complex field of genetic engineering, as a natural development of human exploration of the world. Language engineering can also be seen as a necessity in our endeavour to explain the increasing complexities of other forms of engineering and industrialisation to a wider public.

It is the purpose of this book to present and discuss the process of translation against this background and as part of interlingual communication in the late 20th century where translators work in quite different and more diverse modes than they did until now. The advent of automated alternatives to human translation has fundamentally affected the profession, its products and the relationship between translators and their clients. In order to account for this new situation this book widens the context in which translation is normally studied, re-examines the process of translation and analyses the manner in which the new tools affect the product of translation.

The analysis and description of a process and its product involves us in looking at existing theories and models in order to select those which are still adequate for the changed situation or to reformulate those which can be adapted. Theories, being abstractions, are the more useful the broader their field of application. Because of its many ramifications into linguistics, pragmatics, psychology, communication theory, etc., a general theory of translation risks, however, becoming overburdened with detail. It is therefore desirable to be selective in the factors to be included in order to keep the theory simple and still generally valid. Nevertheless, the number of facets to be considered is quite wide-ranging. An eminent theorist (Wilss 1989) lists factors as diverse as context, culture, originality, speed and the cognitive components of the process itself as the basic facets.

In a scientific environment theories about human activities and their outcome are established in two different ways:

(a) We can observe examples of the process and its products in an attempt to generalise and evolve a theory, in the same way as the biological sciences have evolved from observation. Communication and its instrument, language, are constantly changing and adapting to the environment in the manner of an evolving organism, and may very conveniently be examined in this way. The same applies to the product of translation, which is simply a particular manifestation of the phenomenon of language.

(b) Another approach would start from a general theory of communication, the particular applicability of which would be tested against the analysis of human behaviour in the process called 'translation'. In return, the conformity of 'translation' to such a theory could be assessed.

The history of human translation is rich in analyses of particular manifestations of translation products. The result of this experience, however, can only be exploited with some difficulty because insufficient attention is normally being paid to the human factor which accounts for translators producing different translated versions of the same text. For machine translation, on the other hand, there is only limited experience available and what there is, cannot be considered definitive. It is therefore necessary to adopt the opposite approach and formulate a theory of machine translation, based on the experience of the theory of human translation, which will then have to be corroborated by examples of machine translation or by specifications of existing and speculation about future systems and products.

In order to arrive at a satisfactory theory a number of models are examined and developed. Two ways of modelling translations are available:

— starting from translation as a product, in which case there may be as many modes for getting from source language (SL) to target language (TL) text as there are distinctly definable products; this usually involves a comparison of source and target language texts independent of their use.

— starting from the translation process, leading possibly to a diversity of products; in this case the emphasis is on the phases of the process which diverge in order to achieve a particular, pre-specified product.

Both approaches are adopted at different stages in this exploration of human and machine translation.

In this attempt at providing an industrially oriented analysis of translation we are particularly aware of a number of critical issues.

Existing theories of translation do not make a fundamental distinction between human and machine techniques of production. Nor is there much recognition of the difference between end products with respect to either form or function. On the contrary, most current writing pretends to measure the machine output against the human product, without having a clear definition of what the standard of comparison should be, when there are indeed variously acceptable human versions to be accounted for.

A theory which says something about how one gets from a source language text to a target language text, must justify the stages in this process and must describe these stages in terms of reception and production, cognitive units, psychological processes, matching of equivalents, etc.

Such a theory must also provide criteria for relating the source and the target language texts, i.e. the degree of dependency between the two texts must be established.

If such a theory is to be useful in an industrial environment it must, finally, deal with evaluation in all its many aspects, namely: evaluation of the process, evaluation of the product as text and as message in communication.

Chapter One

The Language Industry and its Raw Material

1 The Language Industry and Translation

1.1 The industrialisation of communication

The basic condition of industrialising a human work process by creating either an automatic or semi-automatic alternative, i.e. a complete or partial substitution for a human process, must be that it is useful and that we can derive direct and tangible benefits from it. These benefits may be expected in the quality of the end product, in the greater cost effectiveness of the process, in the speed of operation, or in some other advantage. At the same time we can anticipate that the industrial process itself will eventually yield other products, which could not have been achieved by conventional human methods.

The industrialisation of communication is the result of the technification of our society and the extraordinary value information has acquired in the process. The new importance of communication and information has introduced new techniques of interpersonal communication and ultimately thereby essentially affected language itself. This development has in turn produced a need for new linguistic products, new language-related professions and new forms of communicative organisation.

We can demonstrate this evolution by a number of social changes which have affected our linguistic habits:

— The rapid evolution of science and technology has produced vast numbers of new concepts which require new multilingual designations and compilation in lexical databases.
— Technological growth has invaded all aspects of society and has led to new economic activities, many of which are dependent on efficient communications and reliable information. Consequently new types of information arise with their own new modes of communication.
— International political, cultural and economic relations have grown considerably and require interlingual contacts beyond the traditional patterns of translation.

— Mass production of consumer goods demands ever larger markets. Consequently there is a move to supra- and international markets dominated by multinational companies with their own multilingual communication requirements.
— Large-scale production is a consequence of and now also a motivating force for standardisation of objects and consequently of language.
— The transfer of knowledge and the exchange of products leads to the creation of a multilingual market for scientific, technical and cultural information. The information market itself has a requirement for standardisation of its constituent elements, including language, which facilitate the exchange or transfer.
— Language itself has become a commodity in the cultural market in which there is now greater consciousness of and willingness to preserve linguistic differences as signs of separate cultural identity. States are now more respectful of their linguistic diversity and many have adopted bi- or multilingual regimes where before there was only one official language.

All these developments have significant effects on the subject of our concern. Information, the substance of communication, therefore grows in importance; the large quantities of information assembled need efficient and powerful support as well as maintenance. Databases are continually updated and need easy and multipurpose access to become economically viable. This encourages efforts towards standardisation of data storage, retrieval and transfer systems. The development of mass media of communication permits a wide distribution of specialised information to a large lay public for which modes of access and instruments have to be designed. With greater numbers of the population participating in communication, and a greater diversity of cultural aspirations having to be satisfied, many governments now actively engage in language planning, thus providing public resources for the development and application of tools of the language industry.

1.2 The scope of 'Language Industry'

'Language industry', is, in the first instance, a loan translation from the French 'Les industries de la langue'. But, like so many slogans it combines the deceptive ease of internationalisms with an, at least initial, semantic vacuity. So we have to interpret the possible meanings of the juxtaposition of these two nouns. Is the language industry an industry 'for' or 'of' language? What are the raw materials of this industry, what are the products or services it provides?

1.2.1 *Support industry*

On the one hand, there has always been a support industry for all manner of communication which has also benefited interpreting and translating. The first major industrialisation of communication came with the invention of printing, which can be called the first support industry for language. The telephone, the wireless, the dictaphone, the typewriter and telex and, more recently fax, word-processors and electronic mail are all tools that we have used to overcome the barriers of time and distance in communication. They are now part of our everyday lives. But they are only tools for human use and do not directly help to overcome the biggest barrier of all, that of a second language, which is the raison d'être of translation.

1.2.2 *Industry for processing languages*

If we interpret language industry as products and processes that manipulate or help us to manipulate language then we are looking at a new industry dependent on computers. Two alternative lines of research have led to industrial developments. If the issues involved are seen from the point of view of linguistics, it is Computational Linguistics (CL) that offers solutions. If, however, the problems are seen from the viewpoint of applications of computer technology, we are in the field of Natural Language Processing (NLP), which is considered part of Information Technology (IT).

While the importance of Information Technology is widely recognised and associated with advances in computers, videos, satellite transmission and a host of other innovations, few directly associate this work with language, as identified in the new term 'Language Industry'. Yet language is at the basis of it all and language specialists are occupying a very important position in this process. In fact, the more we advance in IT the more we move into the domain of language and are therefore aware of the difficulties encountered by computers in the process of handling language.

1.2.3 *Industry for the production of languages*

A third interpretation of language industry is an industry which:

(a) produces language, as, for example, in the form of automatic abstracts and of course also fully automatic translation without human intervention; or
(b) produces languages in the form of indexing and documentation languages or the so called 'natural language interfaces' or 'front-ends' to a variety of computer systems.

This form of industry might also, yet wrongly, be seen as a competitor with human translation. The languages which can be produced industrially belong to the realm of artificial or restricted languages for highly specialised communication. The implications of these developments for interpreting and translating are far-reaching. Work in this area has, however, until now been limited to research and a few applications only and is quite a distance away from full-scale industrial development.

1.2.4 *Tools and Products*

In any industrialisation process involving languages we must be concerned with the services to the basic language skills, the active ones of speaking and writing and the passive ones of reading and listening. By another categorisation of the industry we arrive at another division, namely services supporting oral skills and services supporting written skills, which, incidentally, correspond to the professional division between translation and interpreting. These latter skills can also be considered supplementary in the sense that they are associated with a second language, i.e. the various modes of transferring message content from one language to another.

These divisions are useful for a description of the language industry because they permit the examination of the scope for computer assistance skill by skill. Similar to other processes of industrialisation, the tools can therefore be divided into: (i) those that permit users to perform traditional language tasks better or easier; and (ii) machines for the performance of these tasks, partly or completely, instead of humans, in the way robots are employed to carry out mechanical functions.

Tools themselves represent a demonstration of intelligence because it requires intelligence to design, identify their use and maintain tools. The better designed the tools, i.e. the more information is contained in their construction, the more complex they are and the more intelligence is required in their use. Language is the pre-eminent tool because it even permits the construction and testing of hypotheses.

1.3 The evolution of the language industry

Advances in technology have consistently benefited the transmission and storage of language or linguistic data. The earliest achievements were in the area of forms and materials, i.e. writing systems, paper production, and the various forms of printing developed over the centuries. The next big leap forward for written language came with the typewriter, and for spoken languages with the telephone, the voice recording and wireless data transmission. More recent advances were concentrated on the speed of transmission as in telegraphy and on the quality of transmission, as in satellite communication; simultaneously the storage of sound was made possible so that written and spoken language can now be transmitted and stored with equal facility. The main features of the latest advances are not so much speed of transmission, but better and increased access to information via microfilm, facsimile, databases and CD-ROM.

During the 20th century society has actively explored the technical possibilities of data storage and transmission. The broadcasting and television industries have supplemented the press and book publication. The sound recording and video industries permit the preservation of human voices in their original situations. Libraries are being supplemented by databases, letter carriers by data networks. Over the centuries industry has responded to these aspirations for diversification and improvement of means of communication by providing society with the tools and services it expected. In their turn substantial sectors of the economy have evolved around the new services and products that have become available.

In practical applications the repertoire of conventional types of human communication has steadily grown by the addition of such distinctive forms as the following, all of which require industrial solutions for their effective implementation:

— new types of communication: e.g. books and journals in electronic form; libraries with electronic catalogues and access to databases.

— new methods of transmission: e.g. telex, radiotelephone, television, satellites and more modestly, but perhaps with a larger immediate impact, facsimile reproduction and transmission (fax).

— new types of written texts: e.g. telegram, microfilm, teletext, databases, subtitles of films, and now also synchronised running text on electronic display boards in live performances of opera and plays.

— new forms of spoken communication: e.g. the visual telephone call, the teleconference, simultaneous interpreting, voice-over and dubbing of films and the televised interview.

It is, therefore, only natural that attempts should have been made to implement on the computer all four skills associated with communication, i.e. reading, writing, listening and speaking. At a superficial level there is a certain success in this enterprise.

— Reading: Optical Character Recognition (OCR) devices can now automatically capture large quantities of data and make them machine manipulable. Recognition is, however, quite different from comprehension which is normally associated with reading.

— Writing: It is now possible to let the computer produce simple sentence-like statements which can be mistaken for humanly produced text and which can at times fulfill the role of meaningful utterances or messages produced by humans.

— Speaking: Computers can now analyse simple spoken messages and speech synthesizers can produce replies which are remarkably similar to human voices.

— Listening/understanding: So it is equally unexpected that efforts should have been made to employ the computer for the highly concentrated task of text comprehension and to demonstrate comprehension by the direct and effective way always used for this purpose, namely translation, i.e. comprehension demonstrated by reproduction of the text in another code. But it is precisely this task which seems to show up the limitations of the computer in the clearest possible way.

Initially, these developments were only extensions of 'normal' human communications. Input and output were the same and the technology only served to bridge physical distance in time or space or to improve storage. Relatively little, if any, linguistic knowledge was required in the early stages of this development. Telegraphy treated language signals like any other sign, and for early telephone engineers language was just another sound that had to be transmitted with as little distortion as was compatible with economic considerations.

It is evident that all other early computer handling of languages was also minimally linguistic. Speech sounds were analysed like any other acoustic signal and words were treated as if they were isolated items of code which had precise substitutes in another code.

Statistical linguistic knowledge was used by early typesetters and later for the design of the typewriter keyboard, which related frequency and combination of occurrence of characters to the movement of the fingers of both hands. For different languages there are consequently different keyboards, designed according to ergonomic principles. But the application of statistics to language, even with the sophistication of probability theory, did not produce any major breakthroughs in more complex computer operations on language. This can be seen in the early efforts in machine translation by computer which were largely based on statistical evidence. Because of the success of computers in cryptanalysis, it was thought that similar techniques could be applied to the problems of translation. Unfortunately, the idea of simple word-for-word substitution dominated research so long that it seriously jeopardised progress and led to heavy reductions in funding of research in this field at a crucial period of its development.

1.3.1 *The present situation*

It would be naive to assume that all these changes occurred without affecting the nature of the data and our habits of communication. For example, the personal letter has virtually disappeared, being replaced by the telephone call. The informal memo and the phone call at work have been superseded by electronic mail which will also bring to an end a whole tradition of commercial correspondence which in future will be carried out directly by means of the computer without the assistance of secretaries.

Through telecommunications and computer networks transmission and access to information is now more widespread and diversified, as is our ability to store this information in multiple form for re-use at a time of our convenience. Since it is easy to communicate, we now do it more often and in more fragmented a fashion. Since we can now store data in forms other than print, we are diversifying the sources of our information supply, so that, besides printed material, we have collections of images and sounds, which may be either directly accessible or in coded form.

The most important effect of these innovations is that there are now so many alternative modes of communication that they can in some cases even blur the distinction between written and spoken transmission and reception of communication. The individual now has a greater choice than ever before. Information can be produced and accessed on paper, on microfilm, computer screen, video and sound recording. Now the screen, rather than the page, becomes a unit in communication as we see from the example of teletext. Because spoken messages can be stored and accessed at will, they become a more compact and harder item of information than before. With the help of computer networks it is now possible to communicate almost without external control from desk to desk.

A few specific cases illustrate these points:

— We can now bring information onto our screens which before we had to go to libraries for. We can store this information for later reading and reprocess it directly in the form we have copied or received it.

— We listen more to electronically modified voices than to directly transmitted communication face to face.

— Beside long distance voice communication, we can now also speak to absent interlocutors through the wrongly named 'answering' machines, whose function is essentially that of delayed listening.

— We write with the assistance of electronic devices which permit full control, without intermediaries, over the entire communication process from text production to delivery.

1.3.2 *The role of linguistic research*

Such a historical survey shows how much progress has been made without serious recourse to linguistics; unfortunately, today there are still many researchers in the field who believe that linguistics is either irrelevant or that they know everything there is to know about the subject. From now on, however, any progress in the industry depends on detailed study of many aspects of linguistics, and researchers are beginning to recognise this fact.

This orientation towards linguistics which accompanies advances in computer science can be observed in a change of terminology. The new language industry is supported by the new information technology which replaces what was formerly called data processing. The subtle shift from 'data' to 'information' is an indication of the greater attention to the substance that is being processed. Data processing had, of course, already introduced techniques for using computers as sophisticated storage media, but in information technology there is a new emphasis on the involvement of telecommunications, and on the ability to interpret 'information', whereas data processing was assumed to handle 'raw data'. As soon as we speak of interpretation and transmission of information, rather than data, we are essentially concerned with linguistic facts and a language industry which is multilingual, as even the staunchly monolingual English-speaking countries are beginning to acknowledge.

Information technology, concerned with what we now have to call 'natural' language—as opposed to computer languages—is increasingly involved in interpreting and transforming language, both operations which hitherto were considered to be the exclusive domain of human intelligence.

The crucial role of language specialists in this work is, however, still not fully recognised. This is partly due to the fact that language specialists, i.e. theoretical and applied linguisticians were rather late in becoming familiar with, and hence utilising, computer technology. The other reason is that the conventional division of disciplines attributes linguistics to arts faculties which until recently had little if any contact with computing. This division is also largely responsible for the two parallel developments of CL and NLP, mentioned above. While on the one hand linguistics has branched out into yet another interdisciplinary direction, namely computational linguistics, on the other we have, largely emanating from computer science, a mixture of interests in language, pursued by such new disciplines as cognitive science, artificial intelligence (AI), experimental psychology and computer science itself, all engaged in NLP and Speech Analysis.

The relationship with AI is particularly striking. In AI intelligence is equated with knowledge. Intelligent entities have the intention to communicate, for which world knowledge and linguistic knowledge are required, as well as memory from which to select items of both types of knowledge. Since the general aim of AI is to identify behaviour which constitutes intelligence and to differentiate learned from innate behaviour, it must build programs which can learn, and these programs have to be expressed in language. But while AI must study language to deal with intelligence, IT studies language in order to deal with communication.

There is, also, an important difference between the linguistics needed for theoretical work on language and the focus of research in the language industry which adopts a practical viewpoint. Traditional theoretical linguistics analyses a language in order to describe its grammar and lexicon and to formulate rules for the production of hypothetical texts, as is the case in generative grammar, for example. For applications of information technology, linguistic analysis has to start with a coherent set of texts from which pragmatic, syntactic, semantic and other linguistic information can be extracted for the communicative grammars and specialised dictionaries needed for the analysis and production of texts in specific subject fields.

To process this information we also need a theory of information and communication, something which is not recognised as a fundamental aspect of linguistics. There is also a need to redefine 'language' because we observe that information technology sees 'natural language', as in 'natural language processing', in opposition to the language used in and for instructing computers. While the opposition of 'natural-artificial' with respect to languages is not new, it is only now that it acquires a new dimension of meaning. This opposition between natural and artificially constructed languages offers many interesting research perspectives for ergonomic linguistics, a new field of study associated with language planning and with efficiency of communication (see also 2.6 and 4.3). The authentic progress of the language industry must be sought in this perspective. If we succeed in expressing databases in user-friendly artificial languages we shall be able to manipulate the information contained in them with greater ease. If we can write technical reports within the constraints of a computer-controlled restricted language, we can use these texts to make intelligent inferences and can also translate these texts into other languages by fully automatic means.

There are many opportunities for research in applied linguistics in support of the language industry. But the active participation of linguists is still hampered by inadequate training in computational methods and the problems associated with the adaptation to the industrial pressures caused by the increasing need in universities to seek outside finance for the costly research in this field.

1.4 The structure of the language industry

Figures 1.1 –1.3 attempt to show the structure of the elements which contribute to the language industry.

1.4.1 *Science and applications*

A first division of the domain of the language industry can be made by separating the area of pure research from its technology and the area of applications of this research. This is done (in Figure 1.1) by attributing the description of existing languages to the traditional domain of general linguistics now with a computational orientation, and the actual working with language for solving communication problems to a separate area; in other words, the scientific aspect of computational linguistics is separated from its engineering applications.

Theoretical computational linguistics is concerned with fundamental research in the computational description, modelling and representation of languages. Studies of this type provide the foundation for the construction of automated dictionaries, analytical and synthetic grammars, i.e. a whole new linguistics oriented towards the possibilities of the computer.

The insights gained from the study of existing languages and other semiotic systems also provide the basis for the creation of new languages, languages used for limited purposes in documentation and classification systems, or the sort of languages increasingly needed to interact with a computer, programming languages and natural language interfaces.

Applied computational linguistics divides into two areas:

(a) Work with existing languages, i.e. the production, processing, storing and retrieval of texts written in natural language, i.e. the sort of texts conventionally produced with all their diversity and shortcomings; or work with variously restricted, controlled and constructed languages as we find them used by navigation, information science, computer games, etc.

(b) The design and production of new languages, as e.g. in such restricted varieties as the language evolved for efficient international communication by pilots, the language evolved in international research experiments in nuclear physics, satellite technology or space flights or the semi-artificial languages in document storage and retrieval systems, and natural language interfaces to expert or other computerised information systems.

Some of these languages may consist of no more than lists of single words or phrases; others have their own morphology and syntax. The complexity of these languages increases as we attempt to use them for more complex communication and as we learn how to handle greater complexity of language by computer.

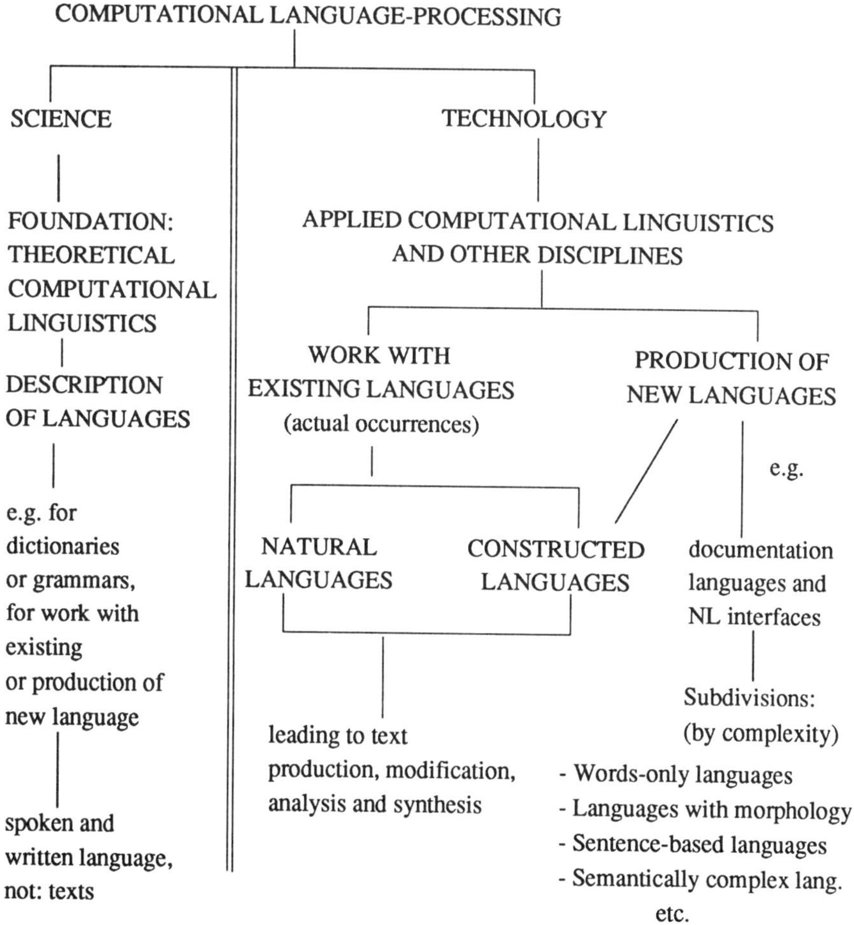

Figure 1.1 *The scope of the language industry*

1.4.2 *Range of written and spoken languages*

Working with either natural or constructed language can be carried out either in the written or spoken form of a language. But there is also a new range of tasks for the computer in the conversion of written into spoken and spoken into written language: e.g. typing out dictated letters, transcribing parliamentary debates or taking lecture notes; or the conversion from written into spoken language that we should like to have in automatic spoken books for the blind etc.

These differences are quite marked in research because the starting point is quite different. In dealing with spoken language another level of articulation has to be added and a completely new system of acoustic sound analysis and description. The range of activities involved is indicated in Figure 1.2. Translation research, traditionally concerned with the written language, will soon be faced with the problems associated with conversion into and out of the spoken language as well.

1.4.3 *Reception and production*

Working with languages, whether written or spoken, whether natural or artificial, implies two types of operations or processes: reception of texts and production of texts—analysis and generation—input and output. We should not say understanding and creating; these are distinct human activities.

Unless it is for simple storage in its natural form, the reception of texts implies some form of analysis. This analysis proceeds to varying degrees of depth according to the intended use. For speech it starts by breaking down a continuum of sound into meaningful segments and transforms them into 'computer-readable' units, which, according to the language in question, may correspond more or less to units of the written language. In a second stage it identifies linguistic units at the level of the word, the phrase, or the sentence, and extracts relevant information on the formal characteristics of the individual items, their syntactic interrelation, or their meaning and place in the text. If text inferencing is required, a high degree of analysis is necessary. If only storage and text compression is intended, the analysis can remain at a superficial level. The types of analysis and synthesis are indicated in Figure 1.2.

1.4.4 *Applications and products*

Analysis is required for such purposes as text excerption for dictionaries, text editing, keyword recognition in document indexing systems, key-phrase recognition in question and answer or expert systems, and in translation systems.

Analysis may lead directly to the production of word lists, indexes, or indirectly to automatic summaries and abstracts, and, of course, translations. When production of text is envisaged there must be some form of generation or synthesis of text to present readers or listeners with something they can recognise as a language.

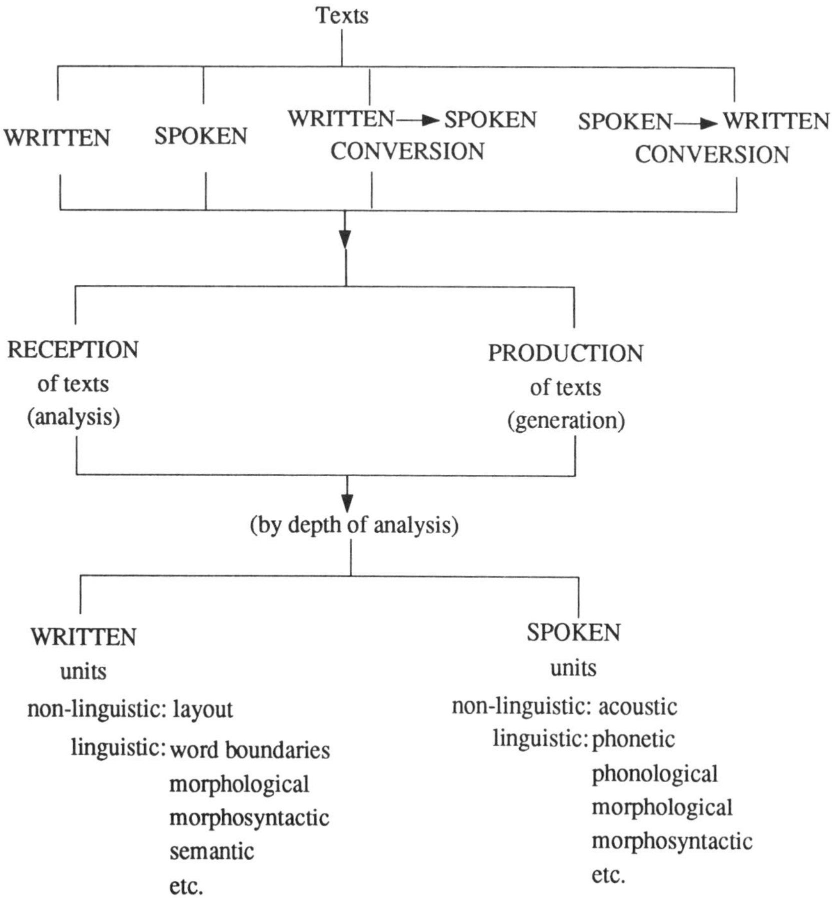

Figure 1.2 *Scope of the texts treated by the industry*

The list of possible analysis and production outputs, given in Figure 1.2, indicates some of the basic materials leading to products of the new industry; these are more fully exemplified in Figure 1.3.

COMPUTATIONAL PROCESSING OF TEXTS

(by purpose/application)

ANALYSIS OF TEXTS

for: editing
- keyword recognition
- key-phrase recognition
- inferencing
- syntactic analysis
- content analysis (transl.)

PRODUCTION OF TEXTS

for: word lists
- indexes
- abstracts
- translations
- text grammars
- new texts

EXAMPLES:

WRITTEN
- spelling checker
- NL interface
- style checker: proof-reading
  text critique
- writer's workstation
- machine translation
- document processing: indexing,
  abstracting,
  etc.
- dictionary production from corpus
- term bank production from corpus

SPOKEN
- word recognition:
  interface to wristwatches,
  cookers, carphones, etc.
- text entry by speech
- telephone access to
  information systems
  etc.

Figure 1.3 *Application of computational linguistics*

Some of these applications, most of which have a multilingual dimension or can be used in conjunction with multilingual tools, are briefly characterised below.

— Spelling checking systems typically incorporate little linguistic knowledge, most of them being based on statistics and the presence or absence of a word in a dictionary. More advanced systems include one or several of the following features: (i) the structure of words, also called orthotactics, which characterises natural languages, can be exploited to eliminate non-occurring combinations of letters, in general or in particular positions in the word; (ii) morphological rules of word formation may permit accepting combinations which are not in the dictionary but nevertheless acceptable forms of words; (iii) syntactic rules may permit the detection of errors of agreement but also arbitrate between noun and verb (e.g. practice and practise), according to the possibilities of word class in a particular position in the sentence; (iv) some shallow semantic processing can also help to resolve cases of doubt, but this is as yet an area of research. Greater sophistication through linguistic analysis can also identify 'correct' forms which we must read as misspellings because of their role and position in a sentence.

— Text critiquing involves assessing a text for such features as general legibility or more particularly, consistency, coherence, structure, or even sequence of ideas. Indicators for these features are sought in the use of punctuation, sentence length, the use of active vs passive voice, the combination of tenses, the depth and number of embeddings, reference, generally ill-formed sentences and such lexical features as the use of correct terms and over- vs under-use of some expressions.

Such systems can also offer suggestions for improving a text, to bring it into line with an image of an adequate text for the declared purpose. Text critiquing systems can be used to enforce consistency of expression and terminology. They can also render texts more informative and so enhance their communicative value.

— Text scanning serves to identify 'important' or 'relevant' concepts contained in such texts as news flashes or announcements made by major news agencies, financial news services or in the printed press. Such scanners may concentrate on a narrow range of items, e.g. movements of prices, but may also scan for events which may have an impact on prices such as armed conflicts, natural disasters, changes of government, takeover bids, bankruptcies, etc. Text scanning can be rough or sophisticated. In its simplest form it categorises texts by importance and according to keywords as they are processed, so that detailed analysis can be carried out by specialists. It can be more detailed by extracting, abstracting or paraphrasing text segments for later human evaluation. At an advanced level, as yet only in experimental form, knowledge gained from one text can be integrated with knowledge gained from others in order to produce some sort of weighted report.

— Natural language interfaces are modes of access to conventional, generally relationally structured, databases. Interfaces may be portable, i.e. usable for more than one database, or usable for a single application. Modern interfaces may have some degree of intelligence, but typically not so much as natural language components of advisory systems, which work on the contents of the database.

For many databases, rather than a natural language interface, it is enough to have a sophisticated menu system that allows the user to build up questions step by step. Such an approach can give the appearance of a natural language query, but is simply a means of expressing the query language of the database in a user-friendly fashion.

— Advisory systems, also called 'expert' systems, accept questions in natural language on a particular topic, e.g. the state of a bank account or, at a more advanced level, advice on investment, and generate language output in the form of factual answers, statements, reports, recommendations etc. This type of system is heavily dependent on the quality of the knowledge base, and the complexity of processing involved.

— Dialogue systems are based on the assumption that speech can replace text in many applications or obviate manual operations as, for example, in speech to-text systems which 'take dictation' and display the results on a screen. Speech systems can be important for database consultation where a query can be made over a telephone line to a computer equipped with a dialogue component.

— Terminological databanks differ from machine-readable dictionaries in two respects. They were initially designed as databases for on-line consultation and limited to vocabularies of specialised subject fields of which they attempt to give full coverage. They are therefore linguistic databases specially designed for particular user needs. Such collections were then also seen to be useful for spelling and style checking, e.g. to preserve consistency of usage, or for indexing systems etc. They have a special role in most other applications which need some kind of dictionary and in which terminology occupies a key position. The flexibility of databases also permits easy updating and extracting of subsets of lexical information for special purposes.

— Machine translation is a generic concept for a variety of translation tools and independent systems. In such an environment it can no longer be seen as a single, stand-alone, black box, but is a requirement of any one of the above exemplifications when they are adapted to multilingual use. Indeed, most document processing and retrieval is today multilingual and many documents contain words and phrases from other languages which may require translation to make them comprehensible.

The integration of facilities and tools can be seen in a few simple examples:

- A multilingual termbank is an essential tool for any machine translation system, but may also be the only recourse a translator has when machine translation fails;
- text editing before translation is a feature of many translation systems;

— style checking is often incorporated into post-editing procedures of translation systems;
— interactive machine translation systems incorporate elements of expert systems and can themselves be part of workstations which link a translator to other databases or advisory systems. A full discussion of MT tools can be found in Hutchins & Somers (1992).

Currently, such tools as spelling checkers, style checkers for proofreading and text critique are already being widely marketed. Some of these tools are incorporated into word processors; other products come as separate items on CD-ROM disks or as fully manipulable lexical databases of general or specialised vocabulary. For translation there are a number of tools and independent systems on the market, and more are currently under development. Various versions are being developed of what has been named 'workstation for translators', which will offer them a variety of tools including access to dictionaries and interactive editing.

In voice production tools there is less available for assisting with interlingual communication, though talking dolls and miniature speaking dictionaries have been selling quite successfully.

From the point of view of fully automated translation and even the services available to a multilingual community, the picture is less positive. While word-processing is generally established, it is far from adequate as far as multilingual facilities are concerned. Even monolingual communication, especially across national boundaries, is still being hindered because there is not yet a standard for operating systems, size of disks, keyboards etc. which would make the transfer of text in machine-readable form as easy as, or, as we might expect, easier than, the transmission of paper. Facsimile transmission and optical character recognition have an indirect impact on the communication across languages. Fax facilities can help overcome the problem of inadequate character sets in computers but only at the expense of removing it from a magnetic computer-readable form. While OCR has radically improved over the last decade, most systems are still heavily conditioned by characteristics of individual languages and therefore do not provide a general solution.

The minimum facility translators can now count on are wordprocessors with dictionary making facilities. There are commercial software packages available and some specialised dictionaries in database or CD-ROM form; but many translators have learnt to develop their own facilities which fit into a convenient textprocessing environment. Some of these are then offered commercially.

More recently large CD-ROM dictionaries of both general language and terminology have become available for the major languages. For the moment most of these tools still consist of simple electronic copies of the printed pages which were prepared without the benefit of computational control. Only when they adopt a structure which benefits fully from the available electronic resources, will it be possible to evaluate their relative advantage over conventional dictionaries. The large terminological collections specially constructed for electronic use which are now being offered, e.g. the Canadian database TERMIUM, certainly appear to promise a revolution in the production and the use of specialised dictionaries.

1.5 Conditions for the design and application of industrial tools

Industrial tools must take into consideration the unique complexity of communicative situations and hence modes of communication. There are a number of parameters which influence the nature and type of assistance the industry has to plan for, if it wants to offer effective tools.

There are firstly the four basic techniques already listed in Figure 1.2, namely written, spoken, spoken for writing down and written to be spoken. Secondly, there are the time intervals between producing and sending and receiving of messages, which are sometimes useful for reflection, while at other times they are a hindrance. Thirdly, there are the physical distances that have to be bridged. The industry can now provide visual contact over long distances, as in teleconferences which will significantly modify our attitudes to such contacts.

Regarding the participants, the numerical relationship between senders and recipients is of industrial relevance and varies from one to one, to one to many, but also from any number of simultaneous senders to several recipients with or without immediate role reversal. In most aspects of the technical design of tools we can probably assume that the relative social status of the recipients cannot be a determining factor, but in the application of the tools it is important to bear in mind that in many communicative situations in industry the social status of the participants is important, if only to decide who has access to certain types of tools, and who is in control of the speech act and its situation.

There are many textual parameters that influence the design and the use of tools. Most of these are discussed in detail in the following chapters. Here a few general factors that shape any design are listed. Firstly, it must be taken into account that most communications and texts are connected to, or at least have a precedent in, other texts and that many texts actually form part of series with their own situational and formal patterns. This fact, then, distinguishes routine occurrences of texts, for which industrial assistance can be provided, from one-off or highly original pieces of text or communicative situations which cannot be planned for. Other factors which can influence design are the need for privacy of communications and messages and the distinction between tools for official and private use.

A last parameter, which is often overlooked, is that of the use made of texts, which in turn can have an effect on the time and money spent on their production, transmission and storage. Most newsprint, for example, is for rapid consumption and the relationship between number of copies produced and the few copies that are actually put into archives is a very unequal one. Other texts are produced in single or duplicate copies only, but all have to be preserved in their original form for a limited time, e.g. the duration of a contract. On the other hand, such documents as textbooks and manuals are produced in large numbers of copies, and are intended for repeated reading and reference but are usually replaced or re-written after a few years, according to the state of the art of the subject matter in hand. The type of use, the degree of social importance, the physical quality of the document, the shape in which it has to be preserved, and the length of its validity in general use or archived form, can all influence the design of tools for communication, especially if they are coupled with such other factors listed here which have implications for the cost of the design and the cost of the use of the instrument or tool to be designed.

1.5.1 *Conditions for the development of the machine translation industry*

Machine translation (MT) is an industrial process performed by machines designed and constructed by computational linguistics engineers. These machines process a very complex substance: language, which differs from other industrial materials in that it is entirely man-made and symbolic. The machines that carry out this industrial process are computers which have to be designed in their material form, the hardware, and their mode of operation, the software instructions, so as to be capable of accepting and processing this particular substance.

To the extent that MT is seen as an alternative to the human translation process, it can only be justified if the end product is in some way 'superior', e.g. in quality, cost or speed of output. It is therefore necessary to define the characteristics of the end product of MT so that it can be distinguished from the alternative human product it seeks to replace or parallel.

In order to have adequate criteria for designing appropriate machines, a theoretical design specification or framework is needed both for the description of the material input to the process and for the process itself. For the specification of the substance undergoing the process, language, there are many models in theoretical and applied linguistics which can be called upon to provide adequate explanations. This is not the case for the specification of the process. Existing work on translation theory does not offer an adequate model for machine translation because it is based on the assumption that translation is an exclusively human process and therefore conveniently explained by heuristic and hermeneutic models, which are of little exemplary value for MT.

It is now widely recognized that the human translator does not provide a possible model for a translation machine. We can therefore attempt a reformulation of the problem, and say that a design specification for machine translation (MT) must be based on a theoretical model of an automated linguistic and pragmatic transformation process whose specific initial product is modified to become a different, but related, end product.

The theoretical model must identify the initial product the MT transformation can operate on; support, explain and justify the various stages of the transformation; and define the characteristics of the end-product. It is further expected that there is an interdependence between the input product and the processes that can be performed on it; equally, it is accepted that the chosen process will have an impact on the end product. The success of the transformation is measured in terms of a particular relationship between the initial and end products. The model must also include criteria for the assessment of the quality of the end-product, which is expressed as the acceptability of the end product to groups of users.

Finally, a design specification for machine translation systems must be fitted into a theory of translation in general, because the objectives of both operations—the facilitation of translingual/interlingual communication—are, in principle, the same. Translation theory, in its turn, has a place in a theory of communication because the phenomenon of translation, i.e. the transformation of written documents (texts) from one natural language into another, only makes sense in terms of communicative objectives and can ultimately be measured only in terms of its communicative value.

2 Theoretical Aspects of Language

Language engineering is concerned with the design and use of tools for activities involving languages. Tools are designed to be purpose-specific, to facilitate activities and to solve problems arising from activities. They are applied to the substance of language in general and to manifestations of languages in documents selected for particular applications. This section examines this substance of the engineering activity for which tools are being designed. Our concern is with the definition and differentiation of existing languages rather than with language in the abstract, because the language industry deals with specific instances of languages, be they national or regional languages, official or working languages, technical jargon or colloquial speech; hence criteria are needed for the distinction of types of languages which enter into texts and messages.

For the purpose of this section we initially accept a distinction between general language and sublanguages for particular subject fields, which we shall attempt to identify and differentiate further. In the process we shall introduce the concept of 'artificial language', which is both useful as a contrast to clarify issues and necessary for discussing language in an industrial environment.

2.1 The nature and uses of language

It is convenient to start with a classical definition of language which permits the identification of the elements that separate types of languages.

> Language is a purely human and non-instinctive method of communicating ideas, emotions and desires by means of a system of voluntarily produced symbols. (Sapir, 1921:8)

According to Sapir language is ''symbolic'', hence referential, ''systematic'', hence rule-governed, ''non-instinctive'', hence voluntary and deliberate; and it is used for ''communicating'', hence it is communal. These four properties, referentiality, systematicity, deliberateness or voluntariness and communality are inherent to all types of language in all manner of uses (see Figure 2.1).

In general language there is a rough balance between the exploitation of these four complementary properties. Special subject languages are characterised by maximising certain possibilities of reference and certain systematising features. For example, in general language it is sufficient for 'toothpaste' to refer to a cleansing compound of a particular consistency; in the special language of chemistry the reference must be to a particular chemical composition, a certain density, consistency, etc. Also, in the naming system of chemical compounds, the systematic nature of language is exploited to a maximum degree in order to reflect in language the structure of the special subject area as far as language permits. Subsets of a language may, for example, emphasize systematicity in their lexicon or syntax, or stress greater precision of reference. Word-formation and derivation techniques in particular are used in order to support the systematic structure of the names given to the concepts of a subject field. For example, Gastromyotomy = surgical cutting (tomy) of a muscle (myo) in a particular part of the body (gastro). When the systematising devices of a language are considered inadequate, special subject languages develop ancillary semiotic systems such as graphs, formulae and other notations; some of these are language-based, e.g. the biological nomenclatures, others are completely independent such as the chemical notation (though it too uses signs of language). A very special case is the mathematical system of writing which is a translation of spoken language into another, language-independent code. This tendency to create supplementary codes can be identified as the first reason for setting up separate categories of special languages.

The differences among types of languages become more marked when moving from the essential properties of language, identified by Sapir, to the uses, frequently called functions, of language. Sapir recognises the communicative role of language as well as its emotive and social use. Every speech act has an inevitable social dimension because writers and readers cannot separate themselves from their environment and their emotions. His definition does not specifically mention, but clearly implies a classificatory use—which has also been called 'ideational' (Halliday 1973). At its most basic level, this appears in the simple process of naming items of our experience in a systematic manner. These natural and inevitable uses reveal language as a multifunctional tool, and it is in the nature of this tool that any one user in any one speech act is able to stress one use more than the other. In addition there are a number of special and deliberate uses, such as the poetic, phatic or the metalinguistic which need no further examination. In the relevant literature there are many different categorisations of functions of language. For example, Bühler (1934) recognises three functions, namely "Darstellung" (representation), "Ausdruck" (expression) and "Appell" (usually translated as 'vocative'). The number of three appears most frequently, for example in Halliday's (1973) "textual, ideational and interpersonal" and Lyons's (1977) "descriptive, expressive and social" functions. Malinowski (1966) speaks only of two, a "scientific" and a "magical" function, whereas Jakobson (1960) gives the most complete list to date with his "referential, emotive, conative, metalinguistic, phatic and poetic".

Close inspection of these lists shows that many authors seen to confuse properties, which are basic, i.e. inherent, to the nature of language, and functions, which may or may not be evoked. Speech acts are by nature referential and every use of language has an emotive aspect, because human beings cannot separate themselves from their emotions, though they can try to minimise their impact. But they can freely choose whether to make an expressions poetic.

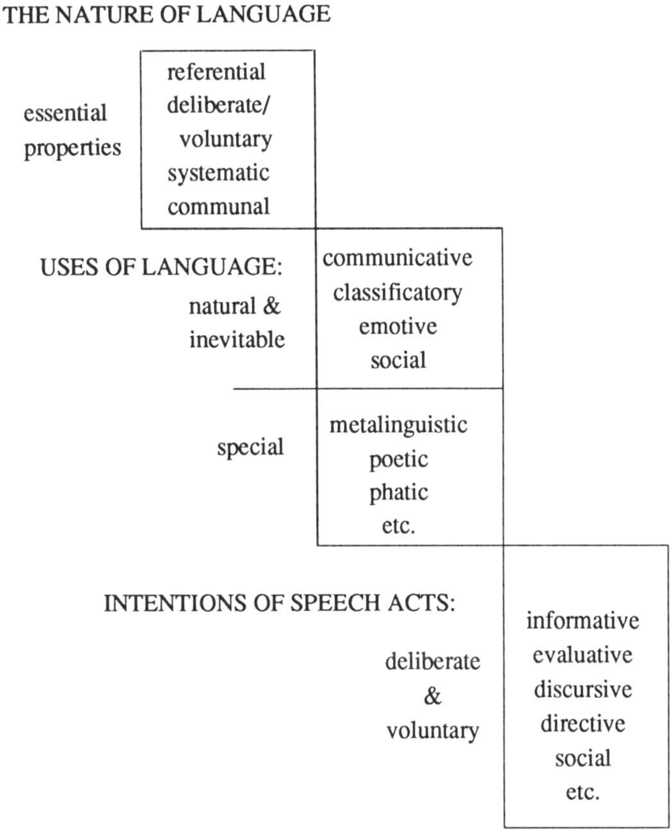

Figure 2.1 *The nature and uses of language, and the functions of speech acts*

It is a convention that in the usage of special subject languages the communicative and classificatory uses are maximised and the emotive and social uses are deliberately minimised or neutralised. The difference between general and special speech acts lies in the degree of emphasis on any one function and the balance between the uses. It can, for example, safely be asserted that special subject languages are used more self-consciously than general language. The justification of the development of special subject languages can also be sought in the overriding aim of using language to convey information, to transfer knowledge and then emphasizing the uses that will further this aim.

2.2 The intention of speech acts

Closely connected with function is intention—the two are often confused—which is a deliberate exploitation of the possibilities offered by language for achieving communicative goals. While functions or uses are inherent in any natural language, intentions derive from the voluntary nature of language and dominate specific speech acts.

A number of basic intentions are supported by direct linguistic evidence, namely, the 'informative' intention is reflected in simple statements and its reverse, the 'interrogative' intention is expressed as requests for information; the 'directive' intention is reflected in imperatives; the 'evaluative' intention is reflected in the grammatical feature of comparison; the 'discursive' intention, for which modality is essential; the 'social' intention has no specific linguistic feature for its representation.

The informative intention deliberately exploits the communicative use of language. The evaluative intention concentrates on the classificatory use of language, but normally also involves the communicative and emotive uses. Speech acts with directive intention are designed to cause or modify behaviour and in order to specify that behaviour they draw upon the referential nature of language. The language of science is essentially concerned with the extension of knowledge and in its purest form, therefore, involves the informative and evaluative intentions, but does not contain directive speech acts. The teaching of science—part of its application—is pursued with a directive intention. Directive speech acts are frequent in technology. Discursive speech acts are essential for human interaction; they may be formal as in speeches and philosophical speculations, or casual as in domestic arguments. The social intention is never dominant in the special subject languages but does occur and is as difficult to control as the evaluative intention. General language speech acts can have a whole range of mixed intentions even in a single sentence. Special language speech acts tend to avoid phatic and poetic communication altogether and often divide texts according to intention, e.g. informative continuous prose followed by directive exercises in textbooks; the division of reports into main body (informative), conclusions (evaluative), recommendations (directive). Other authors have established categories like 'narrative' and 'descriptive' which can be considered as subclasses of informative.

Our society has set up an elaborate system of associating speech acts with particular circumstances and locations and giving them names indicative of the intention, e.g. lecture theatre, conference hall, debating chamber, court room, interview room, audience chamber.

2.2.1 *The pragmatic dimension of speech acts*

In order to identify the pragmatic situation of a speech act, it is convenient to represent its position on a particular point of several axes of expression, which some people also refer to as registers.

Figure 2.2 shows the axes on which any one speech act can be located to determine its pragmatic setting. The roles of these axes of expression in the speech act is discussed in section 3.3.6ff.

The first axis is geographical and has a range from standard national, which is better named 'common', to locally restricted language or dialect.

The second axis is concerned with degrees of specialism which are determined by the nature of the topic, the writers' knowledge, and their perception of the readers' knowledge. Any discourse is expressed at a certain level of generality or specialism according to the circumstance of the situation. This choice in turn implies a choice at the level of another axis, which ranges from natural to artificial language and is discussed in section 2.5, below.

The third axis is one of mode of expression and ranges over gradations as identified by such labels as: frozen - formal - consultative - casual - familiar - intimate, derived from Joos (1967). In order to avoid any particular association with any set of labels we call this opposition 'formal' and 'colloquial'.

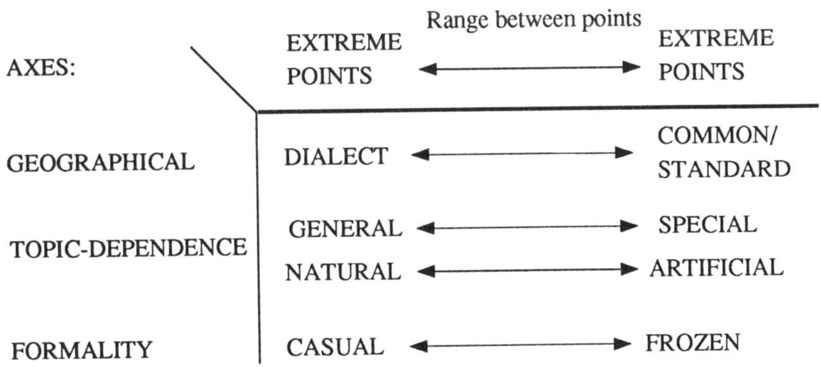

Figure 2.2 *Axes of expression*

For any one speech act we can represent the three axes as intersections and so produce a picture of any one pragmatic speech situation. See Figure 2.3 for an example.

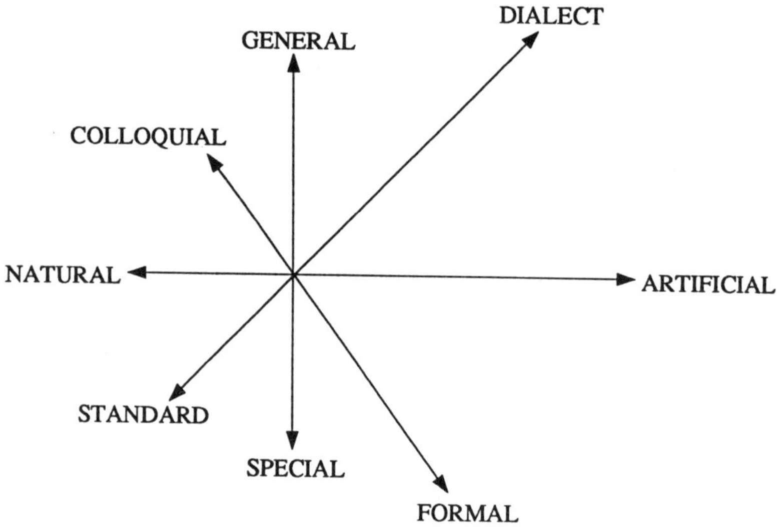

Figure 2.3 *An example of a speech situation*

The intersection of parameters illustrated in Figure 2.3 can indicate a speech act which is semi-specialised, using more natural than artificial features, with few regional characteristics and roughly half-way between formal and colloquial. A discussion between a specialist, a lawyer or architect, for example, with a client on professional matters would fit this conjunction of features.

2.3 The concept of sublanguages

Moving from considering language as a symbolic system to actual usage implies moving from the abstract rule system represented by a grammar to the more limited but more flexible set of social norms which determine the actual 'accepted' occurrences of utterances in textual units.

To clarify this point we postulate four levels of speaking about language, as illustrated in Figure 2.4. The first level represents what is in the nature of languages, what all languages have in common. At the second, still theoretical level, we locate historically and linguistically coherent systems of particular languages used by a community seen as a whole. This level is represented by books on the phonology, lexicology, syntax or semantics of, e.g. English or French, which can describe the linguistic rule system that differentiates one system from others, e.g. the difference between Welsh and French. The concept of language does not, however, by itself entail such concrete objects as written grammars or dictionaries. There are probably still more languages in the world entirely based on oral culture than there are so-called 'languages of culture' which have written forms, whose grammars are codified and whose lexicons are collected in dictionaries. As soon as the forms of a language are unified in order to create, support or justify political, social or economic unity it gives up some of its natural creativeness and flexibility. In order to maintain its openness as a general tool of communication for a large body of people, natural language is then variously regulated and controlled by social norms. It is therefore theoretically possible to postulate two extremes: a completely natural language, ruled by linguistic norms only and very few social norms and a heavily restricted, almost 'artificial' language which does not permit the individual any freedom of variation within the social norms, as we find it, e.g. in the language of court ceremonial. The Occidental concept of language, as it is known from such languages as English or Norwegian, has relatively rigid spelling rules, standard rules of pronunciation and syntax and even word-formation rules.

LEVELS:	language universals	a language e.g. English	sublanguages, dialects, techno-lects, sociolects	idiolect
language systems	→	rule system ↓		
potential speech acts		ling. norm →	social norms ↓	
actual cases of speech acts			usage →	individual discourse

Figure 2.4 *The levels of language analysis*

The next level of description accounts for the differences of usage within any one language. It accounts for the degree and type of restriction imposed on usage by the social norms which govern all sublanguages. This level deals with coherent systems of sublanguages which may share with others a number of linguistic rules, but are differentiated from each other by social norms which determine and control the linguistic rules actually accepted by the respective speech community, and also fix the boundaries of such separate features as pronunciations and spellings in dialects and sets of vocabulary or terminology used only by this group of users. The most interesting aspect of this level is that it has both a practical side and a theoretical side of system description which is directly based on the observation of actual realisations of language in context. The practical side of language realisations deals with usage in discourse with its language varieties which can be described in terms of situational subsets of a language, e.g. the range of dialogue used between nurse and patient, bank-teller and customer. The upper levels of analysis depend on this level for their examples which they use after abstracting the sublanguage-specific elements, often with unsatisfactory consequences. The fourth level, is theoretically that of the individual's command of a language, which is of great interest to psycholinguistics but not to the subject matter of this book. Actual instances of discourse are essential for any exemplification because linguistic behaviour can only be observed in individual speech acts. The identification and description of sublanguages is in effect nothing more than the abstraction of common elements of real speech acts by speakers belonging to a coherent social group defined by professional, situational, geographical, historical or other criteria.

For a description of language by subsets criteria are required. The degree of independence of the subsets has to be determined; the relationship of one subset to the other has to be decided and the levels of the system of language affected by this subdivision, i.e. the grammatical, semantic or pragmatic level or any combination of these.

There are many reasons for establishing divisions at the pragmatic level, such as separate user groups, different topics and different situations. But while it appears easy to divide manifestations of language into written and spoken, with a special category written to be spoken (formal lectures, plays, etc.) and spoken to be written (dictating), or prose and poetry (as demonstrated by Molière in his comedy 'Le bourgeois gentilhomme'), no speech act is ever completely described by being identified as 'dialect' or 'standard' without taking into account the topic of the speech act and its mode of expression.

Any manifestation of language is the result of complex decision processes which involve, firstly, the semantic choices that determine the topic and content of a message, secondly the linguistic choices required by the various levels of articulation, and, finally, the choices determined by the pragmatics of a particular speech situation. Pragmatic and semantic choices determine grammatical choices, even though the particular linguistic rule system of a language puts some constraints on the realisation of what is intended.

There are geographical, social and occupational variants (sublanguages) for some topics like farming and old-established technologies like pottery and weaving, but levels of expression only and few variants for science or other subjects used by a small number of speakers whose education has been more linguistically homogeneous. The use of variants depends on the social conventions governing the use of language. The means available are further restricted by the command the participants have of the topics, codes and forms.

2.3.1 *Criteria for establishing sublanguages*

In any applications of linguistic theory to genuine problems of usage, a theory of sublanguages based on linguistics, pragmatics, semantics and communication theory is essential. Linguistic criteria alone are insufficient for justifying a separate treatment of sublanguages. On the grammatical level there is a tradition of stressing unity rather than diversity by ignoring syntactic differences between written and spoken language and morphological and phonemic variations between dialects—the domain of theoretical linguistics. The fascination of general and theoretical studies of language lies in the system of language as such, the structures of grammars, the interaction of grammars with the lexicon and the multilayered articulation of language. This unitary view is reinforced by research methods which permit the use of constructed examples, as long as they can be identified as grammatically well-formed instances of a language system. This approach gives rise to the well-known conundrums like the contrast between 'climbing boots' and 'climbing roses', ambiguous sentences like 'Time flies like an arrow' or non-sense constructions like 'Colorless green ideas sleep furiously'.

From a pragmatic and communicative point of view of language description and analysis, it is highly desirable to establish various segmentations of languages by such concepts as subject field or topic, social and geographical distribution, function and mode of expression.

From the point of view of communication, it is easier to justify the existence of separate languages, in the form of dialects or technolects, than the existence of single languages like Italian or German, which in some of their non-standard spoken form are incomprehensible within distances of some 500 miles; because they have been unified, their written forms are usually recognised as being an instance of that language, even though the content of a written document is not necessarily understood. In this case people are simply able to identify the forms and structures of a certain symbol system, but this identification then stops short of using the referential nature of language.

At the semantic level of language alone, the borderline for a subdivision is prima facie less obvious because all types of sublanguages share common lexical items and find it difficult to attribute lexical items unequivocally to special subject fields. We note this particularly in the hesitation of dictionaries to use subject labels. The case for justifying the existence of special languages lies in giving priority to the pragmatic and semantic dimensions of language, whereas the unitary view tends to stress the syntactic and morphological dimensions.

In the practice of communication the case for sublanguages is accepted at all three levels, and, according to the application, one or the other level is given priority in classification. If speech acts are ordered on the basis of domain of discourse, the geographical and formality levels cannot be ignored, but they are then used as modes of subclassification. Sociolinguistics, by contrast, is either more interested in geography, ethnicity or social structure and this determines the priority given one or the other level.

2.4 Evolution and types of language varieties

Having established a case for the consideration of sublanguages, there is a need to relate this concept to others as diverse as standard language, jargon, colloquial English, ESP, EAP, the King's—or now the Queen's—English, national language, official language, slang, sociolect, technolect, etc..

'Language' on its own is an abstract concept as there are only individual languages and sublanguages. The most common qualifiers for languages are ambiguous adjectives, such as German or English which can be interpreted geographically, politically or etymologically. Through hundreds of years of conditioning in nationalist thinking, most people do not question such vague and unscientific designations as 'the English language'. Only when confronted with the need for a definition of such alternatives as 'the Australian language' or 'British English' does it become necessary to reflect on the classification of languages. In general, 'dialects' signal a geographical classification of languages until this is used in a political contexts. Thus French politicians consider Corsican a separate language while any historian of the language would classify it as an Italian dialect. Unity of language as proclaimed by constitutions or ministries of education is only a very broad specification which at best safeguards channels of communication in a community and at worst fossilizes the language of schools and other institutions and adds to the linguistic division of a society.

Groupings of languages into families and divisions of languages into sociolects, technolects and other group languages, determined by the characteristics of language users, proliferate but are not sufficiently developed to relate to the textual units needed for discussing concrete instances of texts for translation. To trace the evolution of language varieties we need to postulate a concept of 'language in its natural state'. This concept can be variously defined. Historically speaking, it describes a language at an early stage of evolution when it exists in spoken form only and before it develops to the sophisticated and diversified instrument now represented by the so-called 'languages of culture'. In its natural state a language can be defined as the means of expression evolved by a simple homogeneous society before that society codifies its social and knowledge structures and consequently its language by written means. Even today, there are languages in something akin to their original state in small isolated communities that have not yet acquired a unified written form of expression and therefore have neither a grammar nor a dictionary in written form which can be used as a measure of correctness or control. In the European experience this state occurred in an early historic period where such languages had largely natural geographical boundaries only, inside of which there was considerable variation of usage in pronunciation, meaning and even syntax. Only at a much later stage, through closer inner cohesion on the one hand and social or geographical separation on the other, did some of these groups evolve greater individual identity until the moment when such distinctions as Polish and Ukrainian, Swedish and Norwegian, German and Dutch became linguistically meaningful, which in turn was long before these purely linguistic concepts were converted into the political concepts of national languages.

Even in simple or early societies there is already evidence of subdivisions of language for purposes of ritual, by age groups or sexes and activities. The evolution of sublanguages, therefore, occurs parallel with the development of social structures and is governed by social norms, which determine levels and modes of expression as well as lexical items which are characterised by their appropriateness or even mandatoriness in certain situations. The most obvious example of this form of language is to be found in early incantations and in religious scriptures, many of which eventually got a written form, which itself may be quite distinct from other forms of writing.

The evolution of a language from its natural state into a 'language of culture' always entails some form of limitation of freedom of variation and creativity. This process is associated with the creation of a written linguistic rule system and can be postulated as occurring along a sliding scale of increasing constraints. One extreme is represented by the theoretical concept of 'natural language', which, evolving along an axis of increasing restriction of freedom, reaches the other extreme represented by the theoretical concept of 'artificial language'. Actual languages or manifestations of language would occupy a wider or narrower section on this axis and be located closer to one or the other polarity, as shown in Figure 2.5. For example, a highly codified and formalised language like that of nuclear physicists would be located closer to artificial languages whereas a language of a small Amazonian tribe without a written grammar and dictionary would be close to the natural language extremity. The same placement could be applied to other types of sublanguages. For example, we recognise the sublanguages of traditional crafts to be less restricted and in a different way than the sublanguage of air traffic control.

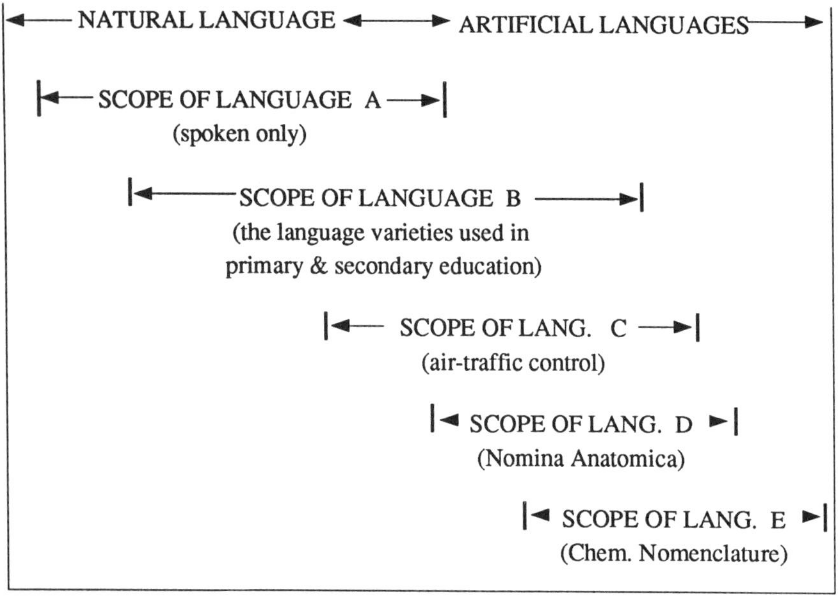

Figure 2.5 *Language types by degree of constraints*

2.5 Natural and artificial languages

In the environment of information technology the concept of natural language has recently gained a new dimension which highlights and illustrates the dichotomy here established. In computation and particularly in data processing, 'natural language' is used in opposition to 'computer languages' or 'programming languages'. This dichotomy is then exploited further by saying that the computer can process natural language only by means of instructions written in the 'artificial' computer language. In this case we can say that the computer instructions act as a metalanguage to convert natural language items and rules into a code acceptable to the machine. It is precisely those elements of natural language a computer cannot readily handle that constitute the essential characteristics of natural language.

2.5.1 *Characteristics of natural language*

The theoretical concept of natural language is characterised by a maximum freedom of formal variation at all levels of articulation, according to criteria of usage and function. This freedom of variation is founded on the absence of an external, socially conditioned, codification which can be used as a point of reference and which introduces the formal criteria of acceptability of the text of a speech act as a genuine manifestation of a particular language. Some linguistic theories call this acceptability by such names as 'grammaticality' or 'well-formedness'. The growth, diversification and variation of natural language is only limited by the boundaries of mutual comprehensibility among speakers. A fully natural language is therefore eminently flexible, open to change (for reflecting new experiences of its users), unhampered by the grammarians or lexicographers who would decide what is permitted in the way of spelling, morphological variation, syntactic structure or lexical item.

The creation of a 'standard' language requires a series of specific interventions by groups or individuals whose influence is accepted by others as being generally beneficial towards achieving the goal of a broader-based means of communication. Haugen (1966) defines the ideal goals of a standard language as "minimal variation in form" and "maximal variation in function". Standard languages thus represent a conscious and deliberate form of control and exploitation of a natural language in the direction of providing a flexible means of primarily written communication for the largest number of literate people.

A standard language can emerge over a long period of time by piecemeal adoption of unifying features proposed or created by individuals which successive groups of influential users find to be advantageous. An influential dictionary, a widely-used school grammar, or a guide to pronunciation can all exert standardising influences which may then be assisted by the recommendation of such works for adoption in schools, the prescription of usage in official documents or the social imposition of their content in influential circles of government or the Church. The slowness and the gradualness of such processes are essential for the widespread acceptance of standard languages and at the same time for the preservation of the decisive characteristics of natural language which are so important for keeping the standard language flexible and responsive to social change. This description fits the emergence of the standard versions of the major European languages which in the case of French and Spanish, for example, was officially supported by the creation of national academies of the language. However, the absence of such institutions for the German or English language has in no way impaired the speed of development nor the scope of influence of standard varieties of these languages.

2.5.2 *Characteristics of artificial languages*

At the other extreme of the polarity of formal constraint, we locate the characteristics of the concept 'artificial language'.

The BSI Glossary of Documentation Terms (BS 5408) defines this concept as "a language whose rules are explicitly established prior to its use". From a structural point of view this definition is sufficient to distinguish artificial languages from natural language, but in order to cover the external form or function of artificial languages it is necessary to add "...and whose function is to supplement natural language by greater specificity of reference, greater economy of expression and greater appropriateness to its community of users". It should further be stated that these languages have a fixed repertoire of lexical items and associated meanings and rules for their formation and combination, which can only be added to by another deliberate act of creation.

Theoretically, the creation of artificial languages can be perceived as resulting from the application of extreme constraints to a natural language so that it loses its inherited properties and adopts all the rules successively established for its restriction. This would require 'freezing' both the forms of the language and the reference of its items to the outside world and subsequently fixing form and reference by means of a new grammar and a dictionary with definitions of all possible meanings. In practice this happens in very small segments of language used for legal or ceremonial purposes, e.g. oaths, certificates, formulaic expressions, often limited to particular situations where the speech act itself represents the action.

Artificial languages are not "historically given" (Lyons 1977:118). While natural languages are grouped into historical families and are geographically distributed, artificial languages, even though many are derived from a natural language, are used in different patterns by diverse user groups. Historically, artificial languages are created in response to two major necessities which support the two major uses of special subject languages, namely the communicative and classificatory use. This development can be attributed to two motivations:

(a) Members of a speech community become conscious of the limitations of natural language in terms of (i) the efficiency of language use, e.g. the economy of expression, and (ii) the deficiency of their particular natural language, e.g. the absence of words or phrases for the expression of specialist knowledge.

(b) Members of a speech community want to record and so stabilise and order, or classify the specialist knowledge of their group. In this case the polysemic properties of natural language are perceived as an impediment to the unique identification of objects or concepts of the special subject.

These explanations exclude artificial languages whose motivation differs from these objectives, e.g. artificial ritualistic or secret languages.

Both theories of origin presuppose an advanced stage of evolution of language and linguistic theory, because they require their creators to understand the characteristics of language, the functions of levels of articulation and indeed a perception of the limitations of natural language.

These theories can be illustrated by a number of practical realisations of this concept. There are, for example the languages, commonly called nomenclatures, designed for detailed identification, designation and description of physical entities across a number of national languages. Different techniques and principles have been used for their creation. Botanical Latin, for example, created in the 17th century was inspired by the natural language model provided by the Ancient writers who had already seen the need for a systematic description of plants. Today's European botanists no longer have the background of classical Latin learnt in school and are therefore in the same position as their colleagues in other continents for whom the natural origin of Latin was never apparent. It will be interesting to observe the fate of the Latin and Greek-based nomenclatures in biology and medicine when there are no longer any links—through conventional education—with classical antiquity, its languages and cultural values.

Another international artificial language is the chemical notation; it originated in the 18th century, and recognises national language characteristics in the spelling of lexical items because it was felt that this was a better way of keeping some relationship between written and spoken form, of avoiding mistakes and of keeping the system under control. The management of this increasingly complex artificial language is now under the control of the International Union for Pure and Applied Chemistry (IUPAC).

A more modern example of artificial languages is given in documentation or indexing languages, as, for example, presented in documentation thesauri, which have both a limited vocabulary and a limited set of rules for combining words. Though these languages use lexical items and semantic relationships derived from the special subject languages they serve, they do establish a new framework of reference from lexical items to documents, i.e. by means of restrictions on the meaning of lexical items in titles or running text. The grammar of these languages is given in the rules of indexing which prescribe the possible syntagmatic combinations of elements. The lexicon of such languages is contained in the list of permitted keywords or descriptors. The lexical structure of such languages is established through a thesaurus which may also contain grammatical information. The translation from the natural language of the documents to be indexed into the language of document description is carried out through a reference from non-descriptors, i.e. natural language words with their free semantic associations, to the descriptors, with their prescribed relationships to other descriptors. The interesting point to be observed is that the artificial language is narrower in every sense than the natural language it is derived from and that it is this narrowing which constitutes the superiority of this specific language.

The most striking exemplification of the interaction of artificial and natural language comes from information technology. A computer processes, i.e. operates on, data in response to instructions expressed in a particular language. This language is artificial, by virtue of its fully human design, and restricted in scope, in accordance with the limited means of operation of the computer. The data can be linguistic or non-linguistic. When they are linguistic the success of any operation is limited by its nature: when the operation deals with strictly rule-governed aspects of the language a high performance can be expected; when it pretends to deal with norm-governed manifestations of language or even the implicit elements of a discourse, the success will be minimal.

Artificial languages can be based and related to national languages or be independent of them. Because of homography between natural and artificial languages, it is impossible to identify a single reference item, e.g. 'mile', 'billion', 'HP' or 'meningitis', as belonging exclusively to one natural or even one single artificial language. Nor is it often possible to identify a list of terms as belonging to one or another type of language. For example, it is not obvious whether the sequence 'hepaticus-badius-rufus' belongs to classical Latin or to Botanical Latin. Only the use of these items in an appropriate context identifies them as belonging to a particular linguistic system or language.

These examples permit the formulation of design criteria for artificial languages which will counteract perceived deficiencies in natural language. The measurement of efficiency has been made by three values, namely economy, precision and appropriateness (Sager, Dungworth & McDonald 1980). They can be applied to the justification of the design of artificial languages or alternatively to identify the characteristics of this trend of linguistic behaviour.

2.6 The evolution of restricted languages

Between these two extreme concepts of natural and artificial language, all languages of culture have adopted some restrictions. The motivation and the evolution of these restrictions, briefly summarised in this section, explains the development of language varieties and sublanguages of which special subject languages are of particular concern for the language industry and translation.

In its unconstrained form natural language diversifies and creates variants; if users of a common language then spread over a wider geographical area without close regular contacts, dialectal variations appear which may eventually lead to a lack of communicability and transparency. As societies evolve, we witness two trends, arising from opposing motivations, exerting their influence on the shape of the language: (i) language stratification tending towards the creation of sublanguages resulting from an internal diversification of the speech community caused by such factors as the formalisation of knowledge, the division of labour, the establishment of social classes; (ii) language unification in order to maintain social cohesion and at the same time to create larger political and administrative entities leading eventually to the creation of a 'national' language, which can then become identified with the concept of a nation or even of a nation state.

Both trends use the instrument of restrictions or constraints on language forms and functions. In order to create a national language, it is necessary to codify its written form and even, though to a lesser degree, its spoken form and control written and spoken variation. This work can be carried out overtly, by a national academy of the language with legislative powers, or covertly by assumed authority of a number of publishers, or in a mixed fashion whereby the work of a group of self-styled 'authorities' is officially acknowledged and imposed by such bodies as ministries of education, the civil service, the Law, the Church etc. The scope permitted by these rules is then called the domain of 'general', 'common' or even 'standard' (i.e. a restriction through consensus) language, acknowledging thereby that there are other forms of the language required by other areas of usage which are different both in form and function. The principal characteristic of such a 'general' language must be its openness and its dynamism which permit it to respond to the changes in society, continue to provide a common link among all members of the language community and serve as a source of inspiration for the more specialised communicative needs of the community. Translation from one standard form to another is relatively unproblematic if both standard languages cover the same areas of usage. Where these diverge, the translator is faced with the problem of choice at the level of axes of expression.

Within these general constraints of a codified general, possibly 'national', language, sublanguages evolve in response to a variety of motivations, e.g. religious practices, the social and administrative structure of a community. The motivation provided by the dual movement towards the division of knowledge into subject fields and professional specialisation of user groups leads to the establishment of special subject languages. These sublanguages are often defined in terms of the further constraints on the general language because they are somehow considered subsets of the general language, occupying a narrower range of linguistic forms available and a narrower set of areas of usage and purposes of use. This is a rather restricted view because it does not include the possibility of special languages having both quantitative and qualitative features not contained in the general language. It would therefore be better to stretch the concept of national language to include both its general language and its various sublanguages and to define special subject languages with respect to their position on the two axes of restrictions given (i) by subject specialisation and (ii) by the contrast of natural and artificial language characteristics (see Figure 2.2). This approach also avoids creating a separation between 'general' and 'special' in the sense that one would start where the other leaves off, but rather there can be overlapping usage domains, with one domain being closer to natural language features and the other to artificial language features, as illustrated in Figure 2.6.

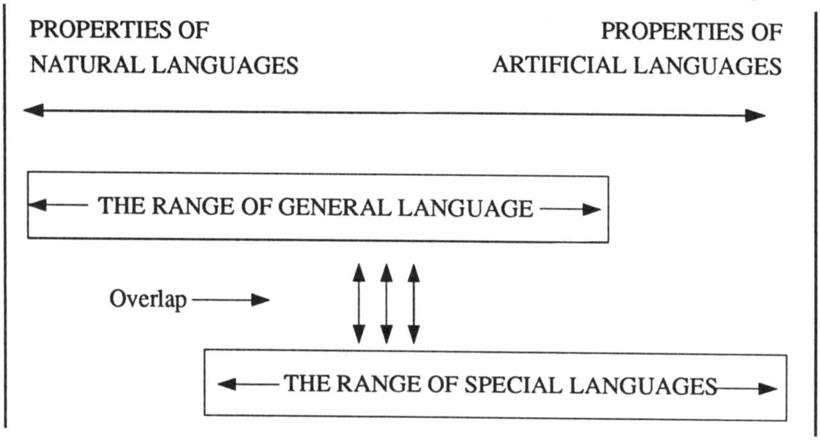

Figure 2.6 *The overlapping domains of general and special languages*

A trend towards adopting features of artificial language can be seen in every special subject language. This trend towards incorporating artificial language features in functionally and topically restricted languages is supported and encouraged on the one hand through scientific commissions which lay down rules for naming, guidelines for the writing of theses and scientific articles etc., and, on the other, through industry-supported standardisation committees who in a series of posthoc decisions attempt to consolidate earlier standardisation processes through the issue of glossaries in an effort to maintain the widest possible economy and efficiency of communication. It is, for example, common for a standards organisation to make attempts to unify and standardise the vocabulary at the basis of several connected standards documents, produced over a period of years, which show the natural proclivity of language users to diverge. The value of this work can be measured in the degree of adherence to the rules that are established. An influential journal editor can insist on strict conformity to rules and some university style manuals have been adopted by other universities with the result that the external form of academic theses and papers is very similar in each subject field. Normally it is powerful user groups of language which impose their syntactic rules or their vocabulary on others. If, for example, it is said that a particularly successful manufacturer has set a virtual standard for such products as television receivers, video recorders or personal computers, the implications are that this manufacturer has also created or re-defined the vocabulary associated with these products, their operation and parts. The simple launch of a new sophisticated product may thus introduce overnight hundreds of new items of an artificial language which may then gradually be absorbed into the general vocabulary through progressive circles of diffusion.

The trend towards the incorporation of artificial language elements is increasingly also at work at the international level where formal treaties on linguistic cooperation between such countries as France and Canada, Belgium and the Netherlands, France and Belgium or Malaysia and Indonesia have led to the creation of subject committees which regularly attempt to maintain a unified vocabulary. Their efforts are guided specifically by principles of artificial languages because they deny or avoid the development of spontaneous regional forms of language. More recently efforts are also being made to unify the language used in databases in order to increase their retrieval effectiveness. This work has a monolingual and a multilingual dimension and may use thesaurus-like devices to create bridges between the natural language of the searchers and the artificial language of the query system. Regular users of such systems readily adopt the artificial language expressions which will ensure success in consultation of the database.

Purely socially conditioned sublanguages, for example, sociolects of subcultures, do not develop in the direction of artificial languages, but rather adopt such features as heightening types of meaning, phonological variation and morphological and syntactic deviation from the national, general language.

2.7 Definition of special subject languages

The evolution of special subject languages is of special importance for the language industry because it is a special case of language creation by means of restrictions, motivated by the social structures of language users. We can now attempt a separate definition of special subject languages in terms of their function, knowledge and difference from general language. The term 'special language' is here used as a compromise designation, chosen for the sake of simplicity.

The elements which justify the existence of special subject languages belong to quite separate areas.

(a) In relation to the general language system, special languages represent a development along the axis of topic dependence, described in section 2.2.1. Special subject languages are 'special' with respect to the content of the discourse, since they serve to express what is commonly conceived as subject knowledge, as opposed to general knowledge, e.g. the language for the description of chemical or geological phenomena and speculation. Special content assumes a division of knowledge into subject fields or disciplines and is semantically expressed by the concept of special reference, discussed below in section 2.7.1.

(b) Special languages are 'special' with respect to usage and users, since they are used by people in their professional capacity. The specialism manifests itself by the different emphases on intentions of speech acts and the uses of language in relation to the nature of language, introduced in section 2.2 and discussed further in section 2.7.2, below.

(c) Special subject languages are 'special' with respect to the tendency to restrict forms in the direction of artificial languages as indicated in section 2.5 and presented in section 2.7.3, below.

The unifying aspect of these elements is the view that language is a consciously developed tool which can be planned and controlled and that it is shaped according to our perceived needs. It is the technological/engineering view which has taken over the purely scientific view of observing language as a natural phenomenon.

2.7.1 *Disciplines and subject fields*

Reference to special knowledge areas presupposes that knowledge is divided into subject field or disciplines. Such a division is equivalent to defining a set of subspaces of the overall knowledge space of a particular society. But, just as different disciplines overlap, the special knowledge spaces can be said to intersect.

The definition of what constitutes a special subject is a matter of social convention and changes over time. For example, prevailing educational policy for schools determines whether physics and chemistry are taught as separate subjects or as a 'science'. Equally, subjects like geography, considered as one subject at a certain point in time or at a certain level of education or specialism, are later divided up into constituent elements and even distributed over a wider range of major subject fields, so that, for example, geography can be found in Arts faculties and in Social Science faculties. In each of these cases the individual items of the knowledge structure remain the same, but the ordering of and the entry point into the knowledge structure is different. An individual's assessment of which item of knowledge belongs to a particular discipline is highly subjective and depends on the education received.

General language serves for the expression of general knowledge, which is whatever society defines it to be at any one time. General reference is used in communication between individuals who want to communicate and express personal attitudes to a topic in every day discourse such as conversations, letters, diaries. Beyond that, society organises itself into groups, associations, professional societies etc., each of which is characterised by specific degrees of special knowledge for which special language features and items are created.

2.7.1.1 *Special knowledge reflected in texts*

While it is theoretically important for the identification of knowledge structures to relate special subjects to disciplines, the knowledge represented in documents considered relevant to translation and the language industry is rarely of one single discipline and the knowledge possessed by specialists is also a mixture of knowledge structures.

The body of knowledge commonly known as the discipline of chemistry is not identical with the body of knowledge expected and acquired by the professional chemist. The communicative needs of a professional chemist are much wider, as can be seen in the academic curriculum, which will include courses in mathematics and physics, computing and management, and, even more clearly, in the range of documents chemists have to handle as professionals. In day-to-day contacts, they may have to deal with health and environmental protection, instruments and plants which involves engineering, transport, finance and marketing.

Special language texts diversely combine areas of special knowledge. In messages knowledge subspaces overlap and interpenetrate. Single subject messages usually only reflect the purely theoretical aspects of a discipline. In all other cases we are dealing with a subject, e.g. chemistry, and an aspect, e.g. administration (see section 3.3.1). In the so-called 'interdisciplinary' areas these combinations are accepted without hesitation; e.g. statistical linguistics is a form of applied statistics, which combines the vocabulary and the phraseology of statistics and linguistics.

A more practical way of demonstrating the difference between special subjects and the texts associated with their applications is to cite the example of translator specialisation. While there is room for a few highly specialised translators who translate the research output of a few specialists in a narrow field of enquiry, the bulk of translation is required in fields of applications covering wider areas of knowledge. While there are special vocabularies of such narrow fields as nuclear physics and molecular biology, there are very few, if any, special message forms peculiar to nuclear physics or molecular biology. In both fields we find research reports, articles, abstracts etc., the various forms of scientific discourse as distinct from the forms of engineering applications. Any classificatory approach to special languages relevant to translation must ultimately be based on the observations resulting from detailed examination of actual text occurrences.

2.7.1.2 *Special knowledge and reference*

In order to account for 'special reference', language items are classified into terms and words on the basis of the concepts to which they refer. In the environment of the language industry it is appropriate to examine how a British Standards document defines the concept 'term'.

> 'Every day words', it has been said, 'tend to become vague in meaning and rich in associations. The scientific writer wishes a word that he can define exactly and that has no irrelevant associations'. Such a word, a technical term, needs to be selected and formed with considerable care......
> A technical term keeps its life and its meaning as long as it serves the system of thought that gave rise to it....
> ...behind each term there should be a clearly defined idea or concept, systematically related to the other concepts that make up the body of thought in question.
> Moreover, the chosen term should express this concept effectively and unambiguously, and the outward form of the term should be generally acceptable.
>
> (BS 3669:1963)

The 'body of thought', can be perceived as a knowledge structure containing the concepts of our world. The concepts in this space are either conceptual primitives, or complex, in which case they are formed by linking primitives into new combinations. There is scope for an infinite number of concepts, very few of which are realised in language. While each concept occupies a point in this space, its linguistic realisation is on the whole that of a range because, as a discrete medium, language is restricted in its available expression forms. The characteristics of denotation in language permit a certain latitude as exemplified by broad references as 'table', 'energy', 'light', which are normally interpreted as referring to both a particular member or instance of the broad class and to a particular instantiation of the reference. Reference can, of course, also be special, i.e. more pointed, in such cases as 'quadruped' and 'triangle'. For highly specific reference there is, in addition, the phenomenon of proper names which permits unique and individualised reference.

Each individual acquires through his education both the general structure of the knowledge space of his society and the linguistic expression forms for accessing it. We understand 'passively', when we have only a vague idea of the place of a concept in the knowledge space. We understand 'fully' when we know the precise place of a concept in relation to others.

In general language situations it is unlikely that two individuals will refer to precisely the same region of knowledge when using a word. A certain consensus is provided by the social norms which set the confines of a traditional knowledge structure, the bounds of disciplinary subspaces and the configuration of concepts in any one discipline. It will, for example, say when a table-like object can no longer be called a table, whether the word 'breath-group' is acceptable in phonemics, and whether 'dialectology' is or is not part of sociolinguistics. In a discipline or subject field where there is a large number of concepts to be accommodated, there is usually a greater need for differentiating terms. At the same time the need to avoid overlaps between concepts will reduce the degree of flexibility admissible in their delimitation. For example, in general reference a 'lion' can be qualified as fierce, aggressive, majestic, heraldic etc. In special reference a lion is either heraldic—in which case he can be qualified as 'rampant' and 'red'—or a species of the genus 'felis', in which case a much wider selection of such qualifiers as 'old', 'mangy', 'starving', 'ferocious' or 'frightened' can be applied, but not vice versa. There is thus a difference of degree between the structure of concepts in a special subject field and the less well-defined, less 'disciplined' structure of general knowledge. This does not mean that general knowledge cannot contain well-defined facts, but only that within a special subject field there are more rigorous constraints on the overall delineation of items of knowledge.

Special subjects are therefore differentiated from general knowledge primarily by the nature of reference, and also by the fact that they contain additional concepts. This difference is one of degree and it is therefore more appropriate to speak of general reference and special reference as extremes of this distinction than of general and special knowledge.

In order to differentiate between general and special reference in linguistic terms, a distinction has become accepted between 'terms' which have special reference within a particular discipline, and 'words' which function in general reference over a variety of subject fields. Further distinctions are made on the basis of frequency of occurrence. This yields such groupings as 'the vocabulary of science and technology', which are not very useful for translation.

In order to heighten the specificity of reference, agreements are concluded on the precise meaning and expression forms of lexical items by means of processes of regularisation, harmonisation and standardisation, as well as by means of new term creation.

2.7.2 *Special usage*

The feature of special usage is partly covered by the following definition:

> Special languages are semi-autonomous, complex semiotic systems based on and derived from general language: their use presupposes special education and is restricted to specialists for conceptualisation, classification and communication in the same or closely related fields.
>
> (Sager, Dungworth & McDonald 1980)

It is important to note that only the language used by specialists among themselves provides a sufficient theoretical basis for an adequate identification of the distinctive features characteristic of this type of sublanguage, i.e. when they are communicating with other professionals at a professional or otherwise expert level, e.g. the language of chemists, or the language of dentists in their role as specialists. As subject matter, chemistry or dentistry are also talked and written about by all manner of people in a variety of circumstances generally, in semi-technical terms and in popular scientific discourse.

For internal communication by the specialist community the degree of constraint and hence previous knowledge required of the restricted rules of the language is greater; for communication with outsiders a lower range of restriction is adopted with a greater number of natural language features, for example, in the language of popular-science writing. The growing involvement of artificial language elements in specialist discourse is exemplified in Figure 2.7.

2.7.3 *Special restrictions*

For the purpose of translation and information processing in general it is important to recognise the characteristics of natural and artificial languages as they occur in special subject languages.

(a) Temporal dimension

— Natural languages are open systems which have diachronic dimensions; their history is shaped by the evolution of their rule system and their interaction with and response to social norms.

— Artificial languages can only be considered synchronically; they are created once and can change only when a modification overrides and invalidates parts of the previous system; they have a limited repertoire of rules and items which cannot be altered or added to without deliberate action. Their usage is strictly prescribed without any flexibility of norms.

— Special subject languages partially accept this property by restricting the form and range of meaning of the accepted vocabulary.

TYPES OF INTERLOCUTORS	TYPE OF LANGUAGE USED FOR: GENERAL TOPICS	SPECIAL SUBJECT TOPICS
general, non-professional	general language	general with occasional semi-technical terms
lay-person to specialist	general language	general with semi-technical & technical terms
specialist to lay-person	general language	artificial lang. elements in general discourse & popularised specialist discourse
specialist to specialist	general language	artificial language & special subject language in specialised discourse

Figure 2.7 *The pragmatic progression of specialised discourse*

(b) Acquisition

— Natural language is primary, i.e. it is learnt as a first language.

— Artificial languages are created by users of natural language and have to be learnt consciously, as a second language through the medium of the first language, which serves as the metalanguage of access.

— This is also true of special subject languages, and distinguishes them from general language.

(c) Flexibility

— Only natural language has the flexibility of paraphrase and can therefore be used as metalinguistic discourse, both for itself—English grammars and dictionaries are written in English—and for other languages we want to describe or comment on.

— An artificial language cannot function as the metalanguage in which to discourse about this language or any other; for this function a less restricted language is required.

— Special (subject) languages tend to expand in the direction of artificial languages, i.e. as they evolve they adopt a greater number of features of artificial language in their effort to consolidate the scientific basis of the subject. They may even incorporate artificial languages specially constructed to refer uniquely to concepts and functions exclusive to the subject. The special language of botanists, for example includes the artificial language of botanical description, in the same way as the language of mathematicians includes the artificial language of mathematical symbols.

(d) Forms

— Natural language is essentially spoken, its written form is secondary and represents a step in the direction of restriction.

— Artificial languages are designed to be written in the first instance. Some can be spoken but where this is possible the spoken form is always derived from the written form.

— This does not apply to special subject languages, but the principle that the written form is primary, and not as in natural language, the spoken form, has important consequences for the use of special languages.

(e) Range of functions

— Natural language is not limited in function; it is essential for the expression of emotive, aesthetic, social and phatic meanings.

— Artificial languages are usually monofunctional; they are often designed for a strictly descriptive, classificatory or communicative use and for primarily informative and directive intentions.

— These features are adopted with more or less rigour in the special languages of science and technology.

(f) Lexical features

— The lexicon of natural language is based on the complementary principles of polysemy and homonymy. Words acquire and accumulate a variety of meanings in addition to a diversification of connotations. At the same time one wordform may be used for the expression of several meanings.

— Artificial languages establish monosemic reference, avoidance of synonymy and homonymy, i.e. one word one meaning and one type of meaning, the denotation, and one reference is associated with one lexical item.

— Special subject languages pursue the same aim with less rigour; there is a degree of synonymic variation in certain types of special discourse necessary for the functional diversity of usage.

(g) Polysemy

— Natural language needs polysemy as a vehicle for the development of thought.

— Artificial languages do not permit polysemy, which excludes their use as metalanguages.

— In special subject languages polysemy is restricted because of their division according to fields of knowledges; there is also a limitation on the acceptable degrees of polysemy in different types of texts. Special subject languages need a metalinguistic function for innovatory speech acts, teaching and learning; for this purpose they keep their link to general language open.

(h) Rules and Norms

— Natural language distinguishes between linguistic rules, which determine what is an acceptable form or structure of the language, and the social norm which narrows down the range of choices to a smaller range of socially appropriate and acceptable items.

— This distinction between the rule system and the norm is inapplicable to artificial languages. Since rules and their scope are explicitly designed before the language comes into existence, they are one and the same. Hence artificial languages are strictly governed by rules which do not permit any deviations. This property makes for the conciseness and precision of artificial languages, but the concomitant absence of any redundancy makes artificial languages unsuitable for certain types of communicative situations.

— Special subject languages adopt special rules only to the extent that they do not inhibit communication.

In summary it can be said that special subject languages adopt certain properties of artificial languages, but a special subject language without any general language features would be an artificial language. The threshold between general and special subject language can, however, be delineated only by pragmatic criteria derived from usage.

In order to create a special, i.e. restricted, language, artificial language elements can be inserted in a natural language, when the forms and functions of these elements have been specifically designed prior to use. This can happen when language users agree to freeze a language in a particular state, document it and do not, after that codification, permit additions, modification or deletion of either form or reference, except by a special act of linguistic and semantic legislation. This is the case of the languages of sea and air navigation control and other special codes derived from natural language. Artificial languages, can, of course, also be generated by computer, or more precisely, all language generated by computer corresponds to the definition given above, i.e. the very act of specifying a grammar and a lexicon for a computer system is identical to the design of an artificial language. The difference lies in the production process: the computer, knowing only the limited rules it is given can only produce within them, regardless of the mode of triggering off the production process. The special case of machine translation is then a conversion process of a natural language text into an artificial language derived from another natural language.

The number of artificial language features in any one text varies with the degree of specialism and hermeticism of the discourse. In adopting features of artificial languages, special language users introduce a degree of pre-planning into their language, which is usually motivated by a desire for greater efficacy of communication and greater classificatory and evaluative impact. This is, of course, only possible with elements of language that are used for recording established experience and knowledge considered common among the specialist community and therefore no longer open to discussion, redefinition or redesignation.

This recognition leads to a further differentiation in specialist discourse according to the degree of previously codified knowledge and hence terminology encountered. Acts of consolidation of knowledge as expressed in manuals and textbooks for the advanced learner can contain a high degree of artificial and standardised terminology. Encyclopaedias and other means of popularising specialist knowledge also adopt fully regularised and even standardised forms of expression for technical concepts, though the general language element used to explain scientific knowledge to the layman retains its metalinguistic function and is, therefore, inevitably subject to potential variant interpretations.

On this basis it may be possible to distinguish between speech acts according to the degree of artificial language elements they contain. The higher the proportion of such elements, the more is the discourse concerned with restating known facts; the lower the proportion of such elements, the more is the discourse concerned with the presentation of new knowledge for which there is as yet no definitive designation or fixed place in a knowledge structure. It is therefore possible to speak of retrospective and innovative speech acts respectively to mark these two positions from the point of view of their place in communication.

Retrospective speech acts serve the purpose of confirmation and consolidation of knowledge and thus constitute a reservoir of knowledge (as in a knowledge base) and could, in their purest form consist of formal descriptions or definitions of the concepts and relations between them in a knowledge structure.

Innovative speech acts are then those which develop new theories, express speculative judgements and hypotheses, many of which require the full range of natural language phenomena to deal with the new ideas as they are being developed.

Speech acts associated with teaching occupy an intermediate role between these two form of discourse. For the learner the discourse is innovative and has then to be consolidated by reference to the established knowledge structure, so that the learner progressively acquires the artificial language elements of the subject he is studying.

The particular nature of special subject languages lies in the fact that they can consolidate knowledge in a relatively rigid system akin to artificial languages and sometimes even in full artificial sublanguages, while maintaining the flexibility of natural language for developing and transmitting new knowledge or whatever is considered new to the recipient of a message.

The implication of this distinction for translation, and especially machine translation are considerable (see section 10.7).

Chapter Two

Communication Theory for Translation

3 Elements of a Communication Theory

A theory of communication is a theory of human interaction by means of semiotic signals. These signals can be more or less direct or symbolic. For the purpose of a theory of translation, only those written symbolic signals which are exclusively produced by humans and which are called linguistic signals are relevant. Non-linguistic symbols not attributable to a particular semiotic system associated with one language require special consideration.

Communication is a deliberate human activity. Messages, i.e. written units of text, are produced with a purpose, i.e. a writer intention and a reader expectation, both briefly explained in section 2.2 (for a fuller discussion see section 3.3.2). A number of modern theories use the concept of 'messages', but do not then clearly distinguish messages from such concepts as text and document. Document is used here to mean a physical entity and is therefore generic to both text and message.

3.1 The environment of communication

Written communication takes place between individuals or groups who are thereby assigned exchangeable roles as writers and readers. Communication has a social function: it is a conscious and deliberate and hence purposeful human activity. For scientific and technical communication the purpose can be simplified by stating that it is concerned with affecting the knowledge structure of the participants. Communication also occurs in time and space—it therefore has a historical dimension. The basic condition for communication to take place is that the participants share a common code. This may be a shared writing system, a common dialect or both, but it may also be a non-linguistic code, such as musical notation or symbols of formal logic.

The name 'speech act' to designate functionally coherent interactions performed by means of linguistic signals represents an important recognition of the fact that the production and reception of language is a form of human activity and behaviour; it also indicates that production and reception constitute a communicative unit, regardless whether the act itself, as happens in translation, is physically or temporally split into separate parts.

Linguistic signals occur in messages: language as an instrument must be capable of expressing what is expected of it. In section 2.1 it was pointed out that besides communication, language has several other possible functions, e.g. classification, ideation, expression of emotion and social contact, and that these uses cannot be strictly separated. The mode of language use concentrated on in this book, i.e. translation, always entails communication and we therefore use the word 'communication' for the type of linguistic interaction captured in a theory of translation. In order to achieve this objective, however, the process of translation itself can involve the translator in other uses of language.

While message production is a primary semiotic process, translation falls in the class of secondary processes together with (i) copying, which is the verbatim reproduction of input; and (ii) transcribing, which is the reduction of coded input into another code.

3.2 Preconditions of communication

Every speech act is produced in a particular environment existing prior to, and independently of, that speech act, and every speech act is received in the same or another environment, which is the general condition of translation. The preconditions of speech acts are listed in Figure 3.1.

When the environments of production and reception are the same, the participants are less conscious of the environment than when, for example, reading a document from centuries ago, or when reading a document in a foreign language. When encountering an unfamiliar document, for example, one produced in a background other than our own, a reader's first reaction is to ask when and where it was produced. For example, translators of Goldoni's La Locandiera must be aware of the environment of 18th century Italy and England before they can decide whether to attempt to re-create the atmosphere of 18th century Italy, or to demonstrate the universality of the theme by placing it in a 20th-century English setting. The performance of a play by Shakespeare in modern dress offers an interesting contrast between a modern setting and the language of a different age in a modern pronunciation.

Within the broad environment every speech act occurs and is received against a particular background. The background is not only a physical place in time, but includes the whole range of human concerns that can be reflected in speech acts. The knowledge available in a particular period, the stratification of its society, the customs prevalent at the time, all influence what is said and written, and its form of expression.

ENVIRONMENT:

BACKGROUND OF SPEECH ACT PRODUCTION

era: historic period

setting: a. available store and classification of knowledge (topics)
governed by PERCEPTUAL, COGNITIVE,
EVALUATIVE NORMS

b. available store of language (codes) dialects, sociolects, technolects, text units, syntactic & lexical forms
governed by LINGUISTIC, PERCEPTUAL,
EVALUATIVE NORMS

c. available means of communication
governed by BEHAVIOURAL NORMS
i. set of conventional forms
ii. technical means

PARTICIPANTS:

a. social characteristics of community:
e.g. group allegiance, social class

b. individual characteristics:
FIXED: family origin,
age, sex,
VARIABLE: education,
occupation,
ideology: religious
political

c. knowledge and experience:
i. command of topics
ii. command of forms
iii. command of codes
iv. access to means

BACKGROUND OF SPEECH ACT RECEPTION OF A TRANSLATION

Figure 3.1 *Preconditions of the written speech act*

For example, a presentation of the theory of relativity in an undergraduate textbook shortly after it had been formulated in the early 1900s would have been highly complex, if not unlikely—in 1990 it is mentioned in schoolbooks, because totally different assumptions are made about the readers' knowledge. Before widespread and compulsory education, certain social groups—and not only poor ones—could communicate in writing only by employing a full-time or ad hoc scribe: this situation has now virtually disappeared in industrialised countries and with it the concomitant speech act. Knowledge of this situation is, however, essential in the study and translation of certain historical documents if we are not to draw erroneous conclusions. Technological advances influence speech acts, or create new situations in which new speech acts become possible. The technical advances in telephone services now allow intimate conversations when previously the noise level was too high for subtleties of expression. On the other hand, socio-economic factors determine access to telephones. Simultaneous interpreting facilitates the new speech act of multilingual conferences; electronic mail is another new speech act; fax transmission and television broadcasts of parliament or court proceedings are new dimensions to existing speech acts.

3.2.1 *Communicative situations*

The state of knowledge in any one era and the means of communication available establish a number of conventional forms of communication which are adopted by its users without hesitation. The form of communication itself is semiotically meaningful. For example, the formal and the usual forms of address of 17th-century letters must be known in order to understand what the writer was saying as a matter of course and in order to give proper attention to deviations from the pattern. Each society has its set of forms and appropriate codes, the deviations of which are also meaningful.

Since a text is produced by someone of one background, and received by others whose background in a translation is frequently not the same, the identities of the writer and the reader are important; just as in a conversation the interlocutors 'size up' each other, so in reading a text the identity of the writer has to be established. The following example shows the complexity of background in a multilingual setting.

An English member of the European Parliament, born of working class parents and with a university education in economics, for example, may know the regional and occupational dialects of his home town or region, and acquire different dialects during his secondary and university education. He will acquire the occupational dialect of his discipline or profession, and become familiar with the regional dialect of his eventual place of work. The language he uses within his own family may differ from all of these. When speaking in parliament all these influences are present but, as a politician, he will also be aware of the fact that few, if any of his listeners in a multilingual parliament can appreciate this rich linguistic variety and will probably adjust his mode of expression to what he perceives to be an effective common ground. After some experience he will adjust his utterances to the three potential audiences, namely to other English speaking members of parliament, to other members who prefer to listen to English rather than be dependent on the interpreter and finally to what he believes the interpreters being capable of conveying. The same considerations will affect his writing in the international environment because he can anticipate that his text will be translated. He will not usually be conscious of any of these influences—although he is likely to be conscious for a time of the dialect he learns at school—or of the ways in which he shifts from one variety of dialect to another. All of these dialects merge into his idiolect, his own blend of all these influences. All people react consciously and unconsciously to these varieties of language; translators must be able to recognise and identify them.

In any environment there are a multiplicity of writers, readers and topics. They come together in the particular situation of the speech act, and speech acts vary according to the social differences between the participants and the factors of the situations.

Figure 3.2 shows that communication can only take place in the area where settings overlap—the shaded area in the figure which represents the overlap between the two environments—and inside this setting only to the extent of shared codes. In all other cases translation requires some degree of adaptation.

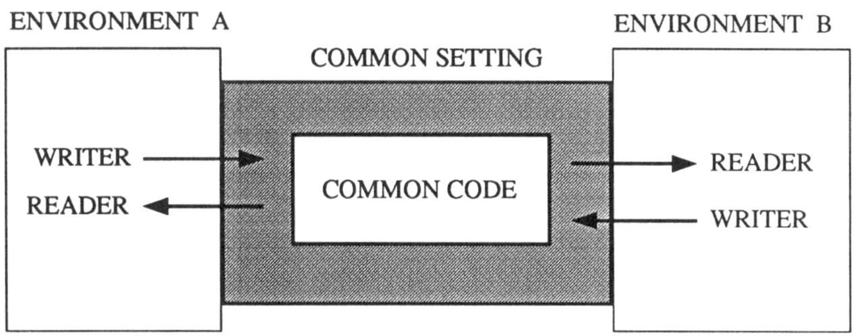

Figure 3.2 *Communication across cultural and linguistic environments*

Communication cannot take place unaided when the participants do not have some parts of a common code, hence the need for interpreters and translators. Participants from different environments can communicate only on those levels on which they share at least some forms, codes and knowledge or topics. For example, Shakespeare is still read in the original but the reactions of a modern readership cannot be the same as those of his contemporaries. Anthropologists who live among primitive tribes may acquire their language in order to become independent of interpreters, but their understanding will be impaired by their own environment which they cannot deny or forget. If they translate from such a language into a language with a written tradition, they almost invariably infiltrate erroneous cultural assumptions into the translations.

3.2.2 *The situation of the written speech act*

A combination of writers, readers and topics creates potential patterns of speech acts. By realising one of these combinations at a particular time and in a particular place a situation for a speech act is created. This is illustrated in Figure 3.3. A speech act is then the product of a particular situation and may be influenced to a greater or lesser extent by any or all of the factors of the situation.

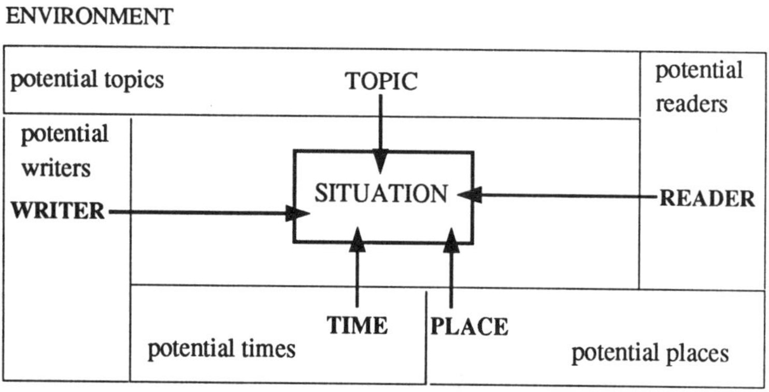

Figure 3.3 *The factors constituting a speech act in a situation*

The speech act itself is triggered off by a stimulus which may be provided by any factor of the situation or by the speaker, using a convenient situation. Every society organises situations for specific speech acts, e.g. a classroom with teachers and pupils, a call from a telephone box, the interview in a police station, or the hearing of witnesses under oath.

In any other situation which is not designed for speech acts the participants may, but need not, interact; as soon as a written speech act is about to occur, the participants separate into writers and readers. This separation is accompanied by a conscious or unconscious assessment of the relationships which are formed between them. Writers tend to be fully aware and conscious of this, but readers seldom pay attention to all the factors of the situation. In many instances such a full attention is unnecessary and undesirable, but the critical analysis of texts for the purpose of translation demands full attention and consciousness.

3.2.3 *Components of the speech act*

The situation of the speech act is initiated by a stimulus and composed of a topic, time, place, and the participants. It is further shaped by the number of participants, the roles they occupy, the relationships between them and their individual psychological states.

In all written or recorded communications, the speech act results in a 'document' which is the physical manifestation of the intended message of the writer; as soon as it exists it gains a relative independence. Documents have a temporal existence which may be very important. Dates of appearance, duration, renewal may be important as, for example, in the precise hour of a press release, the re-issue or new edition of a book, the withdrawal from circulation of a report or standard. Equally the physical characteristics of a document can be significant; for example, the position on a shelf, the place on a noticeboard, the layout of a page; the form as, for example, microfilm, tape, luxury edition; the number of copies, for example, in mass circulation, in a limited edition, in the writer's file, with copies to named persons only. The physical attributes of the text, and the personal factors, are listed in the Figure 3.4.

All these factors of the situation exist before communication takes place and are essentially independent of it. The condition of the communication, and the new situation of the speech act is, of course, modified by the communication as it evolves. According to the type of speech act chosen, there is more or less time available to assess these various factors. In an application for a post, for example, some decisions are pre-empted by the environment which specifies certain conventions, and by the situation which confines the topic on which to write. There are books with models of such letters. The choices to be made are, however, surrounded by a greater degree of uncertainty than in spoken communication. Since writers do not know the situation in which a letter will be received, they have to make a number of assumptions which may prove to be false and which cannot be corrected.

All speech acts are conditioned by a number of situational and environmental factors beyond a writer's control or influence. Only novelists or dramatists can create freely the situations of their characters' speech acts, but even they are conditioned by environmental factors.

STIMULUS to the speech act: (subject to change during the act)

— arising from the situation

— incidental to the situation

	EXAMPLES
TEMPORAL FACTORS	
— point of time	— date of production, publication, reception
— duration	— time for writing, copying, reading
— time-lag	— interval: production ⇔ reception
— regularity	— unique, occasional, regular
	— first time, last time
SPATIAL FACTORS	
— location	— position on page, in book etc.
— proximity — distance	— nationwide vs. local press
— private — public	— home vs. un-restricted circulation
— familiar — unfamiliar	— office, new job, unusual layout
— number	— rare book, limited edition, mass circulation

PERSONAL FACTORS

Relationships (real or assumed)

— numerical	— 1 to 1, 1 to few, 1 to many, etc few to 1, few to many, etc.
— psychological	— attitude of writer and reader (not necessarily reciprocal) admiration, sympathy, dislike, etc
	— mutual knowledge acquaintance, friend, stranger, etc
— cognitive	— specialist — layman equals in knowledge teacher — learner
— professional	— judge-defendant, dean-professor doctor-patient, lawyer-client
— social	— class: equal — different
	— role: patient, applicant, client
— cultural	— same, similar, alien

Psychological state in the situation: (variable in speech act)

e.g.- depressed, optimistic, cheerful, uncertain, etc.

Figure 3.4 *Factors of the situation of the speech act (variable and dependent on the environment)*

3.2.3.1 *The stimulus*

Since language is voluntary and non-instinctive, a speech act leading to a document must be triggered off by a stimulus. A writer needs some form of impetus to start a text production process: i.e. something must happen to connect a particular writer with a specific topic and a specific reader at a given time and place. The stimulus may arise out of the situation, but different participants can react differently to the same situation. For example, an ornithologist and a geologist see nature differently and therefore react differently to the same stimulus. The stimulus to a speech act may be incidental to the situation; for example, a visual impression may stimulate an observer to draw the attention of others present to this scene. A comment overheard in a train may stimulate someone to make a note in a diary. The stimulus that gave rise to a particular speech act may be explicitly stated in the message itself; this occurs most frequently in letters; for example, in letters to the press or letters of complaint it is essential to state the cause of the letter. The stimulus may only emerge in the analysis of a text. If the stimulus is not stated and cannot be detected, it is futile to speculate on what it might have been. In professional writing the stimulus is frequently provided by another document since most documents are interconnected in some way. The stimulus for a translation is an important indicator of the purpose of the new communicative situation.

Pragmatic analysis of documents brings out clearly the double stimulus of many speech acts: beside his purely poetical inspiration, Shakespeare wrote plays because he had to provide material for an existing dramatic company, just as leader writers or a columnists write because they are paid to do so.

The immediate stimulus gives way to the choice of a topic and a purpose, and these are clearly discernible. Because some speech acts are dynamic in respect of both the writer and the reader, the original stimulus may not account for the whole document. Additional stimuli may arise, as, for example, in the new thoughts which are formulated during the planning and drafting of a written document. The investigation of the stimulus is a matter for psychology, and has no bearing on the linguistic choices made in the production of the speech act.

3.2.3.2 *Temporal factors*

Point of time and duration of both production and reception, frequency of occurrence of one type of act, and incidence, all constitute the 'time factor' of a speech act.

Point of time

The time of production and reception is almost identical for spoken communications that are not mediated, but differs for writing for there are time lapses between production and completion of a document and between availability and reception. Knowing the point of time may be crucial in understanding a historical document; time references may be comprehensible only in relation to the date when a document was produced.

In translation the point of time assumes particular importance because of the inevitable time-lag between production in the source language and reception in the target language.

Duration

The significance of the length of time available for a communication, determining its duration, is obvious. Journalists usually write to a deadline, and so do many writers of reports. In journalism, in particular, there is a critical relationship between production, and reception: the form of a news story is determined by the assumption that many readers will not read the whole text.

Translation may be strongly conditioned by the time available for its production. Techniques of conference translation, in particular, are largely determined by the time constraints under which translators have to work.

Time lag

Written communication is fundamentally characterised by the physical—temporal and spatial—separation of the communication process into two separate activities: writing and reading. The most important consequence of this separation for the process of communication is that writers and readers both act under separate conditions and can therefore determine their own circumstances of production and reception of texts. Temporal separation gives writers time to reformulate a text, to construct it in consultation with others, to ask others to revise it, to delay sending it and indeed generally offers the opportunity of introducing a separate sender of a text and finally to separate the writer both spatially and temporally from the reader of a text. Readers, in turn, can choose the moment for reception of a text, repeat reading and share the action of reading with others.

The time lags, assumed or known, between production, issue and reception vary widely and are either fixed and known or totally uncertain, especially when secondary readers are involved. Different time references are required in documents that are to be presented to an audience a day or a week or a month later.

In most translations a time lag is an essential feature of the new document; but it may also occur that a time-lag has to be hidden so as not to disturb the impact of the translation.

Regularity
The relative frequency or regularity of occurrence of texts in a particular format conditions not only the way in which writers produce texts, but also our response. Serial publication differs from unique publication. In some pre-printed forms standard formulae or multiple choice questions are used which permit only individual variation of such information as the name of an applicant and date of the document. A daily newspaper contains much repetition of information and refers to previously provided information. Books are relatively self-contained and bibliographical and other references are largely given for accuracy. The more unusual the format of a book the greater is the need for indices and other cross references. Translations which do not follow the same regularity of occurrence as source language documents may have to take into account different reader expectations and may, therefore, have to make adjustments to compensate for the novelty of the situation.

A related time factor is the position of a document and its place in a sequence. A final article of a series sums up the previous ones. Such a summary will be omitted if later these texts are published as one unit. Because readers have to adjust to a new type of publication, writers tend to proceed more slowly in the first chapter of a textbook until the readers have got used to their idiosyncrasies of expression.

Since documents to be translated are often separated from their surrounding texts, attention to this factor is important.

3.2.3.3 *Spatial factors*

The importance of spatial factors which require the substitution of a translated document for a source text is self-evident.

Written documents have a physical existence and location of their own. They are produced and received in different places, except in special cases such as the legal deposition. Often the place of production can be categorised as widely as the English-speaking world: as in the case of a technical manual which deliberately avoids constructions and terms specific to British or American Standard only, and aims at an internationalised English. There are often economic and legal restrictions on the circulation of publications. The sale of certain editions of books may be restricted to either the United Kingdom or the United States and appropriate spelling adjustments have to be made to translations.

Location also means the place of an essay in an anthology, the position of a news feature on the page, whether an advertisement appears in a glossy magazine or a specialised publication with a limited but homogeneous readership, as well as the format and size of print used. Some of these elements are predetermined by the situation, others cannot be decided by the writer but depend on an editor. In translations it is important for the translator to know the physical circumstances of the target language text so that appropriate adjustments can be made.

Length of text is usually associated with types of documents. In frequently recurring texts, convention has established average lengths which are reflected even in the size of paper used. Greeting cards, telegram forms, the format of newspapers and journals are examples of such conventions. A questionnaire conditions the length of the expected reply by the space it allows. Calendars and diaries for business and office use may provide separate lines for each hour of the working day, but rarely allow much space for Saturdays and Sundays.

Newspapers vary the width of their columns in accordance with the length of the text—leaders usually have a two-column spread, short ads are often printed in very narrow columns. News features may be as short as one sentence, but there is also a maximum length beyond which a feature must adopt the form of a story or a news item. A memo may be very short, but for an essay or a report a minimum length is expected and therefore an appropriate time for production and reception is usually considered.

Where different conventions exist regarding length of texts and other physical characteristics between source and target language, this information is most important for translators.

3.2.3.4 *Personal factors*

The personal factors are divided into those which are more or less stable before and during the speech act and those which may change rapidly.

Relationships

The relationships of age, sex, education etc. of the individual participants do not vary from speech act to speech act, and hence form part of the background. Other relationships between participants change, however, not only with different speech acts, but can change in the course of a single speech act. They are dependent on the other elements in the situation.

The relationships between the participants are perhaps the most important aspects of the situation, and are influenced further by the number of participants. They are subdivided into numerical, psychological, cognitive, sociological and cultural relationships.

Psychologically, the relationship may be one of love, admiration, sympathy, neutrality, dislike, fear or hatred, etc.; it occurs between people who are or are not social equals, or have the same or different roles in their society. Severe difficulties can arise in translation from a wrong evaluation of this relationship.

Cognitively the relationship is one of inequality or of equality of knowledge between participants. Writers may be experts on a particular topic, but they cannot write like experts unless they are addressing other experts; if the readers are not experts, writers must adjust to the degree and kind of knowledge they know or assume their readers to have. Divergent levels of knowledge between cultures may require major adjustments in translation (see section 7.3).

The social role of writer and reader also determines their relationship. The reader may be addressed as a citizen, a motorist or a student by a judge, a policeman or a professor. All members of society have a very great number of roles and the situation determines in each case what role they have as writers or readers. Social role can also be expressed simply as superiority and inferiority of authority between sender and recipient in a particular speech act, e.g. the relationship between soldier and officer, employer and employee which not only determines forms of address, but what sort of demands, order or requests can be expressed. Translation is most problematic when social roles are either not fully recognised or difficult to replicate.

Cultural differences can significantly influence a speech act. For example, textbooks of English as a foreign language written for Europeans are unlikely to be effective in Asia. The cultural relationship between author and reader may involve a totally different background. On the other hand there are texts which are meaningless outside their immediate area of use simply because there are no readers for them. By contrast, some international advertising agencies produce different copies for the same product in different countries. Translation is most difficult when cultural barriers have to be surmounted.

The greater the number of participants, the more difficult it becomes to define the relationships closely, and the readership is depersonalised into broader social, intellectual and economic categories, as in newspapers, advertising and television which are addressed to particular income groups or social classes. Most written documents, especially publications, are produced by one writer for an unspecified but certainly very large group of people, hopefully, in some cases millions. Literary works may, on the other hand, include direct addresses to imaginary individual readers.

Psychological state

The psychological state of the participants in the situation and during the speech act also affects the situation. A letter may convey the irritation, anger, amusement the writer felt and which may even have prompted the letter. It is equally important, although not so often remarked upon, to note the psychological state in which documents are received. Often, a reader initially finds something tedious or hard to understand which on re-reading can be understood with little effort and even be found fascinating. Writers may even make assumptions about the psychological state of the readers which influence their planning of the message, e.g. inserting a joke or an anecdote in a lecture, or attempting to arouse anger and indignation in a speech.

Secondary readers, which is the position of the translator and the reader of the translation, have to take into account the writers' psychological state, and that assumed in their primary readers as well as their own at the time of reading. In printed texts the psychological relationship is assumed to be neutral, except in explicit polemic and argumentative writing. In written documents which have gone through several stages of revision, or are of joint authorship, the psychological state of the writers is irrelevant, unless it is deliberately contrived.

3.3 Choices in communication

In order to arrive at a speech act in a given situation, writers must choose a substance for the communication. A message is always about something, which we here call the topic. In addition they must choose a technique of communication in which this topic is conveyed and received. The range of available topics and techniques is provided by the environment. This combination of topic and technique is not arbitrary, they are dependent upon each other. They are made on the basis of the situation and may change as situation and speech act influence each other.

Choices in the speech act are made in response to the assessment of the situation, and are therefore simultaneous with it. Figure 3.5 lists these choices as a sequence, an inevitable consequence of tabular presentation; in reality these choices are made simultaneously, especially in spontaneous communication, and are as difficult to separate from each other as thought and language.

These choices determine the linguistic coding and the compositional coding of the communication inasfar as these are not pre-conditioned by the conventions established by the environment. Besides topic and technique, which both have their linguistic and non-linguistic side, there is a third major area of choice which is most strongly situation-determined, namely the purpose of the communication.

3.3.1 *Choice of content of the message (its topic and aspect)*

Writers, readers and content exist in a particular environment and converge in a particular situation which is defined by time and place and the relationship between the participants which is known or assumed.

Choice	Examples
Topic	
1. conceptual field, subject presuppositions about the reader's knowledge	politics, numismatics
2. aspect	personal, administrative, didactic, testing, descriptive, historical, publicity (journalistic, advertising, propaganda)
Purpose (communicative use of language)	
1. purpose of whole text	social/informative/directive/ discursive derivative: translation, summary, precis
2. purpose of text segment	id.
Affectivity highly emotional ◄──► neutral	
Language — native language — foreign language — sublanguage by topic	
Text type	memo, schedule, essay, report
Techniques of communication	
1. type of code:	
— non-linguistic	drawings, formulae, musical notation
— linguistic + non-linguistic	
2. external form	written to be spoken, written to be read, etc.
3. technical means	holograph, photograph, print, fax, telex
4. axes of expression	
— geographical	dialect ◄──► common/standard
— topic-dependence	
— level: elementary — intermediate — advanced	general ◄──► special code
— degree of restriction	natural ◄──► artificial
— formality	frozen ◄──► intimate

Figure 3.5 *Choices in the speech act (interdependent, limited by environment & situation)*

3.3.1.1 *Topic*

The writers' knowledge decides the range of topics to choose from, their assessment of the relationship decides the assumptions they can make about the readers' knowledge or interest in the topic, and this in turn allows them to select what knowledge they can express implicitly and what has to be presented explicitly by variation of the level of expression.

The choice of topic is closely linked with the stimulus, and is initially pre-linguistic since it is concerned only with the choice of a conceptual field. The stimulus causes a person to select a subject field such as mathematics, music or cookery, before a decision is taken to either write a talk about mathematics or write formulae, whether to write in musical notation or in prose about music, whether to demonstrate a cookery recipe or write it down. This second choice is then influenced by the purpose of the speech act. The topics we can choose are the conventional areas of knowledge, the school or university disciplines, whose conceptual relationships are already established prior to a particular speech act. These relationships among concepts can then, of course, be modified by speech acts.

Each society has its own structure of knowledge. These structures are similar in the pure sciences and diverge the more they are influenced by social structures. This can have an effect on translation.

3.3.1.2 *Aspect*

All topics are, further, treated under different aspects, i.e. from different points of view. For example, art can be discussed from a historical point of view, a personal point of view, or a didactic point of view. The broad subject of education has a theoretical aspect, a practical aspect, a financial aspect, and an administrative aspect, as well as the journalistic and historical aspects which every subject possesses.

The choice of aspect of a topic, like that of the topic itself, arises directly out of the whole situation. It is circumscribed by the environment, and directly reflected in the semantic coding.

Texts can be modified by a change in aspect. For example, a scientific description can be adapted for a textbook by ordering the material according to didactic principles. Such changes in the aspect of a document may also be made by the translation.

3.3.2 *Choice of purpose (Intention + Expectation)*

The next stage in the process of communication is that of choosing a purpose for the speech act, identified in 2.2 as the convergence of a writer's intention and a reader's expectation. Whereas the choice of topic can be dependent upon the writer alone, the purpose of a communication must be chosen with regard to the reader. It is the presence of an intention which converts a text into a message.

It is clear that, as a conscious human activity, every message is produced with an writer's intention and is received with a reader's expectation. For a theory of communication, it is, however, also necessary to accept that intention and expectation need not coincide in the same message, since, once the text is produced, the writer rarely has full and absolute control over its destination and acceptance. Since texts, once they are produced, can have an independent existence, any reader can utilise them at will, quite independent of the writers' original intention. Especially in multilingual situations, a message can be associated with several intentions addressed to different reader communities. This is a further reason for speaking of documents as a generic category with two subclasses of texts and messages respectively. Figure 3.6 is a summary statement of the structure of messages.

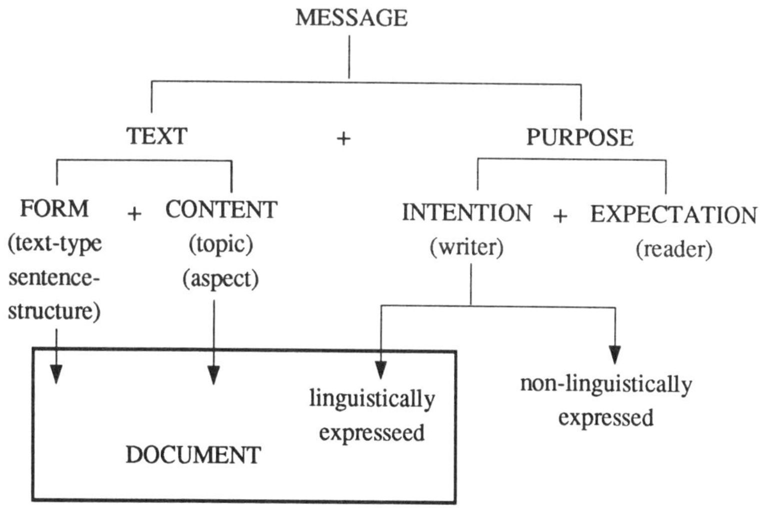

Figure 3.6 *The structure of messages*

For translation in particular it has to be noted that purpose can be expressed linguistically or may have to be assumed through choices made at the level of the text type or the communicative situation. Identical documents may represent different messages according to the intention with which they are sent or the expectation with which they are received, e.g. a regulation which is binding for one group of people but not for another, to whom it is not specifically addressed. This distinction can be influential for the interpretation of a translation, where, e.g. an election leaflet, which is naturally meant to be persuasive for the monolingual potential electors of one linguistic community, loses its former purpose because for another community it can only be received as informative of the type of persuasion used in that election. The same applies, of course, to the leaflet as soon as the election is over.

Purposes can be, and have been, classified in many ways: here we identify five major ones for messages used for written communication in special subject fields and these purposes clearly determine the linguistic coding.

Special subject texts which are translated can be said to be produced for five distinct purposes:—social—informative—directive—discursive—evaluative. A single purpose may inform a whole text, but many texts are multi-determined, the purpose changing from sentence to sentence in the same way as there may be shifts in subject and aspect. It is important to distinguish between the overriding purpose of a text and the purpose of a sentence, paragraph or other text segment of a text. For example, an overall discursive editorial must initially inform or state the presuppositions that are made. This informative purpose is, however, generally mixed with discursive elements, as is clearly seen when the opening sentence of a leader is compared with the news-item it refers to. A leader often concludes with a recommendation to policy-makers. This directive purpose is, however, seldom realised as a list of "do's and don'ts", but it is part of the overall discursiveness. An experimental report which is usually informative, often has a directive section pointing out procedures to be followed. A discussion paper for a meeting may have as its main purpose the direction of the committee to adopt a certain course of action, but this proposal is preceded by a discursive analysis of the various arguments that have led to the decision.

Purpose is defined in relation to the four main factors: writer, reader, topic and situation (time and place). As in other stages of analysis, purpose has to be established both from the point of view of the writer and from the point of view of the reader. The writer's intention may not be acknowledged or understood by the reader, who may interpret an informative memo as directive and take offence. The writer may discursively raise a number of questions and hope that they are interpreted as directions by some of his readers. A regulation written for a limited group of readers becomes informative for those not affected. Point of time also affects the purpose: a law, which is directive as long as it is in force, becomes informative once it is superseded, even though this was not the original intention, and the information conveyed may be correspondingly inadequate. A secondary reader very often has a different expectation. For example, a secondary reader of original source-materials, may read an old copy of a Baedecker not to plan a trip, but for a description of the country at that time. The factors which influence the selection of purpose are represented in Figure 3.7.

Purpose	Writer	Reader	Topic	Situation
Social				X
Informative			X	
Directive		X		
Discursive	X	X		
Evaluative	X		X	

Figure 3.7 *Factors determining orientations of purpose*

3.3.2.1 *Social purpose*

The social purpose is situation-oriented, and attuned to the social roles of the participants in the speech act; there are exclusive social topics, such as greetings and other socially obligatory exchanges, but otherwise the social purpose is only a dimension of varying importance attached to other intentions. For example, employees talk differently to their superior at an annual party than at a formal interview. Translators must be able to recognise messages informed by a social purpose, although it is highly unlikely they will ever have to translate messages with an exclusive social purpose because such messages are usually written only by and for people with an intimate knowledge of the social environments in which they occur and on which they depend. Such messages include the formal address, the social page or column of a newspaper, the printed message in a greeting card.

3.3.2.2 *Informative purpose*

Informative messages are topic-oriented, writer, reader and situation all ranking equally second in importance. The eliciting and furnishing of information is paramount, and this information may be of varying degrees of objectivity. A stock list or a library catalogue are in principle neutral and objective, as is the classified advertisement for a job or a film. A news-item may, superficially, seem objective: in fact, so many different choices and selections will have been made prior to its appearance, that its objectivity is deeply suspect.

3.3.2.3 *Directive purpose*

Directive messages are reader-oriented: if readers respond in the expected way, or more specifically, do what they have been told, the communication has been successful. Such an immediate test of the efficacy of a communication is not usually available in other speech acts. The topic and the situation vary only the form of the message. The most basic example of the directive purpose is seen in requests, orders, instructions, prohibitions, exhortations, warnings and their distinctive formal requirements are obvious. The directive purpose is often phrased as a statement, a wish or even a question. A writer may enquire whether a reader feels cold as an indirect invitation to request assistance; or in a political pamphlet, an analogy may be drawn with a historical event in order to encourage readers to emulate this example. The directive purpose may apply to a limited number of readers only, as in laws and regulations where the purpose is informative for the general reader and directive for the specific group of people listed, or falling into the categories set out.

3.3.2.4 *Discursive purpose*

The discursive purpose is the most difficult to describe; it is heavily writer-oriented, and depends on the interaction between writer and reader. Unlike the other purposes its nature is bi-directional, since the writer must involve the reader in the speech act. The relationship between writer and reader is of fundamental importance and is appealed to in the message. The writer requires the approval of the reader and constructs the message to obtain it. In developing the argument of the discourse, the writer must anticipate and direct the reader's thoughts. Topic and situation are unimportant, although it is obvious that certain situations are less likely to call for a discursive approach. An essay most strongly shows the discursive purpose.

3.3.2.5 *Evaluative purpose*

Evaluative speech acts exploit the classificatory use of language but may also involve emotive and informative uses. The writer relates to the topic either as an individual, a social role player or a subject specialist and expresses this relationship in a deliberate evaluation of a topic. The distinction between general and special language evaluative speech act lies in the degree of self-awareness with which the natural classificatory use of language is exploited and controlled and, on the other hand, in the reference to pre-established types of assessment and criteria of evaluation. A regular meat inspection report, for example, is an evaluative speech act for the laboratory specialist who produces it; passed on to an office, it can become both purely informative of the fact that a job has been carried out and evaluative and directive for the recipient of the report, who may have to issue a health warning or a reprimand to the producer.

3.3.3 *Choice of affectivity*

All purposes vary in the degree of personal involvement, i.e. in the degree of affectivity displayed by the writer. A writer can use a pre-printed greeting card or write his own message; a military command differs significantly from a polite request, a definition in an encyclopaedia is affectively neutral, whereas the explanation of the same phenomenon given by a mother to her child may be highly personal and emotive. The larger the number of writers involved in the production of a message, the less affective it will be. The communique issued by an official to a mixed crowd of journalists and the general public at the opening of a new hospital has a social purpose but is minimally affective.

Affectivity allows writers to vary the message. In an informative text writers may impress a reader to believe, rather than state a fact, in a directive text they may persuade rather than command, beg rather than demand; in a discursive message they may show real or assumed personal engagement in the argument, enthusiasm rather than perfunctoriness.

Affectivity is reflected in the choice of words and the mode of expression (see 3.3.6.4). A switch from a casual to a formal tone in an otherwise informal exchange of messages signals a distancing between a writer and a reader, in the same way as, after formal introductions at a reception, participants sometime tentatively increase their affectivity by adopting a more familiar tone in order to get to know each other better.

Purposes are rarely pure in any one text and coexist with varying degrees of affectivity. Even a dictionary which is one of the purest form of informative message, can be affective, if, for example, it is produced for children.

Affectivity may become irrelevant in an industrial translation environment, when it is simply an expression of unintended idiosyncrasy of a writer. Translators must nevertheless be aware of it because it can affect the degree of formality of expression suitable for the target readership.

3.3.4 *Choice of language*

The choice of language does not normally arise nor does it appear to be problematic in a monolingual society, but for multilingual mediation it assumes a major importance.

The language chosen can be a 'national' language, i.e. a language which is accepted as the official vehicle by the government of a speech community and in most cases this is the language chosen for translation.

In communication with people of another cultural setting the choice of language is surrounded with complex considerations of courtesy. This is particularly true in the increasing cases of correspondents who have a good command of each other's languages. For example, when writing to someone in a foreign country, it may be polite to use the foreign language: to do so may, however, be construed as a slight on the correspondent's command of the writer's own language, especially if he has replied to the writer on a previous occasion in the writer's native language, and the writer then does not do him the honour of replying in the same language.

Special problems arise in countries which admit parallel linguistic systems; there may be two official languages, there may be accepted minority languages with a limited range of accepted application and there may be variants of the same language or alternative languages, the use of which has political or cultural implications. Countries and institutions can have complex linguistic regimes which are safeguarded and protected by legislation. For example, there are some variations of the same language in two countries, e.g. German in Austria and Switzerland; and there may be variants in one official language, e.g. in Norwegian.

In translation for international use there is further the question of language variants by country. For example, a choice may have to be made between US, UK, Canadian or Australian English, between European or Canadian French, between Swiss, Austrian or German German.

Most languages have a national standard which is established and maintained by some official or quasi-official body. This usually extends to spelling, sometimes pronunciation, the morphology and rules of syntax. There is usually guidance rather than rules in matters of larger textual units, and there is only a limited possibility of a generally acknowledged lexicon. Very few languages are stable enough and can afford to maintain a regularly up-dated dictionary that a writer or translator could rely upon.

While up to this point choices were general, or at least not specifically related to linguistic realisations, the subsequent choices all involve linguistic features at some level of expression. In most cases of non-sophisticated monolingual communication these choices are largely automatic and heavily preconditioned by the previous choices for professional communicators. They are, however, of particular significance for translingual communication.

3.3.5 *Choice of text types*

Once these externally conditioned choices have been made there are the choices which directly affect the form of the message itself and which immediately precede coding. These are first the choice of the overall form for the message in the shape of a text type, for example a letter rather than a note, a telephone call rather than an electronic message, a summary rather than an abstract or a critical review. All subsequent choices are conditioned by the conventions governing traditional text types. For example, having chosen a telephone call rather than an electronic message, a participant becomes a speaker in a dialogue at a level of formality appropriate to this form of contact and the relationship with the listener.

In a simple model of communication, messages consist of a knowledge content and an expression form (see Figure 3.6) which come together in a document of a particular structure, namely a text type. Text types are historically and socially conditioned modes of organising knowledge in spoken and written discourse. They are fully discussed in section 4.1, below. Here it is sufficient to indicate this choice in the sequence of decisions leading to the production of a message. This choice entails selection from a large number of patterns established by tradition and habits for particular user groups and situations.

3.3.6 *Choice of techniques of communication*

At this stage of planning the speech act a potential sender of a message has to decide on the technique of communication. This is fundamentally either written or spoken and usually both linguistic and non-linguistic. The choice between written and spoken communication is conditioned by the situation and by tradition. The means to choose from are provided by the environment.

Even though we are only concerned with the detailed analysis of written language, it is useful to summarise the available techniques.

3.3.6.1 *Choice of non-linguistic vs mixed linguistic/nonlinguistic communication*

At some stage in the communication process a choice has to be made regarding the system of communication, i.e. (i) whether to communicate non-linguistically by means of some semiotic system or other; or (ii) whether to communicate primarily linguistically.

The choice is not between linguistic and non-linguistic means, because linguistic communication by its very nature requires the vehicle of a script or voice which both can only be realised by the inclusion of non-linguistic elements.

Non-linguistic communication in the form of gestures, signs, diagrams, illustrations is of no particular interest to a model which aims at describing translation. Since, however, language cannot be produced in a vacuum, every linguistic communication is inevitably accompanied by some type of non-linguistic communication which is either purely incidental and vehicular, such as voice or script with its individual physiological variants; it is deliberate, but nevertheless inevitable, such as facial expression and gesture in speech and by the kind of paper, size and type of print etc. in written communication. These extralinguistic factors can be quite important in the planning of communication. They are very significant for translation and interpreting because so many of them are culture-conditioned. For example, the type of script to be selected from a variety of possible printed typefonts in the transliteration of words from other scripts; the presentation and layout of texts on the page; the intonation and emphasis in interpreting.

3.3.6.2 *Choice of external form*

Participants not only have the choice of speaking or writing but in each of these groups the alternatives of immediate or mediated communication, i.e. whether to speak unaided or through instruments like a hailer, a microphone, via a tape, radio, telephone etc. or alternatively whether to write in long-hand, on a typewriter, or whether writing goes through several stages of correction before it appears in print.

Participants are aware of the time lag between the production and the reception of a text and adjust their expression accordingly.

There is another fundamental choice in written language: whether it is written to be read or to be spoken. If it is to be spoken, it may be produced to be uttered by the speaker himself (a speech, a lecture) or by somebody else (a 'ghosted' speech) and further, the speaker may want to give the impression that he speaks without a script.

Recipients hear directly or indirectly with varying time-lags, the voices often distorted; or they read the text in the writers' own hand or in some printed form. Reading itself is, however, differentiated by degrees of attention which range from casual and cursory reading (scanning or skimming) to repeated reading—the difference between a short news item or an advertisement, and a learned article or an entry in a reference work.

For texts to be translated in the conventional manner it is assumed that a choice has been made to write for 'mediated' production; this choice excludes anything whose final form is handwriting or single copy typing by the speaker, such as personal letters, diaries, or any matter whose final form is not on paper, such as signs, posters, inscriptions and grafitti. 'Mediated' also implies that there is a time-lag between production and reception, and that the production process goes through several distinct stages which allow for correction or change of coding. Regarding reception, translations are also restricted, namely to a range between casual and repeated reading which is, nevertheless, considerable in diversity.

The choice of external form is, on the other hand, already situation conditioned, and for translated texts, i.e. writing to be printed and read, the situational factors are, of course, of varying importance. The inevitable time gap implies that there is always a different place for reception, which, however, is also under the control of the reader. As far as number is concerned translation deals mainly with the one-or-few to few-or-many relationship, which entails that the individuality of the reader is mostly disregarded, hence social and intellectual groups are addressed rather than individuals. The range of mutual knowledge is limited and the psychological state tends to be neutral.

The choice of external form not only restricts the subsequent choices of means and mode of expression, but also implies a distinct set of coding procedures. For mediated writing in an industrial environment a writer is restricted to existing typography and the conventions normally associated with it, i.e. the meaning of hyphens, semicolons, italics or underlining instead of italics, etc. It also means adhering to such conventions as govern the use of apostrophes, complete sentences, exclamations etc.

3.3.6.3 *Choice of technical means*

The technical means at the disposal of the participants are determined by their social position and role (a type-writer, a short-hand typist, access to printing, broadcasting, etc). In modern communication the means of sending messages have diversified, and so partially blurred the traditional distinctions between written and spoken communication. The difference between the informal electronic message and a conversation or a telephone call are newly available alternatives which are changing existing conceptions about the nature and choice of message forms.

Not all of these techniques and combinations of techniques require separately identifiable forms, but they certainly influence the coding of the message and the way of presentation. The listener normally hears a message once only. The absence in written texts of supporting aids to comprehension, such as facial expression, gestures and intonation, require a more careful planning of the message so that an even distribution of information is achieved. Good writers, who have acquired the appropriate rules over many years, make these adjustments intuitively; but rhetorical techniques vary from language to language and have to be consciously learnt for full reception, understanding and efficient production.

3.3.6.4 *Choice of axes of expression*

There are further choices to be made which are best explained as several axes of variation within a linguistic system. Any speech act would then be located on a point of any of these axes, as described in section 2.2.1. A combination of such points can be said to characterise a document.

3.3.6.4.1 *Geographical variation*

The axis of geographical variation has the common, national language at one extremity and a local dialect at the other. In between, according to the ethnolinguistic structure of the environment, there will be dialects of regions and such diversifications as town and country variants and in some cases even age variations. In some languages with wider distribution, there may be some sort of a supranational form of expression in speech and/or writing. This is the case for Arabic, Chinese, English, French, Malay, Russian and a few other languages. Translation in an industrial environment is normally assumed to occur at some undefined level of standard common language. This can cause considerable problems in languages like German which have to correspond to three national standards or Spanish which has national standard variants all over Central and South America.

3.3.6.4.2 *Topic dependence*

For a satisfactory theory of communication we accept that any one speech act does not occupy the full range of any one language, even within particular geographical confines, but operates within the special language of the particular topic.

For some topics, like farming and old-established technologies like pottery and weaving, there are geographical, social and occupational variants or sub-languages; for science or other subjects used by a small number of speakers whose education has been more linguistically homogeneous there are levels of expression only and no geographical and formal variants. The use of variants depends on the social conventions governing the use of language. The means available are further restricted by the command the participants have of the topics, codes and forms.

Choices at this level involve the writer or speaker in the selection of the special language appropriate to the topic of communication chosen. According to the requirement of efficiency of communication and the hermeticism of the community of its users, these languages adopt more or fewer characteristics of artificial languages. It is therefore possible to locate speech acts or texts on the axis of greater or lesser restriction or artificiality (see Figure 2.5). This important fact has to be recognised in translation because the corresponding sublanguage in the target language system may not have developed along similar lines of restriction.

The remaining choices are more in evidence in the individual expression form than in the linguistic system.

3.3.6.4.3 *Level*

According to the previous knowledge presupposed among their readers, writers refer to their topic in a general or a specialised way, i.e. they choose a level of expression. While topic and aspect are clearly choices of content of communication, the choice of level of expression is more linguistic than a matter of knowledge content. The level of expression ranging from general to special according to the difference of knowledge between the participants has been described in section 2.7.3.

For efficient communication with a general readership, writers choose concepts which are readily understood by non-specialists and these concepts are expressed in words belonging to the general language (also referred to as the 'common core'), shared by the majority of participants in the environment. Levels of expression can be illustrated by the example of teachers who guide students from one level of language to the next higher one in specialisation. They must assume the lower level to be known in order to explain the concepts of the next higher level, which they do in terms of the lower one before actually naming the new concept. Generally speaking, the choice of the level of language to be used is determined by the degree of identity or difference in the background and by the type of relationships which exist or are assumed.

Communication across cultural barriers cannot include the same number of presuppositions as when a cultural and cognitive equal is being addressed. A university textbook in physics presupposes a secondary school level of knowledge and therefore uses the special language of physics at an intermediate level. A teach-yourself book in physics is addressed to the lay reader and therefore has to start off with general language and gradually introduce the special language required for the topic.

Many translation difficulties arise because of inadequate attention to the level of a topic. For example, newspapers presuppose some knowledge of current affairs presented in previous issues and while they do not normally use highly specialised language, a great number of their presuppositions on the cultural, social or psychological plane have a similar effect and can make newspaper articles difficult to comprehend for secondary readers.

3.3.6.4.4 *Formality*

The choice immediately preceding coding itself concerns the mode of expression. This choice is again preconditioned and depends heavily on the participants and the situation, and to a lesser extent on topic and purpose. It is made on the axis of formality, identified in section 2.2.1. The modes identified here, are often called stylistic levels, a description which has to be rejected because style is a much wider notion than modes of expression and tends to be associated with qualitative judgments, whereas modes of expression only deal with varieties. These modes, frozen – formal – consultative – casual – intimate (Joos 1967), are points on a continuous scale, like the colours of the spectrum, which merge into one another, but have been given distinctive names to mark points on that scale. The words are used here with their customary denotations; 'consultative' having the smallest intension because it is generally defined by elimination. All five modes are characterised by organisational, syntactic, lexical and morphological features.

From intimate to frozen, pre-planning of the speech act increases. The intimate tone is normally spontaneous, the consultative is individually planned, whereas the formal and especially the frozen are planned in advance. For example, legal documents may not vary in mode for centuries, and formal addresses are usually a generation or two behind casual usage. Casual or intimate utterances which are carefully planned exist; e.g. the 'aside' in a lecture, or ad-libbing by an entertainer. Rather than contradict, these phenomena strengthen the argument, since spontaneity is expected and, to be effective, the pre-planned utterance must be presented as if it were spontaneous. Planning is dependent on the technique of presentation, and consequently frozen and formal texts are usually written, and casual and intimate texts usually spoken. If frozen messages are spoken, as still occurs in some legal and liturgical formulas, they are usually read aloud from a printed document to ensure accuracy and hence legitimacy. The written-intimate or rather the pseudo-intimate is also found in commercial greeting cards, but the very variety of such cards emphasizes the point that the intimate tone has the greater freedom of expression normally associated with spoken language.

The complex interaction of influences on modes of expression can be seen in Figure 3.8.

	FROZEN	FORMAL	CONSULTATIVE	CASUAL	INTIMATE
TIME	neutral	→ of increasing relevance →			most important
PLACE	general public	→ of increasing specificity →			particular most differentiated
INDIVIDUALITY	disregarded	←——→			most differentiated
NUMBER	one:many	——→			one:one
RELATIONSHIP	unknown/general strangers		colleagues	friends	intimates
TOPIC	unlimited	← wide range →			limited range
Examples	contract patent	annual will	textbook instruction	gossip column	diaries letters

Figure 3.8 *The interaction of mode of expression and situation*

Frozen & formal

Speakers of a formal message have little freedom of choice; they must use certain forms of address, and certain words and phrases because their meaning has been established by the legislature, the court, a written constitution, or by custom and usage: there are, for example, accepted conventions for drawing up wills and contracts.

Freedom of choice is a function of the role of the participants. Frozen and formal documents are impersonal because they are produced by role players, by people not writing as individuals, but as holders of some office or position. The casual and intimate tone is employed by individuals addressing other individuals and the degree of intimacy is dependent on their degree of mutual acquaintance.

Frozen and formal documents are further distinguished by grammatical completeness, and a high degree of repetition. Formality is associated with a hyper-correctness of syntax and morphology, an intolerance of mixed or loose constructions to the extent of supplementing linguistic means by compositional ones. Frozen documents often use different formats and sizes of type as well as numerals. This is to minimize misinterpretation and ambiguity and since it is a normal tendency of language to economize and simplify, such documents use archaic and more complete constructions. For example, a hire purchase agreement may have the following phrase: "If the buyer ..... ii. sells, pledges, lends, lets on hire, or otherwise parts with the property in or possession of the goods....". Pronominal reference is generally avoided; this leads to repetition, and thereby redundancy. Words often appear in pairs or strings so that one defines the other and thereby limits its denotation, e.g. "to bestow and award", "to order and command", etc..

Casual & intimate
Casual and intimate modes, on the other hand, rely on the detailed knowledge speaker and listener have of each other so that an almost private language is created which can tolerate great simplification, because the situational references are very narrowly defined. The intimate mode, also, supplements linguistic means by non-linguistic ones, but for different reasons. Gestures and facial expressions supplement the intonational patterns to express the extreme complexity of affectivity present in the intimate mode. Non-linguistic sounds serve as pause-fillers as do vacuous phrases like 'sort of', 'you know', 'I mean' etc., and are used to maintain continuity, to forestall interruption, or simply to avoid silence. Repetition is also found in the casual mode, and to a greater extent in the intimate mode, for phatic reasons.

This slackness and looseness in intimate speech is reflected in the lexical range of the modes. The formal and frozen mode have a wide lexical range, the former encompassing all technical languages, the latter technical languages, and legal/archaic terminology; whilst the casual mode has a much more restricted range, closest to the boundary of educated common core. Because of the extreme freedom of 'intimate' its lexical range is unpredictable. Two people whose social relationship is such as to determine that their style of conversation be intimate are likely to share common interests, and may very well employ the technical language of those interests, as well as a highly developed private vocabulary of general language words with unusual meanings, private neologisms, and typifying, evocative, place names. Finally, profanity and slang can occur only in 'intimate' and 'casual'.

Casual and intimate, because of their predominant occurrence in spoken language, use contracted and elided forms, which, when written, are indicated by an apostrophe. The contracted forms 'don't', 'won't', 'we're' etc. are invariably present in intimate but never found in frozen or formal. It is at the level of 'casual' and 'intimate' where the greatest difficulties occur in translation across cultural barriers, because of the different interpretations of certain signals.

Consultative

The consultative tone has hitherto been defined only as the central area between two extremes. It is often described as the normal or neutral tone. It is the written and spoken language used by speakers who address the listener as an equal with the same level of education or professional or social standing. It is also used by speakers with a lower degree of education to address listeners of a higher degree of education and social standing. It tends to be affectively neutral, especially in the latter case, and is concerned with all aspects of a topic except the personal one, where often a casual tone is preferred.

Its outward signs are complete, but not overcorrect, grammar, planned utterances, a full range of lexis to reflect the full range of topics available, but without either archaisms, slang, or private denotations. For special effects it can borrow features from formal and casual speech, and this is often done in a didactic or a publicity aspect as well as in its use for social purposes. The consultative mode is the one foreigners usually learn and consider the only mode available. It is also the mode most commonly chosen by translators when they are unsure of the appropriate mode of expression. Translator's inability to vary the mode of expression in accordance with the source document is the main cause of heaviness of expression, and absence of fluency and spontaneity in translations.

4 A Theory of Text Types and Messages

The choice of text type is that step in the production of an autonomous or dependent text, i.e. a translation, which determines the macrostructure of the coding itself. With a topic and a purpose chosen, the writer must decide on the order, structure and pattern of communication before choosing the techniques of communication and actually starting to write. Recognition of text type is also the reader's and translator's first reaction to a document.

Traditionally, messages are considered autonomous units of communication. Since, however, a message can be a single word, a sentence, a paragraph or a number of any of these, such a definition is inadequate. It, therefore, becomes necessary to examine the question more closely.

Since a message is usually identified with the product of the activity called 'speech act', it may convey the idea of a temporal and spatial unity of production which in many cases is unjustified. Production of written texts is rarely limited to a single period of time, but may be interrupted, delayed, planned to occur in stages etc. It is therefore necessary to have criteria which determine when we are dealing with a complete entity and when there are interim stages in the production which yield products which can play a separate role in communication. There are several criteria and approaches to determining what constitutes a message.

4.1 Text types

Since writing is a motivated human activity, the writer always has a more or less specific pragmatic situation in mind. In our structured society such situations have become conventionalised; regular patterns of communication have produced typical text types associated with particular intentions, e.g. birth certificates, application forms, instructions, manuals, grammars and encyclopaedias. These text types signal part of the intention of a text; if the writer sends the text directly to a reader, as e.g. in personal hand-written correspondence, the original intention with which the text is written, is the sole intention of the message and in this instance it coincides with the reader's expectation. Such a situation, however, is a rare occurrence in an industrial environment where texts are usually the result of multiple authorship, undergo various stages of modification, known as revision and editing, and are then used for a variety of communicative situations by different user groups over a period of time, a division which is increased by translation.

Conventional categories of text types are identified according to such features as topic, intention, mode of expression and situational factors, but mainly according to the social and knowledge relationships between writer and intended reader. These general categories are pre-scientific, and there is no single generally agreed and established classification of text types that is usable in discussions of translation. Neubert (1985:125) offers an interesting explanation of text types by calling them "socially effective, efficient and appropriate moulds into which the linguistic material available in the system of a language is recast".

There are hundreds of names for conventional text types and dozens in any one area of human activity supported by speech acts. In any one field of activity users handling numerous documents need names for their identification and consequently coin names to this end. Information scientists and documentalists have created certain classifications of documents, which are, however, made for the specific purpose of storage and retrieval. Some text types, especially literary ones, have undergone extensive analysis so that there are detailed descriptions of types of poetic and narrative texts, for example. Zierer (1979) classifies text types for translation and lists three major classes of text, i.e. expressive, persuasive and informative texts, and exemplifies them. He gives play, novel, poem, satire as examples of expressive texts. He characterises tendentious novels and didactic poems as lying on the intersection of informative, expressive and persuasive texts, and sermon, advertisement, political pamphlet, commentary and leaders as fully persuasive texts. In his scheme, purely informative texts are scientific treatises, reports and memos. But narrative reports and biographies already overlap with the expressive function. A definition of some hundred text types from the fields of science and engineering can be found in Sager, Dungworth & McDonald (1980:147-182). While the lay person usually associates text type with content, e.g. medical report, police report, book review, cookery recipe, in many cases, the same content permits a variety of text types, expression forms and more than one pattern of syntax or choice of words. There are, for example, a great variety of reports on diverse topics which are based on the same overall text structure. Written documents are one possible form of expressing content beside spoken language (dialogue, monologue, talk, etc), drawings, pictures, moving pictures, etc. Knowledge content can also be expressed by non-linguistic means and many messages consist of a combination of such forms. Text types and their associated expression forms can also be ordered by sociolectal, technolectal, dialectal and rhetorical features occurring in communicative situations and, to a lesser extent, by personal idiolectal (stylistic) elements.

4.1.1 *Macro text types in science and technology*

In the absence of a generally accepted, cohesive and wide-ranging categorisation, text types are exemplified here by the broad classification developed for scientific and technical English and first presented in Sager, Dungworth & McDonald (1980:134-147). The essence of these observations is that text types are seen as highly conventionalised patterns of general purpose and organisation of content suitable for specific situations, which provide the external form of speech acts.

As pattern of content organisation, over a wide range of topics, text types can be defined in terms of the manner in which they arrange and represent a conceptual field, i.e. in the way they represent and reflect a writer's view of reality. As far as linguistic choices are concerned, these authors group the mass of written texts, usually occurring in technical and scientific environments requiring translation, into four broad categories with distinct formal characteristics independent of topic. These categories show distinct coding procedures depending on a number of situational factors and on the way they organise and structure the content of the communication. These broad categories are schedule, memo, essay, report.

The basic functions of the four broad text types imply certain pre-conditions in the preceding choices which are presented in Figure 4.1.

4.1.1.1 *Schedule*

This broad class of texts is used for organising and detailed structuring of a conceptual field according to criteria emerging from the situation and the purpose. This is done through listing items in units of disconnected prose. Dictionaries, catalogues, indices, sets of rules and regulations are simple instances of schedules. There are very specific problems of mediation associated with this text type, because only if the same conventions of presentation of information on a page apply to the source and target language communities can translation be limited to linguistic matter only. A language in which the order of importance of elements is expressed from top to bottom and from left to right, following the writing conventions of that language, requires adjustment in non-linguistic elements if a source language does not accept the same tacit value assumptions.

The macrostructure of schedules is predetermined by convention, the order of elements is determined purely by the content. Typical examples of schedules are address lists, time tables, agendas or road safety regulations.

	STIMULUS		
SCHEDULE	The writer's wish to order a topic appropriate to the situation or in general		
MEMO	The writer's wish to create a new situation as a result of this speech act		
ESSAY	The writer's wish to interpret a topic in general or situation-specific terms		
REPORT	The writer's response to a reader's request to record an observed situation		
	PERSONAL FACTORS		
	Writer	*Reader*	*Text*
SCHEDULE	often anonymous/ collective	situation-conditioned	written for a reader in a situation
MEMO	acts in social role	spec. role	addressed to reader
ESSAY	acts as individual	general	unspecified reader
REPORT	subordinate to reader expectation	known & specific	independent of situation
	TEMPORAL/SPATIAL FACTORS		
SCHEDULE	general or situation-specific		
MEMO	specific		
ESSAY	general		
REPORT	specific to recorded situation		
	TOPIC		
SCHEDULE	detailed structuring of topic by aspects		
MEMO	establishes relationships between writer and reader		
ESSAY	personal, subjective interpretation of topic		
REPORT	representation of topic in another defined situation		
	RELATION TO REALITY		
SCHEDULE	may be based on a situation, but the speech act may create a new situation, e.g. a new classification		
MEMO	writer and reader know the situation; or writer constructs it, e.g. a new commercial contact		
ESSAY	writer knows situation, reader does not		
REPORT	record of a separate situation		

Figure 4.1 *Preconditions of the four broad text types*

4.1.1.2 *Memo*

This broad class of texts covers messages which establish a connection between participants and a conceptual field under any aspect and for any purpose. By relating participants to a specific topic, memos directly create new situations, and can therefore be called the most direct realisation of speech acts as linguistic 'action', as it occurs in letters, textbooks, notices, manuals, advertisements etc., which are all concerned with the immediate interaction of participants and topics.

The macrostructure of memos is largely convention-bound, the internal order of the message is determined by the situation as seen by the writer. The memo may consist of several separate parts of inter-connected sentences.

Translation of texts belonging to this broad class needs careful situational analysis in order to ensure that emphasis of attention on participants is duly observed in a changed linguistic background.

4.1.1.3 *Essay*

The generic class of essay is concerned with the personal interpretation of a conceptual field and hence of the experienced reality reflected in it. It is the writer's view of reality without any other constraints than the communicative intention stipulated here for all categories described. Examples of essays are leaders, columns, articles and dissertations.

The macrostructure of the essay is free; the writer determines the internal structure and produces closely inter-connected sentences.

Translation of this class of texts corresponds most closely to the conventional views of translation, because it focuses on the writer, rather than the reader and the situation.

4.1.1.4 *Report*

Texts of this broad class create a record of the reflection of a conceptual field in a particular situation which is separate from the situation which produces it. It is not limited to organising linguistic reality and adapting it to a situation, like a schedule, but is a description, a narrative, a statement with or without evaluation of reality as it is manifested at a particular time and place. It may be the report of a past event, a football match, a concert, an experiment, a contemporary event, minutes of a meeting, or a future event like an economic forecast. It is further differentiated by being a speech act commissioned by a reader who entrusts a writer with a specific job of observation, the results of which are collected in the report. The writer therefore organises it according to existing expectations which are enshrined in pre-established conventions.

The macrostructure of reports is either specified by the reader or otherwise bound by convention. The reader as commissioner of the report also determines the internal sequence of the sections of reports, which are clearly divided into sections of 'recommendations', 'conclusions', 'appendices' etc.

Translation of reports responds to varied demands. Heavily situation-oriented reports rarely require translation, unless they occur in multilingual environments. Topic-oriented reports, like book reviews or scientific conference proceedings, are frequently translated in industrial settings.

In industrial settings, these broad, generic text categories are realised only in specific types which can be associated with the conventional text types established in any one society, with possible restrictions according to topic and aspect. For example, an advertisement is always of the generic type MEMO but its specific form of job advertisement, election poster or leaflet depends more specifically on the choices the participants make in the speech act.

4.1.2 *Reader recognition of text type*

Since the text type itself has a meaning, its recognition conditions the readers' response. Text types can normally be identified immediately from their compositional features and produce an initial effect on expectation. Readers recognise the message as, for example, belonging to the class of schedules, reports or essays etc. and this recognition arouses certain expectations. The text type tells them how they are addressed: as individuals or as members of a group, and who addresses them. Identifying a message as a schedule, readers know that the items listed in a vertical column may be of equal importance or in preferential order; and also that they follow a logical rather than a syntactic order. In a report, they know they can decide to read certain sections only, such as the conclusions or findings, and they are conditioned to finding them in a certain place. In a memo they know that they must read the whole text before they can judge which parts are of interest to them. In an essay they know that they must start from the beginning to find the approach to the argument, before they can read selectively.

Readers can, however, react to the documents they receive from two different angles. If they consider them as personal messages, they must receive them in relation to their individual background, involving the writer and possibly a sender. Texts isolated from an intention and hence from senders and recipients need not be considered by a theory of communication. But when texts become messages they are objects of a communication theory, because a specific sender has attached a particular intention and/or a recipient has associated a text with a certain expectation in the pursuit of communication.

There are, however, many documents in existence about whose origin and original intention we have little, if any, information. Such documents are deprived of their original message function and we can only study them as static objects, i.e. as texts. Once a text is thus divorced from writer and reader and finds itself outside its original pragmatic circumstances, it is simply an item of writing, a document which may be re-used by another writer, by any reader, sender or recipient with a different intention, and thus re-enter the domain of communication.

Much literary criticism is concerned with discussing texts independent of their original environment and the lasting value of literature is based on the assumption that the original message is either universal, or otherwise transcends the temporal and location boundaries of its period of creation.

4.1.3 *Criteria for defining a textual unit*

Since speech acts can be iterative, for example, a sequence of letters, and extend over a period of time with interruptions, as, for example, in the stages from a white paper to drafts and so on to a final piece of legislation, independent criteria are needed for deciding what are textual units and how they can be defined. In the sequence of linguistic elements from word to text which can constitute a message, the text type is the largest unit which is entirely determined by pragmatic criteria and is thus the prime class of units. But text types on their own do not provide us with sufficient criteria for identifying textual units since there is no clear distinction between single items and items in collections and groups. For example, a "yearbook" contains many separate messages, all with their own unity, and the text type "encyclopaedia" provides the external unity for what is otherwise a more or less arbitrary number of articles written by a multiplicity of authors.

The unity of a document has been sought to be given by purely linguistic, semantic, pragmatic, i.e. personal or situational criteria. Purely linguistic criteria are normally inadequate, since almost any linguistic unit can constitute a message and consequently a text. Semantic unity is also an inadequate criterion since texts can cover a wide range of topics. Features of unity have, therefore, to be sought in such global characteristics as aspect, level, mode of expression and the very elusive concept of 'style'.

4.1.3.1 *The concept of textuality*

Some authors have created the new concept of 'textuality' in an attempt to come closer to the elusive concept of a textual unit. Beaugrande & Dressler (1986), for example, stipulate a number of characteristics or "standards" of textuality which they divide into text-centred and user-centred criteria. It is obviously not necessary that all the criteria be fulfilled, but the authors do not indicate priorities nor do they give quantitative criteria to determine minimal conditions for their concept of textuality. The following elements are considered to be text-centred:

— Cohesion: which is exemplified by grammatical dependencies, such as pronominal reference;

— Coherence: which the authors define as the ways in which the components of the textual world, i.e. the configuration of concepts and relations which underlie the surface text, are mutually accessible and relevant.

The following elements are considered to be user-centred:

— Intentionality: defined as the writer's or speaker's perception of beginning and end of a message;

— Acceptability: defined as the reader's or listener's acceptance of a message as being a unit of communication;

— Informativity: defined as the extent to which the occurrences of the presented text are expected vs. unexpected, or known vs. unknown;

— Situationality: defined as the factors which make a text relevant to the situation of occurrence;

— Intertextuality: defined as the factors which make the utilisation of one text dependent upon knowledge of one or more previously encountered texts.

The so-called user-centred criteria are highly subjective. While writers usually have a perception of what constitutes a complete text, they do not necessarily express it explicitly in a single message and at a single moment in time, as we can see from many texts which receive later additions. Readers, according to their education and familiarity with writing conventions, also have a perception of what constitutes a complete texts, but this may be dependent on their expectation. Otherwise they can only assume that the message they have received is a complete message. 'Informativity', as defined here, seems hardly relevant, because there are many completely vacuous texts. The notion of using 'intertextuality' as a criterion for determining textual unity looks like a circular argument. If a text depends on a previous text, it is possible that both texts form a unit, rather than constituting two separate texts. This leaves 'situationality' as the only genuine criterion, but even this is weak and no more than a probability rather than a certainty.

We conclude that these criteria offer no significant advance on our ability to determine textual unity, and that we have to fall back on the conventional criteria of text type and the respective textual markers for beginning, end or continuation of text and text segments.

4.1.3.2 *Text types as efficient units of communication*

In order to strengthen the arguments for considering text type as units, they can also be defined as a set of features we utilise for producing, predicting and processing textual occurrences. Inasmuch as the production of a message, expressed via a text type is purposeful, a text type can be said to act as a predominant determiner of economy, cohesion and appropriateness of a message.

Text types are economical units because their form conveys a meaning which is conventionalised and hence generally known, so that the participants in the speech act do not have to spend effort in decoding its meaning. They are cohesive units because many contain strong signals indicating the unity and inner coherence of parts of the message. They are also appropriate because they can signal the intention and thus create favourable conditions for message reception. Many text types are closely fitted to communicative situations and therefore ensure their appropriateness to the speech act.

In translation not all criteria of communicative textual quality may be equally enforceable. In fact, the derived nature of translation-specific text types introduces different standards for measuring the efficiency of texts.

4.1.4 *Inter-related texts*

Texts rarely occur as isolated and unique creations. Texts and messages are related to each other by the various people who are involved in their production and reception, by the situations in which they are used, by the topics they deal with and finally by the form chosen for their expression. All writers are familiar with a large number of sequential texts which directly or indirectly influence them; therefore, most conventional writing can be said to be shaped by the text forms and segments individual writers have personal experience of producing and receiving, thus providing continuity and stability at the macro level of communication. The existence of set phrases and idioms is a further confirmation of this repetitive nature of text production. Even in the field of literature, authors who seek a certain originality have to make great efforts to free themselves from the models of the many forms of writing they are surrounded by.

For a theory of communication and translation we have to discuss relationships that exist between documents at the level of expression forms (text types, fixed phrases, etc.) and at the level of the content (sequences of pragmatically related documents).

4.1.4.1 *Formal inter-relation*

We can distinguish three sequences of formal inter-relation relevant for translation in an industrial setting:

(a) The sequence 'pro-forma ⇒ text ⇒ message' can be found in pre-printed forms and pro formas, but also in what is called standard letters and similar fixed-format documents suitable for stereotype situations.

(b) The sequence 'model ⇒ text' is less formal; it occurs when a writer has a model document as a guide or independently chooses an existing document as a pattern for modelling a new message on.

(c) The sequence 'draft ⇒ text ⇒ message' is the normal pattern when a complex document is being produced.

If the production is entirely in the writer's hands, there is no clear separation of the phases; in many cases, however, drafts and intermediate versions are seen by others and formalised patterns of revision and modification exist for such composite processes of text production. Formalised processes of text modification are discussed in section 4.4.1. The specific case of translation revision is examined in section 8.8.

In order to teach them writing, learners are given guidance and models of text types, such as reports, essays, précis, etc. Guidance is expressed in such documents as style manuals, handbooks for writers etc. and is often accompanied by model texts. Many of these models are deliberately produced for the occasion and constructed to exhibit a graded progression of complexity. They are meant to teach good and accepted usage, are variously prescriptive and in some very special cases even represent narrowly defined standards, as for instance in rules of classification and cataloguing and highly repetitive test or inspection reports. Patterns of organisation of texts are usually established for small groups inside a particular firm or institution, e.g. rules about writing standard specifications or other standard documents.

4.1.4.2 *Content inter-relation*

Documents can also be interrelated by content. In industrial environments writers usually have to fit the documents they produce into a sequence which is part of a more complex communication event. A draft final report, for example, reflects the interim report and foreshadows the final report. An undergraduate textbook must take cognisance of existing textbooks for schools, in the same way as an advanced course-book assumes the knowledge conveyed by an undergraduate textbook. Documents also refer to each other by such devices as footnotes, citations, quotations and bibliographic references; they logically succeed each other as, e.g. in the many documents that make up the sequence of court proceedings, contracts or official enquiries. Sometimes documents are collected into a new form and so constitute a new message type, e.g. proceedings of a conference. Writers, just like translators and interpreters, need to be informed of the content of previous related messages.

4.1.4.3 *Inter-relation by imitation*

Imitative writing such as literary parodies, travesties and other forms of emulation are special texts dependent upon the form of others. The imitation of forms is frequent and institutionalised in literature, education and advertising. The imitation of text forms in literature and advertising is irrelevant to our concern as this mode of writing does not cause any additional problems for translation. Recipients of the message are expected to recognise the text as an imitation of other known texts, and this purpose does not change in translation, though it becomes a major issue to decide what target language models, if any, are suitable candidates for imitation while maintaining some relationship with the source text. Imitative writing in education is part of the normal learning process and not a subject of translation.

4.2 A model of document production and reception

In the model of communication developed here for the purpose of translation it is assumed that documents are constructed on the basis of abstract contents which can be expressed by linguistic means (natural languages), by non-linguistic means (artificial languages, e.g. mathematical, chemical notations) and by a combination of the two. Writers produce documents with a certain purpose which partly determines the text type they choose. This purpose is translated into the original intention of the message, but since the intention need not be overtly expressed in the message and since the intention of a message can be changed without affecting the expression form, we do not consider it at this stage.

4.2.1 *The role of participants in production and reception*

A theory of communication of written messages distinguishes between the several functional agents participating in the act of communication. These are:

— Producers of texts and messages: the professional or occasional but always subject-specialist writers who convert an abstract content into language.

— Mediators: such diverse agents as editors, translators, revisors, abstractors, conference translators, who all introduce some form of modification of a text. They add to, delete from or transform documents with respect to their content, intention or form. Their function is a double one, they are recipients of texts which are not addressed to them and they are producers of modified texts at the same time. Translators are recipients and producers, always on behalf of others; information scientists may combine the function of recipient and communication agent. Further discussion of their functions and types of activities follows in section 4.4.

— Communication agents: commissioners of texts, senders of texts, who either instruct producers or mediators, or use existing texts to send to recipients; they can be publishers, or officials requiring their subordinates to produce texts for public distribution, advertising agents, etc; their function in the communication process can best be described as initiators of messages or agents ensuring the conversion of potential into real messages.

— Recipients of texts and messages: the end users, i.e. the people addressed by the messages, or indeed people who read other people's messages with a different expectation (see 4.2.3.1).

These functions are interchangeable and several functions may be performed by any one or the same person at a time, except, of course, those of producer and recipient. Recipients may, however, act as their own communication agent, for themselves or for others when commissioning a translation. They may also carry out the function of mediators, if they decide to edit, or translate a document. They are unlikely to produce a fully edited and typed or printed new version or a written translation for themselves alone. As soon as a document is modified for the use of others, the roles would change again, producers becoming mediators, and possibly also communication agents at the same time.

Each agent has a different approach to the fundamental operations performed on documents, viz. creation and writing, understanding and reading. Modification is a dependent speech act, considered here as a secondary operation to writing. This approach is conditioned by its role in the communication process.

4.2.2 *Production*

Writers convert the abstract conception of the content of a text or message they have conceived or that has been suggested to them into a linguistic form. This process is usually called writing or drafting.

The coding process brings together all the environmental and situational influences and the choice of topic, purpose, text type, technique and mode of expression, and transforms them into the linguistic and compositional features of the message.

— Linguistic features are not only those elements normally described by grammar, but include, on the one hand, the more fundamental ones of logical patterns of presentation, i.e. the choice of referent and proposition and, on the other, the selection of word categories and of individual words, terms, idioms etc.

— Compositional features are all those elements in written and spoken language which are not strictly linguistic in realisation, such as tone of voice, volume, pauses, emphasis etc. in spoken messages, and their written counterparts, e.g. capitalisation, underlining, punctuation, paragraphing, layout, etc.

Figure 4.2 shows the various modes of referring and their types of coding. Only those signals which are linguistically expressed are usually subjected to translation. What is left unexpressed, because it is assumed or presupposed in the setting, needs consideration when a change of culture and conventions is involved in the circumstances of translation.

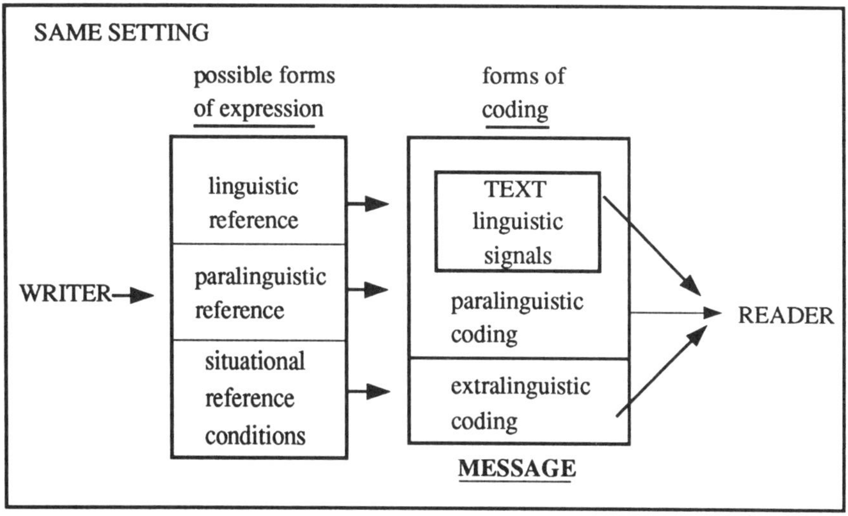

Figure 4.2 *Modes of coding*

Figure 4.2 also shows the difference between text, the linguistic expression only, and the message which includes the non-linguistically expressed parts.

Coding itself can be structured into separate phases which in practice, of course, are inseparable:

(a) Semantic coding involves the conversion of concepts into words and the appropriate word categories, which permit the expression of the relationships intended between concepts and their formulation into syntactic units. A writer may want to express something as a process, verbally, as a quality, adjectivally, etc., relate two observations causally, or as a condition operating at a certain point in time. This selection is controlled by the rules of word formation, pronominal representation, the choice of prepositions, conjunctions etc.

(b) Syntactic coding takes these semantic elements and connects them into 'acceptable' units. This process is subject to the rules of what is normally called 'grammar', but this concept is wider than most conventional descriptions allow. For example, English has two grammars, one for the written and one for the spoken language with their separate rule systems for different text types. Syntactic coding uses the social norms governing the particular text type to restrict the possibilities offered by linguistic rules. The rules of grammar guarantee what is usually called the 'well-formedness' of a sentence for the respective text type, so that it can fulfil all the various functions and purposes required of it. Syntactic meaning is subsumed under semantic coding, so that syntactic coding comprises only formal aspects such as agreement, sequence of tenses and morphosyntax as well as phono-morphology.

(c) The last stage of coding is determined by the technique of presentation chosen, i.e. it is either phonological or graphemic. The major choice, particularly relevant to translation, is between linguistic and non-linguistic coding because non-linguistic coding is also culture-conditioned and rules may differ. For example, there are different practices concerning the use of commas and full stops with numerals in several European languages.

(d) The activities of re-reading and correction, editing or re-writing offer no problem of interpretation to original writers because they can refer back to the abstract content they have conceived. The revision of translation is a double process of text comparison and correction.

(e) Communication agents—in rare cases, writers themselves—address the text to recipients, thereby providing it with a specific intention. If they have control over document production, they can ensure the expression of their intention in the document itself. If communication agents have to rely on existing documents, e.g. a librarian conducting a literature search for a scientist, they can choose material written for a broadly specified readership, e.g. an article in a learned journal, or messages originally intended for a different readership, e.g. an accident report, a doctoral thesis.

4.2.3 *Reception and understanding*

Reception of messages does not follow the reverse process of production. Hearing or reading a message, recipients first of all have to recognise a particular graphemic or phonological code which they can assign to a language they know. Understanding the syntactic coding allows them to accept what they have received as coherent units of this language. With reference to their own semantic code readers interpret the referential meaning of the individual words, the relations among those words, and the general meaning implied by the mode of expression and the text type. Analysis of the syntactic coding permits the recipients to understand the relationships among concepts created by the arguments of the text. The broader, pragmatic meaning of the message can be understood only by reference to the situation and the environment. Only if recipients can operate within the same code, i.e. have as wide a range of the code as the sender, can the communication succeed at all these levels.

Reception of messages is based on the following data:

— the presuppositions and assumptions in the background and the situation;

— the conventional meaning of the words used together with the identity of any references that may be involved;

— certain psychological preconditions which are explained below, in section 4.3, under the heading of principles of successful communication;

— the context, linguistic or otherwise of the message;

— the fact, or supposed fact, that all relevant items falling under the previous headings are available to both participants and both participants know or assume this to be the case.

Reception itself is a selective process, in the sense that it is rare that the complete message, as deliberately conceived by the writer, ever reaches its destination. Traditional communication theory speaks of noise in the channel of communication, which can be interpreted as interference during transmission or as the form of the message not being suitable for the means of conveyance. In a more linguistically explicit theory, noise can be identified with external impediments such as either or both (i) a discrepancy between intention and expectation at the outset and (ii) the absence of shared elements of knowledge, including shared knowledge of code among the participants in the speech act. Another way of expressing obstacles to reception is by the degree of precision in the determination of presuppositions about the readers' knowledge and by the degree of appropriateness of the assumptions made by the sender of the message about the reader's expectations. In a message addressed to a wide readership, individual recipients, after analysing the intention and relating it to their expectation, decide whether the message is relevant to them. If the intention of a message coincides with their own expectation, there is a good match, and decoding of content can begin. If it does not, recipients superimpose their own expectations, or in the rare case of professional readers, e.g. critics or book reviewers, suspend their own expectations and attempt to read the message with the original intention or the expectation of a putative readership. These conditions for reception are illustrated in Figure 4.3.

Reception is followed by understanding of the message which is again a selective process. Theoretically, understanding consists of an analysis or interpretation of the content of the message through the filter of the reader's expectation which eliminates what is unwanted and registers expected elements of information in a certain priority. In technical discourse, for example, connotations of words are usually excluded from this level of interpretation, while in poetry they may be considered of equal importance to denotational meanings. In practice readers are influenced by their prejudices and hear what they want to hear. The ability to select what best fits expectations and to order information input by degree of relevance is a matter of experience. Readers improve and accelerate their reading-understanding of texts as they progress in their study of the appropriate subject field.

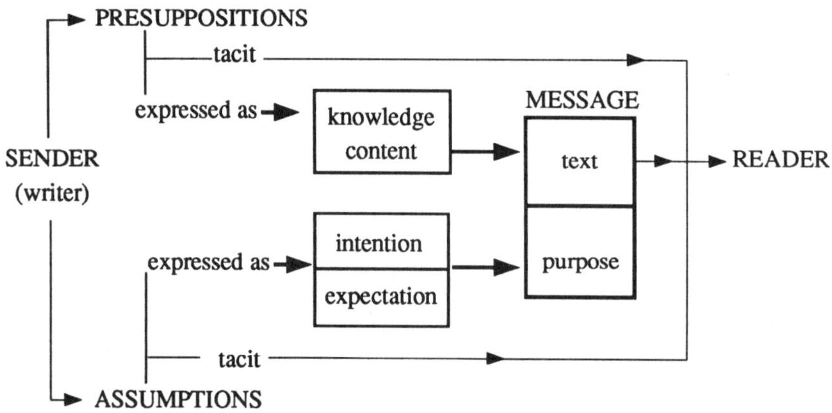

Figure 4.3 *Presuppositions and assumptions in the speech act*

Difficulties in the analysis of messages arise out of the fact that the linguistic realisation may have introduced an ambiguity caused by the rules of the code or by any of the features influencing coding. An article, the choice of an adjective or a colon may serve as an indicator for several features, as well as being a basic requirement of the code. Often only the frequency of indicators and their distribution allows a conclusion about their function. For understanding readers must know more than the rules of the code before they can ascribe the choice of a tense, the use of a pronoun or the omission of a conjunction either to the requirement of the code, or to the communicative intention of the speaker. Writers must have a full command of the flexibility of the code to represent all the environmental and situational constraints they want to reflect. For understanding a lesser degree of knowledge is required, the so-called 'passive' knowledge.

It must also be recognised that reading is not a single undifferentiated process but varies from detailed and repeated reading to simply glancing at a document in order to identify it or to decide on its relevance for a particular purpose. Consequently, the understanding associated with reading can either largely ignore the details of linguistic realisation or concentrate on the mode of expression and the choice of linguistic items and features. Text production can be geared to particular reading habits or demand certain modes of reading. For example, newspaper paragraphing and column presentation techniques are intended to facilitate rapid reading; manuals are carefully structured to permit repeated reference and easy finding of isolated sections.

The communication process is only completed by the readers' reaction to what they have understood, and this depends on their recognition of and response to the chosen purpose. For example, the informative purpose has succeeded, if a reader believes or accepts the information given, in the same way as the directive purpose is accomplished, only when readers have carried out what the message has directed them to do.

Reflections on the possibility of total reception and the inevitable selectivity of understanding are of considerable consequence for a theory of translation. If translators, like any other readers, inevitably select in reception and subsequently further select in understanding, it becomes a matter of personal experience whether translators can satisfy the information needs of their clients or not. This point is discussed more fully in section 7.3.

4.2.3.1 *Primary and secondary reader*

The distinction between coincidence and mismatch of intention and expectation is vitally important for measuring the success of communication. In cases where there is a general match of presuppositions and assumptions writers address a primary readership. All recipients not included in the writer's intention are secondary readers who have to evaluate the communication accordingly.

The distinction between primary and secondary reader is vital for all communication, but it plays a particular role in certain types of translation: readers who ask for a translation of a message addressed to them directly, may be primary readers, if it can be assumed that writers intended to but could not address them in their own language, or did not know that the readers do not understand the writers' language. If readers ask for the translation of a message addressed in the first instance to someone else, they are merely the recipients of a text and are, therefore, by definition secondary readers; worse, since they cannot identify the intention they cannot even be sure whether a translator can help. Translators can then translate the text while maintaining the more distant role of secondary reader, or they can modify the text so that it fits the readers as primary readers; the translators' ability to transform the document for either purpose partly depends on the nature of the document, for instance, to what extent the intention is explicitly expressed and therefore discernible by translators. It is clear, however, that secondary readers may have to deal with intention signals of documents that are addressed to primary readers. In such cases the writers' contribution to the success of communication can be evaluated fairly, only if the role of the readership is fully taken into account.

4.2.3.2 *Assistance in reading-understanding*

In order to overcome the difficulties of selection in the process of reading understanding, elaborate techniques have been devised for assisting readers. Mediators, for example, provide abstracts and summaries and translators regularly provide summary translations of business letters or relevant current awareness information. In regular dealings with documents written in another language most professional readers have also developed habits of expectation. It is in such an environment of expectations and assistance in understanding that a theory of translation has to place the translation process.

4.2.4 *The product*

The product of communication can be examined from three different positions, that of writers, readers and mediators. Communication agents are not assumed to affect the content or expression of a document directly; their influence on documents is indirect through one of the other three agents.

4.2.4.1 *Text and message from the writer perspective*

In an industrial environment writers see text or message production as work of a certain value. While the work may, in the first instance, be produced by one person, it is rare for the finished product not to have undergone some process of control and modification in the form of approval, editing, mark-up for printing, proof-reading etc., which involves other professionals. Writing is either undertaken on an independent basis, i.e. a text or message is produced to be sold to a publisher, e.g. as a book or an article, or in a dependent position where writers are employed and writing is part or the whole of their occupation. Publishers usually have editors who control the final version of the document. In a dependent position there is greater control over every aspect of the writing process and the product, and it is common for editors to eliminate traces of personal style in favour of an institutional mode of expression. As writers, translators are even more strongly incorporated into the production process and rarely have full control over the product.

4.2.4.2 *Text and message from the reader's viewpoint*

All writing is based upon the presuppositions writers make about the knowledge possessed by the recipient of the message and upon the assumptions writers can make about the proper interpretation of the intention of the message. Writers can make their presuppositions and assumptions specific to an individual, or general to a group of potential readers.

Readers are conditioned by all the documents received and read over years of professional training and experience. They develop reading habits which permit them to cope with the volume of routine reading material that occupies their professional lives. Readers know when they are addressed as individuals, e.g. in personal notes, when they are addressed as members of a small group, e.g. in a memo to all employees over 60 years of age, or when they receive communications as members of the general public, e.g. as tax payers. Any deviant or unusual document requires greater attention which is willingly given, if the content of the document justifies the additional effort and is resented, if it is not. The translator as reader must identify the role of the intended reader of the source language document and judge whether it is appropriate for the new reader of the translation.

4.3 Criteria for successful communication

Successful communication depends on a number of heterogeneous elements, some of which are the result of successful choices made in the setting up of the conditions and the realisation of the speech act. Senders have to make the right assumptions about recipient expectation and the right presuppositions of knowledge in terms of recipient knowledge and then choose the elements of code they know the recipients to possess (see Figure 4.3.).

It is against this background of presuppositions and assumptions that are appropriate to the participants that any speech act is made, and it is against this background that its success has to be measured. The actual realisation in linguistic, para-linguistic and extra-linguistic forms of signalling then depends largely on cognitive and psychological factors, and these are briefly discussed here.

4.3.1 *Knowledge*

The most basic condition for success in non-phatic communication is that the sender has something to say or write which the recipient wants to hear or read. But the knowledge content of the message must be tuned in such a way that the gap between the knowledge configuration as expressed by the sender and that of the recipient is not too wide. Three basic conditions can be envisaged: (i) the sender knows more than the recipient, and the communication aims at narrowing this gap in at least one respect; (ii) the recipient generally knows more than the sender about the specific chosen topic, in which case the speech act must be concerned with eliciting some detail of information; (iii) both can be said to have the same level of knowledge, in which case communication can only serve to confirm the existence of knowledge.

Knowledge referred to here belongs to what has been defined as topic and aspect in section 3.3.

4.3.2 *Cooperation*

The need for identifying certain principles which guide the production, reception and modification of texts and messages has been recognised in the philosophy of language. So, Grice, in examining the phenomenon of implicature in conversation, postulates a "cooperative principle" which is required for conversation to be maintained. Though particularly formulated in connection with conversation or "talk exchanges", the principle can be shown to apply to normal written exchanges as well, and to any other forms of social interaction and cooperation. The requirement or expectation of cooperation grows with the directness of the exchange and with the temporal duration of the cooperation, as a mutual dependency between the partners is being built up. Grice formulated the principle as follows:

> Make your conversational contribution such as is required, at the stage at which it occurs, by the accepted purpose or direction of the talk exchange in which you are engaged. (Grice 1975:45)

While this injunction does not add anything that has not been said before in connection with intention and expectation, Grice goes on to express a number of maxims, intended to elucidate this principle, and which are required for successful conversation, and by extension, for any successful sequence of communication. He groups them under four categories intended to qualify the nature of the conditions, namely quantity, quality, relation and manner.

Under quantity he has two maxims. The first, "1: Make your contribution as informative as is required", is understood as applying within the intended purpose of the speech act. There may, in special cases, be a conflict between other principles and this maxim, e.g. in the case of someone being asked deliberately or unwittingly for some confidential information the speaker/writer is not at liberty to disclose. "As required" is exclusively concerned with reader expectation; we would have to add "as informative as possible" to cover the situation where the writer knows less than the reader assumes he does. The quantity of information required for any one text is determined by convention. A statement like e.g. 'children are children', is clearly acceptable only in particular circumstances.

Equally a personal reference letter of only two sentences would not be considered adequate, without some additional explanation to account for this brevity. It can be the purpose of modification of messages to supplement information, so that a message can be made suitable for another group of recipients.

The complementary maxim, "2: Do not make your contribution more informative than is required." provides a brief for mediators, as it is often the case that over-information is reduced by editing and translation.

Grices's quality maxims are dominated by the super maxim: "Try to make your contribution one that is true.", which he then explains as meaning "3: Do not say what you believe to be false". Any violation of this maxim would mean flouting the first maxim of quality. There are however cases, in rhetorical figures, for example, where this maxim seems to be violated. This occurs in the following figures of speech:

	EXAMPLE
Irony	X is a fine friend.
Metaphor	The speaker lost the battle.
Meiosis(understatement)	Rather cold (for: Freezing!)
Hyperbole	Every rule has its exception.

The fourth maxim, "4: Do not say that for which you lack adequate evidence.", is only of limited validity, because it would appear to exclude any expression of suspicion, doubt or indeed exaggeration to which a speaker seeks a reaction, e.g. 'They are probably economical with the truth'. The violation of this maxim could again be attributed to the rhetorical figure of hyperbole.

Under the heading of relation, Grice introduces the brief maxim "5: Be relevant". This maxim is rather vague and it would be necessary to define more closely various types and kinds and focuses of relevance.

By "manner" Grice means how something is said, and here again he has a supermaxim "Be perspicuous", a rather polysemous word, which can mean many things to many people. There are standard ways of flouting the individual maxims grouped together here, as "6: Avoid obscurity of expression; 7: Avoid ambiguity; 8: Be brief (avoid unnecessary prolixity); 9: Be orderly". Obscurity and ambiguity are stylistic devices which may be essential for the proper conveyance of intention. Besides, some ambiguity is unavoidable in any natural language. Nor is succinctness an objective concept because it depends on reader expectation. Brevity is therefore not always a virtue, nor may it be intended. Orderliness falls into the same category.

While a speech act, to be successful, requires cooperation, it must be possible to opt out or deliberately flout any of the maxims and still achieve highly successful communication. Only the unknowing violation of a maxim may be harmful to effective communication.

The principle of cooperation is not the only one that can be identified but is probably the most important one. Cooperation can, of course, also be interpreted more broadly as including politeness and other social virtues known to be influential in achieving cooperation. Cooperation is not something that can be demanded of every speech act, because the social distinctions between participants and their roles in the speech act determine the degree of cooperation participants are willing or even permitted to give. In some speech acts in legal proceedings, for example, cooperation is deliberately withheld because the prosecution has to prove a case against the defendant who is assumed to be innocent until found guilty, and this requires the defence not to give information it may have or to admit statements that might be considered incriminatory. Therefore, the social role of the participants in the speech act has to be attuned to the other factors, in order to produce what is considered 'successful' communication in any one case.

4.3.3 *Relevance*

The maxim of relevance has been singled out by Sperber and Wilson (1986) and developed into a separate theory, governing the efficiency of communication. They shift responsibility entirely to the sender of a message when they say:

> It is left to the communicator to make correct assumptions about the codes and contextual information that the audience will have accessible and be likely to use in the comprehension process. The responsibility for avoiding misunderstanding also lies with the speaker, so that all the hearer has to do is go ahead and use whatever code and contextual information come most easily to hand.
>
> (Sperber & Wilson 1986:43)

They also deal with the problem of conflicting assumptions, claiming that a stronger assumption ''automatically'' (p.114), eliminates a weaker one, without clarifying why and how.

Their chief principle has a certain tautologous ring about it when it states:

> Every act of ostensive communication communicates the presumption of its own optimal relevance. (Sperber & Wilson 1986:158)

Relevance is measured with regard to its contextual effects and the effort required for processing information contained in a message. The optimal relevance is achieved, according to Sperber and Wilson, if the contextual effect of an assumption is large and the effort for absorbing the information is small.

4.4 Text modification

Next to the production of new texts and messages, there is an even larger, highly industrialised, activity concerned with text and message modification, which we define here as any text or message created on the basis of a pre-existent one. Text modification is based on three basic needs: (i) texts are modified in order to improve them; (ii) texts are modified in order to re-use them as a whole or in parts; (iii) texts are modified in order to make them accessible to other recipients than those first intended. Such modifications of texts are secondary operations to original writing and can be called dependent speech acts. In essence they consist of addition, deletion and/or substitution of text elements; in the third case, modification can be so substantial that it is necessary to speak of a new text production method, namely text derivation, the products of which are derived texts. The meaning of 'derived texts' has here a somewhat wider scope than in information science.

Text improvements range from the individual's spelling correction of personally produced text, to editorial proofreading and editing to make texts conform to house-styles. There are now a great variety of tools available for spelling correction and editing. In so far as they affect the work of translators, they are discussed in more detail in sections 7.5. and 8.8.

In a structured society situations recur with a certain regularity and therefore many communications are repetitive to the extent that writers do not often engage in original conception, but re-use existing texts or segments of language. Therefore, texts, once produced, are often re-used on other occasions with minor or major modifications in the same way as idioms, proverbs, sayings etc. are repeated. In its social function, communication serves to consolidate established patterns of behaviour and therefore introduces novel forms only on the basis of familiar expressions. Written communication is by its nature more reflective and therefore more given to repetition than spoken language. Writers tend to repeat, copy, or imitate speech acts, e.g. when they elevate texts of previous, successful communications to the status of pro-formas which they simply complete and adjust to fit a new situation.

Modelling can lead to the systematic creation of pro-formas, and all manner of forms and questionnaires (exemplified in section 4.1.1), and ultimately to regulation and prescription of a narrow band of closely defined subclasses of particular text types, such as diplomatic notes, legal notifications, contracts etc. On the individual level it is common for writers to follow precedents closely, which often means copying a complete speech act with simple substitution of expression of time, place, objects etc. The activity of using precedents or copying patterns is common to all forms of writing and is therefore also present in translation. In an industrial environment this activity is well-established and has recently found its recognition in the field of machine translation under the heading of example-based translation (see section 10.4.2).

Beside the activity of modelling, there is the large, heavily industrialised sector of text re-writing, with the objective of making texts available in their entirety, in translation, or in part, as abstracts, with or without translation, with varying degrees of other modification.

4.4.1 *Types of document modification*

4.4.1.1 *Correction*

The most obvious form of text modification is that commonly known as correction, in which a text is contrasted against a linguistic rule system and the social norms governing a particular text type in a particular setting in order to establish conformity with accepted practice of writing. The purpose of correction is multiple: to ensure efficient and unambiguous communication, to demonstrate what is considered to be polite and civil behaviour, to show respect to recipients by conforming to rules which are assumed to be expected, but also to have the freedom to deviate from the norm in special cases and so maintain the flexibility of the system of communication. For example, if a particular norm prescribes that capital letters are used only for proper names and after a full stop and the writer is normally respectful of this rule, then any deviation will not be considered a mistake but a deliberate act of drawing attention to the word spelled with an initial capital letter.

4.4.1.2 *Editing*

This activity has an extremely wide range. It can consist of no more than what was called 'correction', above, or of major re-writing or over-writing of parts or whole sections of text, to make them conform to the canons of expression chosen by an 'editor' who usually acts on behalf of an organisation or institution. In a professional environment, the general meaning of 'editor' is that of a person responsible for issuing a particular text. But this role can vary from responsibility for content to responsibility for form and even extend to selection of readership. Some editors do no more than make a text conform linguistically to generally established rules and perceptions of norms. Others, as in journalism, take responsibility for the content and its expression, to the extent that they consider all possible legal implications of statements and opinions expressed in the document they edit.

In their contact with editors, who usually cannot read the source language text, translators find themselves in an ambivalent position. An editor, in this case, reacts to the content of the original text, as expressed in the target language.

If such a monolingual editor wishes to change the content of a translated text, the decision is entirely based on its target language expression; in this case the translator must provide the necessary guidance since the editor cannot distinguish between the content in the original and in translation. In reaction to the form, the same editor is entirely dependent on the translator because only the translator can indicate what is the author's idiosyncrasy and what is a matter of the translator's interpretation. This problem is critical in literary translation. The special case of revision of translation is discussed in section 8.8.2.

4.4.1.3 *Derivation*

Any operation which goes beyond correction and editing, as here defined, can be grouped under the heading of derivation, by which is meant a modification of text motivated by a desire to improve acceptability. The different techniques of modification are best treated according to the type of operation involved.

Theoretically, text modification is required if the writer has made an erroneous presupposition or assumption about a reader, or, if a reader or an agent wishes a text to be adjusted to a different level of reader expectation or another expectation. In the first case, modification is then concerned with correcting a writer's erroneous or inappropriate presuppositions with respect to a reader's knowledge and with correcting a writer's erroneous or inappropriate assumptions about the reader's expectation. In the second case, we are usually dealing with a secondary readership, or a secondary expectation of a readership, e.g. one which wants a summary of a report rather than the full report it has received.

The most common reasons for requiring regular patterns of modification can be found in the following situations:

— Temporal or physical distance between original document and reader can determine a change of text type, e.g. a move from written to spoken communication or vice versa.

— A change in the purpose of a text may require the same content to be expressed in two different text types; e.g. an instruction may require a lengthy explanation for some but not for other readers. The same content can be expressed in an informative leaflet and in rules, regulations or instructions.

— A change in the content of a text can lead to a change in purpose; a simple informative text may become imperative for a particular group of readers and may therefore require a change in text type in order to be effective.

Within such a theoretical setting, we then identify several types of modification:

— Modification affecting the content: this applies to commentary or annotation or reduction of the content of a text, which may incidentally also involve a change of expression form;

— Modification affecting the purpose: this applies to changing the intention, which may involve some changes of the expression form of a text, e.g. to inform rather than direct, but may also involve some change in the content of the text.

— Modification affecting the code: this applies to changing the symbols of a linguistic system, i.e. transliteration, or to changing from one conceptual and linguistic system to another, i.e. translation.

Translation can, in fact, be interpreted in two ways: (i) as the consequence of a correction of the writer's erroneous presupposition about language knowledge; or (ii) as the consequence of a different code expectation of a secondary readership. The simplest form of translation would then be seen as introducing an alternative code, so as to fulfil the common code requirement of successful monolingual communication.

For a theory of translation we are interested in the particular set of modifications required in connection with the transformation of the linguistic code of a text. This activity can also be described as substitution. While substitution can be defined as consecutive acts of deletion and addition, the special form of substitution that is translation is best treated separately.

4.4.2 *Types of derived texts*

In order to differentiate between original and derived texts, the latter are defined as texts in which the substance of the content of the texts remains constant, permitting variation of all other elements. Thus derived texts are dependent for their content upon another text or message; consequently the core knowledge contained in the derived text never exceeds the knowledge in the original. But no dependent text can introduce anything—information or argument—that is not in the original. Any text, even derived texts themselves, can become the source of a derived text: there are, e.g., abstracts of translations and translations of abstracts.

The class of derived texts includes translations, various types of abbreviated texts and texts with modifications of form. We speak of derived texts, when we want to refer to their mode of production; we speak of textual dependence, when we want to characterise them in relation to the text which has given rise to the derivation. The physical object is the same; the designation reflects the different way of looking at it.

The greatest variety of derived text types is produced by modifications of the length of a text:

(a) text types produced by reduction to a fixed percentage of the original length, i.e. the summary or précis;

(b) text types by reduction to a fixed length, independent of the original, i.e. abstracts with subdivisions by author, treatment of content and mode of expression into author's, descriptive, informative, indicative, telegraphic abstracts;

(c) text types characterised by both reduction in length and a particular treatment of the content, i.e. the adaptation, the commentary and the slanted abstract;

(d) text types which convert spoken to written language. These are the transcript, which seeks to represent an original as closely as possible, the compte rendu and minutes, which have developed techniques of their own and can therefore be considered written text types in their own right.

While all these text forms are clearly derived, they are variously dependent upon the original. A transcript or minutes, for example, become the only lasting record of the spoken speech events they record. Most summaries and précis are read in their own right and only rarely do readers then go back to the original for fuller information. This is even more true in the case of translations. It is social conventions which determine the degree of dependence, and therefore also the degree of freedom, the mediator has in altering the text.

4.4.3 *Methods of modification*

In the process of producing derived texts, we distinguish two major types of modification, which for practical purposes we call transformation and translation, though translation may, and often does, include transformation. Transformation is acknowledged to be a very diffuse activity, but translation is equally complex. Analogies with transformation are useful to identify the many types of activities which go under the name of translation.

4.4.3.1 *Transformation*

As texts consist of content, purpose and expression form, text modification can in principle occur either at the level of the content (with constant expression form), or at the level of expression form (with constant content), or both; or at the level of purpose with subsequent need for changes at both other levels. Minor changes to either content or form may be required subsequent to the modification of the form or content, but on the whole this division of form and content is valid for this model.

Modification of content within the same expression form, is, of course, the normal condition of writing according to particular patterns; this type of modification is of no interest here.

Modification of the expression form with constant content can be done by writers or mediators. The writers' own modifications, e.g. the correction and finalisation of draft texts, are of no particular interest, if they are done as one and the same text production process. If they are done at a later time, they may be relevant as a stage in the life of a document and thus be of interest to professional mediators in determining the content of a text.

Text transformation is frequently also associated with redefining the intention of a text. It occurs when a potential sender or a potential recipient of a message wants to use an existing text for a message but finds it unsuitable for his intended purpose. In such cases, texts, i.e. their content or expression form or both, are transformed by writers and professional mediators into more appropriate ones, so that the intention with which they were originally written is modified to suit the communicative situation of the moment. This type of derivation may be minimal and affect only some textual features, or it may be more substantial and require the choice of a new text type, which, in effect, means recasting or rewriting the entire text.

Transformation can also involve converting linguistically expressed written content into non-linguistic forms, e.g. the conversion of running text into tables or diagrams or, on a larger scale, the conversion of a lecture text into overhead projector sheets and vice versa.

Transformation varies according to this mode of approaching texts. A dynamic approach permits contact with the writer, a static approach requires separate decisions on the purpose of the transformation to be taken by the translator or editor.

4.4.3.2 *Translation*

Text derivation produced by changing the language is called translation, but it is necessary to distinguish at least two types of translation. There is the translation which aims at preserving both content and intention, i.e. the conventional concept of a translation, as can be seen in the translation of novels, plays or filmscripts for dubbing. The result is a dependent text. The preservation of content and intention can, in this case, be judged by comparing the effect of the translated text on the new readership with the effect the original has on selected readers among this new readership, who are able to read the text in its original form. In this type of translated text, the dependency may, but need not, be acknowledged, once the text has been produced. It therefore has a different status potential than the next type of translation.

The second type of translation, that which in addition to a change of code also involves a change of function, i.e. purpose of the text, involves, in effect two separate processes, namely (i) change of function of the text, and (ii) translation, in either order of sequence, according to the technique used by the translator, who in this case is clearly doing more than is conventionally understood by translation. Though in practice, summarising and translation is carried out in one operation, such a theoretical division of activity is essential for a theory of translation, especially one which embraces MT, because it must be assumed that a machine will deal with the two operations separately, if at all. This theoretical position towards abstracting—translation is also useful, because it permits us to differentiate types of translated texts by the process of production. This type of translation might conveniently be called by another name, since the change of language may be considered only as a second level operation.

The first type of language modification assumed a constant content, a constant intention and consequently also a constant text type. There are, however, languages which do not have matching text types. In such a case, the translation is limited to smaller units than the text, perhaps only sentences. The finished translation, however, is then a product sui generis, a type of translated text expressed in an innovative text type to that linguistic community. Original translation text types can also be produced as a result of a reduction of texts which are not reduced in their monolingual form, as is the case of the gist translation (See also section 6.6 and Figure 6.4).

4.4.4 *The professions concerned with text modification*

Mediators are professionals who perform their work only as a result of specific instructions received by communication agents. While it is possible to conceive of text producers as working without a very specific purpose, this is not possible in the case of mediators who are usually employed in order to fit texts to new and more specific readership expectations, i.e. to bridge the communicative gap that exists, or is perceived to exist, by a communication agent.

Mediators can receive documents the time and location of which is quite distant from the readership because of cultural and linguistic barriers. In order to be able to modify texts, mediators must first read them. This is a different operation from the reading carried out by the recipient of the message. Since they are neither primary nor secondary readers, mediators approach the text with their own expectation, which is the result of the definition of the modification task they are to perform on the text. As professionals, they either have a standing brief in their vocational role as, e.g. abstractors, editors, revisors, translators, which provide them with an approach to the document, and/or they receive specific instructions by a communication agent. This is the mediators' situation of text reception which is always given. Mediators must also receive, or have as part of their regular vocational role, a specification of the readership that is to be addressed by the modified text.

The mediators' expectation is therefore quite specific and distinct from that of end-readers. They must, first of all, identify the text type of the original and interpret other factors associated with it. They must also identify the original intention of the document. They must therefore be able to filter out those text elements which are intention markers. They must then 'understand' the text, and in some way or other separate the abstract content from the linguistic expression form. Once they have absorbed this abstract content, mediators can re-code it. This they do by modifying the content (addition or deletion of information), expressing it in a different form (redrafting), by summarising or translation.

A document sent for modification is invariably and inevitably taken out of its regular sequence in a process of communication and becomes a draft for a new document which stands in a different relation to the original. The most immediate effects are that of altering the time sequence of communication and introducing another writer into the process, so that a mediated text is by definition less direct than a text transmitted without intermediaries. Assuming, for the purpose of this model, that mediators can separate content from expression forms, it is possible to separate several modes of working. They may:

— work with the objective of improving the text, in the same way as the author;

— change the text type, which implies a change in intention, e.g. the conversion of proceedings into a report, the conversion of a report into a summary, the conversion of various minutes into a single report;

— change the language of the text, i.e. translate the text, while maintaining its text type, e.g. translate a letter into a letter, a technical manual into a technical manual;

— translate and change the intention, probably involving a change of text form, e.g. an L2 abstract of an article in L1, the L2 gist translation of a L1 letter.

In each case mediators must consider the texts they are modifying, i.e. transforming or translating or both, as a draft. The reading of drafts can therefore be defined as a special activity which differentiates the mediator from the end user.

Mediators are thus concerned both with the conversion of drafts into texts and messages, and with the production of documents on the basis of documents which for them are drafts for derived texts and messages. As far as their public role is concerned, mediators either remain anonymous because they produce texts on behalf of others, who then are identified as authors, or they produce texts which permit their identification as modifiers of texts in such categories as abstractors, synopsis writers, adaptors or translators.

4.4.5 *Criteria for successful modification*

It has been shown that there are several possible modifications to a text, e.g. several equally valid informative abstracts, summaries or translations. In fact it is known that no two mediators will ever produce identical derived documents, just as no two authors will ever produce identical texts. Generalising the situation, we might even say that two texts written or translated by the same person, at different times, can never express quite the same content. We would, however, also have to admit that there are degrees of matching content which are independent of identity of form. While it is unnecessary to go into the psychological reasons for this difference, this fact must be taken into account when it comes to evaluating the relative merits of mediators' work, and their motivations for this work must be subject to assessment.

In their role as readers, mediators are in principle, subject to the same constraints as other readers and consequently are doubly selective in what they absorb from a document. Firstly, interpreting a text signifies selecting certain items of information for closer attention than others; secondly understanding a text signifies selecting certain semantic and pragmatic values associated with the selected items. These two selections are then reflected in the modified document produced by the mediator. It must be assumed that the particular form of expression chosen by different mediators reflects their particular type of reading, their interpretation of the task they are expected to perform and their command of codes.

Because theirs is a professional activity, the modifications chosen by mediators must be assumed to lie in the interest of the improvement of the text for the specific readership addressed. (We leave aside here the special case of rewriting of texts for the purpose of mis- or dis-information.)

It is therefore possible to postulate a further principle of successful communication, which is specific to text modification, namely 'the mediator principle', which underlies and motivates the professional activity of text modification and which can be expressed as follows:

> Any modification of a text is carried out in the perceived interest of an improvement of the text as part of a specific message. It involves making texts more effective for and in a particular communicative situation.

Accepting this principle, any divergences that occur between modifications produced by different mediators are then only attributable to differences in their understanding of the content, perception of the original intention, interpretation of their professional brief or perception of the specified new readership.

There are well-established patterns for text mediation with their own rules, and there are, in fact, also text types associated with the different modes of modification of text. To test this work of mediators, it must be possible for a third person to say that the modified text expresses the same content as the original document, and that the two documents only differ in expression form, and in intention, where this was required.

Chapter Three

Theoretical Aspects of Translation

5 The Nature of Translation

5.1 The scope of theories of translation

The previous sections have placed translation in the context of its wider communicative environment so that it is now possible to concentrate on the situations that demand the particular form of text modification identified as translation in section 4.4. Since translation has for many centuries been considered an independent activity, we have to demonstrate the limitations of these views of translation in order to justify developing a new model suitable for the involvement of information technology.

Section 5.1 briefly summarises the elements that are fundamental to any theory of translation. Subsequently, in sections 5.2–3, a number of existing definitions of translation are analysed, in order to examine how they treat these elements, before describing those appropriate for an industrially-oriented model of translation in section 5.4.

5.1.1 *Two aspects of translation*

Before defining 'translation' itself, the nature of the concept has to be identified, i.e. the term 'translation' itself must be disambiguated, since English, like a number of other European languages, permits the same formation pattern for both product and process nouns. In a technical environment where the same product may be obtained by different processes, this distinction is crucial and needs explicit clarification. In this case both meanings comprise a wide range of concepts, many of which do not yet have separate names, as they are insufficiently delineated in current theories.

5.1.1.1 *Process*

Viewed from the industrial and professional stance adopted in this book, translation can be described as a range of deliberate human activities, which are carried out as a result of instructions received from a third party, and which consist of text production in a target language, based, inter alia, on the modification of a text in a source language to make it appropriate for its intended new purpose. These various steps which convert one man-made product into another, are collectively called 'translation'. They are carried out separately or jointly by people such as secretaries, information scientists, academics, engineers and, of course, professional translators. The one common element among these activities is that there is a shift in language between the conception of the task to be performed and the actual realisation of the task (see Figure 5.1).

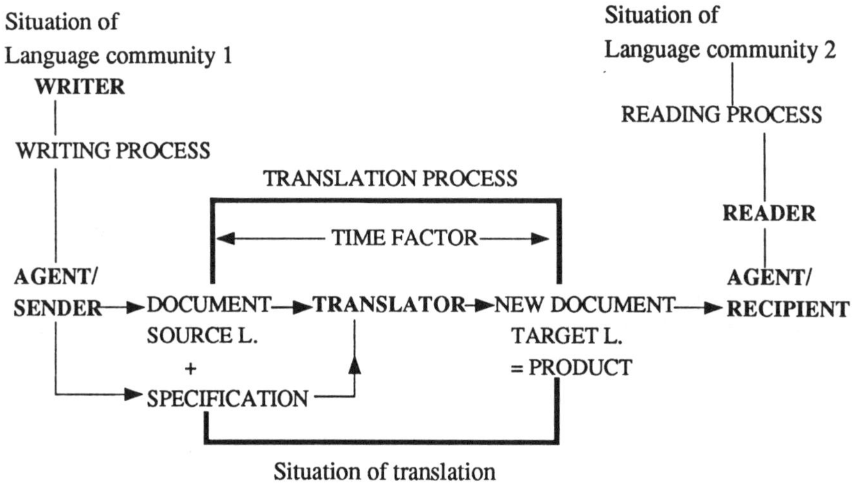

Figure 5.1 *A model of the translation process*

5.1.1.2 *Products*

Secondly, there are a range of documents, such as parallel texts, multilingual instructions, foreign language abstracts, gists, prose paraphrases of poetry, which are all generically called 'translation' because they are written in a 'target language' on the basis of texts in a 'source language' and because they maintain a certain similarity with their source language text. A document for which we cannot postulate some sort of source language text, cannot be considered a translation. Therefore the ultimate criterion for identifying a document as a 'translation' is its derivation from a document in another language. Hence, a 'translation' can also be defined as a derived document which maintains a certain degree of similarity of content with its source document while being clearly dissimilar in language from its source.

This very cautious description of a well-established set of practices by a very old profession and the evidence of whole libraries of documents called 'translations' is even more justified in the age of information technology when communication can no longer be considered as being exclusively confined to an interaction between human beings; a contemporary definition of communication must now also include the interaction between humans and machines in a variety of natural and restricted languages, such as dialogues in question-answering systems and even texts produced entirely by machines, all of which involve and include some form of 'translation'.

5.1.2 *Dimensions of a theory*

As indicated in Figure 5.1, a theory of translation must incorporate several dimensions, the separate identification of which helps to circumscribe the scope of the theory.

5.1.2.1 *Communicative/author dimension*

Translation involves a communication shift between two languages, which implies a dynamic situation initiated originally with a particular purpose by a sender, an author or another agent.

5.1.2.2 *Document or product dimension*

The product itself is complex and has several important constituents:

(a) Sublanguage: A translation is written in a particular sublanguage of a specific language community and is based on a parallel sublanguage in a source language. Existing theories do not fully distinguish between all the varieties and sub-types of language, established by textual analysis, which are relevant for translation. In this book we concentrate attention on the types of sublanguages called special subject languages as the type of language involved in industrial translation.

(b) Text: In communication, language occurs in units, known as texts, or documents, as defined in 4.1.2. Translation is concerned with such units and their parts, in the first instance. Texts have characteristics that allow the establishment of types. Every document to be translated is of a particular text type. Textual characteristics, either as linguistic phenomena of any one language or as common elements between language pairs involved in translation, are therefore of overriding importance as it must be accepted that there may be different modes of translation for different types of texts.

(c) Extra-linguistic features: Communication occurs by means of language and other semiotic codes. A document must be considered as a single entity of both linguistic and other means of expression which complement each other.

5.1.2.3 *Reader/agent/recipient dimension*

While in a theory of communication we can accept that texts, like personal diaries, are written by a text producer for him or herself, for a theory of translation in an industrial environment it is essential to postulate a recipient of the translation who is neither the writer nor the translator. Besides, in translation it is essential to distinguish clearly between the intention with which the text is produced and the readers' expectation because readers of translations may have another expectation than readers of the source language document. Most translation theories make some reference to readers, but do not admit that readers may have diversified expectations of a text, resulting from their different cultural backgrounds and communicative needs.

5.1.2.4 *Motivation/translator dimension*

An industrially oriented theory of translation, as distinct from a general theory, must be concerned with explicit reasons for this activity so that goals can be defined and assessments of success in reaching them can be made. Since all rational human processes, and for that matter the design of substitute machines or tools, are motivated, we identify the basic need to overcome a barrier in communication as the motivation or purpose of translation. Since this need is permanent and widespread, a specialist profession has evolved, which, unlike scribes who became redundant with the advent of general literacy, has flourished and expanded. Following Old Testament chronology we could date the original motivation for translators and interpreters precisely to the destruction of the Tower of Babel which, at a stroke, transformed a monolingual society into a polyglot one in need of assistance for communication. Translators and interpreters can therefore claim to belong to one of the oldest professions.

5.1.2.5 *Situational dimension*

As an activity, translation has a temporal and a spatial dimension of its own, thus creating a third situation, which may be closer to writers or readers, according to the language community from which the initiative to commission a translation is taken. The time gap is particularly significant because the process of overcoming the language barrier always requires a certain amount of time; we can thus also speak of a temporal barrier in the communication process which, beside the act of translation itself, permits other types of modification which alter the sequence of the process. The situation of a translation is also made more complex in that it has another participant, so that beside the sender and the recipient of a message there are now mediators, i.e. interpreters, translators and their agents. Obviously, additional participants between the writer and reader, can add their own perspective to the speech act.

5.1.3 *Machine translation as a new activity and product*

In an extended theory of translation which covers all modern techniques and approaches, a place has to be found for new tools and especially for machine translation (MT) systems. Such a place can only be allocated on the basis of a clear understanding of the meaning and scope of this new industrial process. The allocation must distinguish clearly between the MT process as an independent activity and as a supporting tool for a human activity; it also has to accept the dual function of MT products as finished documents and as semi-finished documents, as aids, drafts or props for human finishing. These alternatives are illustrated in Figure 5.2.

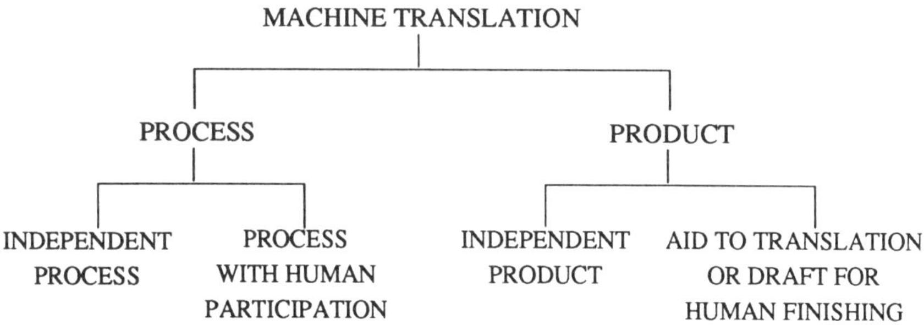

Figure 5.2 *The scope of meaning of machine translation*

Computers have long been recognised as tools which assist in performing intellectual tasks like writing letters, diagnosing illnesses, keeping stock of materials and commercial transactions and so on. For a more substantial place of MT in a theory of translation, deeper reflection is required. With the introduction of independent MT, computers no longer only assist, but perform on their own the activity of generating texts which was hitherto considered to be an exclusively human intellectual capability. The question, therefore, arises in what sense this machine 'translation' activity is like any of these diverse human activities which are globally called translation, and what other text modification functions it can perform. An alternative interpretation is to postulate that the computer does something else, which may be similar in some respects, and the outcome of which is a derived document for which we have yet to find another name.

The key issue is, consequently, to define what precisely the computer can do and hence how it can be used in the way people generally use machines, either (i) to ease human labour; or (ii) to provide a service that human beings cannot provide in terms of accuracy, consistency or precision; or (iii) to increase productivity and thereby to recover with profits the investment made in machines in the first place. The second of these alternative possibilities, that the machine may be able to do things we are ourselves incapable of, is an important aspect of the potential benefits of MT which must also be included in a theory of translation.

5.2 The meanings of translation

In this section a number of definitions of translation are contrasted in order to clarify the scope of the phenomenon under discussion.

The range of possible interpretations is very wide. Nida (1976) was the first to distinguish clearly between a philological, a linguistic and a sociolinguistic theory of translation. Neubert (1991:17-27)) identifies six perspectives under which models of translation are created: (i) His first perspective is result-oriented and hence concentrates on the TL product. He calls it the 'critical' model because traditionally translation critique was devoted to the target language text. It partly covers the reader dimension described above. (ii) He contrasts this with the 'practical' model which, starting from the source language text, is prospective and dynamic in its exploration of translation possibilities. This perspective—corresponding broadly to the document dimension—would also have to accommodate a didactic perspective, not mentioned by Neubert. (iii) The perspective which concentrates on the linguistic mechanisms of transfer leads to Neubert's 'linguistic' model in which translation is a particular type of language use. The main concern under this perspective is with the reconstruction of linguistically expressed meaning. (iv) By extending the linguistic model to include pragmatic aspects and communicative values, Neubert arrives at his 'text-linguistic or holistic/discourse' model in which the complex sign system represented by the target text is related to its stimulus, the source text, as the original complex sign system. (v) The emphasis on problems associated with translation barriers caused by cultural and social differences, characterises Neubert's 'socio-cultural' model, which broadly corresponds to the situational dimension, introduced above. (vi) Finally, he lists the psycholinguistic perspective or model which concentrates attention on the mental processes of the human translator. Neubert also speaks of a computer model which we do not accept as appropriate in this type of consideration. Machine translation is a parallel technique to human translation and must therefore be considered from the viewpoint of all the perspectives here mentioned, with the exception of the psycholinguistic one which obviously would not apply. These perspectives have varying degrees of relevance for the description of industrial translation. They do not include the consideration of motivation for translation and its role in communication in general.

5.2.1 *Existing definitions of translation*

The examination of a number of contemporary definitions of 'translation' shows the evolution of thinking on the subject and the many different points of view currently still being held. By contrasting them we hope to illuminate all the various perspectives identified above, that, somehow or other, belong to the concept of translation.

Most older definitions concentrate on the creation of some form of equivalence without going into details about the sort of equivalent that is being pursued. This emerges clearly from the well-known definition by Nida:

> Translation consists of producing in the target language the closest natural equivalent of the source language message, firstly with respect to meaning and secondly with respect to style. (Nida 1959:19)

The keyword in this definition appears to be the word "natural"; this word must be contrasted with 'appropriate' in our own definition (section 5.1.1). Whereas 'natural' has the quality of absoluteness, the substitution of 'appropriate' would imply a relative quality, dependent on some external factors, thereby widening the scope of the concept. Mounin (1963:278), commenting on Nida, already pointed out that this "natural equivalent" could not be taken as a fixed entity for all times.

The reader dimension emerges from the definition formulated by Flamand (1983:25) for whom translation means rendering the SL message with precision (faithfulness to the author) in a correct and authentic form of the TL, adapted to the content and the recipient (faithfulness to the reader). In this definition the old and usually unmodulated demand for 'precision' or 'fidelity' is tempered by a call for attention and adjustment to both topic and reader. The weakness of the definition lies in a lack of qualification of the otherwise rather emotive-sounding 'faithfulness'.

The translator dimension is stressed in a definition by Jakobson (1966:233): "Translation is the interpretation of verbal signs by means of another language". By avoiding the issue of equivalence altogether and stressing the need for human cognitive processes, Jakobson has provided the element so far missing in the other definitions. His choice of "interpretation" must be understood as a generic term for a whole series of cognitive processes which occur in the translator's mind, and which are associated with three major activities, namely:

— problem-solving—previously identified as 'selection' in the reading-understanding process—for establishing meaning and intention;

— decision-making for the choices in the new production process;

— evaluation for assessing the decisions taken in relation to previously defined objectives.

These activities involve such skills as planning, inferencing, schematising, mapping, comparing, intuiting, formation of rules and strategic planning.

The recognition that texts are very complex entities when it comes to viewing them as the objects of translation is demonstrated in the definition by Vermeer (1986:250-263), summarised here. He speaks of "interlingual" translation and calls it a special form of linguistic transposition. The text to be translated is seen as a partial verbalisation of a situation. What has to be transferred is the global meaning, ("Das Gemeinte"), a unit of situation and verbalisation; the verbalisation is a unit of meaning and form, the meaning is a unit of reference of intellectual meaning, ("Darstellung, Verstandesbedeutung") and expressivity, emotive meaning ("Gefühlsbedeutung"). In this summary some of the original terms have been paraphrased and their originals given in brackets in order to show the different conceptualisations underlying the author's thinking. Vermeer's concept of the global meaning of a text can be presented diagrammatically, as in Figure 5.3.

Under global meaning Vermeer distinguishes further between 'usual/customary' and 'style', which he considers as resulting from both the general and specific situation (i.e. attitude, status, role). Vermeer is also flexible about the principle of fidelity. He demands "fidelity of effect", which he considers to be variable according to the cultural, linguistic and communicative community. He thus interprets fidelity very widely by admitting the possibility of restructuring the relationship between the situation and verbalisation and consequently between presupposition and information.

Vermeer also establishes three general rules for translation, namely that a translation:-

— must re-order the above mentioned relationships;

— should keep the speech intention constant as far as possible;

— must not aim at identical information only.

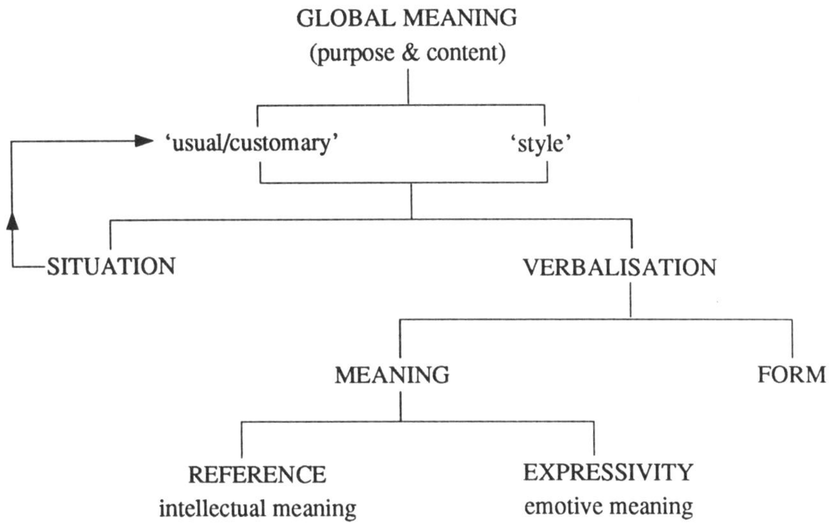

Figure 5.3 *Vermeer's model*

The weakness of this position is revealed in the second requirement. Constancy of speech intention cannot be an absolute aim; the 'possibility' of constancy is ambiguous because he does not make it clear whether this is a matter for the translator to decide, or, as we shall postulate, a result of reader expectation. Vermeer's last requirement is a partial recognition of the need for the adjustment of a translation to the needs of the recipient.

A more general philosophical position is adopted by Frawley (1984:160):

> Translation means 'recodification'. Hence, a theory of translation is a set of propositions about how, why, when, where (...) coded elements are rendered into other codes. As such, translation is nothing short of an essential problem of semiosis: it is the problem of transfer of codes.

This general position is undisputable. Only in his attempt to formulate a theory of translation, when he speaks of a "matrix code" which provides the essential information of a text and a "target code" which provides the parameters for re-rendering this information, does Frawley become specific. The act of translation is seen by Frawley as a "perpetual shuffling" back and forth, or bilateral accommodation, between the matrix and the target codes. The translation itself, Frawley calls a "third code", which is a subcode of each of the codes involved. This model would seem to support the view that translations are not only text types of their own, but constitute a separate semiotic code.

Numerous other definitions could be added here. The examples discussed show the considerable diversity of scholarship in this field, but also that until now little attention has been paid to the industrial situation where machines can assist human workers and where translators can take on the role of facilitators in communication beyond the scope of the traditional view of mediating in multilingual situations.

5.2.2 *Other meanings of translation*

It appears useful to look briefly at the many activities or views of activities which have been called translation but which are either peripheral or totally outside the meaning of translation in a professional and industrial environment.

(a) A distinction is often made between interlingual and intralingual translation; 'intralingual' refers to diachronic updates of texts belonging to the same language; for example, the translation of 13th century English texts into modern English; and 'interlingual' refers to translation between languages. While both are genuine cases of translation, we are dealing here only with 'interlingual' translation which can be qualified further by saying translation between national, official or otherwise well-established languages which have a substantial volume of translation needs.

(b) 'Translation' is often loosely used to refer to the translation of words and sentences as part of language teaching. This activity is clearly different from the translation of complete 'authentic' texts and is therefore excluded from consideration as it does not fulfil the requirement of a document satisfying a particular communicative need of a genuine TL situation, given above.

(c) In some countries and in some traditions, often associated with teaching, translations have been distinguished by different names according to whether they were from or into the translators' first language. The words 'theme' or 'prose' have been used, especially in traditional schools and universities for translation from the native into a foreign language and 'version' for translation into the native language. Since these terms were coined in connection with Greek and Latin in the first instance, the motivation behind these separate names is no longer very clear but indicates a recognition of the distinctive nature of the two tasks. From a professional point of view we are here concerned only with translation into the language of habitual use of the translator, recognising that translators usually work into one language only, though they may be able to work out of several source languages. The special case of the fully bi- or pluri-lingual translator is not considered here.

(d) Many people confuse translation and interpreting by extending the meaning of translation to cover also the mediation of spoken messages. While the ultimate purpose of overcoming a language barrier is the same, the circumstances of mediation and the techniques are quite different. Between translating and interpreting there are, however, a number of mixed activities, e.g. on-sight translation and conference interpreting, which mix written and spoken forms as source and target languages.

(e) Translation has nothing to do with the process of transferring natural language texts to artificial codes, such as semaphore or morse, which is sometimes called translation. The transliteration of texts from one script to another, such as Cyrillic to Roman, has also been called translation, and is also excluded here.

There are, however, some genuine borderline cases in which a clear definition of translation is difficult, since, especially in literature, adaptations, paraphrases and imitations of texts in other languages are sometimes difficult to separate from translations. A fairly wide scope of translation-related activities, given by Gouadec (1990), is discussed in section 6.6.5.

5.3 The concept of translatability

Though this book postulates the feasibility of translation as axiomatic, it is useful to examine the arguments for and against the possibility of translation because they are relevant to a definition of translation itself, and especially, because they regain new interest when machine translation is talked about as an alternative to human translation. The main arguments against the feasibility of translation have come from the view that language and culture are intrinsically connected and that cultural diversity makes translation either impossible or meaningless. It is worth noting that discussion of translatability has so far been considered mainly in terms of the distance between linguistic systems and cultures. However, the relative proximity between linguistic systems can also present obstacles to translation. In order to translate reliably between two languages, translators need two separately identifiable grammars and lexicons. It is notoriously difficult to translate from one dialect to another or to the standard language.

There are numerous authors who question the possibility of translation on cultural, linguistic and philosophical grounds. Such reservations have a long historical lineage and can be traced, from the classics via Humboldt to Whorf but can be countered by the evidence of the existence of actual translations of highly culturally sensitive texts and an equally distinguished list of writers on translation from St. Jerome to Schleiermacher and Ortega y Gasset.

The greatest number of untranslatable concepts which have been identified in the domain of culture are geographically determined. For example, names of plants, animals, weather conditions, minerals are rarely translated but initially borrowed directly, with some adjustments later, if the concepts become common property in the new culture. If texts are seen as representing a community's values, i.e. as objects which respond to certain pragmatic assumptions and connotations belonging to a community in which they are created, the non-equivalence of many items, which are not matched by the same cultural assumptions, must also be accepted.

The limitations of the medium are most obvious in the translation of poetry where often the metres and rhyme of one culture and language would have to be re-invented in another and are instead rendered in prose paraphrases—a well-known compromise which, however, only indicates that the translation of poetry cannot deal with all aspects of language at once. But as all the aspects of language may be considered equally important in a poem, it is not reasonable to say that satisfactory translations of poetry in the same poetic form are more or less impossible: a translation of a poem as a poem must be considered like a new but original poem in the TL that is a suggestion of the SL original, or an aid to its comprehension.

The seemingly contradictory alternative demands made of translation have been summarised by Savory (1957:49) and stated as simple juxtapositions:

A translation should......
— render the words of the original;
  — render the ideas of the original;
— read like an original piece of text;
  — read like a translation;
— reflect the style of the translator;
  — be written in the style of the original;
— read like contemporary work of the translation;
  — read like a contemporary work to the original;
— must never have deletions or additions;
  — may have additions and deletions.

5.3.1 *The legitimacy of translation*

Translation has even been considered to be unnatural or ungodly, as can be seen in some religions who prohibit the use of translations of their sacred texts for religious purposes. Jews and Muslims, for example, do not attempt, and even discourage, the translation of their fundamental religious texts or scriptures. In the Christian tradition there is an ambivalent attitude to translation. Initially there was a strong movement of translation until there was a complete Greek and later Latin set of scriptures. At the end of the Middle Ages, however, translation into the languages of the believers became associated with breakaway and reform movements. For many centuries the Catholic Church did not encourage the vernacular in religious services and only in the 1970s was the universal practice of the Catholic mass in Latin abandoned. The Protestant movement, on the other hand, was built on the individual's need for direct access to and interpretation of the scriptures. Over the centuries this attitude has led to a proliferation of versions of the Bible into all sorts of languages, dialects and pidgins in a true 'pentecostal' spirit. As the most translated set of documents, the Bible not only exists in the largest number of languages, but has undergone alternative translations and regular modernisations in many Western European languages.

Another aspect of legitimacy of translation is founded on purely practical considerations. In order to avoid legal disputes, commercial contracts with multiple language versions frequently specify that only one language has legal status. Such contracts then usually also specify the country and the courts of law in which any litigation must be conducted, thus confirming the fundamental legitimacy of one language only, in relation to which all other versions are unofficial.

5.3.2 *Cultural arguments*

If language is considered as the product of a particular society which inextricably links language and thought, then the re-expression of thought in another language is at best an interpretation, but not a translation, which would require identity or equivalence of content. Translation would, therefore, be some form of 'explicitation'; any act of transference of messages between cultures or even between techniques of communication is, of course, subject to some degree of modification by the simple fact that another human intelligence is reprocessing and reproducing a message, the full complexity of which is never consciously captured by the reader, nor, for that matter, by the translator. In practical terms, this observation combines three separate issues: (i) individuals, including translators, do not necessarily take in and comprehend every part of a message and re-convey it (see sections 7.3 & 8.1.2); (ii) a cultural barrier which may require paraphrases or other forms of explanation to convey concepts unfamiliar in the target culture; (iii) languages and techniques of communication are inherently more or less explicit and information conveyed explicitly in one language may become implicit in another and vice versa.

This third argument can be exemplified further by the inclusion of the concepts of 'literacy' and 'orality'. These concepts have been used to distinguish characteristics normally associated with written language from features typified in spoken language. High literacy is associated with definiteness and logical cohesion devices, and expression is largely situation-independent. Orality on the other hand uses situational reference and prefers hidden and vague statements in contrast to the relatively more openly-stated and clear-cut sentences of literate language. It is obvious that languages with a strong written tradition will, in this view, be more literate and languages with a strong oral tradition will be less so. 'Importing' translations on a large scale would, therefore, change the balance of an orally-oriented language through the creation of new forms of written language. On the other hand, translation into an oral tradition would have to take on board a transfer from highly literate to highly oral form which is similar to the transfer from highly explicit to highly implicit. In either case 'explicitation' would involve modifications at several levels of expression. Conceptually it may mean turning concrete into abstract or vice versa, replacing the specific with the general or vice versa. Semantically, it can involve such changes as replacing pronouns with proper nouns, replacing metaphors with similes, thereby exposing the act of comparison, giving explanatory additions etc. Syntactically it may consist of filling in ellipses or adding conjunctions. While few theoretical positions object to the need for such cases of omissions in translation, caused by the inherently more implicit nature of a language, e.g. the absence of plurals or definite articles, there may be objections in the reverse process because it requires the translator to interpret what is implicit.

To counter the arguments for the cultural impossibility of translation we can point to the history of languages which is full of examples of borrowed concepts, expressions and even grammatical features resulting from the contact of written languages, which can be one of the effects of a policy of large-scale translation. Most European languages have benefited from periods of major translation, for examples the Tudor translations of the Classics and Italian and French authors during the 16th century in England, or the translations from the Arabic sponsored by Alfonso the Wise of Spain. The strong influence exercised by Latin grammar over many European languages and the influence of the Bible and classical literature on the stock of proverbs and expressions provide many examples of what is now a common Western heritage. For example, from the fables of Aesop and Phaedrus parallel sayings exist in various languages, such as "Eine Schwalbe macht noch keinen Sommer/ one swallow does not make a summer". From Martial are derived parallel sayings in several languages, namely "revenons à ces moutons", "um auf besagten Hammel zurückzukommen", "but to return to our sheep". The largest number of parallel sayings and proverbs in European languages are probably of Biblical origin, as, for example, from Matthew 7.6. "Perlen vor die Säue werfen", "cast pearls before swine" and "donner des perles aux porcs". Other examples of biblical expressions in wide usage in many languages are "dead letter", "seventh heaven", "the seventh seal", "a thorn in the flesh", "to speak with tongues" etc.

The existence of differently expressed proverbs and sayings with the same meaning and applicability is at the same time a sign of untranslatability at the purely linguistic level. For example, the German "Zwei Fliegen mit einer Klappe schlagen" has parallel English and Spanish equivalents, namely "to kill two birds with one stone" and "matar dos pajaros de un solo tiro" which constitute single translation correspondences.

Beyond the level of the sentence the notion of untranslatability has been associated with the idea of textuality, i.e. which sees a text as a complete and individual world produced according to particular rules of textuality. In this view the communicative intention in a speech act is achieved through the internal relations of 'textuality' in the text and through external references to the community. The nature of textuality is characterised by 'coherence', marked by recurrence and co-reference of words; 'cohesion', marked by a linguistic framework guiding the collocation of words, and 'closure', the feature which ties everything together.

Culturally conditioned problems of translation are of limited importance in industrially-oriented work because in the field of science, technology, commerce etc., the cultural perspective is considered to be unimportant or compromise solutions have been found which neutralize or eliminate the problems. For legal and administrative texts which offer many cultural obstacles, solutions are being found out of the necessity of contacts between different linguistic communities. An interesting example is offered by Canada which had to reconcile the Roman Law-based legal system of Quebec, expressed in French, with the Common Law-based system of the rest of the country, expressed in English. Another example is offered by the European Community which has to issue legally binding dispositions valid in nine languages in twelve countries. In order to stress the cultural equality of all the member states' official languages, the European Community organisations, including its courts, function in all nine languages and are finding solutions to linguistic problems of translation through special committees of lawyer-linguists.

5.3.3 *Philosophical arguments*

The philosophical arguments concerning the feasibility of translation are concerned with two complementary sets of issues, namely, to show that (i) languages represent and are based on systems of concepts, and (ii) to examine the proposition that the possibility of translation indicates the identity of these systems of concepts. For some philosophers, translation therefore assumes a very important role, as D. Davidson (1984:191) states: "studying the criteria of translation is therefore a way of focusing on criteria of identity for conceptual schemes".

The philosopher Quine (1960:69) admits translation as a possibility only to the extent that there is "identity across linguistic systems" and denies its possibility beyond that. The idea of identity across linguistic systems, however, in reality comprises three separate concepts of identity.

(a) Conceptual identity:
This type of identity presupposes identical conceptual systems or structures of knowledge across cultures. It is generally acknowledged that translation in the natural sciences and technology is possible (i) because of parallel intellectual developments in different linguistic communities in which common conceptual structures coexist side by side; and (ii) because of the transfer of concepts and whole knowledge structures from one culture to another. Often new concepts are created in the target culture through an act of translation. To what extent the process of concept creation and creation of a translation equivalent are identical or in what sequence they occur, is another interesting question which forms part of the philosophical issues connected with the concept of translation.

(b) Referential identity:
This form of identity, also called 'absolute synonymy', would require that both denotational and connotational meaning systems of two languages be identical. In an industrial environment this requirement can, however, be reduced to a demand for denotational identity, other forms of meaning being frequently deliberately ignored for the purpose of interlingual identity. Denotational identity works quite satisfactorily at the level of sublanguages, where the meanings of words are deliberately restricted.

(c) Identity based on universals of language:
This demand would limit the possibility of translation to identical grammatical concepts only and would require the establishment of full contrastive grammars prior to translation so as to determine identity and the distribution of patterns between the languages involved. Such contrastive descriptions could be established in general terms as broad syntactic functions, or more specifically within subsystems of, for example, tenses, number, or case. The concept of translation between sublanguages, again, largely overcomes this difficulty.

In a narrow interpretation of 'translation', these three forms of identity must be present for translation to be possible. In all other cases, it would then have to be said that beside translation, there are other processes of text production at work. We are thus faced with the theoretical impossibility of translation and the practical existence of millions of translated documents.

All these arguments for and against the possibility of translation can be reduced to a question of the scope of the definition of this concept. Coseriu (1981) resolves this dilemma in a practical manner. He denies the possibility of an abstract ideal translation. Instead he accepts that there are optimal translations of specific texts for particular user groups, for particular purposes and for particular historical situations. This vindicates the efforts of the thousands of translators who for centuries have contributed to the diffusion of knowledge.

5.3.4 *Measures of translatability*

If translatability is recognised as a relative concept, it is possible to speak of degrees of translatability. This involves a discussion of the existence or absence of units of equivalence between linguistic items of two languages, possibly established according to text type, sublanguage, text segments or whatever other criteria may be considered to be relevant. The detailed examination of such units could lead to ranges of equivalence from 'one-to-one matches' of units, signifying total semantic and pragmatic identity, to 'no match' which would mean that a unit of text is untranslatable in the conventional sense of the word: for instance, it is generally recognised that puns, anagrams, palindromes and other plays on words cannot be translated but, being entirely text-bound, have to be recreated in a target language. Degrees of translatability can be established relatively easily at the level of text types. For example, it is possible to classify texts on a scale ranging from maximum uncertainty, because of conflicting demands, and hence difficulty of translation, to greatest ease of translation because of maximum restriction and prescription of tasks which leads to the use of pre-established equivalents. On such a scale poetry, texts of songs, jokes and filmscripts rank among the most difficult because of their need to balance content with requirements of form; less problematic are advertising texts, especially culture-related ones such as tourist brochures and guide books but also plays, novels and religious texts. Fewer problems are encountered in journalistic, legal, economic and sociological texts, because of the numerous precedents which serve as models. Even less complex would then be legal documents and court proceedings because of the need to fit into established patterns and the existence of precise models. Official documents and scientific and technical texts offer yet fewer problems, for different reasons. They are normally considered to be less context-dependent and therefore less culture-bound. By these criteria, few if any obstacles should be encountered with such specific texts as cookery recipes and weather reports where circumstances of use and readership are the same in the source and target language and fixed models determine the accepted modes of expression. On the other extreme of translatability, such text forms as nomenclature lists, part lists, technical specifications and measurements and labels can only be translated if they already have precise equivalents of text form and lexical items; otherwise translation has to wait until equivalents have been created by subject specialists. Lexical items in this type of texts may, therefore, be considered untranslatable unless there is a fully substitutable target language term or expression available. The knowledge of the limits of human translation, or rather the determination of directly 'untranslatable' units is particularly important for a theory of machine translation. For these reasons objective criteria for determining 'untranslatability' are needed which can then be tested against techniques of MT.

5.4 The basis of a theory of translation

Bringing together the various opinions so far expressed in this section, we can attempt to present a unified view.

The practical feasibility of translation is founded on two conditions affecting the three components of messages, namely 'content', 'intention' and 'form'.

The first of these conditions is the possibility of somehow separating the intention of a message from the text itself. If messages are distinguished by being heavily situation-conditioned because of the presence of purpose (intention and expectation), we may say that texts are more readily translatable because they are devoid of intention. By undergoing translation, messages require situational adjustments which would, in this view, have to be re-expressed in a way which exceeds the limits of what has hitherto been considered translation. On the other hand, it can also be argued that a text, i.e. a message deprived of the situational references which serve to clarify it, may become untranslatable because of its increased ambiguity. But, intentional signals, whether linguistically expressed or not, become neutralised or possibly irrelevant and disturbing when a document is chosen to be translated for a readership not originally addressed. While the changed communicative situation automatically eliminates non-linguistically expressed intention signals, the separation and possible elimination of linguistically expressed intention markers has to be performed by the translator. Within this line of argument, messages are directly translatable into target language messages as long as the same purpose can legitimately be maintained. In all other cases the new intention of the translated text has to be identified so that it can be expressed as appropriate.

The second condition is the possibility of somehow separating the linguistic form in which the document is expressed from the 'topic' or 'knowledge' and its linguistically expressed intention and of re-expressing this content in another linguistic form, in such a way that the two documents, i.e. the original and its translation, can be judged to be 'variously' equivalent by people with a knowledge of both languages concerned. This is the essence of Frawley's definition of translation as 're-codification', cited above.

With the possibility of isolating the three constituents, i.e. (content–form–intention), a number of re-combinations of elements becomes possible of which only two are normally considered to belong to the modification process called translation. Constancy of content but different linguistic form is the basic condition which then has the alternatives of (i) producing a message with the same intention or (ii) producing a message with a different intention. Since we have claimed that linguistic intention markers can be isolated, it must, theoretically, also be possible now to restore appropriate intention markers into the translation, so that any reader expectation can be satisfied fully within the new communicative situation. In fact, a translator who does not know the target reader has the alternative choices of assuming (i) that the target reader has the same expectation as the source reader or (ii) that the target reader has a different expectation. According to this choice, translators either have to re-introduce matching intention markers or different ones in order to convert the target language document into a communicative functional entity, i.e. a message belonging to the target language. The third choice, i.e. not to introduce intention markers into the translation, then leads to a target language text, rather than a message.

The basic condition of the alternatives in this process is illustrated in Figure 5.4, which recapitulates the content of Figure 4.3, adjusted to translation situations.

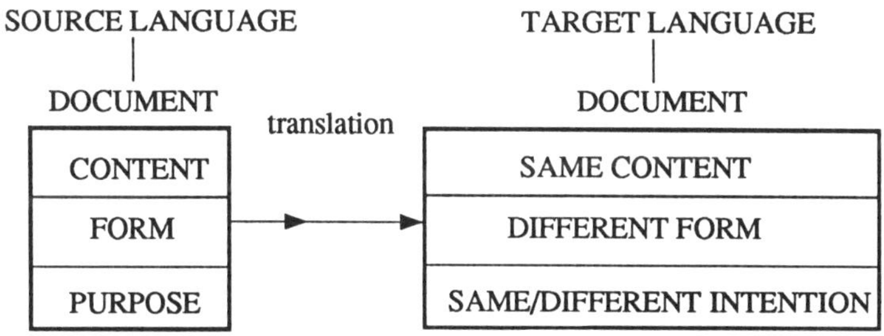

Figure 5.4 *A general model of the relation of source and and target language document*

This first model gives a limited view of translation which has to be developed further, especially with respect to the interpretation of what is understood by content. Linguistically speaking, meaning is a feature of both content and form. We postulate that industrial translation is concerned with transferring meaning of content, if necessary at the expense of the meaning contained in the form. The opposite is not considered to be translation.

Form occurs at several levels: ranging from units smaller than the sentence, such as the word or phrase to units larger than the sentence such as the paragraph or an entire text type. While changes in form introduced by translation regularly affect units below the size of the sentence, most translation theories maintain that there is an approximation to equality of form at the higher levels, which is reached completely at the level of the text type.

In order to deal with the change of form while maintaining the same content, translation theory benefits from the theory of sublanguages. In special subjects and domains of use the meaning of forms is less complex and can thus, under certain conditions, be assumed to be constant between two language communities.

The implications underlying this premiss are the existence of:

(a) socially normalised forms of language from and into which translation occurs. In the simplest of interpretations this means that one must be able to know that a source text is written in language A, the rules of which are known so that a translator can say whether it is in a standard form or represents some deviations from the norm. There must likewise be a standard for the target language against which the translator's effort can be measured.

    Normally both source and target languages of translation can refer to established standards of syntactic correctness and a lexicon with a recorded range of meanings.

(b) a universality of knowledge and other things expressible in any number of languages. This condition is comparable to that expressed by Quine, above, with respect to conceptual identity.

    Knowledge which forms the content of documents must be considered culture-independent; any knowledge which is not available in a target language culture, and hence does not have a linguistic expression form, must nevertheless be expressible through the means of that language. Nida affirms the possibility of universals of knowledge when he says "One important reason for the possibility of interlingual communication is the fact that human experience is so much alike throughout the world.

What people of various cultures have in common is far greater than what separates them'' (Nida 1982:9).

(c) a global translingual synonymy of linguistic forms. This condition is similar to Quine's demand for linguistic universals, or ''identity across linguistic systems'', but it is here expressed less categorically by permitting a wide interpretation of what is meant by synonymy. There is no need for absolute identity but for some sort of balanced equality.

There must, however, be a sufficient number of culture-independent or culture-neutral units within the source text to establish synonymy between pairs of languages so that the possibility of constant content can be realised. (We must be able to say that two texts express the same content, and to justify it by listing items of sameness). It is easy, for example, to show that the tense systems of two languages do not exactly correspond to each other, or that the use of determiners differs, but at the same time that it is possible to express the same time references by a combination of tenses and adverbs. For example, the idea of passivity is variously expressed by means of auxiliary verbs or pronouns in different languages and translators have established conventions of grammatical equivalences to this end.

A theory of translation must test all these assumptions separately.

5.4.1 *Process model of translation*

Seeing translation as an industrial activity, we identify translation as a purposeful activity or process leading to a result or product. In this view, translation is a deliberate human activity, a production process with an input of material, instructions concerning the task, and an output. The material input is a document; the instructions are a specification of the expected product and (possibly) how to produce it. Specifications are discussed in detail in section 6.5. The output is a document which has to measure up to certain expectations, as previously described. The process is a temporal sequence of actions or events which can be broken down into separate stages. Most authors on the subject consider the process as a goal-directed activity consisting of two phases which are named differently, according to the orientation of the approach, namely:

Approach	PHASE I $\Longrightarrow$	PHASE II
Cognitive:	comprehension	reconstruction
Linguistic:	deverbalisation	reverbalisation
Communicative:	decoding	encoding
Pragmatic:	decomposition	recomposition

The critical point is always the transition from the first to the second phase. Describing the process in cognitive terms draws attention to the necessity of relating comprehension to a pre-existing area of knowledge; describing it in linguistic terms, there is a need for a language-independent representation as a meeting point for the two phases. This aspect is fully discussed in section 8.3–8.6. The communicative and pragmatic approaches also require some form of representation into which text can be decoded or decomposed.

In the process model of translation, in Figure 5.5, input, process and output are all variables which sequentially influence each other. These variables are:

a) different types of input which can be processed in different ways, according to the specifications and the nature of the input;

b) different methods of processing, applicable to different input and leading to a diversity of output documents;

c) different types of outputs, resulting from the nature of the input and the processes to which it is submitted.

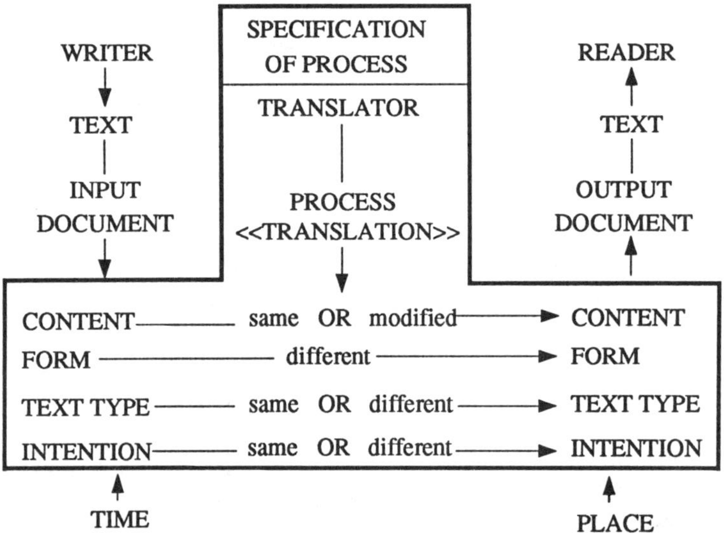

Figure 5.5 *The process model of translation*

This model differs in three important respects from its precursors (Figures 5.1 and 5.4): (i) it adds the specification of the translation task; (ii) it widens the scope of possible products by admitting the possibility of modifications to the source content; (iii) it separates text type from form as an element that can independently change in response to a change of intention. The new possibilities of translations with modified content and text type are introduced in view of the existence of such well-established translation activities as second language abstracting and summary translations (see 4.4.3).

This widening of the scope of what we understand by translation is appropriate at this stage because the development and description of an industrial model has to take real occurrences of products and processes into account. Whereas theoretical models assume that 'translation' is an adequate specification of a task, for a practical model translators require proper instructions to enable them to produce a satisfactory end product.

The basic process consists of the translator dealing with each of four constituents (content, form, text type, intention) of the input document in terms of the specifications and the possibilities afforded by both the transformation techniques available and the cultural-linguistic systems involved in each case. From the point of view of translation practice the analysis of the process requires further detailed description of the activities involved. Since the process is carried out by human beings at a time and place within certain constraints of time and cost, the model should also be given an ergonomic and economic dimension. In addition we must acknowledge the need for criteria for the evaluation of both the process and the product. The stages of this analysis are listed in section 6.4; the process including considerations of cost and evaluation is treated in sections six to eight.

A relatively complex model of the process of translation is here cited as contrast and for comparison. It was developed by Koller (1983) and is illustrated in Figure 5.6.

According to Koller the following relations have to be examined in a theory of translation:

— the relation a—a' between the L1 and L2 texts, which is concerned with textual criticism;

— the relation b—b' between the sender, the translator and their respective products, which covers the translation process, comparison and evaluation;

— the relation c—c' between the two linguistic systems, which is the case for contrastive analysis;

— the relation d—d' between the two respective recipient groups of the L1 and the L2 texts, which examines the translation product from the point of view of 'equivalent effect'.

This process view is increasingly gaining ground but with considerable variance in the inclusion of what are considered relevant features. For example, Roberts (1988) establishes eight principles of translation in which full considerations is given to the various participants in the process, the difference between message and text, the importance of context, the mixed linguistic/non-linguistic nature of the operation, etc. The overriding importance of message equivalence over word equivalence is properly acknowledged, but not the possibility of a change in message function.

KEY

	TYPE OF COMPONENT	DIRECTION
a = text - world	content component	text-oriented
b = sender - text	pragmatic component	writer-oriented
c = text - ling. system	formal ling. component	
d = text - recipient	pragmatic component	reader-oriented
D = text - translator	pragmatic component	

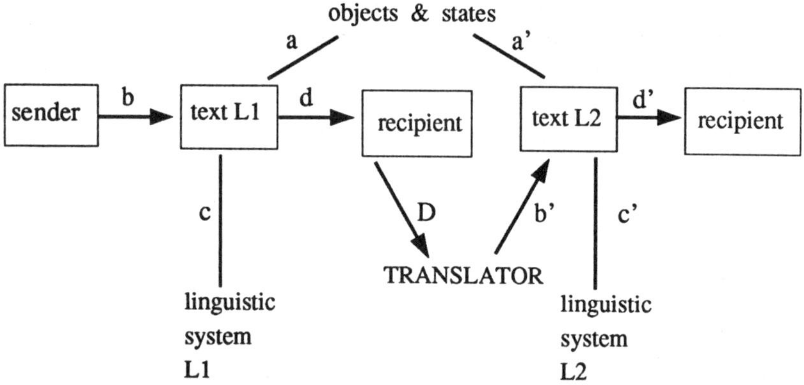

Figure 5.6 *Koller's model of translation*

These principles are, however, still not flexible enough with respect to the circumstances of translation, because they do not provide for recipients stipulating their own motivation, the possibility of translation agents as mediators between sender and recipient, or the collection of instructions to the translator in the form of specifications. On the other hand, Roberts' last principle seems to be rather too general for translation. "(8) Equivalences can be said to have been established when all the ideas in a text have been conveyed in the manner most appropriate in the light of the function of the message involved." (Roberts 1988:166). Here equivalence is implicitly equated with the acceptability of a translation and expressed in terms of 'conveyance of ideas'. This is too broad a statement to be a sound criterion for the success of translation, because it would even admit the transformation of a linguistic code into a non-linguistic code if this were in the interest of the function of the message. While this could be a successful act of text transformation, it could no longer be considered translation.

5.4.2 *Translation situations*

Inside a theory of communication, the various activities associated with translation processes are subsets of communicative speech acts which are distinguished from ordinary speech acts by a situation which requires this type of mediation in order to succeed. As a first approach to the diversity of processes and products of translations, these situations must therefore be described and their characteristics identified.

The process of translation itself constitutes a temporary suspension, of variable duration, of an intended communication process and therefore a separation of the source text from its production environment and the pragmatic meaning that can be associated with it. To justify and sustain this suspension, we must assume a strong initial motivation to communicate or to receive information which cannot be fulfilled in the intended manner because of a language barrier. The need for communication must be considered important enough to wait for the translation to be carried out and to engage other parties, i.e. mediators, to assist. Time and cost factors introduce a certain level of formality into the proceedings and increase the complexity of the task. Within this simplified pattern, translation can be said to be required in the following communicative situations:

(a) when in a temporally concurrent situation a writer fails to communicate with a primary reader, because neither knows the other's language. This is the normal situation of contemporary translation, as exemplified by business letters, diplomatic notes, contracts, etc. There are, however, two variants:

— (i) the case of a communicative situation which is suspended pending the completion of a translation, i.e. 'concurrent' in the narrow sense;

— (ii) the case where a regular time gap between production and reception of the message in translated form is already acknowledged and accepted as routine.

(b) when in a temporally deferred situation a secondary reader fails to understand the language of a document. This is the situation in research on original documents in another language or the case that motivates the translation of a textbook not originally envisaged for a readership of another language.

(c) when in a temporally deferred situation a reader no longer understands the text or message because of linguistic changes of the language. This is the case of older versions of a language which later generations no longer understand, for example, a modern translation of Chaucer's Canterbury Tales or a re-translation, such as a new version of the Bible.

In each case a decision has to be made to employ a mediator whose task it is to bring the attempted or planned speech act to a successful conclusion. The assignment of the translation task comes either from the sender, who wants to reach a recipient in another language, a recipient who has a message he does not understand, or an agent acting for either or both, such as a publisher who commissions a translation, or any other person who assigns a job to a translator. It does not come from the translator, the mediator who must be responsive to the needs of all communicating parties and their intentions; although there are exceptional cases where individual translators prepare translations, i.e. act as agents and translators, before looking for a publisher. This case is, however, largely restricted to whole book and literary translation.

Figure 5.7 gives a schematic presentation of the situations in which translations are commissioned, in the order of the motivation which originates the task.

In the first case the writer looks for a translator to whom the task of translating a message is entrusted. The writer receives the finished document and decides whether to use it as a message. In the second case the (secondary) readers have a document written in a language they cannot read, which was previously written by a writer as a message addressed to someone else. They employ translators, give instructions what to do, and receive the finished product document for their own use. The third is the case where an agent, independent of writer and reader, decides on the desirability of a translation of a document. The agent is at the beginning and the end of the speech act of translation; the previous speech act of writing the document, and the subsequent speech act of a reader receiving the document are both temporally, spatially and causally quite independent. But, the purpose of translation is not fulfilled if there is no final reader.

It can be seen that the circumstances of the task impose several conditions which are specified and discussed in the following sections:

(a) There must be someone entrusting the translator with a task. We call this person an agent.

(b) There must be a genuine and clearly specified reader who cannot read the message in its original form—otherwise the process does not fulfil a primary communication need. This need can be anticipated by writers or agents or discovered by the readers themselves. This condition excludes students' translation exercises from consideration because the teacher is no genuine reader.

(c) There must be a genuine source, a 'translatable' document, within the conventions of what is considered suitable for translation by a community.

Writer-motivated translation

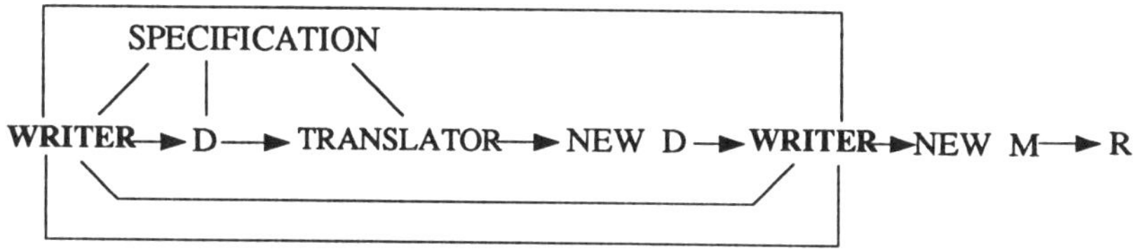

Reader-motivated translation

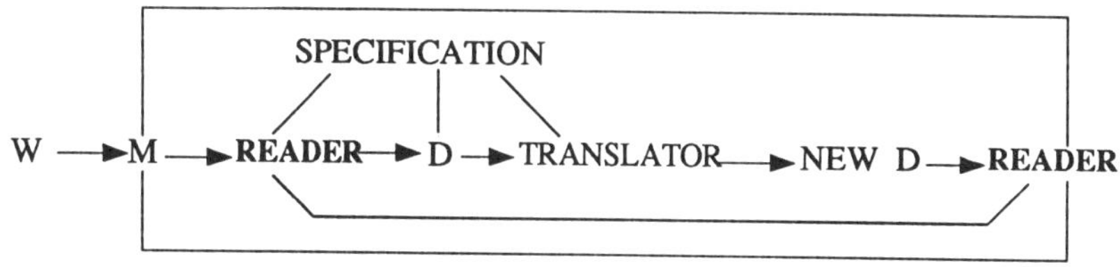

Agent-motivated translation

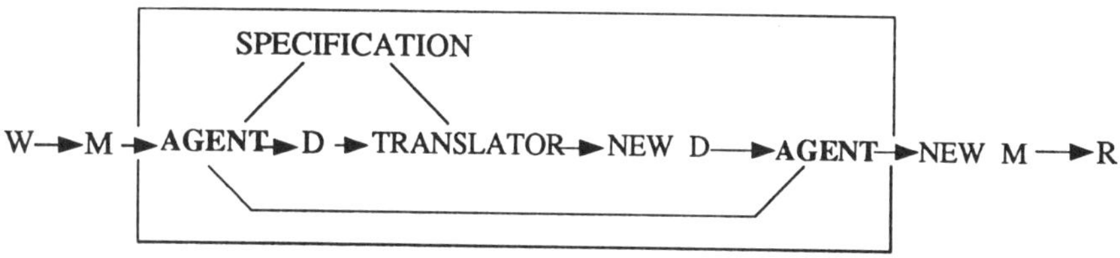

KEY: W = writer R = reader
D = document M = message

Figure 5.7 *Types of translation situations*

(d) There is always a disruption of the normal flow of communication by the various steps of the translation process and hence a time delay between writing and reading, which, incidentally may give time for reflection. The permitted time delay must be specified.

(e) There must be an external specification, a set of instructions, summing up and defining conditions (a)—(d), to which the translator can work.

(f) There must be a translator who delivers a product to a client or a client's agent—otherwise there is no possible control over the process.

This condition also excludes the translation, written or oral, made by readers themselves for their own benefit. This condition excludes amateur translators who translate for personal satisfaction. An exceptional case are some literary translators who produce an unsolicited translation because they anticipate the interest of a publisher and hence work to specifications their experience tells them to be currently valid, or preferred by a particular publisher they submit work to.

The specifications differ according to who provides them: writers can be supposed to know what they want to say, readers are clearly ignorant of the content of the message but know what they hope to read and the way they wish to read; the agent usually acts on behalf of the writer or the reader. Translators must interpret the specification according to the source from which it is received; in some cases they can interact with the provider of the specification—there being also the special case of the translator interacting with both the agent and the writer.

5.5 The concept of equivalence

Fundamental to all theories of translation is the concept of equivalence. There is, however, considerable diversity in the interpretation of what is meant by this concept, as demonstrated in section 5.3.3. It is generally recognised that the relationship of a source and a target language text is one of cognitive, pragmatic and linguistic equivalences. How these equivalences are achieved and how they operate, is, however, far from clear. Equivalence between the two documents involved in translation can also be stipulated at different levels and there is further diversity in the evaluation of what is considered successful equivalence. We review here some of these interpretations.

We begin with the well-established concept of 'dynamic equivalence' established by Nida in the context of Bible translation.

> Dynamic equivalence is therefore to be defined in terms of the degree to which receptors of the message in the receptor language respond to it in substantially the same manner as the receptors in the source language. This response can never be identical, for the cultural and historical settings are too different, but there should be a high degree of equivalence of response, or the translation will have failed to accomplish its purpose.
>
> (Nida & Taber 1982:24)

The whole justification of Bible translation rests on the assumption of the possibility of equivalence of response, and the experienced Bible translator knows that the cultural and temporal barriers cannot possibly produce full identity.

Further clarification of what is meant by "dynamic" in this context comes from another group of Bible translators.

> A translation which transfers the meaning and the dynamics of the original text is to be regarded as a faithful translation. The expression 'transfer the meaning', means that the translation conveys to the readers or hearers the information that the original conveyed to its readers or hearers.... The expression, 'the dynamics', means that (1) the translation makes a natural use of the linguistic structures of the RL (receptor language) and that (2) the recipients of the translation understand the message with ease.
>
> (Beekman et al. 1981:34)

The division into meaning and dynamics is a recognition of the role of purpose in communication, but the vagueness of "natural use" and "understand with ease" are indicative of issues rather than full explanations of phenomena.

Another account of the problem of equivalence, this time in a general environment is given in Larson (1984):

> ... the best translation is one which (a) uses the normal language forms of the receptor language, (b) communicates, as much as possible, to the receptor language speakers the same meaning that was understood by the speakers of the source language, and (c) maintains the dynamics of the original source language text. Maintaining the 'dynamics' of the original source text means that the translation is presented in such a way that it will, hopefully, evoke the same response as the source text attempted to evoke.
>
> (Larson 1984:6)

For Larson, equivalence means "the same meaning" given by the original writer and maintenance of "dynamics", which, in terms of our own account of the communication process, corresponds to what we have called setting, means both background of the speech act and purpose of the message.

Turk (1990) analyses the concept of equivalence and notes that decisions concerning equivalence are alternatively based on the concepts of adequacy, which is indicative of progressive approximation to an absolute value, and correspondence, which would be indicative of progressive homogeneity. He also makes a functional distinction between these values. He proposes that 'adequacy' be used with respect to comparison of translation with expectations in the target language; he also proposes considering 'correspondence' for comparisons with respect to the original source text and by extension to linguistic units between linguistic systems; he reserves 'equivalence' for comparisons with respect to other translation possibilities. Equivalence would therefore also be determinable by the possibility of exchanging units of text with the same range of meaning. He acknowledges the particular problems associated with ranges of meaning of expression forms, i.e. correspondences of one-to-many and many-to-one in general language where subject fields do not impose a filter on the range of denotation. He makes the interesting observations that equivalences can be discovered through translation rather than be presupposed.

For the case of literary translation Turk (1990:66) distinguishes four types or degrees of equivalences. While literary translation lies outside the scope of this book, his observations serve as further illustration of the many dimensions of the concept of equivalence.

(a) Equivalences which do not alter the historical or systematic significance of the range of interpretation of the original.
(b) Equivalences with historical or systematic significance which exploit the range of the one-to-many correspondence between source and target language for the benefit of the semantic content and the state of interpretation.
(c) Equivalences which are explanatory and productive in the target language, because they symbolise the semantic content in a new and different manner, exploiting the many-to-one correspondence.
(d) Equivalences which exploit the one-to-many correspondence in order to diffuse the original meaning.

Some authors have indicated priorities of importance of equivalence in such factors as: rhythm, meter, verse, rhyme, intonation, tempo, pauses, nominal-verbal style, choice of words, proverbs, puns, metaphor, illustration, euphony, grammatical rhetorical figures and syntactic means. Levy (1967:104) postulates three opposite values of equivalence, namely 'general-individual, whole-part, content-form' of which the good translation should emphasise the general, whole and content.

Summing up we can say that the explanations here discussed concentrate on (i) equivalence of meaning and (ii) equivalence of the rather broad concept of 'dynamics', while revealing minor differences of interpretation. They do not deal specifically with the other possible types of equivalence, i.e. of effect and form, which are sometimes presented as conflicting demands leading to different translation techniques. Nor do they differentiate between equivalence of linguistic units at the level of the linguistic system and equivalence at the level of text types, or even the utterance in specific sublanguage situations. Finally they do not accept a change of either meaning or 'dynamics' as part of the process of translation. This is understandable in the case of Bible translation and also in the tradition of literary translation which implicitly underlies Larson's position. Equivalence, then, is a relative notion, because all decisions on equivalence are based on the alternative perceptions of adequacy and correspondence, which, however, themselves presuppose some form of norm against which we can measure equivalence. Such measurements are discussed in the next section. The means of creating equivalences are discussed in section 8.

In more recent writings we note a break with the idea of equivalence. Reiss & Vermeer, for example, reject the concept of 'equivalence' in favour of the more general concept of "adequacy" which they link to "purpose" (Reiss & Vermeer 1984:101). Even more explicit on the subject is Gutt (1991) who speaks only of appropriateness by text type and function. While appropriateness is a valid criterion for measuring the success of a speech act, a concept of equivalence or correspondence is still required in order to deal with the evaluation of the result of the process at the micro-levels.

The critical question of how to determine equivalence is faced by few writers. When translators read a document they first of all identify the pragmatic equivalences required at the level of the message and text type; they understand the document in a very special manner which permits them to identify the cognitive units for which correspondences are sought; at the same time an experienced translator retains a sufficient perception of the linguistic and rhetorical structure so that, for reasons of economy of labour, they can look for equivalences at the nearest grammatical level possible.

5.6 Evaluation of translation

The last basic element of an industrially oriented theory of translation must be a means of determining the success of the speech act, i.e. an evaluation of both the process and the product. There are inherent difficulties in evaluating translation because of the nature of the task. For evaluating the product both writers and end users have only a limited role to play because they cannot assess either the source or the target text; translators are equally unsuitable because they transfer knowledge of the source document into their interpretation of the target document and therefore lose objectivity. Process evaluation has only become relevant with industrialisation. Hitherto, the process was omitted from evaluation because as a purely human activity it depended on the training and experience of the individual translator and was thus highly subjective. With the existence of MT, a theory must, however, contain means of evaluating the relative merits and benefits of one form of process against another. Because machine processes can be broken down into separate phases and evaluated separately, there is now also a greater interest in segmenting the human process in order to come closer to the possibility of detailed evaluation.

In an industrial setting evaluation must be pursued on a very broad front. It serves for the assessment of individual translators, of the relative merit of automated systems, of the cost and relative cost efficiency of a service and can even extend to customer needs. More specifically, evaluation pursues several complementary objectives. It can be communicatively or linguistically qualitative, (i.e. assessing the value of the product), operational and pedagogical, (i.e. looking for means of improvement of both process and product), and finally methodological, (i.e. observing the process in order to determine how it evolved).

Two levels of evaluation have been identified. If evaluation occurs at a general or macro level it is broadly qualitative and can be directed at a comparative appreciation of products with respect to cost, time and adequacy for the intended purpose, which comprises such criteria as acceptability, intelligibility and even reading time by the end user. While macro-evaluation is usually directed at alternative products by different people or produced by different methods, micro-evaluation can concern itself both with comparison among alternatives and evaluation of a single product. At the micro level evaluation is concerned with such criteria as fidelity and more specifically with correctness in terms of choice, order and grammatical agreement of items. Micro-evaluation of the process is essential for teaching improved human translation performance and for the design and improvement of automated systems.

Traditionally evaluation of the translation product is based on text comparison in order to determine degrees of fidelity, accuracy, completeness and felicity. This is often carried out in form of a contrastive evaluation by a single individual of the source and target texts only, without the guidance of objective criteria. Such an individual is in no better position than a translator unless we assume an idealised bilingual and bicultural subject field expert. Even then, the evaluation would be dependent on the individual's preferences of expression and interpretation of content, a typical objection to the conventional assessment of translation examinations of students.

In order to avoid subjective judgements any genuine comparison must contain a third neutral element, the 'tertio comparationis' against which the comparison of source and target text can be made. Without such a neutral standard there is no point of reference for the comparison of content, form or intention. Figure 5.8. shows the different possibilities of evaluation. In this three-element approach, evaluation criteria for the product in relation to the source document focus on four possible types of contrasts:

(a) a comparison between the L1 text, the L2 text and any of the translated versions; (1 –2 –5).
(b) a comparison between the L2 text and several other translated versions; (2 –5).
(c) a comparison between the L1 text, the L2 text and an optimal translation; (1 –2 –4).
(d) a comparison between the source text, the language-independent representation and the target language text; (1 –2 –3).

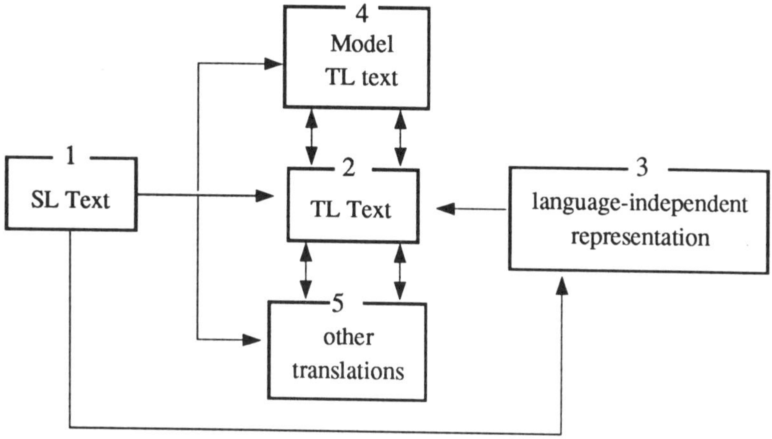

Figure 5.8 *Evaluation criteria (tertio comparationis)*

Most traditional views, and this includes the literary tradition, consider a translated document in relation to its original only, i.e. mode 1-2 in Figure 5.8. In this view documents are seen as finite entities because they deal with discrete segments of language and the evaluator is the sole arbiter of the meaning of the original and consequently of the choice of equivalents. Translation theory therefore can become an exercise in textual criticism, which may lead to an evaluation, i.e. statements about the 'quality' of a translation. Such evaluations may be extended to the assessment of alternative translated versions of a SL text from which an optimal version may be construed, i.e. mode 1-2-4. One of the measurements of success, then, lies in the human assessment of maximal identity of content between the source and the target language texts being at the same time fully identifiable as belonging to two different languages.

This view is undoubtedly appropriate for existing translations of literary works of the past, but of little relevance to the industrial scene, for which a much wider view is needed. Such a straightforward view of translation was also used for the assessment of the early machine translation products, because the machine was simply seen as a text converter in a misunderstood analogy to a misunderstood human process. Early designers of MT, having neither translation nor linguistic experience, spoke of 'recoding' only. Simple contrastive assessment of units of transfer is, of course, still quite appropriate for measuring degrees of 'correct' equivalences contained in the fully automatic MT systems, and an indication of the comprehensiveness of linguistic description contained in the system.

For the language industry, product evaluation must involve user expectation, agent specification and, in order to judge the appropriateness of the final product, also some form of metalinguistic representation of the source text as tertio comparationis, i.e. the pattern 1-2-3, above. The source text itself is of little interest for this type of evaluation, except in the special case of full parallel texts being specified. Alternative versions are accepted as unavoidable but not considered without justification. Assessment of translation in this view is a more complex operation as indicated in Figure 5.9.

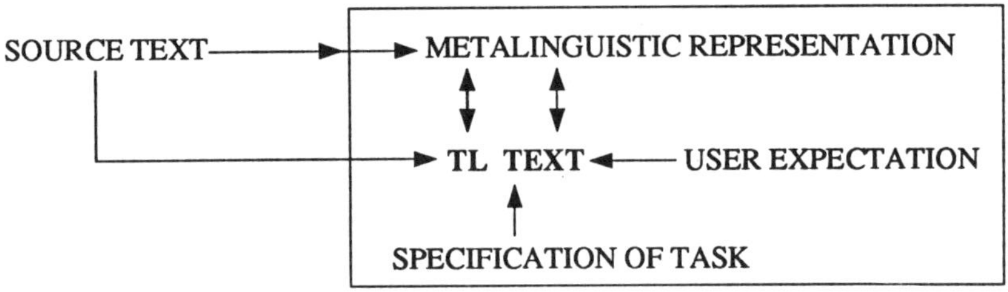

Figure 5.9 *Elements for industrial evaluation of translation*

5.6.1 *Criteria for evaluation*

A number of criteria have been advanced for the assessment of translation in an industrial environment (House 1977, Gouadec 1981, van Slype 1986). Those which are specific to human or machine translation are presented in sections 8.8 and 9.5 respectively; more general ones are briefly introduced here.

The classical criterion for evaluation is fidelity, but beside the problems of who should assess fidelity, mentioned above, there are difficulties regarding the level at which fidelity is to be established. Global evaluation, seeing the text as a single sense unit is strictly limited in scope and usefulness. As soon as the text to be assessed is considered as a sum of lexical meanings restricted by syntax, the assessment must be based on a model of interpretation of the text seen as a complex entity. Prior to assessment a progressively restricted selection of possibilities of meaning must be made, the result of which is then the basis of comparison. This basis of comparison is further shaped by the interpretation of the purpose of the document which is also manifested in the choice and order of the content by means of lexical items and syntax.

The determination of accuracy of equivalence then varies with the form- or sense-orientation of the translation method, even when information is the only or chief criterion of evaluation. In practice such an evaluation would have to be carried out unit by unit at the level of the phrase, clause, sentence, paragraph and the whole text.

In order to involve the end user of the product it has been proposed that intelligibility, defined as the subjective evaluation of the degree of clarity and comprehensibility of each sentence, should be the decisive criterion. The subjectivity of this method would, however, require assessment by a large number of individuals in order to overcome or neutralise the variants introduced by the differences in previous knowledge of the subject matter and the level of education of the assessors. Other obstacles to decisive results of comparison between texts are the intrinsic degree of intelligibility of the source text and, of course, the question of accuracy of the translation in the first place. The measure of intelligibility, though easily assessed through such methods as cloze tests, or multiple choice questions on the content, can at best be carried out after the accuracy or fidelity of the document has been established.

Another approach to intelligibility is the measurement of reading time required for a translation in comparison to the reading time of a similar document in the readers' own language. While reading time is easily and inexpensively measured, the conditions for such an assessment must be carefully monitored. A fair number of testers is required in order to neutralise personal variation in reading speed. It is also necessary to have separate groups of readers: the group whose reading speed has been measured with respect to a particular translation cannot be used to read another translation of the same text since this group is already familiar with the content of the texts. Furthermore the individual interpretation of reading time varies considerably and can sensibly be controlled only through the type of test described under intelligibility, above.

A combination of criteria, still in the interest of evaluation of industrially-based products, can be grouped under the heading of acceptability of a text to its readers, which presupposes fidelity, intelligibility and usefulness. Though still highly subjective, this measurement appears the most globally useful, though even here it will be necessary to distinguish between different users and different uses of different types of texts. For example, a translation required for current awareness only may not be acceptable for storage and repeated reading or for teaching purposes. Acceptability questionnaires might also contain sections asking what is an acceptable cost of production or price for the information obtained and what is an acceptable delays in receiving the information.

6 Specifications: Factors Influencing the Translation Process

This section is concerned with establishing the conditions for the description of the translation process in an industrial environment. For this purpose it first examines existing models of translation and assesses their applicability for the requirements of a new model in which human translation is extremely diversified and variously assisted by tools of the language industry or, in special cases, replaced by other modes of communication. On this basis it analyses the preconditions for translations, here called specifications, which determine the variety of possible operations on texts by human translators, with or without the assistance of machines, and by machines.

6.1 Conditions for modelling the translation process

A model of an industrial process must analyse the input material, the operations that can be and are in practice performed on this material, the scope and capabilities of the operators and machines available and the possible end products that can be obtained. The input material consists of documents belonging to a variety of text types associated to topics. The operations are completely human or completely automatic processes, or combined, in the case of the interaction of human and machine operations. The operators are human translators, or, in some special cases, writers or readers with varying levels of experience and skills. The machines are computers with software in various stages of development and hence diverse quality of performance. The end products are other, related documents that can be described from the positions of: (i) the possible transformations applicable to a particular type of text, expressed as a relation between input and output; (ii) user requirements; (iii) the types of operation carried out.

The inclusion of tools and hence alternative translation methods complicates the conventional modelling of the process of translation in at least two respects. One of these is the possibility of selection from a variety of tools; the other is the optimal timing of the applications of any of these tools in the process. We concentrate on the enhancement of human capabilities in association with the tools provided by the new language industry but must not forget that this enhancement now extends beyond the profession of translators. In order to admit the machine translation product as a full alternative, the model must also allow that there can be several 'acceptable' human and machine translations of the same text, resulting from different methods and techniques of translation. This allowance is simply an extension of the widely acknowledged experience that no two human translators produce identical translations of complete documents even though they may coincide on sentences and phrases.

6.1.1 *Basic approaches to translation techniques*

The first and most important variable in the translation process is that of the diversity of human translators and other people engaged in related activities. This factor affects all types of translation and is therefore discussed here before narrowing the focus of this book to the translation process in an industrial environment.

Based on their varied educational and practical backgrounds and their concomitant differences in linguistic and subject knowledge of the two cultures between which mediation is required, translators have different attitudes to the 'distance' to be bridged between the languages and cultures involved. These different perceptions affect their reading and interpretation of the document to be translated, their preferred method of translation and their view of the target language document. These differences are deeply anchored in the reality of the translation market in which there are many people whose professional profiles do not conform to the theoretical assumptions of most job specifications. These job descriptions usually state linguistic performance requirements in terms of one 'active' mother tongue and one or several 'passive' or source languages from which translations are made. The reality of the market is, however, quite different. In a multilingual and multicultural Europe with greater mobility than ever before, individuals cannot simply be classified by mother tongue or 'language of habitual use' and passive languages when many years of residence, in education and work, in different countries at different ages are quite common and result in a great mixture of command of a variety of sublanguages which can be positively exploited in a professional capacity. The educational background of professional translators, which determines amounts of special subject knowledge and hence familiarity with topics and text types of sublanguages, is equally diverse. While the majority of translators currently working in Europe may, indeed, have joined the profession via a degree in the humanities, oriented towards translation or followed by a vocational training course, there is a large group of professionals who have first and even second degrees in technical or other specialist professional fields, such as law or medicine. Quite a number of these have also had practical experience in the exercise of these professions before turning to translation as a full-time job.

Professional practice and the working environment in which translators receive their practical training exert a further diversifying influence on attitudes. Whether working in their own country or abroad, in a monolingual and monodisciplinary or a multilingual and multi-disciplinary setting, creates different working habits and hence attitudes to the substance of mediation. In addition to such a diverse profile of full-time translators, the many other professionals who translate as part of their regular other professional activities have a strong impact on the industrial scene and influence and shape attitudes to translation. To be accurate, translators' job-specifications would have to be expressed firstly in terms of requirements of command of source and target sublanguages, secondly in terms of the special knowledge of subject fields associated with these sublanguages and thirdly in terms of experience of communicative situations in which their mediation is to be applied. In practice, translators usually work into one language only of which they know some sublanguages and text types and work out of one or several languages of which they are familiar with matching sublanguages and text types.

These different backgrounds, then lead to widely differing attitudes to the task of translation which have to be taken into account in a realistic description of the translation scene. Three major points of focus are here identified:

(a) The first focus is adopted by people fully conversant with the subject matter at hand and results naturally when a subject specialist who can understand specialist literature in a foreign language attempts to translate what he understands rather than what is specifically expressed. Translation in this view is primarily concerned with the transfer of units of meaning rather than with textual units. For subject specialists, especially when they are not full-time translators, the form of the text is secondary or even irrelevant to the process; they read and understand a text in the same way as ordinary readers and then reproduce what they recall without much attention to the details of syntax or rhetoric of the source text. In such a translation the content may even be filtered through the translators' own perception of the subject matter, with the addition of personal interpretations or selections where felt appropriate for the situation of the mediation. This attitude to translation, provisionally called 'conceptual transfer', can also be described as being cognition- or comprehension-based, or as somehow 'restricted' as defined by Newmark (1988:12).

    In its extreme form without linguistic sophistication, this attitude is not considered appropriate for professional translators but in practice much translation is produced from this position and in some cases, such as multilingual abstracting, it has its distinct merits.

(b) The second focus is adopted by the many professional and occasional translators who have a near-equal command of sublanguages and cannot therefore clearly separate active from passive command and use which should be expressed in the direction in which they translate. In fact large sectors of the translation industry, especially in smaller countries, where translators cannot make a living by translating into their mother tongue only, are dependent on translators with bi-directional skills. This necessity, combined with appropriate skills, leads to a translation technique similar to that typically used by the 'bilingual' person who can produce two equivalent versions based on the same communicative intention and situation. This mode is also comparable to the situation of the liaison interpreter in an international environment who has to work into and out of two languages without identifying with either party. The qualitative test of this translation would be the complete reversibility of the process in either direction leading to the same text. To characterise its different basis, the resultant technique is here provisionally called 'bi-directional composition'.

In the particular environment of fully bilingual regimes in such countries as Belgium, Canada or South Africa a great deal of legal and administrative bilingual writing and translation is done by persons with such a background and attitude. It is also found in the large sector of trade and commerce where idiomatic fluency in two languages is required with ease of movement between source and target language.

(c) For a theoretical model a third, background-neutral focus is necessary, and here identified as 'balanced translation'. Such a neutral attitude is the theoretical position that underlies most writing on the subject. It is the position of translators without the natural advantage of a wider linguistic experience and subject knowledge, a condition often found in the beginners in a translation career. Theorists, who in most cases come from university institutes concerned with the training of translators with that sort of background, therefore assume this to be the essential condition of the translator. It is not usually considered that even translators starting from this basis are likely to develop tendencies in the direction of conceptual transfer or bi-directional composition according to their professional environment. The most successful ones develop both attitudes in equal measure and exploit these skills as appropriate.

This focus can be called balanced because it stresses the parallel importance in translation of form and content as expressed in both syntactic and semantic units; it attempts to preserve the syntactic structure of the sentence as far as possible, but differs from (b) in that it goes deeper into the analysis of texts in order to produce what is conventionally understood to be a reliable or accurate translation rather than equivalent sense or effect, regardless of structural comparability.

Figure 6.1 illustrates these three natural and basic attitudes to translation in simplified procedural steps which show the differences of approach.

	FOCUS		
Steps	**Conceptual**	**Bi-directional**	**Balanced**
1. *Reading*	comprehension of content & rhetorical form	content & syntax & rhetorical form	subsentence units content & syntax
2. *Process*	rhetorical units	sentences, unless obvious	syntactic units
3. *Method*	reconstruct rhetorical units	match semantic units	match lexical units and word form, match constructions revise & adapt to TL
conventional name	free translation	free translation	close translation

Figure 6.1 *Methods of human translation*

Traditional translation theory recognises two major types of translation, which are, on the whole, concerned with the dichotomy of emphasis on content versus form. This is illustrated in Figure 6.1 by the contrast between the conceptual and bilateral models one the hand and the balanced, syntax-based method on the other. This contrast, with minor divergencies in interpretation, is also variously called free vs. close, reader- vs. writer-oriented, and more recently by Newmark (1981), semantic vs. communicative translation. The contrast is usually exemplified as lying between greater observance of formal equivalence criteria, on the one hand, and a greater concentration on semantic equivalences, on the other.

The *close translation* is concerned with observing the highest possible degree of formal equivalences at the word, phrase, clause and argument level; this is usually associated with the admission of smaller units of translation and a narrower concept of equivalence. The expression 'literal', as a synonym to 'close', is here deliberately avoided because of its various and diverse interpretations ranging from word-for-word matches to denotational equivalence only.

The *free translation* concentrates on conveying the content in such a form that it becomes easier for the reader to grasp, understand or capture the text, even to the extent of translators disregarding unit boundaries at the sentence or paragraph level. This position is naturally highly subjective, because it requires translators to decide what may and what may not be easy to understand for an often unknown reader, which in turn requires a degree of interpretation of the SL text that may not be required for the 'close' translation.

Newmark (1988:45-47) develops a scale of translation types according to the translators observance of source or target language features. Starting from SL emphasis, his scale moves from word-for-word to literal to faithful to semantic translation; starting from target language emphasis the scale moves from adaptation to free to idiomatic to communicative translation. In Newmark's view, "only semantic and communicative translation fulfil the two main aims of translation, which are, first, accuracy, and second, economy" (1988:47).

As usual in any theoretical opposition there is always someone to advocate an intermediate position, as exemplified by the translation model presented by Bathgate.

> Normative model: First one translates literally; then one asks oneself whether the literal translation conveys the meaning intended. If not, one departs from the original form to convey the right meaning. One then asks oneself whether the translation which gives the right meaning is also appropriate to the situation involved: is that really what you say in that kind of context. (Bathgate 1980:113-114)

This highly practical advice is, however, insufficiently differentiated to serve as a model for a diversified industrial process.

6.2 Existing models of the translation process

Before listing and analysing the steps of the model developed for the extended communicative theory of translation presented in this book, it is useful to examine a number of existing models and to discuss their relative merits.

The simplest process description is that of Flamand (1983:129), who divides the translation process into four steps:

(1) ASSIMILATION/TUNING
consisting of memorizing, not words, but stretches of information—the longer those stretches of information, the better the translation is likely to be;

(2) CONVERSION
consisting of recasting the text as idiomatically as possible;

(3) WRITING

(4) CHECKING

(5) OBJECTIVE READING, CRITICAL READING, FINAL READING

This model was commented by Manning (1983:228) as follows:

> The key notions of Flamand's definition can be summarised as follows:
> 1. Translation involves rendering not just the words or linguistic forms of the text, but the message—those elements that express the intention of the writer.
> 2. Translation requires that one observe the servitudes of the target language (orthography, abbreviations, grammar, idiom, etc.
> 3. Translation should not sound like translation; it should read like a piece of original writing and so avoid overliteralness.
> 4. Translation should, where appropriate, read as if it had been written by an expert in the field.
> The belief behind Flamand's definition is that every message has an intra-textual aspect—the linguistic elements of the text, i.e. the text per se,—and the extra-textual aspect—the circumstances surrounding the production of the message, including expectations and presuppositions of both writer and reader.

Additional steps in the process are identified by Mareschal (1988), as follows:

1. Identification and global reading of SL text
2. Analysis/comprehension of text
3. Transfer from SL to TL
4. Restructuring
5. Re-reading
6. Revision

Bathgate (1980:23) presents a similar sequence of actions:

1. Tuning
2. Analysis
3. Understanding
4. Terminology
5. Restructuring
6. Checking
7. Discussion

The interesting point about these models is that they recognise two reading processes and that they distinguish 'transfer' from 'restructuring', indicating in this way that the search for translation equivalents can be separated from the process of composition in the target language.

A more detailed picture is given by Vernay's sequence (1981: 243):

1. STARTING POINT: a text in L1, i.e. embedded in its communicative background (CB) 1;
2. Attribution of L1T1 to a text type within CB 1;

3. Transfer of the 'parole' phenomena of L1T1 to the 'langue' dimension of L1;
4. Semasiological analysis of sign units of L1 and their attribution to the noematic categories on the content plane;
5. Production of a metatext as 'tertium comparationis', consisting of semantic categories arrived at in stage 4, related to the CB 1 together with the CB 2 of the recipient of the translation;
6. Onomasiological search of equivalents to the noematic categories, arrived at in stage 4, in the language dimension of L2;
7. Confirmation/fixation of the equivalences or divergencies between L1 and L2 systems, with reference to the extra-linguistic categories of the content plane;
8. Production of the L2T2 text according to the target language norms and with reference to the equivalence conditions valid within and based on a comparison of CB 1 and CB 2.

The importance of this model resides in two elements absent in the previous cases: (i) the fact that it identified the text type as a formal entity, comprising both the external and internal shape of a document; (ii) the inclusion of the communicative background of both languages in the consideration of the appropriate choice of semantic categories. Its deficiency, as with the previous models, lies in the lack of recognition of purpose (intention and expectation) as an independent text dimension which then also excludes the possibility of diversifying translation techniques and endproducts according to pragmatic and functional considerations.

The special case of Bible translation is illustrated by the model developed by Nida & Taber (1982:51-55):

SL text analysis ⇒ kernel sentences ⇒ transfer ⇒
kernel sentences ⇒ restructuring ⇒ TL text

(For a discussion of Bible translation, see section 6.3.2.)

It is obvious that for Biblical and other texts that have undergone multiple interpretation over centuries, it is necessary to re-create basic units of meaning. Their expression in the form of predications, independent of the source language syntax, is the original feature of Nida's theory.

For literary translation we cite two models, the very theoretical one of Steiner and a more practical one by Mayoral.

Steiner (1975:312-318) defines four steps in the process of literary translation, which he also calls "hermeneutic motion":

1. Trust; the translator must trust in his assumption of the validity of the message;

2. Aggression (incursion—extraction); this phase is concerned with the extractive process of interpretation and is limited by the translator's linguistic and other knowledge;
3. Incorporation, appropriation; this phase adjusts the text to the culture of the target language;
4. Restitution; to restore the equilibrium between SL and TL texts, to admit deficiencies and compensate for them.

Mayoral et al. (1988) identify roles and activities associated with them.

— Author (sender in source culture) [encoder]
— MESSAGE encoded in source culture
— [decoder] Translator (receptor in source language) [encoder]
— TRANSLATION
— [decoder] Translator (sender in target culture) [encoder]
— MESSAGE encoded in target culture
— [decoder] Reader (receptor in target culture)

All these models exhibit certain limitations which make them unsuitable for our more specific purposes.

(a) They approach the translation process in a unilinear way. The instructions are meant to be followed by an ideal translator for an optimal translation, but do not allow for variation of technique leading to different products.
(b) They approach it in a statically descriptive way which idealises the process. They do not account for the psychological reality of translating. No indication is given of the nature or complexity of the mental processes involved.
(c) They are theoretical-speculative and not based on empirical data. They are constructed rationally by logical deduction and not by empirical induction.
(d) They are not based on the reality of a job situation in which translators work to instructions, i.e. they do not account for task specifications which determine the technique to be chosen, and the nature of the end product to be delivered to the client.
(e) They do not include the possibility of machines intervening, partly or wholly replacing the human process.

6.3 Major types of translation activities

So far we have dealt with a full range of translation products and techniques. The scope of this book is, however limited to translation in an industrial setting which includes the use of machine aids. It is therefore appropriate to characterise the other major translation activities not dealt with in this book, each of which has its own subtypes and different processes and methods. These are literary and Bible translation.

We specifically exclude the translation as language learning exercise as practised in schools, universities and other institutions, because this form does not fulfil the general conditions stipulated for translation, namely a genuine reader and a specification. The translation as exercise is assigned or set by a teacher who knows both languages and then assesses the work on this basis. The teacher is not a genuine recipient and hence a student in the role of translator has no genuine task of communication to perform. Such translation exercises have their value for teaching accuracy of matching lexical units and for understanding contrastive grammar, but they are no substitute for translation exercises done in a real environment of communication as part of an apprenticeship in translation. All aspiring translators are at some stage apprentices who learn in real life situations or in well-constructed simulations.

6.3.1 *Literary translation*

Literary translation is generally considered somehow different from other translations and we instinctively put it into a separate category. This is largely because the purpose of a literary work cannot be specified in the simple terms of the intentions hitherto presented; nor can reader expectation be so analysed. Since in the translation of literary works there cannot be a single specification, the only overriding responsibility is a translator's ethical obligation to the author. Paradoxically, however, this respect for the author, which can only be realised by means of a strong text orientation, demands an exceptional freedom for the translator to move away, where necessary, from the linguistic expression in order to convey what he perceives as the author's meaning and intention. But, as the interpretation of works of literature is highly subjective, every serious translation of a work of literature is another version corresponding to another interpretation, in this case by the translator, of the author's intention and expressed meanings. This view affirms the originality of the literary creation and at the same time supports and justifies the repeated translation of a single work. In the same way as we accept the meaning of Shakespeare's 'Hamlet' to be clarified by the multiplicity of literary comments on this work, we can accept the meaning of

Homer's 'Iliad' or Goethe's 'Faust' to consist of their commentaries and all their translations over the centuries.

But translation of literature has another distinctive feature. Besides being generally poorly paid and undervalued, the literary translator does not have a clearly defined reader. The original writer neither aims at nor envisages a readership in another culture, nor another period in time, but writes in the knowledge of his own culture for his own culture. The translator, as representative of the writer in the target culture and possibly in a different historical period, addresses or, we might even say, creates a new readership. Nowhere is this more clearly demonstrated than in the case of such literary oddities as the 19th century translations of Dante's 'Divina Commedia' into blank verse by Longfellow for an American audience and into 14th century French by Littré for a French readership.

Literary translation is therefore heavily text-oriented. The text is the only reality and there is no other reality outside the reader's own interpretation of the text. Any reference to another world is inappropriate since this would prejudge the author's relationship to his own world which is indirectly reflected in the text. The text-based view is appropriate to literary translation because the only valid comparison and hence assessment of a translation can be made by comparison with alternative translations of which one is taken as the tertio comparationis.

Arguments for the impossibility of translation are reinforced by theories of literature which do not admit a facile separation of form from content. In such a view, 'translation' in the full sense of the word should not even be permissible. The argument could then be put into a rhetorical question: What are Shakespeare or Cervantes without their language? This position is brought into focus when we consider the translation of a literary work of a past culture into a modern form of the same language. For example, in an English literary culture translations of Beowulf and Chaucer into modern English are not considered to be acceptable substitutes for the real thing, but they may become accepted as interesting re-creations. On the other hand, the same society not only tolerates but accepts without much reservation English translations of Cervantes or Tolstoy because we somehow feel the barrier of a foreign language to be more dense and difficult to surmount than one of centuries of what is considered to be the same language. The limits of translatability are reached in the case of the translation of literary works in which the linguistic form is given special importance, as is the case with poetry. In past centuries translations of poetry were often attempted with full attention to content, rhyme and metre. Today it is rare for translators to attempt a full semantically, linguistically and rhetorically felicitous translation of verse, though exceptions exist in the translation of verse drama. The conventional approach to the translation of poetry is now (i) to paraphrase or transliterate in prose, in the manner of a footnote to the source text which occupies its proper place on the page; (ii) to provide a prose translation in parallel, possibly with footnotes, or (iii) to contrast the original with a new, though somehow related, poem on opposite pages, as if it were to attract attention to the difference.

A very special kind of literary translation is the dubbing of videos and films. Here translation proceeds in several stages until it reaches a linguistic form which is compatible with the time allotted for speech in the film and the mouth movement of the actors or speakers. The first stage is the independent translation of the dialogue parts of the script. The next step is the modification of the translation by re-writing or cutting to fit the dialogue into the time available and the mouth movements of the actors on screen, where these are visible. This stage does not, strictly speaking, require a translator, though in practice translators are often involved in this task. When the script is thus adjusted to the visible articulation of the source language, actors speak the script for a new sound track. Even at this stage, adjustments may have to be made to the text so that it is speakable for the actors who are carrying out the dubbing. In dubbing notions of semantic equivalence of an utterance are subordinated to the pragmatic requirements of the situation of the re-enacted speech act.

Similar external requirements occur in the case of the translation of operatic libretti.

6.3.2 *Bible translation*

The Bible in its original untranslated form is a collection of ancient writings in Hebrew, Aramaic and Greek, spanning many cultures and more than a thousand years. The 66 books into which the Bible is divided represent a variety of text types, e.g. historical narrative, prophecy, poetry, instructions and exhortation. Unlike the sacred writings of other religions, e.g. Judaism and Islam, which are considered untranslatable, Christianity has consistently relied on translation for its diffusion. In 1990 the United Bible Societies (Bible Society 1991) recorded that of the estimated 3,000 languages in the world, 318 had complete Bibles and that in over 1,000 languages some Bible translation was in progress. The target languages vary considerably from those with a long literary tradition, to ones which have only recently been codified and finally languages for which a writing system and written forms are being developed by the Bible translators themselves. The scale and diversity of this work and its future scope can therefore be called truly industrial.

Bible translation has historically been perceived as a separate form with its own methods and practices justified by the nature of the source language texts, the historical distance between text and reader, the inherent value and integrity of the texts as a whole and, of course, the use of these texts. The main representatives of modern approaches to Bible translation can be found in the United Bible Societies and the Wycliffe Bible Translators. Modern translation theories, as represented by Nida (1982), use a four stage 'transfer' model in which the source text is analysed to obtain a representation of the intended meaning which can then be transferred in a form suitable for generating from it a target language text. In this model the role of the translator is crucial because translators have to seek to understand the mind and the purpose of the writer, analyse the form of the message, establish and express its intended meaning, transfer this message into the target language and then restructure it in a natural form suitable for the pragmatic situation of the reader.

Bible translation exceeds the capacity of individuals and is, therefore, in the hands of translation teams; collectively these teams possess the range of languages and expertise required. Especially for languages newly codified in their written form, it is in practice impossible to find target language translators who have a solid command of the source languages and the main languages in which commentaries on the Bible have been written, e.g. English, French or German, beside the experience required for interpretation and evaluation of existing exegetical writings. It is equally impossible to find Biblical experts with sufficient command of a newly written language to undertake the task of translation. Normal practice therefore is to appeal to a third language as both a means of communication among the teams and as a switching language for translation.

This requirement has shaped the methodology of translation. When a third language is used, the analysis procedure involves a near-literal translation of the source text into the third language which is fully supported by all the commentaries that exist on this text. The text is then analysed and transformed into small paragraphs, i.e. simple propositions which seek to re-express the content of the text, by methods developed by Nida (1982) and developed further by Beekman, Callow and Kopesec (1981) and Barnwell (1980). These kernel sentences are then translated into the target language and subsequently restructured in a form acceptable to the literary tradition of the target culture.

The analysis into propositions can be exemplified in the following passage from the Letter of James 1:2-4.

Basic Predication:

	SL TEXT	PROPOSITIONS
1-3	For by the grace	1. God showed grace
	are you saved;	2. God saved you
	through faith;	3. you believed (faith=event)
4	and that not of yourselves;	4. you did not save yourselves
5	it is the gift of God;	5. God gave it
6	not of works,	6. you did not work for it
7	lest any man should boast.	7. no man should boast

These propositions, expressed in the source or the third language, are then translated into TL propositions with greater assurance of capturing the essence of the original message.

The last step, restructuring, must be understood as converting the propositional sentences into syntactic structures appropriate for the TL culture. This may require an adjustment of the translation to other forms of religious texts in that culture or simply re-inserting rhetorical devices appropriate to the target language culture.

Bible translation can now be aided by computers which store the vast supporting material required and assist both in the construction of propositions and the control of the transfer between languages. For a full treatment of the possibilities of computer assistance in Bible translation see Truebridge (1991).

6.3.3 *Industrial translation*

The third major translation activity is much less coherent and embraces all professional translation outside these two areas. They are grouped together here as a basis for establishing a model of the translation process which accounts for the regular application of machine translation and other advanced tools of the language industry.

Within this broad range of translations, subdivisions are frequently made according to topics, such as commercial, financial, scientific, legal, patent and in each area a further professional distinction is often made according to whether the translation affects whole texts or whether it involves summaries or abstracting at the same time. Abstracting, for example, regardless of whether mono- or multilingual, is usually considered a professional activity carried out by specialists under the umbrella of information science. The production of commercial letters in another language is also sometimes excluded from the narrower perception of translation. The frequently used label of 'bilingual secretary' and the separately organised training in many countries for such an occupation are signs that this activity is considered somewhat different, often as occurring at a lower level of professionalism, from translation 'proper'. Correspondingly, the skills involved in writing and reading/understanding and summarising such letters are rarely mentioned in studies of translation. By connecting translation with text production in general, it can be shown that writing business letters on the basis of drafts, notes or verbal instructions in a source language is simply another variant of interlingual communication in which the traditional concept of translation is one option among many solutions for overcoming a language barrier.

Another widely used distinction in an industrial setting is that between the so-called 'outgoing' and 'incoming' translation; the 'incoming' translation, also known under the label of 'for information only', is simply a conventional broad specification of a translation task and is generally understood as either a rough, or unpolished translation or a selective one. The distinctive nature of the 'for information' specification usually lies in the acceptance of paraphrase in lieu of exhaustive terminological research and in the omission of the evaluation and revision phase of the process.

An interesting classification of translation tasks according to the nature of the text, user requirements and technique of translation is presented by Simpkin (in: Picken 1983). Texts for publication are subdivided into (i) 'public relations' for which the technique 'translate and write' is specified and (ii) 'factual texts, including specialised books' which are handled by 'translate and edit'. Simpkin then contrasts legal documents as requiring maximal research before translation with texts 'for information' as requiring minimal research before translation. At the less demanding level he specifies selective translation and routine texts handled by gist translation. The more demanding techniques are obviously associated with a higher degree of professional competence and a higher production cost.

What all these translations have in common is that they have a clearly definable origin and use and that they are undertaken as a professional activity to serve a particular communicative purpose specified by the circumstances of the task or an agent.

6.4 Analysis of the translation task

In the rest of this section and in sections seven and eight the translation process is described as a sequence of conditioned choices, similar to the way the communication process is modelled in sections three and four. This mode of presentation permits the indication of both the common elements in the processes and the additional decisions that have to be faced in translation.

The present model divides the translation task into the following phases and stages:

SPECIFICATION PHASE
1. Identification of source language document
2. Identification of intention
3. Interpretation of specifications
4. Cursory reading (see Reading-comprehension)

PREPARATION PHASE (presented in section seven)
5. Choice of TL text type
6. Choice of translation strategy
7. Reading-comprehension
8. Dictionary look-up

TRANSLATION PHASE (presented in section eight)
9. Search for equivalents
10. Matching
11. Compensation
12. Text production

EVALUATION/REVISION PHASE (presented in section eight)
13. Evaluation
14. Revision
15. Presentation

6.4.1 *Alternative views of the task*

The four phases outlined above require a variety of mental operations: in phase 1, the work consists of identifying tasks and conditions; in phase 2, decisions concerning the general objective of creating a target language text have to be taken on the basis of particular constraints, recognised, case by case or translation type by translation type; in phase 3, the tasks consist of comprehension and reproduction which is variously intuitive and quasi-automatic or a fully conscious complex activity, involving stages of information search and learning; in phase 4, the tasks are evaluative, consisting of critical assessment and correction.

These operations are seen differently by different groups of translators because they have varying views of the task they have to perform and these depend largely on their familiarity with the subject matter and the text types in hand. The first phase can become routine or automatic for most established translators, except when they are confronted with an unfamiliar task. In the second phase decisions are taken which narrow down the possibilities of variation in the critical main phase and therefore make it into a feasible industrial activity.

It can therefore be seen as channelling the professional task into subcategories. The third phase is one of guided creativity or ideation comparable to other partly derivative intellectual activities. It requires a mixture of knowledge and skill, or art and craft according to the nature of the text to be produced. The final phase on the other hand requires self-critical acumen and is therefore often entrusted to others.

Many stages can be compared to the monolingual text production activities and can be described adequately. The greatest uncertainty surrounds the third phase because of the difficulty of explaining the mental processes involved. When translators read and understand almost automatically, i.e. when they are utterly familiar with the substance of the document, they also translate almost automatically, provided, of course, that they have a solid command of the relevant sublanguage of the target language. There is therefore little opportunity to observe step by step how professionals proceed in a task of which we can only see the result of stage 12. The fact that every natural language expression admits variation does not impinge on the professional industrial translator any more than it slows down the technical writer who has learnt to write in a particular style. Successful industrial translators have acquired sets of translational norms which permit them to work at speed with a high degree of consistency; this technique can be compared to intuitive actions.

At the same time, experienced translators are aware of the high degree of innovation and variation in language for which no experience can provide total solutions. Beside their intuition about appropriate translation equivalents, translators are, therefore, faced with the need to identify problems and to develop strategies for solving them. Wilss (1988) recognises the dual position of translation between the stability of rule-governed behaviour and problem identification and solution. He cites two models of problem solution which are applicable to the translation situation. Dewey's (1910) five stages (problem identification – problem definition – proposals for solutions – avoidance of undesirable consequences of particular strategies of problem solution – evaluation of results) make the necessary distinction between problem identification and definition which is often muddled in practice. Bunge's (1962) psychological model (the preparation or assimilation of relevant knowledge – the imaging and trial of various hypotheses – the synthesis that seems to solve the problem – the test of the conjecture) stresses the need for acquiring knowledge which enables translators to find solutions. Wilss concludes with two important observations: (i) problems which are new to some translators may not be recognised as such by others whose perception is limited by their knowledge of the subject or the varieties of expression available; and (ii) what may be a problem for some is a routine operation for others who have encountered and solved this or a similar problem already: it is therefore impossible to identify particular problem areas. He thereby confirms the inscrutability of the third phase.

6.5 Specification phase

The specification phase serves the purpose of identifying the task and becoming familiar with two aspects: the document to be processed and the task description. While for many translators, especially those in a staff position, a large part of the work is routine in the sense that they process a small range of documents according to a small range of specifications, freelance translators and others facing unfamiliar jobs must first go through a process of analysis and reflection. The complexity of this initial phase must not be underestimated and is therefore analysed here in some detail.

The first phase introduces the different communicative situations. It places translators in the middle of the situation of speech acts which they must perform in their professional roles and involves them already in their dual role (i) as readers when they are faced with receiving a message, and (ii) as writers when they are faced with the need to re-produce a message. This awareness is accompanied by an assessment of the potential actions that can arise from such a situation. The typical situations in which translations arise are fewer in number than for communication in general, but they are at the same time more complex. This initial assessment can be expressed as a number of questions, the answers to which have to be found by translators themselves or by consulting the other role players in this situation.

IDENTIFICATION OF SL DOCUMENT	What type of document is it?
IDENTIFICATION OF INTENTION	Who is the document for?
	What is the document for?
INTERPRETATION OF SPECIFICATIONS	What type of document is to be produced?
CURSORY READING	What is the document about?

These questions can, of course, be broken down further. In Figure 6.2 a detailed set of the decisions taken before writing are contrasted with the specification phase to show the coincidence of features.

In a regular systematic process of translation production these questions are divided into several steps of identification and analysis, which are described in the following sections. Some of the answers can be provided by the analysis of the source language document, the rest has to be elicited from the task specifications translators, like other technical writers, work to.

Writing	*Translation stages*
Determine the general content of the message (What?)	1. Identification of SL document
Determine the general purpose of the message (Why?)	2. Identification of intention
Define the recipients (Who?) Define the function, i.e. the expected reaction of the recipient Plan the amount and order of content (What is presupposed?)	3. Interpretation of specification &
Plan the realisation (What is assumed?) (What is expressed linguistically, what by other means?)	4. Cursory reading

Figure 6.2 *Specification analysis in writing and translation*

The answers to these questions permit translators to decide whether they are qualified to undertake the task, whether they have the proper resources to carry it out, what translation strategy to adopt, possibly including the use of tools provided by information technology, and what detailed technique to use.

6.5.1 *Identification of source language document*

Before reading a document, all readers form an impression of the text and the topic they are dealing with in order to tune their cognitive processes to the right attitude of receptiveness; otherwise they lack a stimulus for making the effort for looking at it in the first place. Translators receive documents which in some way have already been pre-selected for this activity by someone, and therefore look at such documents only from a professional point of view, but nevertheless need to identify it more closely. This they do in two separate operations of text analysis.

6.5.1.1 *Recognition of text type and topic*

Nobody starts reading a document, book or letter without first having identified the text type, saying, for example, 'this is a letter' or 'this is a novel'. Equally, a translation job begins with seeing the document, or having at least a description of it which permits the identification of the text type of the source document.

This identification fundamentally conditions reading; without it, readers cannot understand a text. For example, nobody reads a segment of minutes of a meeting written in French as if it were a film script simply because it is written in the present tense; readers of such texts know that in French, minutes of meetings are conventionally written in the present tense. Expressed as a translation problem, this can mean that in order to be able to translate 'yesterday' properly, translators must know whether it occurs in a newspaper report which has a precise date, or whether it is a relative time reference. Identifying a document as a letter, translators automatically tune into the recognition mode of letter-reading and writing and expect certain information; professional translators then look for previous letters in a sequence or expect follow-ups to the document in hand, etc. A practical classification is offered by Jumpelt (1961:25).

The analysis can be functional in the sense of Buehler, as is the case in the distinction between content-centred texts, including technical texts of all sorts, form-centred texts and effect-centred (appeal) texts established by Reiss (1981:76-81) or it can be broadly purpose-oriented. Bell (1991:205), for example, divides texts according to the dominant function and envisages further subdivisions, each of which is realised in a number of text forms:

— exposition:	– narrative
	– descriptive
	– conceptual
— argumentation:	– overt
	– covert
— instruction:	– with option
	– without option

In an industrial environment major translation departments take a less analytical view and order texts by a mixture of criteria of topic, text type and intention which can be correlated to conventional texttypes. For example, senior translators at the Commission of the European Communities at different times and for different purposes have issued three different lists of categories of source texts in their areas of work.

(a)

— common communications of the type 'circulars to staff' (simple syntax, undifferentiated style)

— scientific and technical documents (difficult terminology, simple syntax, precision required, undifferentiated style but cause for error of content)

— legal documents (precise terminology, special and rigid syntax, precision required both in substance and form)

— documents of a persuasive nature, e.g. speeches (complex syntax, differentiated style, authors fully use the lexical and syntactic resources of the language)
— minutes of meetings (common terminology, simple syntax)
— reports (terminology sometimes difficult, simple syntax)
— transcripts of parliamentary debates (simple terminology, peculiar and sometimes very complex syntax)

(b)

— publications in the Official Journal and documents sent to the Council of Ministers
— financial notes
— minutes of meetings
— correspondence and telexes
— summaries of projects submitted for financial support
— reports

NOTE: This second list is clearly incomplete because it does not include the important area of support documentation nor any reference to texts dealing with legal aspects.

(c)

— general texts: letters, official correspondence, letters convening meetings, circular letters for internal and external purposes etc.
— agenda and minutes of meetings
— discussion papers for meetings
— Parliamentary debates
— papers to be submitted to the Commission and eventually to The Council
— activity reports
— financial reports, budgets, investments and loans
— technical and/or scientific papers
— public tenders
— decisions, regulations, recommendations etc. to be published in the Official Journal
— reports and bulletins to be published and destined for a wider distribution or even to be sold
— other legal texts (contracts etc.)

While the importance of text types seems to be generally recognised, there is as yet no conclusive characterisation available. Recently efforts have also been made to analyse the characteristics of texts input into machine translation systems, based on a study of sublanguages. No significant results of these studies are known so far.

The recognition of topic is less problematic and calls upon translators' ability to recognise topics and their aspects and relate them to the type of support available to them in the form of documents, dictionaries, databases etc.

6.5.1.2 *Recognition of intention*

Beside the identification of text type and topic, translators also want to discover what the intention of the source document is. Since they know the difference between text and message (see section 2.2), they must first establish whether the document has a relevant intention, i.e. whether they have to acknowledge the circumstances of the message or whether they can treat the document like a text to which a new intention has to be attached.

If translators remove the writer's intention from a message, something which frequently occurs when a document is translated for another readership, it becomes a text which has to be given a new purpose, either in the form of a new intention or by adjusting it to a new, a secondary-reader, expectation. Translations of texts not originally written for a readership in another culture fall into this category as the original intention may become irrelevant. For example, a regulation applicable in one community, if translated, can serve as a model for other regulations but it cannot function as a regulation in its own right.

A change of intention which is not obvious in a working environment must be indicated in the specifications, which are discussed in the next section.

6.5.2 *Interpretation of specifications*

The translator's next step is to define the task to be performed on the basis of the explicit or implicit instructions received. Some regular professional situations are so obvious and some texts are so special that only one form of interpretation, one form of target language text and one method of translation are possible. In other cases simple routine instruction on translators' worksheets refer to well-established patterns of mediation which do not require individual analysis. In large organisations translations can be classified according to the use for which they are intended and which are sometimes marked on the worksheets as, e.g., 'for information' (of an official or group of officials); 'working document'; 'document for discussion' (in a meeting of committees, working parties etc.); 'for publication'. In some cases such indications are only used as a guide to whether a document requires revision or whether it can be sent out directly after evaluation.

6.5.2.1 *The situation of the translation process*

The cases in which there is a choice of alternatives depend on the interpretation of various situational factors, listed in Figure 6.3 and the textual factors, listed in Figure 6.4. The situational factors consist of time and cost factors, a use factor, here called direction, and personal factors relevant to the author, the reader, the mediator and the initiator of the process and their interaction.

SITUATIONAL FACTORS:

TIME:	SPEED; QUALITY; TEMPORAL DISTANCE
COST:	VALUE OF SL TEXT; ADDED-VALUE OF TL TEXT; LABOUR
DIRECTION:	OUTGOING/INCOMING; BI-DIRECTIONAL

PERSONAL FACTORS:

TRANSLATOR:	SINGLE/MULTIPLE; SUBJECT/TEXT TYPE SPECIALISATION
INITIATOR:	WRITER/AGENT/READER
AUTHORSHIP:	SINGLE/MULTIPLE; HOUSE STYLE/INDIVIDUAL STYLE
READERSHIP:	PRIMARY/SECONDARY; MODE OF READING
AWARENESS:	WRITER/READER AWARENESS OF TRANSLATION

Figure 6.3 *Factors of the specification*

6.5.2.2 *Time and cost factors*

The overall time required for producing a translation is theoretically and practically relevant. It is theoretically relevant because it distinguishes translation from simultaneous interpreting and, in practice, a time gap is required both for the task itself and revision; however, an excessive time gap may make a translation irrelevant. In order to reduce the time gap, short cuts to full translation may be introduced in the form of reduced or selective translation. The time gap may be reduced by the use of machine translation. Furthermore, the time interval between source document production and delivery of the completed translation to the end reader can also have a direct effect on the translated document because it may require changes in the temporal references in the text.

Translation tasks themselves vary enormously in the time required for producing a satisfactory end product. For English, Simpkin (1983) has estimated an hourly production of between 300 and 800 'nominal' words or 30-90 'nominal' lines. In his view, a translation produced 'for information' usually takes no more than 60 percent of the time spent on a full translation because preparation, production and even revision can be reduced substantially. In selected or gist translations the time saved is even more significant because the actual text production time can be reduced to a quarter or even less of the time needed for a full translation. A routine gist translation may not take more than 15 percent in relation to a full translation.

There are no studies on the distribution of actual time in the translation process and only some rough indications on the proportions of time spent on preparatory work, translation itself, and editing and revision for different types of translation. The greatest variation in time occurs between translation and preparatory work, i.e. all stages up to and including reading understanding, research or dictionary look-up, which can oscillate between one third to two thirds of the total time spent on a task. Revision, where it is carried out, usually occupies no more than ten percent of overall effort. In legal or other highly technical work, preparatory tasks can occupy between thirty percent and more than half of the total time; in routine work this time may be as little as twenty-five percent. By contrast in 'gist' translation the preparation prior to the actual writing out the gist takes up some two thirds of the total time because the reading understanding of texts takes considerably longer than stating their content and intention in a few words. In selective translations the time spent on preparation and production may be equal, but in 'for information' work, the text production phase tends to occupy more than half the total time.

From an economic point of view the time of the process must also be measured in relation to a translator's overall speed of work. Translation consumers have an idea of the value of the communication they are engaged in and are only willing to pay a price which is proportionately related to the cost of the source text, or related to the benefit they expect to gain from the translated text. Translators who cannot adjust their speed of work to reasonable time and cost expectations will not be able to maintain themselves as professionals.

All texts have a value and translations should sensibly be costed in relation to this value and not only in relation to the labour involved. After all, the effort required for translation varies from person to person; the specialist can deal with a specialised text in his domain of specialisation in much less time than a generalist. It is therefore a question of choosing the right translator for the right job in order to obtain the highest cost effectiveness.

What determines the cost of a translation can be stated in two ways. A sensible cost calculation is based on (i) what is an adequate reward for honest work by a competent and experienced professional; (ii) the years of training required for obtaining the necessary level of skill to function efficiently; (iii) professional responsibility; and (iv) overheads. These factors determine the unit cost of translation which is usually priced as a fixed sum per thousand words of target language document. For shorter units, especially in the case of legal documents, prices are expressed per page or document.

Another, less common, way of considering the price for translation is to relate it to the commercial value of the source language text. In this respect an analogy with other text-producing professions is relevant. Some independent technical writers and especially publicity material writers and advertising agencies set their prices like lawyers, in relation to the value their clients attribute to their services. In this sense, it is obvious that in an industrial and commercial environment, the cost of producing a translation must not exceed the commercial value of the information that is to be conveyed or that can be extracted by the reader. It is, of course, the case, with translation, more than with almost any other product, that in many instances the commissioner does not know beforehand what value a text has. It is here where the translator's estimate of cost and advice on the type of product that can be produced, and its cost, is particularly relevant. Cost is therefore also related to use of the product, its directionality. For so-called 'incoming' information in a firm a lower quality and therefore more translation for less time and money is expected than is the case for 'outgoing' information. On the other hand, and in practice, the unit price of a translation is frequently decided by what the market will bear, i.e. by the scarcity value of the skill, the urgency with which the work is required and by the need of the client.

6.5.2.3 *The condition of the translator*

Translators must assess their own competence in the light of the task in hand. Too many translators tackle too wide a range of jobs and therefore are slower in their work and earn less than they could if they specialised more. Highly successful translators, like technical writers, specialise because this permits them to develop their skills in particular areas to the highest degree. The ideal literary translation associates one author with one translator.

Translators must establish whether they can do the job alone or whether for technical or time reasons they need help. They must assure themselves of the availability of expert advice they need before tackling a job etc. A text written by a multiple authorship can easily be handled by a team of translators, and in some cases may even be better translated if the stylistic neutrality of a group writing effort is considered a distinctive feature of the text.

Initiators of translations who select translators bear a heavy responsibility for obtaining suitable work when in most cases they are not competent to judge the quality of the work. They have to rely on readers' comments and indirect evidence such as the reputation of a translator. For this reason many initiators use the services of a translation agency or company whose greater volume of work has allowed a reputation to become established and known. Another reason for entrusting agencies or companies with translation jobs is that they are legal entities who can be sued for breach of contract with a chance of obtaining compensation and damages.

Translators must now also decide what extent of electronic support is useful for the efficient conduct of their job.

6.5.2.4 *Writer and reader factors*

Translators must find out whether they are dealing with a document from a single author or whether they are translating a composite document, whether the text has been edited to conform to a particular style or to previous documents which have also been translated. For longer documents, and for texts likely to have sequels, translators increasingly prepare glossaries of the terminology and phraseology of the text they translate so that they can control the consistency of the terminology they use and so that the terminology is preserved and ready at hand for future use in new editions or related texts.

Translators must know whether the readers of the translation are primary or secondary readers, i.e. whether they are directly addressed or whether they are incidental readers.

Translators must know whether writer or reader, or both, will be aware of the translation process intervening in the communication. This situation can be illustrated by the following cases:

Case 1: Both the writer and the reader are aware of the fact that the communication is mediated by means of translation. The reader may be primary or secondary and this determines sub-types. For example, in any official professional or commercial transaction, it is a question whether each party has its own translator or whether they use one working language but produce two linguistic versions of the result.

Case 2: Neither the writer nor the reader are aware that translation is involved. The primary/secondary distinction is neutral in this case. For example, the writer may initially have written for a monolingual readership and may never know that this work is translated; the reader may assume that the text is an original and so the fact of translation becomes irrelevant. This is the case in most text books, manuals and scientific articles.

Case 3: The writer is aware of a translation being produced, but not the reader. This would normally be the case when the reader is considered to be a primary addressee. For example, a writer engages a translator, co-operates with a translator, or even adjusts the text to facilitate translation, as, for instance, in much commercial correspondence and publicity material.

Case 4: The reader is aware that the document is a translation, but the writer does not know that his work is being translated. This is usually the case when the reader is secondary. This case obviously applies to literature translated after an author's death; but this also applies when readers want to read scientific articles produced in another language and culture which they cannot read in the original.

6.5.2.5 *User expectation*

From a user point of view we distinguish a number of communicative situations in which translations are desirable:

(a) Users may simply want to know if the text contains any information which may be useful to them. In this case a keyword translation may suffice. If they discover that there is useful information they can ask for a more complete translation.

(b) Users may know that the text is relevant but may only require partial information.

(c) Users may want all the factual information in the text, but may not need the way it is presented, argued etc. In this case a diagram or an abstract may suffice;

(d) Users may wish to classify texts or documents according to a particular indexing system. Again a keyword translation may serve the purpose.

(e) Users may want to know in general what the text contains or what it is about. A reconstructed or commented translation may be needed.

(f) Users may want a full translation, because reference to particular items of text, arguments etc. is needed.

6.5.2.6 *Source and product (textual) factors*

These external factors of the specifications are complemented by the more specific textual requirements of a translation. These are given by the initial status of the SL text, the relationship between the SL and TL and the new status of the TL text.

The various possibilities resulting from these combinations, indicated in Figure 6.4, are diversified further by the alternative possibilities of treating the input text as either a message or a text.

The type of translation that can be produced depends first of all on the status attributed to the original, i.e. (i) whether it is a draft, or considered to be one, leading to the production of an autonomous document; or (ii) whether it is a message, or (iii) a message to be taken as a text, or (iv) a text. On this basis translators can then decide the status of the target language document and its degree of independence or dependence.

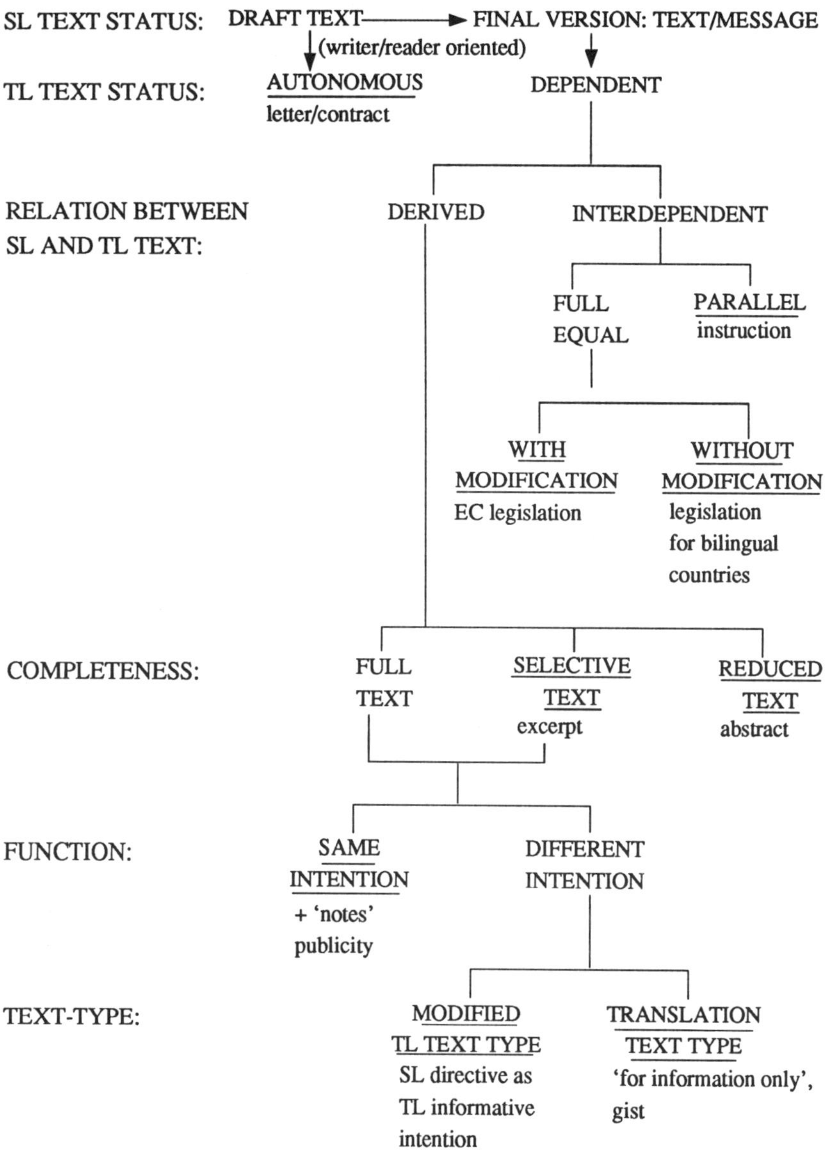

Figure 6.4 *Status and message type of target language document*

Note: Each separate type of translation is underlined, with examples below.

The types of translation are, secondly, defined with respect to their functional role as new products.

The distinction between autonomous and dependent TL documents is based on the status of the original. The subclassification of dependent documents into parallel and derived is already determined by target language criteria, i.e. whether original and translation are equal in status, as in 'interdependent/parallel' or whether this relation is not of any practical importance.

Derived documents must be classified by three separate criteria. On the one hand there is a clear practical distinction between full, selective or reduced translations, and on the other, it is necessary to distinguish them by identity or diversity of purpose between original and translated document. Finally, a distinction has to be made whether the translation adopts a text type which is known in the target language or whether it is expressed in a text form which is only known and used for translations, such as the 'gist' translation.

6.6 Functional types of translation

The analysis of the specifications clarifies the relationship between the source language document and the target language document and at the same time permits the identification of the distinct functional characteristics of the translated documents which translators must take into account. The separate classes of translation products identified in Figure 6.4 can be defined and exemplified as follows:

6.6.1 *Autonomous documents*

Autonomous texts have an absolute value as independent messages which the 'original' did not have because of its provisional status. They are created from SL drafts which, like all drafts, have no definitive status once they have served their purpose. Two types of draft have to be distinguished: those which are drafts in the SL, because they consist of notes, i.e. words and phrases which have yet to be linked into the syntactic form required by the chosen text type; and those which are complete texts or messages in the SL, but, because there are serious cultural or cognitive obstacles to their regular translation, are merely used as indicators of the sort of information to be conveyed. A typical example of the former are notes for business letters, and for the latter, publicity material for certain products which have different customer appeal in different cultures or which are marketed for another range of customers from that of the SL.

All other translations can be said to be variously dependent. Those in which SL and TL document have the same status and which often occur side by side are called here interdependent, those in which the link with the SL document is not normally maintained in communication, are called derived.

6.6.2 *Interdependent documents*

For the translation types here called 'interdependent', i.e. which will co-exist in parallel with the SL document, two major types can be identified:

6.6.2.1 *Parallel documents*

Parallel documents are bi- or multilingual versions which are applicable to exactly the same situation in all settings in which they are used. For the readers there is therefore no recognisable source language text and they can choose which language version they read. The best example to illustrate parallel documents are the multiple versions of instructions or descriptions that accompany products marketed in many countries simultaneously. Translators of such documents assume identical readerships in terms of knowledge and expectation in identical settings only differentiated by knowledge of languages. For official purposes the language of original manufacture is considered to be, and in practice frequently is, the source language. The other languages do not usually have an official status.

6.6.2.2 *Full equal documents*

In ''full equal documents'' the distinction between source and target language completely disappears after completion of the task because both documents are functionally equal. The measurement of equality is by identity of content as measured by the identity of the effect. From the two examples given it can be seen that bilingual or multilingual legislation is (i) only valid if it is available in all its linguistic versions, but also that (ii) in any one country or linguistic region only one version is fully valid at a time. From European legislation we also know that before a European court, all language versions have equal value and judges base their decisions on all language versions in equal measure. Further differences arise according to the linguistic regimes in which the documents have to function. In bilingual countries both versions have absolutely equal status in all circumstances. In the case of EC legislation, a single language version may have to be adjusted to the legal practices of the country concerned, so that in principle there might be, for example, slightly different French versions of a document in order to be acceptable to French-speaking parts of Belgium and France and Luxembourg respectively.

6.6.3 *Derived documents*

All other types of translation are derived in the sense that their production neither enjoys the freedom of autonomous documents nor the extreme restrictions of dependent documents. It is the largest groups of subtypes and also represents the greatest volume of translation of industrial interest. The several types of subclassification yield the following final classes.

By degree of completeness there are full, selective and reduced texts, of which the latter two are identifiable classes.

6.6.3.1 *Selective document translation (Excerpts)*

For selective documents, in the form of excerpts, as a regular technique of translation there are documentary criteria beside the criterion of appropriateness. By this type of translation a special information service can be provided when translators are subject experts and know precisely the information requirements of their clients. Sometimes this type of service is performed by information scientists-translators who go through a document with the potential reader, pointing out items of interest, giving oral impromptu translations which are sometimes followed by selective written translation of excerpts.

Automatic scanning of documents with or without machine translation can replace part of this interaction between end-user and translator and thus speed up and reduce the cost of the information process.

6.6.3.2 *Reduced document translation (Abstracts)*

The production of translated abstract is a regular industry with hundreds of specialist translators engaged in producing copy for the numerous abstract journals in print and on-line. There are several types of abstracts, indicative, evaluative, informative etc. which serve as models for the translators who work in conformity with the stylistic requirements of the publication they serve.

Full texts and excerpts can be translated with the same intention or the intention can be changed.

6.6.3.3 *Translations with the same function*

Documents which retain their function in translation may come closest to the traditional perception of what is a translation and hence be judged by conventional criteria of equivalence and correspondence. But even here the possibility of translator's notes, frequently required in legal texts, gives some room for additional considerations of text type and purpose in the decision of what constitutes an adequate translation. There is also the possibility of glossing cultural or geographically specific references, as for example in literary and journalistic translation, where a SL reference may be too obscure for TL readers, or in translating a recipe for a dish where the TL cook will be less familiar with certain foods, measurements, modes of preparation etc.

Examples for this type of translation are numerous and can range from whole book translations to simple messages. It is commonest in situations where there are few cultural and knowledge differences between the societies and the readers of the translations in question.

6.6.3.4 *Translations with a different function*

Translations with different function are needed when the intention of the source text is so situation-bound that it is not transferable to the new situation of communication created through the translation. A new situation must be given by the specification, unless it is self-evident and known to the translator beforehand. The success of the translation reaching its communicative objective must clearly be judged by its appropriateness for the new intention. Among these a distinction is made between (i) text types known in the TL, (ii) text types for which models already exist in the target language, and (iii) text types which are introduced into the TL culture only through translation. For examples see 6.6.4 below.

Target language text type
Documents addressed to a primary readership in a particular SL culture cannot have the same intention after translation but they can be transformed into types of documents which have a recognised text form in the target culture. For example, an environmental health warning which is directed at farmers in one culture, does not have the same impact in another culture where this phenomenon is unknown and has to be explained through the translation. In such a culture the translated document can be annotated so that the reader perceives this as information rather than an incomprehensible directive.

Translation text type
The best known translation-specific text type is undoubtedly the 'gist' translation of such documents as business letters in which the translator only summarises the content. 'Gist' can be defined as the notification by a translator to the client, in whatever written form is most convenient, of the basic content and intention of a document. Gist can also be conveyed orally as a form of on-sight excerption of the essence of a message. The other widely used translation text type 'for information only', i.e. the provision of a working document for internal use of a firm or client, can mislead the uninformed because the end product may, in part, look like a genuine text type in the target culture. It is therefore a translator's responsibility to indicate the limited functional status of such a translation clearly on the finished document.

The question of translation-specific text types is, of course, much wider if we consider that many cultures have received their first written documents through translation. This can be convincingly demonstrated for European languages in the pioneering work of the Bible societies which gave many languages their first written form. Subsequent commercial contact with the outside world helped to create in such languages an increasing number of functional text types which were borrowed from the chief vehicular languages of traders or colonial powers.

6.6.4 *Functional types of translation by intention*

The last section presented a diverse picture of target language products. Because this diversification presents a major departure from conventional views it is considered useful to analyse the potential types of products further and contrast them with other approaches to this question.

From the conventional definition of translations, presented in section 6.2, it emerges that the target document is always assumed to have the same functional intention as the source document because alternatives are not mentioned. This is an unacceptable simplification as has been demonstrated in the previous section, and exemplified by several functional subdivisions of the translation product, according to the way intention is treated in the source and target documents.

It is, therefore, appropriate to distinguish between intentional parallelism and intentional divergence between source and target document:

— Basic intentional parallelism occurs in the following situations:

(a) The source document is a message directed at L2 readers; e.g. an instruction for immigrants speaking and reading L2 only, a business letter, a scientific paper for a conference with L2 as a working language.

(b) The source document is a message directed at L1 readers and L2 readers simultaneously; e.g. a piece of bilingual legislation.

(c) The source document was originally directed at L1 readers; that readership is no longer available; the text is now to be re-directed at L2 readers with basically the same intention as the original message; e.g. a translation of a historical text or earlier literature into the modern version of the language.

— Intentional divergence occurs in the following situations:

(a) The source document is a culture- and environment-specific message to a L1 reader. To become acceptable to a L2 reader it must be either: (i) given another intention and otherwise adjusted so that it becomes relevant to a L2 reader; e.g. a piece of legislation only applicable to speakers of L1, which can be informative to speakers of another language; or (ii) annotated/translated/edited/re-written in such a way that the L2 reader can come close to understanding the intention of the original message; e.g. a translation of Homer as a model or contrast to our society. (see: Schleiermacher & Ortega y Gasset);

(b) The source language document has ceased to be a message to anyone. As a text it is to be made available for whatever purpose to a L2 reader; e.g. documents from historical archives that are now to be studied as part of a sociological survey of patterns of employment, etc.; or a translation of the Gothic Bible fragments which is now used as the only extant document in that language.

6.6.5 *Other functional types of translation*

Another view of functional types of translation is presented by Gouadec (1990: 332-341), who proposes translation solutions to different types of need.

(a) Keyword translation, i.e. the extraction of keywords from the SL document and translating them into the TL. The result would be comparable to a TL index of the document in order to determine whether it contains useful or relevant information, and, if required, to decide what additional translation is wanted.

(b) Selective translation, i.e. by eliminating all irrelevant information, limiting the translation to one aspect of the topic of the document in order to speed up access to information.

(c) Abstract translation, i.e. to provide a condensed translation of all the information contained in a document. This can take on several forms well known to information scientists, e.g.
(i) translation of the generic themes; (ii) description of the generic content, the objectives of the document and its sub-units and the structure of the document; (iii) abridged translation of all the useful content of a text.
The function of abstracts is to provide fast access to specific information.

(d) Diagrammatic translation, i.e. the transfer of the SL document content in form of a diagram, in order to permit the learner to control his own knowledge of the subject. (This type of information provision exceeds what is here considered translation.)

(e) Translation with reconstructions, by which Gouadec means complete translation of content without regard to form, in order to communicate the content in the most direct way possible.

(f) Absolute translation, i.e. the complete transfer respecting both quantitative and qualitative values of the document.

(g) Sight translation, i.e. to provide a running commentary in order to give information urgently.

Gouadec justifies a staged approach to the performance of translations in professional environments, because he considers the absolute translation to be often an 'excessive' translation. Users may have different information needs which are satisfied by these different modes of presenting information to them.

Chapter Four

A Model of the Translation Process

7 Preparation for Translation

As soon as the general feasibility of a translation task is established, in the sense that the specifications are realistic in terms of time, cost and textual factors, and have confirmed their personal capability of performing the task, the process can progress to the next phase. In practice professional translators usually find themselves in situations in which the general feasibility is given and predetermined for them by the job they hold or by the agent who distributes the work.

The difference between the first and the second phase, described in this section, is that in the specification phase translators assess the situation whilst in the preparation phase they already make choices which narrow down the field of action and so directly prepare for the task of text production. The separate stages of the preparation phase are all dominated by the overriding need to create a new document in a target language, based on instructions, notes or, as in most cases, an existing document in the source language.

The first pragmatic decision in the preparation phase leading towards production is that of choosing the text form of the new product. The next decision concerns the choice of an appropriate strategy of translation which now involves consideration of the use of all possible machine aids to translation. The preparation phase continues with detailed reading of the document, and, where necessary, some separate research, usually confined to dictionary look-up.

Continuing the comparison with the writing process made in section 6.5, we contrast the two sets of decisions, in Figure 7.1, in order to show their great similarity.

WRITING	TRANSLATION STAGES
Choice of text type	5. Choice of TL text type

Consider external constraints
(format, publication, circulation, presentation,
Where, When, How?)

Consider alternative modes of communication

	6. Choice of translation strategy
	7. Reading-comprehension
	8. Research/Dictionary look-up
Determine structure, chapters, headings, paragraphs	9. Search for equivalents
	10/11. Matching/Compensation
Message production	12. Document production

Evaluation
Revision and modification
Presentation

Figure 7.1 *Preparation for writing and translation*

What distinguishes the process of translation from that of writing is that it involves a transformation of code which is based on the search of pragmatic, cognitive and linguistic equivalents at the various levels appropriate for the particular act of communication that is to be mediated. The task of translation itself can, therefore, also be described as a process of establishing and expressing equivalents. While the cognitive and linguistic equivalents are mainly established at the level of the sentence or in smaller units during the translation phase, the pragmatic equivalents have to be selected first in the preparation phase and at the level of the text type before being also realised in smaller units at appropriate points in the document.

7.1 Choice of target language text type

In the same way as technical writers must first decide the text type they have to write in, translators, assuming that the same range and functions of text types are available in the target language, have to decide, on the basis of the specifications, whether to replicate the source language text type or not. The search for equivalents, therefore, begins at the level of the text type. If there is no direct TL text type equivalent, there is then the choice of a different target language text type or the possibility to adopt a translation text type.

(a) equivalent text type:
This choice is automatic if the intention of the translation is the same and if the target language has a corresponding text type. The choice of equivalent text type may predetermine the translation strategy, because there may be no more than one strategy per matching text type. For example, the translation of a text book or an operating manual offers no problems of choice of text type.

(b) different text type:
This choice is usually associated with a change in purpose of the text, e.g. a summary of a longer report, in which the recommendations are purely for information and not for further action, or an indicative abstract. It also arises in cases where the target language does not have the same text type.

(c) a translation text type:
The translator may propose to translate into a text type which exists only in connection with translation. Any text type unknown in the target culture falls into this category, at least for as long as this form is not fully integrated into the target language system of text types. The best-known type of such a form exclusive to translation is the 'gist' translation of, e.g., business letters, but it exists also in the so-called 'for information only' translations. All forms of direct output of machine translation systems clearly belong to this form, though some output may later be edited to look like the first type.

The choice of text type is related to that of translation strategy because some strategies can only lead to specific types of texts, notably forms specific to translation. Figure 7.2 shows (i) that the option of translation strategy regarding machine involvement can lead to diverse end products; (ii) that text types with different functions and translation-specific text types can be produced by two different methods; and (iii) how and at what stage human editing can intervene to convert machine-assisted products and fully automated products back to human products. The possibility of human translators modifying machine output into documents that appear to be a purely human product is indicated by horizontal arrows.

In order to be able to assess the various production alternatives for their ergonomic advantages, translators must combine their knowledge of available text types in the target language with their knowledge of the capability of machine aids. The availability of machine assistance or full MT, presented in detail in section 7.2.2, may lead to a reconsideration of the specifications.

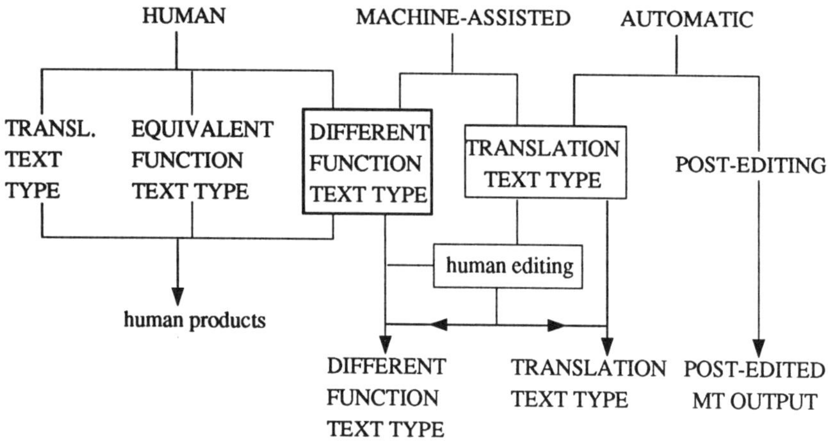

Figure 7.2 *Choice between human and machine translation and target language text type*

In many cases the specifications are unclear with respect to text type because the agents, initiators or commissioners of a translation frequently have no clear perception of what a text type is and what possibilities are available. Decisions on text type are principally based on functional criteria, i.e. the purpose of the translation is paramount, even though it is sometimes only conveyed through the motivation of the commissioner of the translation. When there is uncertainty on this issue, the translator may have to act as communication consultant, explaining the target language limitations and possibilities to the commissioner. Once the scope is clear, a selection can be made and, where appropriate, submitted to the client with a recommendation for approval.

7.2 Choice of translation strategy

Before examining the available translation strategies, it is useful to sum up the various factors which contribute to their diversification.

7.2.1 *Motivation of diverse translation strategies*

Having accepted a diversity of end products, it is natural to accept that there are different modes of translation leading to these products, as, for example, indicated in the types listed in section 6.6.5 by Gouadec. Translation strategies are affected by a large number of factors, listed schematically below. The weakness of some of the translation models discussed above lies in the fact that they do not explicitly allow for the presence of different strategies leading to different products.

FACETS DETERMINING TRANSLATION STRATEGIES

By textual characteristics:
— *Literary*: (diverse intention/expectation)
  — prose: essay — novel — drama
  — poetry:
— *Biblical*: (diversified by section of the Bible and purpose)
— *Non-literary*:
  — culturally specific (not usually translated)
    — legal
  — language/culture independent (often translated)
    — scientific
    — technical
  — target-language-oriented
    — publicity

By relation of source to target document: (as in Figure 6.4)
— autonomous
— dependent
— derived

By intention:
— same content + same intention
— same content + new intention

By content:
— same intention + same content
— same intention + some different content: reduction
  addition
  modification

By precedent:
— documents in a sequence —
  — which will initiate a series
  — which continue a series of related documents
— documents which are likely to remain isolated occurrences

By number of translations required:
— documents translated into one language only
— documents translated into several language at the same time
By degree of revision required:
— documents in definitive original form
— documents likely to undergo stages of re-writing, hence requiring re-translation
— documents used for scanning only and of which a fuller translation may be required later
By user requirement:
— documents for superficial reading, 'for information only'
— documents for detailed reading, filing and future reference for a known reader
— documents used as drafts for other documents
— documents for publication
— texts with the force of legal documents

Some of these factors coincide or overlap. For example, texts for publication are likely to occur as part of an ongoing series for which there are models of translation and precedents of strategies. Not all of these possibilities are exploited in practice, but the combination of factors in even the small number of final products for which there is practical evidence of identifiable strategies of translation can be seen to be founded on a very complex range of requirements. This listing is nevertheless useful because it is a reminder of the diverse criteria which enter into the choices made in the selection of translation strategies and the diverse factors which translators must have in mind in the performance of their work, especially when it come to the decision of involving machine assistance or full machine translation. From a theoretical point of view is it inappropriate, at this stage, to distinguish between human translation and the variations of human-assisted machine translation and machine-assisted human translation because we are either concerned with a product in which the human translator has the last word; or with a machine product, i.e. that which people so far quite wrongly have called 'raw output' and which should simply be called machine-translated documents. At a later stage it may be desirable to distinguish machine-translated documents which are directly usable, i.e. acceptable to end users, from those which are not, and again to distinguish between machine-translated documents which are usable for some kind of human modification and those which are not. Such documents may not be suitable for modification by translators while being usable by an end reader and vice versa.

Existing treatments of translation tend to deal separately with human and machine translation, thus not comparing end products. Other current writing pretends to measure the machine product against the human product, without having a clear definition of what the standard of comparison should be when there are indeed various equally acceptable human versions.

7.2.1.1 *Full, reduced and selective translation*

The greatest diversity among translation strategies is that between full, selective and reduced translation which must be stipulated in the specifications. This choice of strategy decides on the production of (i) abstracts, which reduce a whole article to a prescribed number of words with a particular orientation of the content; (ii) summary or précis, which are reductions of flexible length; (iii) paraphrases of selected passages of a document; or finally (iv) 'full' translations of selected passages. In research establishments and libraries there is also the technique of on-sight, or first-time read-off translation which has been compared to simultaneous interpreting off a script. These strategies, though quite common in practice, are rarely, if ever, considered in translation theory.

The monolingual forms of document derivation are well-documented through manuals of information science which provide models analyses of these processes. While it is theoretically possible to split the activity into a monolingual text reduction, paraphrasing, selection phase, followed by a simple translation phase of an already modified document, this is not how the multilingual process is carried out, because translators combine both phases in a single operation. Psycholinguistic research would be needed to discover how translators proceed with this form of text modification; here it suffices to state that translators do not consciously split the process when they produce foreign language abstracts or summaries. For selective translation, texts are skimmed and annotated following monolingual excerpting methods, so that relevant passages are selected for more detailed attention and translation.

7.2.1.2 *Temporal segmentation of the process*

Even in full-text translation there has been little reflection on strategy because for centuries translation has been considered an entirely human activity combining art and craft in which translators somehow produced a target language document. It was acknowledged that translators sometimes worked in teams or in consultation, especially during the major historical translation periods, but mostly the work of translators was considered to be a unitary hermetic process, the analysis of which yielded no practical insights. With the industrialisation of translation in the 20th century and the grouping of translators in departments of larger organisations, a number of alternative divisions of labour appeared which drew attention to the working process and its temporal sequence. The change from handwriting to typewriter and the involvement of secretaries, especially in the first period when typewriters were exclusively used by typists and not by translators, introduced a clearly visible time gap between handwriting and typing, between typing and revision and again between revision and re-typing. These time sequences were confirmed quite decisively with the introduction of dictating machines in the middle of the 20th century when translators delivered a tape or disk, possibly with several completed tasks, to audio-typists who delivered back a certain amount of typescript ready for revision or checking. These changes have affected the translators' mode of working because in each case, as alternatives became available, translators became removed from their work by the time it takes to type handwritten or dictated work. This segmentation of the process and the participation of an amanuensis was again nullified with the introduction of word processors which permitted instant correction without any external intervention. At the moment, therefore, there are a number of concurrent strategies in use. The alternatives of time segmentation are illustrated in Figure 7.3.

PROCESS	TIME	PROCESS	TIME	PROCESS	TIME	PROCESS
HANDWRITING	—	REVISION	—	COPY		
HAND-WRITTEN DRAFT	gap	TYPE	gap	REVISION	gap	RETYPE
DICTATION	gap	AUDIOTYPE	gap	REVISION	gap	RETYPE
WORD PROCESSING	?	REVISION				

Figure 7.3 *Time factors in translation strategy decisions*

The existence of a time gap forces translators to segment or even measure the units of text on paper, tape or disk which they deliver to typists. In practice the introduction of the typewriter diversified the process in a number of other ways. There still are translators who employ typists or audio-typists and others who type themselves. Among these there are still those who, faced with a difficult document, make a draft in handwriting before typing it out. And, there is the steadily growing number of translators using word processors together with all sorts of checking and editing programs, whose working habits have not yet been studied at all.

The development of dictating machines introduced a further complication into the production process by the simple fact that written documents were translated into speech and speech had to be re-converted into written form by audio-typists. This not only provided occasions for errors due to the introduction of homophones, but more important, a temptation, mainly for the less experienced translator, to introduce rhythms based on spoken language into the written documents, to segment longer textual units into smaller units for convenient oral delivery or, inversely, to adopt the cumulative syntax, without clear sentence boundaries, characteristic of the spoken language. Inexperienced translators needed a long period of adjustment and training before they could confidently handle dictation with the required continuity of speech production if the magnetic medium was to be used efficiently by the audio-typist. Long gaps of silence or breaks in the continuity would not only be irritating to a typist, but also diminish productivity. The experienced translator moves within the confines of the previously selected text type, in the same way as the businessman or lawyer learns to dictate to a shorthand typist or into a dictating machine. This aspect of the dictation-audiotyping strategy has not been studied, even though it represents a major feat of adjustments of speech habits for translators.

The introduction of a division of labour into translators and typing auxiliaries introduced other diversifications of an organisational nature. Especially in large organisations a complex administrative structure became necessary for the distribution of work to translators and typists. In large translation departments, typing also facilitated the introduction of regular and systematic external revision because the typed draft could reliably and efficiently be checked by a revisor.

At the same time another temporal segmentation of the process became evident, that of the dictionary look-up. It is not feasible to interrupt the translation process while dictating, so that translators who use this strategy must do their preparatory dictionary look-up and other research before dictation begins. Another diversification occurs with the use of modern technology when translators have both printed and various electronic media available for information.

7.2.2 *The impact of electronic devices on the choice of strategy*

Beside the typewriter and the dictaphone, the computer has provided the greatest revolution in translation techniques. Computers have affected translators in three ways. First through the provision of terminological databases, then through the introduction of word processing, and finally through machine translation in all its varied forms. Already in the early 1950s the possibilities of computer assistance were clear but only in the 1980s did the technological environment of translation change to the extent that it affected industrial translation. This was signalled by the increased possibilities of core memory and peripheral memories at much reduced prices, the evolution of programming languages, the appearance of reliable networks on a wide scale for the transmission of data, the introduction of text-processing workstations and mini and micro computers which can call up servers of electronic dictionaries, servers with textual databases, and servers of translations. For the future there are the expectations offered by AI. This technological revolution will permit major advances in the near future in machine translation as well as in speech interpretation, especially when this progress is considered in relation to developments in such areas as speech recognition, speech sound production, optical character recognition etc..

Since the computer has also accelerated communication in general, translations are now expected to be delivered faster usually by means of electronic data transmission. In large industrial organisations in particular, there is a trend towards full electronic communication and translation providers are expected to conform to this trend. The concomitant changes in the working habits of translators are gradually being introduced with considerable time savings and reductions in the length of the document circuit. Not many years ago a document for translation was copied in paper form several times and moved physically from the place of the requester through innumerable hands of messengers, secretaries and section heads to the translator and back, being logged for entry and exit from a department many times in the process. Now, when translators receive documents in electronic form it is no longer acceptable to take them out of the electronic medium and dictate translations in order to have them input again by a typist into the electronic circuit. Such a process would be considered too costly in staff effort and too slow.

The integration of document circuits from the writing aid to distribution, passing through translation and standardisation, has been accompanied by a regrouping of tasks, duties and professions so that, incidentally, translators have a wider range of specialisations available than before into which they can channel their talents and which offer varied career orientations (see section 11.3).

7.2.2.1 *Choice of machine assistance or MT*

The most significant strategic choices to be made in a modern environment are the use of computers either to assist in translation or to perform the whole process by machine. In principle, translators have the option of using or not using some form of machine translation. If the choice is for MT they can, again in principle, select any one of several MT systems. Choices currently available include:

— fully automatic systems that claim to produce reader-acceptable output;
— systems that requires pre- or post-editing;
— systems that claim to pre-translate only.

In the case of fully-automatic translation translators usually accept the product of MT as a differently constituted text, which may, however, have the same functional, i.e. communicative potential, as a human-produced translation and a similar place in a chain of communication.

The choice of MT as a viable mode of translation introduces a revolutionary change in the hitherto practised communication process of interlingual communication because the end user of the translation can now bypass the translator altogether. The product of a machine translation system can be given directly to an end user, just like a human translation; or it can be further modified, in the same way as a human translation, though the nature of the modification will, of course, differ. In order to characterise the distinctive nature of the human modification process of MT-produced texts, the term 'post-editing' has been created. This process is not to be confused with 'revision'.

Translators as users of MT systems then have the further choice of using an MT system overtly or covertly, by either presenting the client with a document marked 'produced by system X' or editing the document to such an extent that it becomes undistinguishable, as far as the client is concerned, from a human product. If translators choose to produce the same text type as the SL document they must always post-edit the output, because of the fundamental difference between the functional values of human and machine-produced documents. Only through post-editing can a document be given back the same function and the impact of the machine be obliterated. If the choice is for a translation-specific type direct machine output can be offered. A full discussion follows in section 9.

7.2.3 *The interaction of choices*

The choice of translation strategy is made in the light of the previous choices which were conditioned by the specifications and to a lesser extent by the nature of the source document. A particular document can, through the specifications, be commissioned in two different target language forms, e.g. a report can be required in a full translation, in a reduced version and in the form of an abstract. For each task a separate translation strategy is appropriate.

The interdependence of these choices is illustrated and exemplified in Figure 7.4.

Identification of SL text type	*Interpretation of specification*	*Choice of TL text type*	*Choice of translation strategy*
Examples	Examples	Examples	
1. REPORT	'for information'	derived:	
		full	automatic
1a.		abstract	human
2. TENDER	bilingual	tender	semi-automatic
3. MINUTES OF MULTILINGUAL MEETING	multiple versions	reduced minutes	human with reference to original tapes, full minutes & parallel versions
4. BUSINESS LETTER	selective 'incoming'	gist	human
4b.	'outgoing'	pro-forma	semi-automatic

Figure 7.4 *The choice of text type and translation strategy*

Notes to the examples:

Example 1. A report is required in translation 'for information only'. It has then to be decided whether it is required in full, in which case an automatic translation may be appropriate. If it is required selectively, again the sections selected by the translator may be processable by machine. If an abstract or a summary of some parts of the report are required, these can only be produced through a human process.

Example 2. For a bilingual tender, there is a human model, in the form of previous similar tenders, and it must be assumed that the text type exists in the target language. A machine may be used to assist in translation, but in order to maintain the full functional equivalence of both texts as equivalent messages, the machine-produced translation has to be post-edited in order to maintain this parallelism.

Alternatively the MT output may be translated back into the source language by machine in order to obtain two parallel and equivalent machine-produced versions.

Example 3. Multilingual versions of minutes have to be produced on the basis of meetings mediated by means of simultaneous interpreting. In this case translators are in full control because they have to refer to the monolingual sound recordings of the different speakers in order to be able to report accurately what any one has said during the meeting.

Example 4. The gist of an incoming business letter is required. This is a purely human process, which some people do not even admit to be genuine translation.

Example 4b. If an outgoing business letter is concerned with a fairly routine transaction, it may be possible to use an MT system which presents pro-forma letters from which a letter writer makes a choice of appropriate phrases and inserts the specific details of the communication.

If the decision process leading to the use of MT is presented in parallel with the human decision process that preceded it, it can be shown clearly (see Figure 7.5) how many prior decisions have been made on the basis of human knowledge of texts, long before the machine can get involved.

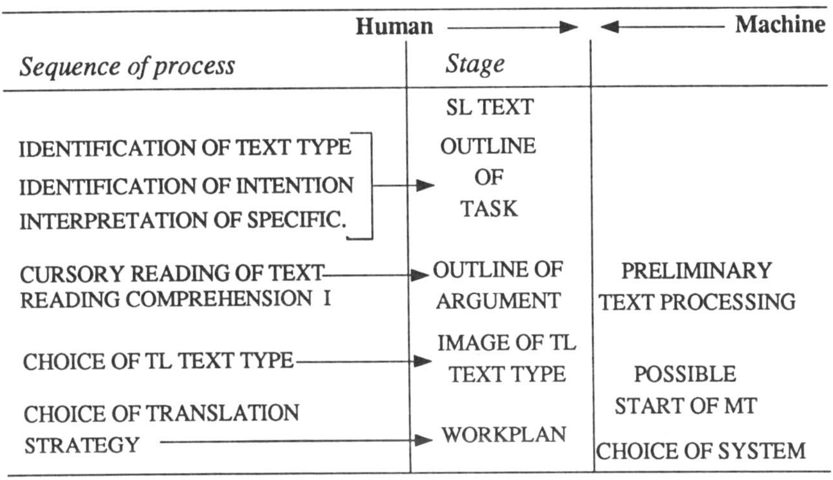

Figure 7.5 *The sequences of the human and machine processes*

Details of the possible MT processes are presented in section 9.

7.3 Reading Comprehension: Human text understanding

The next stage of preparation consists of a detailed reading of the text. The previous steps have cleared up all decisions to be taken on pragmatic issues at the macro level. What remains are cognitive and linguistic questions and pragmatic questions of a lower level. These questions now form the essence of the translation process and while broad principles of translation strategy are decided beforehand, the process of translation itself requires a combination of hermeneutic, heuristic and plain linguistic techniques which may require adjustment and re-combination at every step.

The cognitive process of understanding begins with reading/comprehension, a single or an iterative process of varying intensity. There are many techniques of reading, according to the degree of familiarity with the topic and the subject knowledge of the translator. The technique adopted must permit the identification of the cognitive units of the text while at the same time—according to the pragmatic equivalent of the text type chosen earlier—retaining sufficient perception of the linguistic structure so that the translation can show the degree of recognisable linguistic relationship with the source document decided upon in the strategy decision.

Detailed reading is carried out in the light of the knowledge acquired about the task to be performed and in units which fit the individual's understanding of the specifications and the text, with appropriate breaks for dictionary look-up or other consultations. According to their familiarity with the subject field, translators have to read the whole text in detail before starting translating or they may read segments at a time.

Reading a unit of text, translators relate the new information to their own knowledge structure in general and to the specific knowledge they have accumulated about the document and the purpose of the task. The established knowledge interacts with the newly acquired knowledge and permits the confirmation and expansion of a translator's knowledge structure and the specific subset of knowledge called upon for this task.

In this respect translators' reading and comprehension is no different from other readers and writers: new information is only processed to the extent that it can be related to existing knowledge; existing knowledge can, on the other hand, only be tested if it is confronted with new knowledge, and existing knowledge can only be put to use if it is faced with new comprehension and production situations in which it can be applied.

The peculiarity of the translators' situation is that this knowledge is present in two linguistic modes. Reading source language text expressions relating to items of knowledge, translators connect this knowledge with target language expressions, i.e. the translators' store of knowledge which is normally activated in the target language but reacts to information input in the source language to build up the knowledge structure required for handling the translation task. As reading-understanding progresses, a knowledge structure for the document emerges with two linguistic realisations which are however unequal in strength. The source language store of linguistic items serves only to trigger off the possible target language linguistic realisations and not vice versa. As the work of translation progresses, the translators' target language code and knowledge structure may be consolidated as they interact with the new material and even be expanded to the extent that translators are unfamiliar with parts of the topic.

This stage is the least researched aspect of the process of translation. It is interesting to observe that most studies devoted to translation never even identify a stage required for reading the document. Nor is it clear how a secondary reader, like a translator, i.e. one who is not directly addressed by the writer, understands a text.

There are several dimensions to this understanding. We do not know how translators assimilate the content of documents without becoming experts in the subject matter; nor do we know how to define the form of knowledge translators acquire which permits them to handle highly specialised documents written by experts who have devoted many years of their lives acquiring the knowledge expressed. Most translators do not 'fully' understand a text, in the sense that they could not have written it or could write a similar text after having read it; yet, in most cases, they produce acceptable translations, to the extent that they can claim professional status for their work. We can only assume there to be a particular form of short term comprehension and retention for temporary information to be discarded after use, which may apply to translation, in the same way as it has been partly found to be the case for interpreters. By contrast long-term retention would be needed for learning in order to re-use the knowledge acquired, which in the case of translators only occurs when they regularly deal with the same subject matter. But there are many other uncertainties. Different modes of reading/understanding were at the basis of much early research into Information Science, very often without conclusive results because it lacked a theoretical linguistic foundation. There is also substantial evidence from student exercises—and presumably also from professional practice—of cases where simple transfer of units of discourse by means of a dictionary at the level of syntax has produced acceptable translations without the translator having 'understood' the sentence or paragraph.

We can safely assume that translators read with a greater awareness of linguistic form than other readers. This awareness manifests itself at the same levels as required for other text modification tasks and may require re-reading and in depth reading to find an acceptable solution to a problem. In the model presented here, the first 'cursory' reading carried out in the specification phase must take in major syntactic structures and the logical drift of the argument, but not details. At the subsequent 'full' Reading-Comprehension stage, translators read with sufficient attention to both form and content to convince themselves that they can proceed with the next stage of work. In practice, it is often only at the next stage of processing that translators realise that they have incompletely or incorrectly understood a passage and have to return to more detailed reading of the problem area.

For our model of translation we postulate three dimensions of understanding, the cognitive, the pragmatic and the linguistic, with several levels each. Translators must be able to read and understand at particular cognitive levels and at all pragmatic and linguistic levels. Their own knowledge and experience and above all the specification of the task which they receive with the document permit them to interpret to what level of understanding they must proceed.

7.3.1 *The knowledge dimension of text understanding*

Cognitive reading is independent of language in the sense that, in order to be understood, the information need not be expressed in language. It may appear in diagram, table or other graphic form independent of any one particular language. It is concerned with the following questions:

Level 1. — What is the text about? i.e. a global level of understanding the 'aboutness' of a text;

Level 2. — What does the text say? i.e. a slightly deeper level of understanding the general drift of the argument;

Level 3. — What does the text say in detail?

Level 4. — What knowledge has to be transferred into the TL text?

Level 5. — How does the knowledge contained in the text relate to existing knowledge in the TL society?

Level 6. — What efforts are required to retain this knowledge for active re-use?

A primary reader can stop after any of questions 1—3, he does not ask question 4. Only a subject specialist or a learner of this subject asks questions 5 and beyond. A secondary reader may, in fact, stop after level 2. If such a reader is in a position to commission a translation he may ask question one and then skip to question 4 the answer to which will indicate whether a full or a selective translation is required. Translators cannot stop but must go right to the end of level 4, at least. If translators are involved in the production of evaluative abstracts in the target language, they may also require level 5.

7.3.2 *The pragmatic dimension of text understanding*

This dimension is concerned with the following questions:

Level 1. — What is the purpose of the document? i.e. what is the level of understanding required for the intention, which implies reading the text as a message;

Level 2. — What is the purpose of the translated document? i.e. what is the new intention?

Level 3. — Is the purpose of the new text suitable for the presupposed state of knowledge of the new readership?

For many readers the first question is self-evident. In case of doubt with respect to the answer to question 2, translators are dependent on the specifications or have to ask the agent for clarification. In some cases the answer to question 2 is already partially predetermined by the choice of text type. The answer to question three may give rise to a change in translation technique.

7.3.3 *The linguistic dimension of text understanding*

Reading-comprehension of the linguistic dimension also varies from ignoring the expression form to studying the form in detail. It is concerned with the following questions:

Level 1. — What are the linguistic features of the text type of the text?

Level 2. — How is the text structured syntactically?

Level 3. — What mode of expression, what words are used?

Level 4. — How is the text to be expressed in the TL?

A primary reader need not entertain this dimension at all, or can carry out the linguistic comprehension task to any level of depth and can stop at any level. Linguistic analysis can be subdivided by elements to be analysed. Translators must deal with all levels but usually carry out much of this analysis unconsciously; they concentrate on particular aspects according to the nature of the document and the purpose of the translation. The types of analysis to be carried out are listed below in summary form. The inclusion of these details here is also a reminder of the operations a machine has to perform.

Graphological level:
Spelling — punctuation — capitalization — typographical layout — length of lines — spacing — paragraphing.

Phonological level:
phonological structure — rhetorical devices (rhyme, rhythm, alliteration, onomatopoeia, etc.).

Morphological level:
Word classes and their respective distribution — distribution of active and passive voice — tense and aspect — word formation.

Semantic level:
Choice of vocabulary — denotation and connotation of words — personal pronouns — semantic figures of speech (similes, metaphors, etc.).

Syntactic level:
Word order — types of sentences — length of sentences — linking of sentences — syntactic rhetorical devices (parallelism, repetition, etc.).

Compository level:
Type of introduction — sequence of forms (cataphoric, anaphoric reference) — text structuring (theme-rheme, climactic development, contrast, etc.) — type of conclusion.

7.3.4 *The limits imposed on comprehension*

As socio-culturally determined linguistic behaviour, the reading-understanding practised by translators contains both social and individual components which limit the capacity of comprehension. Translators like other readers select from the information offered according to their own store of knowledge and purpose of reading. Experienced translators have a perception of some of these limitations and develop strategies to counteract those that can be detected as being negative influences on their work. Translators also have the capacity to compensate for interlingual and intercultural differences they are aware of. The problem lies in incorporating this highly individualised skill of adaptation to the task, into a theory of translation. Generalisation on the basis of observed behaviour is difficult because adaptation is made document by document, according to the range of material translators process. Translators may, of course, also wrongly apply adaptive behaviour they have evolved in the case of one document to another situation.

Examining the behaviour of translators, Wilss (1988:60-75) identified two positions:

(a) translation is performed as a reflex action, i.e. it can be defined as being largely automatic because translators are unaware of whatever adaptation they have performed. Inasmuch as it is a reaction applied to any text, this case can be described as being similar to machine processing.

(b) translation is performed as a result of a text-specific adaptive strategy. The adaptation can, however, only apply to the translation problems which the translator has been able to identify.

The question of translators' awareness of their decisions is also observed by Fillmore (1977:61), cited by Wilss, when he states: "The properties of this world may depend quite a bit on the individual interpreter's own private experiences—a reality which should account for part of the fact that different people construct different interpretations of the same text."

In conclusion it can be said that readers in general and translators in particular have in their memory an inventory of patterns for structuring, classifying and interpreting experiences, and that they have various procedures for performing translation processes on the documents they encounter. When the textual environment conforms less to these known patterns and procedures and is, therefore, less supportive, the efficacy of translation is either greatly reduced, or the situation may force the translator to invest more time and effort to achieve a translational result which corresponds to the specifications. If translators encounter totally unfamiliar text types and specifications they have difficulty finding adequate solutions.

7.3.4.1 *Implications for the automatic analysis of texts*

Research into text understanding is of particular interest in relation to MT. In purely human terms translators' understanding can be expressed as reading to the depth necessary for producing an adequate translation. In terms of machine analysis of text, it can then be said say that the machine must analyse to the depth required for eliminating the possibility of misunderstanding, or until all alternative readings have been accounted for. But in particular cases reading/understanding can be relaxed and translators and machines can work up to a much shallower level. Research is then required into how much and what type of analysis can be omitted without endangering text generation. This is different from an earlier approach which wanted to use as little linguistics as possible.

There are a number of areas of text comprehension in which current knowledge is very limited. Particular topics which would require further reflection are:

— To what extent the identification of units of comprehension for which equivalents are sought is conditioned by textual characteristics and to what extent by sense units.

— To what extent translators rely on known phrases and units and to what extent they admit the existence of new units, collocations etc. as genuine new creations by writers.
— What inhibitions of conventionality operate on translators, especially when they are aware of a high degree of novelty of cognitive content. The same problem can be expressed in a different way: To what extent is the translation technique steered by the translators' expectation (i.e. the translators' perception of the expectation of an agent, a reader-client, or their own capacity of cognition and stylistic appropriateness).

7.3.4.2 *Translator competence*

Reading-comprehension is the first real test of translators' professional competence. The combination of theoretical and practical knowledge and experience involved in this particular meaning of 'competence' as distinct from its conventional linguistic meaning is explained in Kussmaul (1986: 206). Accepting the position expressed above by Wilss, competence can be expressed as a balance between the capacity to adapt to novel translation situations (content-form and specification) and the ability to handle with expedience and accuracy, i.e. almost automatically, regularly recurring tasks. In both cases, but especially in the case of regular work, Wilss (1992:47) considers speed to be another sign of professional competence. As experience in translation increases and translation skills become stronger and part of a daily routine, translators encounter fewer novel situations and can therefore develop speed of working. Competence can therefore be expressed as a combination of knowledge and know-how, of intuition and reflection, which express themselves in variable degrees of depth of research and variable speeds of work. Efficient translators look for tasks which permit them to work at speed for most of the time, while leaving some time to widen their experience by dealing with new content, new forms and new specifications. There is a regular process of knowledge acquisition with each text to be translated, but only variety of texts and specifications leads to an enlarged acquisition of techniques.

7.4 Dictionary look-up

Dictionary look-up and other forms of consultation of reference works begin at this stage of the process and continue from then on with varying intensity and purpose. In the reading comprehension phase consultation is oriented towards the source language; in the translation phase the orientation is bi-directional according to the nature of the problem; in the revision phase the orientation is towards the target language, unless there appears to be a need to go back to an earlier phase. Thus, look-up is initially supportive of comprehension, then it becomes concerned with equivalences and moves finally towards control of expressions.

It is impossible to give a comprehensive overview of the full range of support materials translators need for their work because this depends on their degrees of specialisation, previous knowledge, etc., but their dependence on dictionaries can be taken as the most constant need. Nor is it practical to describe a single preferred or optimal mode of this type of research. As long as there were only printed dictionaries available and translators did not dictate their work, dictionary look-up or other consultation could easily be accommodated at any time during the reading and translation process. Some translators annotate their text with the result of their research page by page for the whole document before translating, i.e. writing or dictating, a single sentence. Others, especially with routine work, rely on their knowledge of the topic and only stop for research when a doubt arises. For translators who dictate their work, research of any kind is usually carried out before dictation begins. However, it is also known for translators who regularly dictate, to resort to handwriting when they are dealing with a text which requires a great deal of attention in formulating the target language version and hence unpredictable breaks for consultation of reference tools.

The combination of word-processing and automatic dictionaries offers new modes of consultation during document production because translators can open up windows on their screen for calling up dictionary entries and transfer the found word or expression directly into the new document. The screen may also contain a window for the source document so that translators can transfer automatically any word or expression from a dictionary or a source document window into the target document, thus eliminating the risk of committing typing errors in transcription.

The introduction of termbanks had an impact on translation techniques which is worth noting. These first computer-held dictionaries concentrated on technical terminology and were introduced by large translation departments (Krollmann 1981). As long as these dictionaries could not be accessed on-line translators had to channel their requests for information through information scientists who performed batch searches of the database.

An interesting method of consultation was reported from the Bundessprachenamt of the German Government during the 1960s and 1970s (Hoffman 1983). Translators would annotate a text and hand it in for research at the end of the day. The next morning they would find on their desk the text and the words and expressions requested, in the order of the sequence of the text to be translated. It was found that the interval between annotating and actual start of translation gave translators an incidental and unexpected benefit because it gave time for reflection on the task. These lists then permitted experienced translators to dictate a translation without interruption by making reference to the database printout accompanying the translation task. An interim stage of the development towards on-line access was to provide translators with microfiches of the database or partial printout for personal reference in order to save translators either a phone call to a dictionary mediator or a walk to the library or reference section. Now automated dictionaries come in two main forms, either as on-line databases which can be accessed via the translators' minicomputer with a wordprocessing package or in form of a compact disc via a special reading device. Translators in large organisations now have direct on-line access to the organisation's own terminological database. Others may be connected via modem to such public systems as Eurodicautom of the Commission of the European Communities or Termium of the Federal Canadian Government. An increasing number of translators are converting their own collections of terminology and special equivalents into small databases which they can directly access on their word processors.

It is claimed that dictionary look-up occupied between 15 and 50% of the total process and that the provision of specialised terminology via electronic support can substantially reduce this time while increasing the accuracy and consistency of usage of terminology (Mossmann 1984). There is no doubt that reference to a single information source greatly increases the consistency of usage of terminology and other expressions, but time gained in look-up must be held against the overall need for reflection and continued education which is served by browsing through a dictionary or the shelves in a library in search of an appropriate reference tool. Translators cannot work at top speed for extended periods but need breaks. Dictionary consultation provides such moments of reflection. The instant availability of answers via electronic tools may save search time and be less tiring on the eye, but translators will then require other modes of interrupting the strain of continued intellectual work.

7.4.1 *Modes of dictionary consultation*

Contrary to popular belief translators do not often look up source to target language dictionaries to find out the translation equivalent of a word or expression. For the experienced translator dictionaries are more like a memory aid which comes into play especially when translation fatigue sets in.

Of the many modes of dictionary consultation there are a few which are almost standard for most translators. Most frequently dictionaries are used to confirm choices of equivalents made in a particular context or to examine the alternatives the dictionary may offer outside the context in which the translator is working. Experienced translators have developed their own modes of overcoming the known limitations of dictionaries. For example, when a dictionary offers several alternatives, none of which are sufficiently differentiated, translators reverse the process and look up the found words in a dictionary of the opposite directionality in order to obtain more contextual information. When encountering complex noun phrases, translators know how to break them down into their constituent parts under which they appear listed in the alphabetic sequence; when such units are not found, experience tells the translator under which separate parts information may be found for creating an acceptable paraphrase. Automatic dictionaries increasingly permit interrogation via permuted indexes and truncated parts of lexical items which considerably increases the hit rate of searches. The growing availability of full text databases will permit translators to verify the existence and acceptability of expressions via searches of KWIC indexes.

Modes of use tend to be associated with particular types of dictionaries and also types of translation. General dictionaries are only indirectly useful in translation because they offer a list of isolated lexical items out of context with a range of possible meanings, in the best of cases confirmed and exemplified by actual textual occurrences; but translators need words and expressions in a particular context, which may not even be recorded in the dictionary. Dictionaries, after all, are based on existing and known usage, and cannot therefore offer advice on all the semantic innovations that regularly occur in novel texts. Bilingual general dictionaries have the same limitations and offer even less certainty because they are usually conservatively selective in the range of equivalent pairs they offer. Specialised dictionaries are of more direct use especially when, as often happens, documents cross borders of specialisation of which a translator is less familiar or contain source language expressions outside common usage. It is the large diversity of subject matter occurring in some documents which occasions the greatest amount of dictionary use and consequently explains the heavy effort in building up translation-oriented lexical and terminological databases in the last fifty years.

Of special interest to translators are general language thesauri and other collections of synonyms, paronyms and antonyms because they offer opportunities to browse and so support the need translators often feel of trying out alternative modes of expression. This is particularly the case in literary translation where a translator attempts to re-create the stylistic idiosyncrasies of the author. Beside general language thesauri, translators find terminological thesauri particularly useful because they offer a glimpse of the knowledge structure of the subject field. Even documentation thesauri can prove useful because they list the most important terms of the field and often also differentiate between preferred and non-preferred terms.

In certain areas of engineering, technology and recently also in areas affected by environmental protection there are national and international standards, some of which are even supported by glossaries, that provide definitions and terms as used and agreed by the specialists who have collaborated in the production of the standards. Since most standardisation is a matter for consensus among industrial members, sometimes with the support and guidance of national authorities, these documents are particularly reliable concerning actual usage and meaning, but may be rather limited in the scope of application.

7.5 Electronic tools to support dictionary consultation

Among existing tools, on-line data bases are an important source of linguistic information and an aid to translation which is as yet not fully explored because of the difficulties of accessing them. Use of these facilities will be greatly assisted when translators, their clients or agents have a tool which permits the transfer of the result of an on-line interrogation to a server of translation, and to obtain a raw translation which in certain cases can be used without post-editing, e.g. for browsing through titles and abstracts in order to verify the content before ordering a translation.

The most important lexical databases for translators are terminological data banks, which exist at national, institutional, commercial or individual level (Brinkmann 1980). In Quebec, for example, the government provides a public terminology service in order to support the use of the French language in all areas of life. The first institutional term banks were set up by the Commission of the European Communities and the Bundesprachenamt of the German Government for their translation departments. The first terminology service for industry was created by Siemens in Munich to support their international marketing and service efforts. The French standardisation organisation Afnor created the first database of national and multilingual ISO and IEC international standards and standards glossaries. These large term banks store millions of terms in the main languages of translation and are growing rapidly. Now some of these data collections, and other smaller ones, are available commercially and in addition there are software packages which enable translators to build up their own collections.

An increasingly common tool is provided by translators themselves. For large contracts translators now often propose to their clients the compilation of a document-specific glossary before translation begins, so that all the terminology which is to be used in this and future related translation contracts can be agreed beforehand. This arrangement has proved most useful for such large translation contracts as the manuals needed for the construction and maintenance of off-shore oil drilling platforms or multinational aircraft projects like the Airbus or Concorde. These glossaries are important tools for future translation jobs which the clients can use as general reference tools, or as indexes to the manuals, and may even give to other translators.

In the future, the most important new tools for translators will be collections of existing translations. When more source and target texts are in machine-readable form it becomes interesting to develop search techniques to find models of previous translation pairs at the level of the sentence or matches of smaller, lexical or terminological units. The direct transferability of found precedents makes their use much more efficient and attractive than the previous possibility of referring to a good translation archive or collection of phrases which had to be hand-searched and the results had to be typed out by hand again into the new document. The use of powerful search and matching techniques on substantial collections of coherent documents will also make a major contribution to our understanding of the process of translation because we shall be able to examine the linguistic units which provide the greatest incidence of actual identity between source and target language.

8 Steps in Translation

The four steps of the translation phase, identified in section 6.4, constitute the core of the translation activity which is concluded in phase four, by evaluation or revision. This third phase is conventionally considered to be the only activity relevant for a theory of translation. For an industrial model this is unacceptable because as a commissioned task translation starts with a need for communication and ends with a finished product like any other form of text production.

8.1 The translation process

Once the specifications have been interpreted, every subsequent step in the process of translation is heavily conditioned by pragmatic considerations and therefore all translators' choices on the semantic and linguistic levels are strictly limited. Models of translation which do not make allowance for these preconditions are weak and consequently also of little use for the teaching of translation techniques: translation exercises used for training usually leave too many options open, and long debates can ensue about the possible alternatives, which in a realistic situation are mostly precluded by prior decisions.

The translation phase proper can best be explained in terms of the assumed cognitive states and processes and the resultant linguistic activities. This approach also clearly distinguishes human from machine translation, which is specifically considered in section nine.

8.1.1 *Translation units*

Since very little is known about the human process of translation, it is generally assumed that translators proceed by somehow identifying cognitive units in the SL and finding equivalent TL expression for them. Recognition of units is assisted by knowledge of the subject matter of the document. These units are usually limited by phrase and sentence boundaries in the SL, but this is not obligatory and depends very much on the SL text structure. Units can be larger, if translators are subject specialists; they are usually smaller if translators are not experts, because they have to make sure they have segmented the source text correctly to find the semantically 'right' lexical and terminological units.

The concept of 'translation unit' has received as much attention in the literature as the concept of 'equivalence', discussed in section 5.4. But, whereas equivalence can be explained by linguistic and pragmatic criteria, units of translation also touch upon psychological questions and the techniques of translation chosen. This concept has to be analysed from two viewpoints: one is the practical one of the units translators select for processing at any one time; the other is the unit chosen in the search for equivalents. This latter aspect is discussed in section 8.3.2.

Like any other human being, translators are limited in the task of text handling by memory, which according to Miller (1968:21), is plus or minus seven items. According to (i) the stylistic conformity of the text to pre-established patterns, (ii) translators' familiarity with the text type in both source and target language, and with the topic under discussion, and (iii) their mastery of the technique of visually controlling two texts in different media, or both on screen, translators can retain in their short term memory what are for them more or less complex units within the rough memory span identified. Speed of work is largely determined by the ability to recognise and process such units as a whole. If mistakes occur in the recognition of units, translators have to analyse or decompose complex units they are unfamiliar with, i.e. which they do not understand. Familiarity with textual units within a particular text type is therefore the chief element that determines speed, and incidentally accuracy of processing.

The units translators work with are not easy to detect since they work intuitively and do not consciously segment the text they process. The only reliable way to find out what size of units are processed is to analyse existing translations and identify transposed sections that permit conclusions about their unity to be made. For example, in the following alternative translations the units can be seen by their changed position.

On 10 August,	The Spanish government decided
as a result of the damages	on 10 August
caused by heavy avalanches	to ask for an international loan
in Spain	as emergency aid
earlier this year,	for basic reconstruction
the government decided	in response to the damage
to ask for an international loan	caused by heavy avalanches
to give emergency aid	earlier this year.
for basic reconstruction.	

Another way of detecting units is by contrasting multiple translations, e.g.

This request by the Federal Post Office |
This demand of the Federal Post Administration |

is given the emphatic support |
is now also widely supported |

of the communications industry |
by CDU-led Land governments |

and the conservative-led governments. |
as well as by the communications industry. |

8.1.2 *A psycholinguistic model*

The actual process of translation has frequently been explained by reference to such words as transformation, re-expression or re-coding, all of which stress a particular aspect of this unique operation for which the global designation 'translation' is commonly used. Neubert (1991:25) lists a series of cognitive acts or mental operations alternating in the translator's mind: — problem identification — comprehension — retrieval — monitoring — problem reduction — decision taking, by which he means actual re-expression in the TL. According to him, translators pass through all or a smaller number of these steps, according to the nature of the SL text material, for example, by not requiring 'problem reduction'. He also recognises that the process can undergo certain iterations of retrieval and monitoring in difficult passages of a SL document. In what follows we detail the process in psycholinguistic terms, interpreting, in particular, the work of Loerscher (1991).

Since we are dealing with a theoretical rather than an experiential model, it is useful to start with a caveat. The translation method chosen by an individual translator is not so much determined by the type of problem as by the perceived complexity and difficulty of the problem, i.e. what is a problem for one translator is no problem for another (see Wilss, 7.3.2). This perception depends on the translator's skill, familiarity with the text and topic and, of course, on the translation strategy originally chosen.

With this reservation we can set out a number of basic principles which characterise the process.

(a) Experienced translators use mentally less complex techniques before more complex ones. For example, in the process of comprehension simple observation is preferred to reformulation of content and, in production, simple substitution of equivalent elements is preferred to rephrasing. Only if these simple techniques do not succeed in solving the problem in question do translators employ mentally more complex strategies.

(b) Translation is best described as a forward and backward looking mental operation. Loerscher (1991:101) calls this "retrospective-prospective", meaning thereby that translators move forward in the text they are translating, keeping in mind what they have processed and go back, when and if required. In terms of the present model we can call the preparation phase linear and progressive, whereas the actual translation phase is iterative, in so far as the search for equivalents is repeated for each unit, and discontinuous, in so far as each unit for which an equivalent has been found has to be assessed for the adequacy of its link to a previous one. If this link proves unsatisfactory the present, or a previous unit, has to be modified.

(c) Each new translation task is performed with varying speed. As translators produce more target language text, they gain confidence in translation and can translate faster. This is similar to reading, which usually also gains speed as a reader becomes familiar with the author's mode of expression.

8.1.3 *Modes of processing*

The mental activity of translation proceeds at the level of a declared intention, knowledge acquisition and linguistic expression. The initial stimulus and orientation which give the activity its direction is provided by the specification which, in psychological terms, states the goal of the activity. The specification permits translators to form an image of the new text, i.e. a modified form of reader expectation. This expectation is confirmed and strengthened as work progresses and the translator gains a clearer image of the totality of the new document. As translators process more content of the source text, their knowledge base of the subject matter grows and hence their power of prediction of the remaining content and its form. The likelihood of understanding the text coherently or, at least, in one particular orientation, increases. In practice this means that translators feel greater confidence about their choices of target language units as they develop more knowledge about the linguistic features of the source document itself. With each formulation of a target language unit, translators have an increasing certainty about the form of the next one, which obviates rephrasing and going back on previous decisions.

Translators systematically move from source to target document and vice versa in order to both confirm and add new semantic and linguistic information and so build up a new text, which is provisional until a larger pragmatic unit is completed, so that the argument structure and other supra-sentential features of the text can be tested. The size of units tested at any one time depends on translator competence in handling a particular type of document and its specification.

Forward-looking activities consist of such steps as:

(a) more detailed reading to confirm previously acquired knowledge;
(b) testing a provisionally chosen form against a form occurring later in the SL document about which there is greater certainty;
(c) looking up a lexical unit for confirmation or clarification, etc.

Backward-looking activities consist of such steps as:

(a) testing a provisionally chosen form against the continuity of already translated units;
(b) verifying conformity with a syntactic pattern previously chosen;
(c) checking conformity with a lexical unit previously established as being mandatory;
(d) verifying that there is no unwanted repetition or redundancy, etc.

The technique of looking back makes the passage in hand provisional, until it is rejected, modified or confirmed. This movement can be illustrated, as in Figure 8.1, as a series of circular movements of smaller and larger extension. Variations occur according to translators' concentration on content or form.

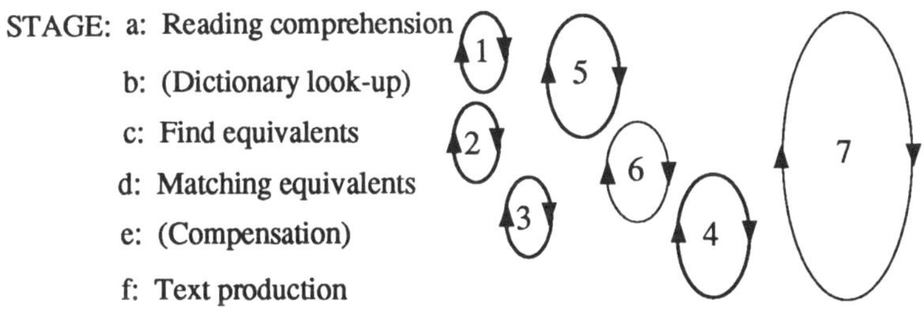

NOTE: (i) The stages b and e, indicated in brackets, are optional which renders circuits 1 and 3 also optional.
(ii) The circuits can be run through one by one or in combination.

Figure 8.1 *Modes of processing (Controlled ideation and invention)*

When a target text segment is formulated immediately after the reception of a source segment the correspondence is produced with greater attention to formal characteristics, because other information is absent. The principle involved in this process is that of the one to one match of lexical units which underlies the formulation of simple bilingual dictionary equivalents. We can also compare this technique to the simple game of formal associations across two languages.

At the purely formal level of the whole document, on the other hand, translation is conveniently exemplified by such formal documents as birth certificates, in which the requirements of form of the target culture have to be satisfied and nothing else.

When translators have larger text units available within a pragmatic situation of their own range of experience, they can proceed in the normal form of reading-understanding, i.e. they separate form from content and attempt to find equivalents for concepts or other units of content, regardless of form, according to the model of conceptual transfer, described in section 6.1.1. If translators are unfamiliar with the knowledge structure of the subject field of the document, translation which proceeds via complex patterns of correspondence of units of knowledge is an arduous and even risky task.

If translators are dissatisfied with a solution found at the formal level, i.e. that it does not meet their intuitive expectation, they have to proceed via a fuller form of reading understanding in order to detect the weakness or error in their intuition and rectify it. In some cases, however, translators have simply forgotten the appropriate form of the target language expression; in such a case they may reach the right solution by a series of rephrasings which eventually lead them to remember the required form. Translators can also proceed on the formal level alone, namely when they encounter problems they have already resolved previously. In such cases they can refer back to lexical or syntactic units and reuse them without having to go deeper into content analysis of the passage in hand. Alternatively, in order to avoid repetition, they may rephrase a previous passage in order to discover formally different versions of similar content. They then have to chose between the two similar passages for the two textual instances into which they have to be fitted. In such a case the choice is determined by both the existing context of the previous passage and the new context yet to be created for the textual unit in hand at the time.

The technique of rephrasing has a number of benefits. It permits translators to get to the cognitive essence of a passage and to find the most appropriate linguistic expression form for the occasion. Only by testing alternative phrasings can translators be sure of the rightness of a decision for a particular context. As a translation progresses the number of choices becomes reduced as previous decisions are consolidated. This is one of the reasons for the increased speed of work as a translation process gets into its stride.

Figure 8.2 attempts to represent the translation process from two points of view, namely the separate parts of the process and the stage reached at the end of each separately identifiable activity. This breakdown of the process should permit the identification of the separate activities and decisions involved in successive stages and to assess the outcome of each stage separately. Such a modularisation can then be used for reflecting on possible machine assistance at any one stage, for designing automated modules and finally for monitoring any interactive man-machine models of translation.

Sequence of process	**Stage**
Specification phase	SL DOCUMENT
IDENTIFICATION OF TEXT TYPE →	
IDENTIFICATION OF INTENTION →	→ OUTLINE OF TASK
IDENTIFICATION OF SPECIFIC. →	
CURSORY READING OF TEXT →	OUTLINE OF ARGUMENT
Preparation phase	
CHOICE OF TL TEXT TYPE →	IMAGE OF TL TEXT TYPE
CHOICE OF TRANSL. TECHNIQUE →	WORKPLAN
READING COMPREHENSION →	SEMANTIC REPRESENTATION
LOOK-UP AS NEEDED →	ID.
Translation phase	
SEARCH FOR EQUIVALENTS →	PAIRS OF EXPRESSIONS
MATCHING EQUIVALENTS →	TL PHRASES & CLAUSES
COMPENSATION OF EQUIVALENTS →	ID.
TEXT PRODUCTION →	TL DRAFT TEXT
Evaluation/Revision phase	
EVALUATION OF CONTENT →	ID.
REVISION OF FORM →	TL TEXT/MESSAGE

Figure 8.2 *The sequence of the human translation process, divided into separate stages*

8.1.4 *Extension of the existing model*

All models of the process discussed in section 6 are limited by the fact that they do not consider the regular working environment of a translator. This also applies to the approach taken so far which models a single translation process. In the reality of industrial practice, the individual translation has to be placed into the professional environment of ongoing translation tasks.

Since in practice, translations seldom occur on their own, a procedural model is needed which includes consideration of the use of existing translations as actual substitutes or as examples for new assignments. This is attempted in Figure 8.3, which is expressed as a flow-chart of decisions permitting the alternatives of using previous translations or having to translate without a precedent.

8.2 Resolution of ambiguity

At the stage of interpreting the source language document and just before they start translation proper, translators are influenced by (i) their own perceptual limitations with regard to understanding the SL text, and also (ii) by the way they interpret their task with respect to the specifications. Even within this narrower objective, they usually find instances of multiple interpretation possibilities, which we group together under the general label of ambiguity. It is at this stage that the problem-solving approach to translation seems most appropriate.

Every reading-comprehension of a text by professional mediators involves a benevolent and neutral interpretation in the first instance. They must assume that the text makes sense (Grice's principle of cooperation) but be open to the possibility of factual error; they can only judge the text with respect to its expression of the content as they understand it. As professionals they can and must make assumptions about the care taken in choosing expression forms and must be critical of certain types of texts. They will, nevertheless, face a number of problems affecting the knowledge content of a text when they encounter text segments permitting more than one interpretation, caused by ambiguity. These problems can be described as either: (i) Sentences or other textual segments that can be given more than one interpretation in the source language; or (ii) sentences or other textual segments that require elucidation when being translated into another language.

Translators may or may not detect such a possibility of multiple interpretation. In practice every mediator will recognise some but not all ambiguities. When an ambiguity has been recognised the next step is to interpret it. Translators have to decide whether, (i) it was intended by the writer or an editor, or (ii) created accidentally by the writer or a previous mediator of the document in hand.

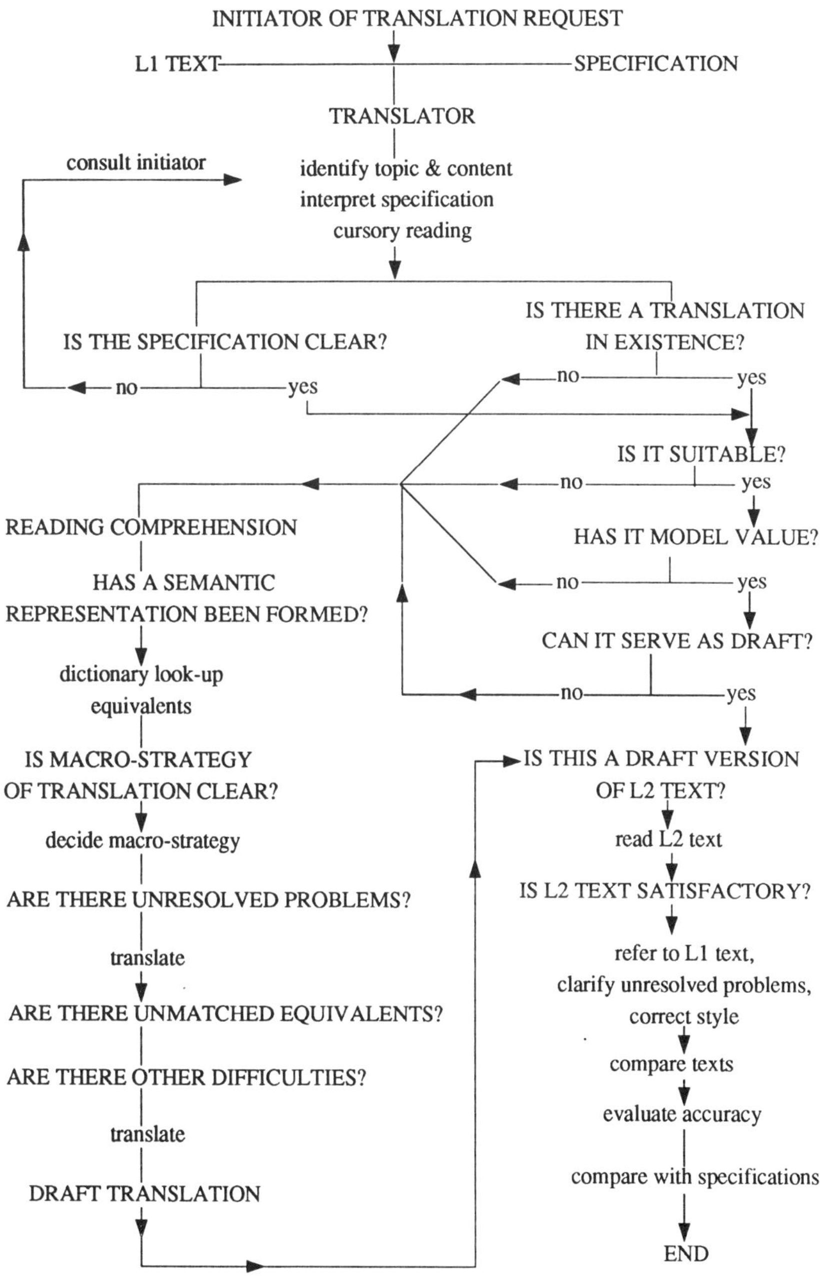

Figure 8.3 *A flow chart of decisions in the translation process*

If the ambiguity is judged to be accidental, an attempt has to be made to resolve it as part of the text modification task, unless it is considered to be a positive value of the text. This could be the case in texts of belles lettres, political discourse etc.

If the ambiguity is judged to be deliberate, translators are faced with a number of possibilities to be resolved in a number of ways.

For ambiguity arising from the SL:

(a) the ambiguity is resolved, if it is felt that it improves the text;
(b) the ambiguity is preserved by finding an equally matching one in the TL; this is not a very common solution;
(c) the ambiguity is resolved because it cannot be preserved but an attempt is made to recreate a similar opaqueness of expression through the introduction of — preferably the same type — or another type of ambiguity elsewhere in the text.

For ambiguity arising in the TL, i.e. in the case where an unambiguous statement in the SL would produce an ambiguous statement in the TL:

(a) the translation is modified to the extent of avoiding ambiguity; this may require as little as adding a gender-specific pronoun or a repetition of a noun, an adverb clarifying the modal status of an utterance etc.;
(b) the ambiguity is admitted because it is not distracting or offensive within the special subject context in which it is found;
(c) the reader is offered an explanation, in the text or in the form of a footnote, of the difficulty and given the possible interpretations and their translations.

Without a specification, telling in which direction to work, translators can choose any of these methods for resolving difficulties. In practice, however, translators are directed by the knowledge they have of the end users of the text. The interpretation of the specifications will, therefore, provide translators and mediators with the necessary criteria to choose among the several possibilities indicated above.

Ambiguities judged to have been introduced accidentally into a text are usually eliminated, unless the text is considered to be of such importance that such an interpretation has to be excluded. If the authority of the SL text precludes an interpretation of an ambiguity as 'accidental', translators are entirely dependent upon the specification or a consultation with the commissioner of the translation about the course of action to be taken.

Most cases of ambiguity fall into the category of ambiguity in general reference which is resolvable in subject-specific interpretation of the text; e.g. 'climbing roses', 'climbing boots'. It is equally common to resolve an ambiguity judged to be deliberate in the text, simply because the readership of the TL does not expect it.

Literature is a special case. In a literary text translators traditionally have the choice of translation in the conventional sense, paraphrasing, adapting and finally annotating a text, thus providing a multiple interpretation. In full translation of literary works it is generally accepted that translators can only provide one possible version, both because of their limitations as interpreters and readers of the text and because of their limitations as writers. In the same way as we accept several critical interpretations and commentaries of a literary work as being, on the whole, complementary and in their totality constituting the 'meaning/significance' of the work in question, we can accept that multiple translations of a literary work, constitute the meaning/significance of that work. This position makes translation of literature theoretically possible, and indeed justifies it as a valid enterprise of elucidation of texts and a valuable cultural activity. Multiple translations of the Bible can also be justified in this way, i.e. as an attempt to come closer to the 'true' or 'full' meaning. Preservation of ambiguity is desirable in persuasive texts, that are built on a certain playfulness of language, (the ludic function of language).

The resolution of ambiguities is not identified here as a separate step in the process of translation because it overlaps both reading-understanding where some cases of ambiguity are first noted, and the search for equivalents which shows up interlingual ambiguity and potential ambiguity in the target language. The active resolution itself takes place at the stage of matching because it is here where the results of any decisions on resolution become visible and can be tested for their effects.

8.3 Search for equivalents

The concept of equivalence between cognitive units which are expressed linguistically can be approached in various ways. An abstract concept of equivalence can be postulated and broken down into component features so that a source and a target language lexical unit are reduced to their basic conceptual components and that the relationship between these components becomes clear. For example, the words 'horse', 'cheval', 'Pferd' etc. can be reduced to their scientific denotation as'quadruped Equidae of the family Equus L.', thereby excluding associations of use or emotive connotations. The concept of equivalence can also be attached to functional units of speech, which can be as large as whole utterances for which identical situational parameters exist. The most striking example of this form are multilingual notices which direct, enjoin, prohibit, permit etc. the same thing to all language users who find themselves in the situation referred to. The conceptual identity can then be demonstrated by the instances in which linguistically expressed signs are replaced by another semiotic code, as for example, in the many sign in international airports which do not use language, but only drawings.

Units of translation and the search for equivalents for these units lie at the heart of any theoretical or practical discussion about translation. But, just as units of translation are flexible and a matter of cognitive and linguistic factors, there are many types of equivalence (see section 5.5) the choice of which is determined by cognitive, pragmatic as well as purely linguistic factors.

We summarise here the basic assumptions about the concept of equivalence, explained in section 5.5, which alone make it relevant for translation, namely:

(a) more or less the same, i.e. equivalent, content arising from one culture is expressible in the language evolved by another culture;
(b) different language systems are sufficiently flexible so that they can express content transferred from another culture, in what can be considered to be equivalent linguistic forms;
(c) translations are guided by norms which establish permitted ranges of matches at conceptual and linguistic levels. The most commonly accepted equivalents at the lexical level are recorded in bilingual dictionaries. Document and situation-specific equivalents and correspondences are recorded in specialised glossaries.

In a static 'product' view of translation, the criteria for determining equivalence are established exclusively in relation to the source language text; in a dynamic 'process' view, they are moderated by the specifications which decide the status of the target language document (see Figure 6.4), and with it the importance of one type of equivalence or another. The important difference of the dynamic view is that it is both wider and narrower, ranging from full identity, e.g. in parallel legal texts, to situational adequacy according to the specifications and the status of the new document. In addition, the dynamic view includes translators, who in the search for equivalents, are limited by their understanding of the document and their command of target language forms, which put practical constraints on their work.

In autonomous documents, as well as in reduced and selective translation, there is a general requirement of equivalent cognitive content. Equivalence is therefore only pursued to the extent required by the conditions of the text type to be created, which are usually laid down in target language rules of writing in general or according to certain specific precepts. In translations with different functions only a very loose concept of parallelism of cognitive content may be pursued while equivalence of the linguistic expression is superseded by the requirements of the text type chosen for the changed purpose. Because translators work from the basis of a source text, there will be some lexical equivalence but even here the requirements of text modification predominate over those of translation. In summarising or abstracting translations, for example, there is a systematic shift required from the specific to the generic which overrides any concern for linguistic equivalence. At the other extreme, translations with full equal status already stipulate full intentional and cognitive identity in the specifications as well as very close linguistic correspondence at the word, phrase and sentence level. For such translations there are usually already models and norms provided by the bi- or multilingual society which demands this type of documentation. Where such norms of equivalences do not exist, they are determined, or have to be determined, by mutual agreement between the respective linguistic communities as a whole. Caught in such unprecedented situations, i.e. situations without a clear precedent of equivalents or previous translation models for the creation of correspondences, translators can only interpret the linguistic norm and seek external guidance; the social norm which sanctions and consolidates the equivalence, is created by others. In these cases, translators can then only have an advisory role because there is no room for the interim solution of a translation equivalent, which is permitted in other types of translation. A convincing example of this case are the regular meetings of lawyers and linguists in the institutions of the European Community to discuss and formulate the multilingual versions of EC legislation so that they becomes acceptable in the members states while still maintaining their cognitive and intentional identity.

This leaves the large field of dependent and derived documents with equal intention for which equivalence poses both theoretical and practical problems; these are solved by one of the methods described below.

In searching for equivalents, translators are faced with the difficulties of (i) comprehension caused by psychological factors of understanding, (ii) cultural interference and (iii) maintaining the balance between the effect the text has on them as recipients and readers of a SL document and their intention as producers of TL messages.

This balance — the essence of translators' intuition and know-how — is, however, the precondition for the successful creation of the three general types of equivalence.

(a) Pragmatically, successful implementation of equivalence is a matter of knowledge of text types and the correct interpretation of the specifications.
(b) Cognitively, successful implementation of equivalence depends on translators' knowledge of the subject matter of the document. Since cognitive equivalence is only measurable via its linguistic expression, it can only be assessed as part of linguistic equivalence.
(c) Linguistically, there are two ways of considering the attainment of equivalence:
— We can say that full equivalence is achieved when equivalents are interchangeable in a given situation. This condition can only be tested by means of comparison with other translations of the same document and therefore subjective factors of interpretations are also involved.
— We can assert equivalence as a relative value by defining it as an approximation between two messages. Because of the characteristics of natural language, perfect equivalence, in the sense that a message evokes identical responses in the speakers of the two languages, is theoretically impossible, and in practice, only attainable in brief pragmatic messages. (see also 5.5.).
— A third approach is to let normative criteria dominate, by establishing conditions of equivalence prior to actual translation and to measure achievement against such predetermined values of equivalence. In some cases the simple norm of a bilingual dictionary is often considered to be a valid measure.

8.3.1 *Units of equivalence*

In our judgement of what is a cognitive equivalent in any one document, translators are guided by, and generally refer to, the prior existence of such equivalents between two cultures, which have been recorded in grammars and in dictionaries. But grammars tend to be over-permissive of constructions, and bilingual dictionaries, by preference, concentrate on the smallest units, i.e. words, whereas translators must fit constructions into the text, and therefore prefer to work with larger units. They must, in addition, decide for themselves which semantic aspects or possible meanings of a linguistic item are required in the context.

In their judgement of linguistic units of equivalence translators must, according to the translation technique chosen, take into account, or ignore, that

(a) linguistic form systems differ because they are the result of different historical evolutions, e.g. the association of certain personal forms of the verbal conjugation with polite forms of address;

(b) linguistic forms themselves, beside their denotation of reference, can have additional meanings which may not have an equivalent in another linguistic system, e.g. the political and emotive connotations of colour adjectives.

When a conflict arises between units of equivalence at the content level and at the formal or linguistic level, translators must decide which is more important.

The size of units of linguistic equivalence translators operate with is decided by the technique chosen. It can be established at the level of the text or the message, or at the lower levels of the sentence, phrase or word. Vinay & Darbelnet provide the linguistically correct definition of translation units when they speak of the smallest segment of discourse the cohesion of which is so strong that the parts cannot be separated (''le plus petit segment de l'enoncé dont la cohésion des signes est telle qu'ils ne doivent pas être traduits séparément''. Vinay & Darbelnet 1968: 37). A special type of unit are proverbs and sayings in which the same sentiment is expressed by quite different associations. For example, the Spanish ''A quien madruga Dios le ayuda'' can be taken as a full equivalent for ''God helps those who help themselves'', whereas the English ''The early bird catches the worm'' can be considered an equivalent for the German ''Morgenstund hat Gold im Mund''.

In practice, as we have seen in section 8.1, translators work with translation units that suit their cognitive capacity and establish equivalences at this level or as close to it as possible. Translators are, of course, aware of the fact that messages are the ultimate units of meaning for which equivalence has to be established, but, as Baker rightly observes: ''meaning is realised through form and without understanding the meanings of individual forms, one cannot interpret the meaning of the text as a whole'' (Baker 1992:6).

The size of the text segments for which translators have to find equivalents also depends on the nature of the document. In certain documents the entire text represents a unit, e.g. a preformulated pattern of a multilingual certificate, into which certain items are inserted (Hatim & Mason 1990). In others, units can coincide with syntactic units or may have to consist of individual words. There are particular difficulties associated with the segmentation of noun phrases in technical texts into terminological units as opposed to free syntagmatic combinations.

8.4 Translation techniques

Units of equivalence lie at the heart of many theoretical statements about translation techniques. One of the most developed of these was presented by Vinay & Darbelnet (1968) when they defined stages of increased complexity of equivalents. Their categories are adopted here because they seem to be widely recognised.

According to these authors equivalence can be established at the word or expression level by the following techniques:

— Borrowing, i.e. direct taking over of words from the source language; this technique can be used for culture-specific items or for items for which there is not likely to be a TL equivalent, or for effect; e.g. haute couture, dolce vita, tequila, Wanderlust.

— Loan translation or calque, i.e. by word for word translation of the constituents of an expression; this technique is used for new terms or for stylistic reasons and permits simple changes of word order; e.g. La perfide Albion > perfidious Albion; the title 'Secretary General' which is formed according to the French language sequence of noun followed by adjective.

— Literal translation, i.e. word by word matching, which is possible in some cognate languages; e.g. 'I accuse' from the French 'j'accuse'; 'I came, I saw, I conquered' from the Latin 'veni, vidi, vici'.

Larger units usually require what Vinay and Darbelnet call recasting of thought, which is carried out by a variety of changes, classified by these authors as follows:

— Transposition, which they define as a form of syntactic paraphrase or alternative linguistic formulation, which obviously affects the TL syntax.
(NOTE: The following examples are expressed as alternative forms produced by transposition in English rather than in another language which some readers may not understand).
Examples:

noun > preposition: Sender=From (at the back of an envelope)
noun > verb: After devaluation=after the currency has been devalued
No Entry=Do not enter
With the loss of=Losing....
verb > noun: When he arrived=Upon arrival he...
adj. > noun: In the early hours of the morning=at dawn
adv. > verb: Little by little he tired=he grew tired

— Modulation, which is defined as semantic paraphrase. Lexical modulation helps to overcome differences in the semantic structures between SL and TL. In general language it is easy to find synonymous expressions, but in specialist discourse the exact term for the conceptual equivalent is expected. Modulation is often used improperly when translators do not know the precise expression and attempt to get over this difficulty by a paraphrase.

Examples:

tooled leather = raised leather,
firewood = wood for heating,
shooting party = hunting party,
note book = exercise book,
wall cabinet = hanging cupboard,
cheap = inexpensive, easily affordable

Other modes of modulation are to change from abstract to concrete, from cause to effect, changes in form/aspect/use and change of geographical reference.

— Equivalence, i.e. to look for parallel values of expression, a technique which changes the reference of a situation and affects collocations, proverbs, standard phraseology etc., so that the meaning of metaphors, for example, can be translated into different metaphors.

Example:

a house of cards = hollow triumph
castles in Spain = fantasies = castles in the air
my cup of tea = something preferred

— Adaptation, i.e. a pragmatic paraphrase, a technique suggested for changing cultural reference. If the SL text uses a specific term with a general meaning, it may be possible to create a TL analogy. An example of adaptation would be to equate the national sport of cricket in England with baseball in the United States or football in Italy. Adaptation also covers the substitution of idioms or proverbs which convey the same basic meaning.

— Explanation, i.e. making explicit what is implicit in the SL text.

(a) semantic explicitation, i.e. expressing something previously implied, for example replacing a pronoun with a proper noun, or replacing a metaphor with a simile, thereby making the comparison explicit, or adding an explanation;

(b) syntactic explicitation, i.e. such processes as filling in ellipsis of relative pronouns or verbs, adding conjunctions etc.

— Allusion, i.e. selective adaptation, as for example, by only partly translating dialect.

Wilss (1975) summarises these techniques into two broad types, 'word substitution' and 'paraphrase' with a smaller number of subtypes, listed in Figure 8.4, thereby excluding Vinay & Darbelnet's techniques of adaptation, explanation etc. from his narrower perception of approaches to translation. These techniques can either be considered to be expansions of the technique of modulation or be explained as arising from an intuitive rephrasing of the source text by translators who cannot automatically establish a direct match.

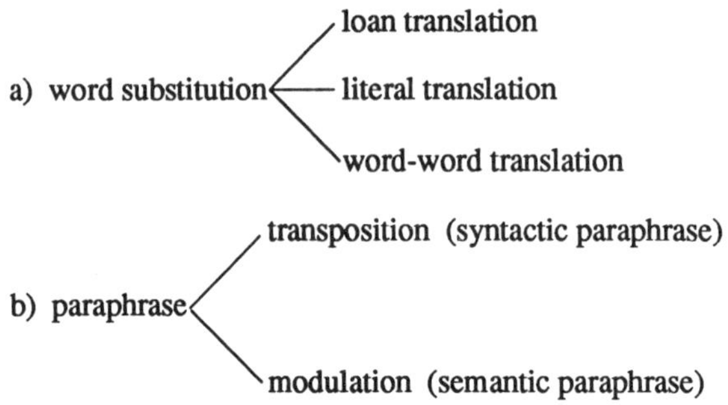

Figure 8.4 *Wilss' translation techniques*

Reiss (1990) also identifies 'paraphrase' as a generic technique under which she classifies some global approaches to translation, i.e. 'literal', 'communicative', 'philological' and 'editing', which she characterises as consisting of particular combinations of specific techniques (see Figure 8.5). In the process, she adds the new supplementary techniques of 'commentary' and 'annotation' which have to be acknowledged as important techniques in the more flexible view of translation adopted here.

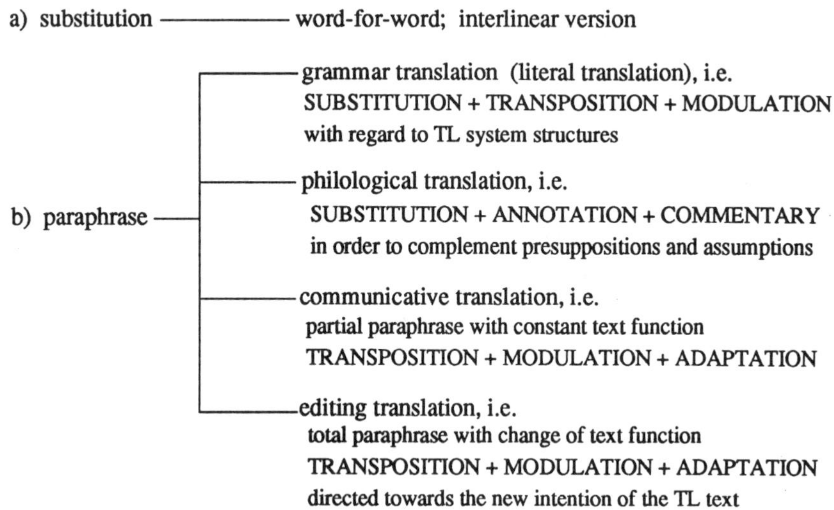

Figure 8.5 *Reiss' translation techniques*

The translation technique chosen in each case is finally also a matter of judgment, because there are cases where there are no recognisable equivalents within the particular subsystem of the grammar or dictionary. In such a case the limitations of pre-established descriptions in contrastive grammars and dictionaries provide a fall-back position and the translator's skill of compensating for unachieved equivalence comes into play.
As time goes by, translators build up their own store of equivalent units in parallel with their increasing familiarity with the subject. e.g. for phrases of business letters, legal formulations or journalistic jargon translators have ready stores of matching expressions and do not require lengthy reflection. Whether the successful establishment of equivalence is more likely to be triggered off by a cognitive unit than by a linguistic surface form is a matter for research.

8.5 Matching

The process of searching for equivalents is confirmed through matching a source language unit with an appropriate target language unit. In conventional perceptions of 'translation', matching is obligatory for certain linguistic units; otherwise the process would be called paraphrasing.
Obligatory matching is expected for lexical items through the recognition of semantic units; syntactic matching is expected for sentence units through the recognition of sentence patterns. These are also the only levels most amateurs consider the ones involved in translation. The other levels are more or less expected in certain techniques and certain types of documents, especially in literary translation. These are: the rhetorical level, where modes of argumentation are recognised, e.g. irony, hyperbole, etc.; the ideological level, where idiosyncrasies, including sound associations are treated; and the aesthetic level.

All analysis of text has to be performed at the lexical and syntactic levels (see section 7.3). Some translation processes stop there and then produce target language text by simply matching the units identified. In practice, units identified as matches at one level must, in turn, be adjusted to the requirements of a match at a higher level, i.e. the choice of a word may be influenced by the requirements of matching syntactic patterns. Syntactic sequencing, in turn, may be influenced by rhetorical considerations.

The 'perfect' translation matches one by one at every level, but this can occur with simple texts only. It is possible to match sentences, or one-sentence messages, but even there we encounter limitations. It is obvious that rhetorically and pragmatically 'RAUCHEN VERBOTEN' is an exact match to 'PROHIBIDO FUMAR', 'NO SMOKING', or 'DEFENSE DE FUMER' but lexically and especially syntactically, these expressions are quite different. From these examples one might conclude that matching at the rhetorical and pragmatic levels takes precedence over matching at the lexical and syntagmatic levels. The reality of running text seldom permits such neat solutions.

8.5.1 *Lexical matching*

At the denotative lexical level simple matches are given in dictionaries and in such documents as schedules, which do not have syntactic structures, e.g. parts lists, etc. In normal situations, however, semantic matching of several types of meaning has to be considered, i.e. denotative and connotative meaning, at least; for example, 'dove' may have the connotations of 'loving', 'pure' or 'peaceful' 'peace-loving, conciliatory' and 'sacrificial' which its synonym 'pigeon' has not.

More complex is the question of collocational meaning, because translators have to interpret degrees and shades of meaning from context. For example, 'corrupt' in association with 'ruler' may simply mean 'bad' or 'exerting corrupting influences', or 'corrupted'. 'Rotten' in 'rotten egg' may have to be taken figuratively or simple as 'inedible'. Collocations have a syntagmatic and a paradigmatic dimension. For example, semantic fields have to be matched rather than single expressions.

Other meanings to be considered are:

— Stylistic meaning, e.g. passed away, died, deceased

— Implicative meaning, i.e. meaning which is implied, presupposed, reflected or contextual

— Sentence meaning vs. utterance meaning.

8.5.2 *Syntactic matching*

Here we are concerned with sentence structure in general, rather than word order. In related languages it is usually possible to match according to the logical or functional structure of a sentence.

8.5.3 *Pragmatic matching*

The previous discussion of text types has already clarified what is meant by pragmatic matching at the highest level. Within functional text types, matching is concerned with thematization strategies and textual cohesion.

8.5.4 *The need for pre-established matches*

In an industrial environment where most activities are subject to some form of regularisation, there is a strong need to go beyond the matches proposed in dictionaries. This need is most strongly perceived in situations subject to standardisation of manufactured goods and processes. Industrial standards are created if, for a variety of economic reasons, it is felt desirable to achieve identity or compatibility of the measurements, quality, types of performance, tolerance and safety in industry or other human spheres of endeavour. In order to communicate the results of standardisation it is then essential to designate the new standardised product or process by a new name which becomes firmly associated with measurable and clearly defined properties, i.e. the semantic reference characteristics or features of artificial languages. The name of a standardised object is therefore entirely artificial and can only be used correctly for other objects with exactly the same characteristics. Standardised names with their peculiar reference to identically defined objects, therefore occupy a special place between the individualising proper names and multifunctional general words.

In particular cases manufacturers set their own limitations and develop what can only be described as their own, functionally limited, restricted language. For example, the engineers employed in the Technical Publications Department of Perkins Power Sales and Services in England found that their workshop manuals, aimed at the competent mechanic, benefited from being written in a 'simplified' form of English. Perkins Approved Clear English (PACE) was introduced in 1980 "for those persons using English instead of their native language and to aid translation, whether traditional or computer-assisted" (Pym 1991:6). Pace was based on ILSAM (the International Language for Service and Maintenance) which in turn was inspired by Caterpillar Fundamental English (CFE) which consists of about 800 words and a body of technical terms. PACE has a dictionary of some 2500 single-denotation words, including some 250 verbs, e.g. 'pass' only means 'to proceed to'. Separate words are chosen for transitive and intransitive verbs; compounds are limited to two, exceptionally to three elements. '-ing' forms are avoided unless specifically sanctioned in the dictionary. The syntax is also severely limited to short sentences, and there are special rules for the conjunctions 'and' and 'or', ellipsis etc.

8.5.5 *Criteria for efficient matching*

In an industrial environment the efficiency of a process of text production, modification or transformation can be evaluated by three simple criteria, namely economy, precision and appropriateness of expression for the intended purpose.

Economy can be established by testing whether the target language text has a higher degree of redundancy than the source language text which cannot be justified by a change in the specification. A language which is maximally economic with respect to its rules, forms and reference can fully exploit a much smaller set of signs and thus require a much smaller repertoire of items. It can also concentrate reference by establishing more complex units of meaning which the users of this language are expected to have acquired before communication.

Lexical precision is guaranteed through the avoidance of unnecessary synonymic variation and of paraphrase where matching lexical items can be found, and through the confinement of types of meaning to the referential. Syntactic precision is established through the restriction of syntactic combinations and their meaning. Where a user can, in case of doubt, refer back to an established source of reference, precision is vastly enhanced. Such a requirement leads to the necessity for translators to be guided by a fully active and complete grammar and dictionary of the target language which satisfies all communicative needs of its users in terms of production of language and interpretation of messages or texts. If, in large translation projects, translators do not observe usage and respond to user needs, there is a danger of the development of variants and ultimately deviations from the target language which undermine the unity and therefore the usefulness of the language.

Appropriateness is achieved by the improved functionality that can be gained if a document is translated in accordance with its specifications.

8.6 Compensation

Existing translation theories are ambivalent about how equivalence is to be determined and recognise differences in the extent to which content and formal equivalence respectively are required for a satisfactory translation.

For units that cannot be matched with normally accepted translation equivalents, the translator has to compensate with alternative forms. These forms of compensation operate at all levels and across all levels of articulation and are usually achieved by a heuristic process. How compensation fits into the process of matching equivalents is illustrated in Figure 8.6.

It is generally accepted that some texts are more 'difficult' to translate than others. The associated matching problems usually derive from differences in the linguistic or the cultural systems of the two languages involved. At the linguistic level there is, in principle, no unsurmountable difficulty because we must assume that any language has or can develop the flexibility to express anything that another language can express. It is, of course, then also obvious that the imposition of linguistic features not normally present in one language, will make the translated text clearly recognisable as a transposition of the characteristics of another linguistic system. For example, untranslatable words are often left in the original, especially in texts where the readers would be already familiar with the meaning of the words in question. Or, detailed time and aspect specification, which in one language is carried out through a combination of verbal inflections and adverbs, may appear clumsy in another language system which expresses time and aspect only adverbially, i.e. a language which is not normally required to give such detail. Similar difficulties occur frequently at the level of definiteness and in the use of the passive.

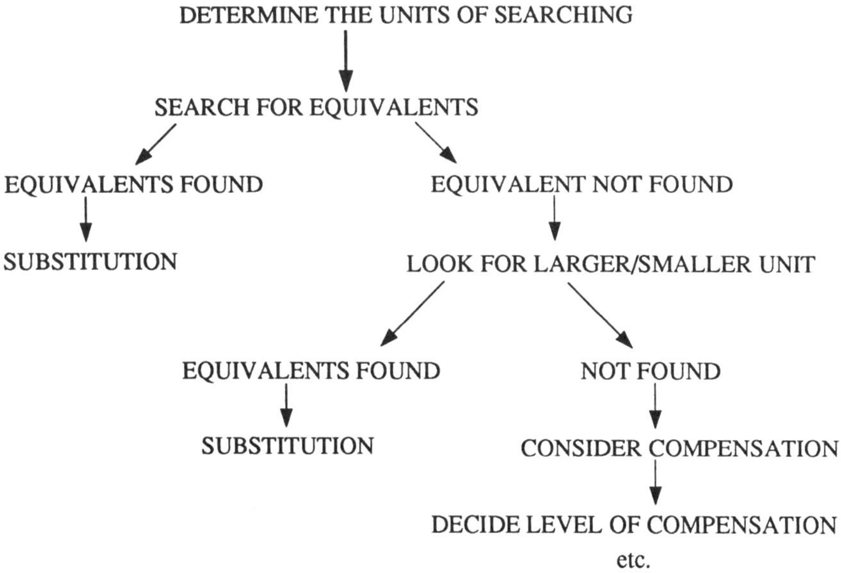

Figure 8.6 *The process of matching equivalents*

In an industrial environment difficulties of translation at the content level usually occur in the following cases:

(a) When concepts are shared between two cultures but the target language lacks a lexical item, equivalence can be achieved by means of:
— literal equivalence, e.g. White House = Casa Blanca;
— descriptive paraphrases, e.g. to sleep an afternoon siesta;
— related words as equivalents; synonyms, doublets;
— use of the generic for the specific, e.g. 'cousin' for a more specific designation of kinship;
— use of secondary and figurative senses.

(b) When concepts expressed in the source language are unknown in the target culture, the problem can only be resolved by the introduction of the new concept into the target culture. There are several techniques for doing this in a translation, some of which are contained in Vinay & Darbelnet's scheme, above. Others require —

— the description of the concept without naming it, e.g. 'one-piece (blue cotton) working clothes' for 'boiler suit';

— the description of the concept in conjunction with the name of the SL, e.g. animals of burden called camels;

— the identification of the concept with an existing one, and the widening of its meaning/reference (without change of name), thereby adding to existing words implicit and/or explicit components of meaning, e.g. a peach-like fruit — a bar-type gauge;

— the formation of a new word according to patterns customary and appropriate for particular subject fields, such as:

- — the creation of compounds, preferably transparent ones, derivatives and the invention of new forms;
- — lexical borrowing, e.g. to drink mate (tea), to cook paella;
- — a loan word or calque, e.g. German 'Fasching or Fastnacht' for English 'carnival' — 'Lisboa' for 'Lisbon';

— modifying a loan word by a classifier, e.g. a bird called 'dove' — the city of Lisboa;

— modifying a loan word by a description of form or function, e.g. 'priest', the person who conducts religious ceremonies; — the Holy city of Rome — the legendary empire of Kubla Khan;

— loan adaptation, e.g. the French Foreign Ministry at the Quai d'Orsay — the siesta hour — siesta time;

— translation of explicative names, e.g. Fronleichnam, or Corpus Christi, the feast of the transsubstantiation of Christ;

— a definition, e.g. the harvest festival in Iceland;

— a generic word together with a descriptive phrase, thereby:

- — making explicit the form of the item, e.g. 'flat' pancakes
- — making explicit the function of the item, e.g. pancakes eaten on Shrove Tuesday
- — making explicit both form and function, e.g. flat pancakes for Shrove Tuesday
- — modifying with a comparison to some thing or event which is known in the TL, e.g. eat pancakes, a habit similar to eating Krapfen or Kraeppel in Germany

— a cultural substitute such as replacing an unknown animal or plant or custom by one known in the target culture, e.g. a red-breasted robin for a red-headed cardinal — morning coffee for merienda — acacia for robinia; — 'God be with you' for a greeting in Arabic or Hebrew.

— anachronistic substitutes, e.g. substituting a metric measure for an imperial measure which is no longer understood.

Whereas in literary translation translators enjoy considerable freedom of compensation for unsuccessful matches, in an industrial setting these problems can seldom be resolved satisfactorily by translators on their own. Optimally, they require agreement at the level of the target language community. In practice, however, translators take ad hoc decisions, unless they have many years of experience of similar problems and regular feedback from clients of what is wanted. There are, of course, cases where the target culture imports whole sets of new terminology to accompany the importation of new technology. When such a situation is controlled by the translation department of a large firm responsible for this new technology, a large number of new terms has to be created for the new concepts that are to be introduced into the target culture. If the new technology imposes itself, it can come about that the translation equivalents created by the translators will eventually become accepted as genuine target language lexical items. In such situations, machine assistance in the creation and control of terminology, e.g. in the form of a term bank, can introduce greater consistency into the individual translators' work and also facilitate consultation inside the community with fellow-translators, language planning agencies, publishers, editors, authors, subject specialists, etc.

Source language words are sometimes preserved in the target language for reasons of snobbery but mostly out of a desire to reproduce local colour. Hence translators may use original forms of address (don, signor), placenames (Roma, Wien), first names (Georges, Pablo) in the spelling of the source language; measurements (pints, hectares); monetary values (dinars, Thaler). Importance is given to foreign elements especially when trying to reflect a situation of intense cultural exchange (e.g. foreigners speaking their own language, & other bilingual situations), when trying to present a foreign culture, or when the source culture differs greatly from the target culture.

When, however, there is a conflict of values between source and target culture concepts, e.g. different ethical or aesthetic values attributed to concepts, the problem is hidden and can only be brought to the surface by the translator. The translator, on the other hand, is not the most suitable person to find a solution to such translation problems because we are dealing with fundamental decisions regarding transfer of knowledge.

Knowledge of cultural differences can help to predict the areas in which such difficulties may occur, and knowledge of the purpose of a translation can provide solutions case by case. For example, the translation of a book on family planning and birth control for a society which has religious objections to such practices can be carried out for two purposes. If it is a translation for the scientific community it can be translated as if it were written in the target language for the same scientific purpose; if it is intended as a guide to social workers to make them aware of developments elsewhere and to sensitize them to these 'new' ideas, the book has to be adapted and this falls outside normal translator competence. This example points out the wider responsibility translators have for collaborating with other specialists who can assist in the work of facilitating intercultural and interlingual communication.

Some of these difficulties are well known since they occur regularly. Missing concepts are identified because of differences in climate, topography, ecology, the presence of natural substances, methods of agriculture, crafts, customs and leisure pursuits, religion, moral values, social structures and institutions, such as the family, legal systems, education, and of course, also artistic manifestations. Even simple descriptions of gestures and facial expressions may require adaptation or explanation in order to be conveyed with their proper meaning. All these problems areas also have a historical dimension which can cause further hesitation. A relatively full treatment of these issues is given in Larson (1984). For the special case of compensation in Bible translation see Beekman, Callow & Kopesec (1974).

8.7 Text production/encoding

In a model of the translation process, text production, though in practice it is the only visible realisation of the previous steps, must be presented separately because a choice of clearly identifiable activities is involved. This process can be defined as conditioned writing, more or less restricted by decisions taken earlier in the process. In principle, it can be carried out simultaneously with matching, or cumulatively when a sufficiently large unit is assembled to give the translator the confidence that a complete syntactic structure can be formulated.

Writing the TL text is variously handled by translators according to the production technique chosen. Modes of encoding are by hand, typewriter, wordprocessor or dictation. The means of encoding chosen, by dictation or writing, decide whether the textual units are encoded phrase by phrase, clause by clause, sentence by sentence or paragraph by paragraph. Particular attention has to be paid to punctuation conventions in different languages where the value of such simple marks as commas, semicolons and colons may not be the same.

Encoding is also the time when non-linguistic material such as drawings, figures and tables that were left aside for translation have to be re-inserted into a document. In some instances this involves translation of captions, conversions of units of measurement and cross references to numbered items in the document.

8.8 Evaluation and revision

When the written, typed or dictated translation has been completed, translators re-read their work, in the light of the job specifications they have received or established themselves, in order to check for omissions, inconsistencies of phrasing, or simply errors of spelling. Two separate processes are involved, (i) relating the new product to its origin and to the specification and (ii) checking the new product for its intrinsic quality or merit. These two processes are not always clearly separated and vary in technique according to textual, pragmatic and personal circumstances. Brief, routine items rarely need this double control; minutes or contracts, on the other hand, may be checked several times by a variety of people before they can be issued in final form (see 6.5.2.). There is also considerable variation of technique between free-lance translators, agency translators and staff translators depending on the degree of confidence or trust that exists between translators, agents, heads of department and end users. For descriptive purposes, the tasks can be divided into:

(a) the control and adjustment usually carried out by translators themselves, which is normally done immediately upon completion of the task;
(b) 'revision', i.e. control and adjustment of content and form which is frequently carried out by others.

8.8.1 *Content comparison and control*

The first process, and the one which is exclusive to translation, is a form of parallel reading of source and target document in order to verify that the content of the source text is reflected in the target text according to the instructions derived from the job specifications. This type of reading may, at one extreme, be a detailed phrase by phrase comparison to ensure the production of full equal documents, or, at a more relaxed level, be as general as checking that the main ideas of the source text have been adequately represented in the second language abstract or gist. In special cases global adjustments may have to be made to expressions, terms, proper names and other special items which during translation were left deliberately open in order to evaluate the final impact.

In the case of routine tasks this work is usually carried out by translators themselves. In other cases other professionals such as lawyers, technical writers or engineers of the target culture may be required to read and comment on the acceptability of the new document. The evaluation phase is also used in some cases to obtain clarification from the author of the document about ambiguities or inconsistencies that have been found and which, after evaluation, require external resolution. In literary translation, for example, it is mainly at this stage that translators contact the author to propose global solutions to cultural problems that affect the acceptability of the text in the target culture.

Once the process of comparison has been completed, any further adjustment is virtually the same as for any other form of text production, in which the emphasis is on the target text. Adjustments of content are made in view of the specifications of the task. Adjustments are reflected in expression form and can be considered as part of the revision process.

8.8.2 *Revision*

Revision can be defined as a process of control of document production for accuracy, completeness, stylistic appropriateness, etc. and the necessary modification of the translation product. It applies equally to all manner of documents and all manner of previous text modification. In practice, where the previous stage of evaluation has been omitted, revision is also concerned with accuracy and completeness in terms of the source document.

Revision is concerned with form at all levels. It starts with spelling, moves to punctuation, then to paragraphing, and finally, to layout of the document. The importance of this function may be shown by the fact that some organisations are said to have one revisor for every two translators. This would signify that revision regularly constitutes one third of the total translation effort. An internal study related to the introduction of text-processing techniques, carried out by a large international organisation, also indicated that approximately half the lines of documents translated in that organisation required some revision and that there were then 2.5 corrections per line. It was concluded that even a saving in retyping half of all documents, which could be made through the introduction of word processors, would represent a considerable economy in time and cost.

Revision can be carried out in three modes: by translators themselves, by revisors or automatically. Computer technology now provides assistance with revision in the form of spelling and style checkers. They are useful for general purposes, but they are generally still too unsophisticated to be used entirely without human intervention. Especially in the case of translation, where there may be a higher incidence of loan words, calques and other items not contained in spelling dictionaries, caution is required in the use of spelling checkers.

Many translators carry out their own revisions and prepare the document for final presentation. In special cases, e.g. book translation, publishers employ independent readers who check the text for interferences from source language expressions. Such readers simply mark sections of text which in their opinion do not conform to target language usage, so that the translator can decide whether the form should be adjusted or not.

In most large translation departments there is a separate group of revisors who control all translations before they are sent out to clients. The control of translators' work by a rank-superior is a normal expectation in any hierarchically structured job environment. It is particularly important in large organisations with a steady turnover of staff. Revisors thus fulfil a training function for junior translators and help newly-employed experienced translators adjust to a new environment.

Though revision is seen as a single process of text improvement, as described in section 4.4, it serves various separate functions. It is usually also accompanied by stylistic modification of the text according to the revisors' personal idiosyncrasies of expression. The specific purposes of revision can be itemised as follows:

(a) Control of the accuracy of translation equivalents, including control of the completeness of a translation, e.g. omissions.
(b) Quality control of style, e.g. for eliminating anglicisms, gallicisms, and other form of source language interference which can creep into a text.
(c) Restoring written language characteristics in texts which were dictated.

These three functions can also be carried out by translators themselves, if they can return to their work after a reasonable interval of time. The intervention of another reader eliminates this time requirement.

(d) Harmonisation of texts by a single author translated by different translators and long texts shared out among various translators. This is a very important function for all manner of documents which require unity of terminology, expression and style. While term banks and reference to archives of previously translated texts can provide some assistance in the pursuit of consistency, the role of the revisor as the representative of the human end user cannot be ignored.
(e) Adjusting the translation product to a particular level or style of expression characteristic of the organisation. It is this revision function which is the most controversial. While it is recognised that outgoing documents may be required to be written in a particular house-style, in many other situations a revisor's stylistic rephrasing of a document may be detrimental because it can lead to a recognisable two-author document of what was clearly a single author original. It can also unnecessarily increase the cost of translation and furthermore lead to stress for the translators who find their

phrasings being revised simply because they differ from that preferred by a revisor. If revisors work to a generally agreed style, whether expressed explicitly in a manual or tacitly understood, translators can be expected to acquire this housestyle. If translators regularly work with the same revisors they can adjust their mode of expression to that preferred by the revisors, so that this aspect of revision work becomes minimalised or unnecessary. If, however, as often happens in large organisations, translators work for several revisors and/or if translator do not know who will revise the translation, they cannot write to expectation, as the phrasing preferred by one revisor may be deprecated by another. This uncertainty can lead to frustration for translators or, even worse, to indifference, since they may feel that their work will be amended in any case. It must also be recognised that a document that exhibits the stylistic preferences of a particular revisor is not necessarily better than one which exhibits those of a translator. In recognition of these difficulties some organisations have created a class of senior translators who are responsible for their own revisions.

8.8.3 *Criteria for evaluation*

In its simplest form traditional evaluation worked with the concept of 'error' of translation. Various levels are generally identified, e.g. three levels of gravity of error: distortion of sense, omission and minor errors such as stylistic infelicity, orthographic error etc. House (1977) proposes three types of "overtly erroneous errors", namely, omissions, additions and substitutions which she subdivides into wrong selection and wrong combination. These she calls denotational errors, beside which she recognises system errors, such as ungrammaticality and unacceptability. The class of covert errors would then include the mismatch of situational dimensions.

A more elaborate, but still traditional, system worked with five classes of error which were further identified as being either lexical or syntactic, as follows:

— reversal of meaning or 'contresens'
— omission of elements of content or 'non-sens'
— addition of elements of content or over-translation
— deviation or distortion of meaning inside the topic or 'faux sens'
— incompleteness or under-translation.

The distinction between these last two types of error is not clear. Distortion may be interpreted as simply a milder form of reversal of meaning, or as the wrong selection of an equivalent. Incompleteness may be interpreted as a partial omission.

A slightly more sophisticated system of counting errors is to differentiate between structural errors and part of speech errors. The first approach would require identifying structural units of a source text and assess their adequate rendering by equivalent structures at some level or other. Within structural units, parts of speech can be identified and their rendering checked to get a finer identification of error. It is, of course, difficult to decide what represents an adequate match inside a verb group, a noun group, complements or attributes. In the second case it would have to be assumed that there are fully matching lexical equivalents for the language pair being translated, which is perhaps possible in some technical registers of cognate languages of a similar degree of technical development, but hardly likely beyond that.

Larose (1989) discusses a detailed evaluation system developed by the translation department of the Canadian Federal Government. Gouadec (1981, 1982) also develops a complex system of error identification, the principle of which is that errors have parameters which are weighted by their origins and nature in a text. He proposes to distinguish between lexical and syntactic errors. Specific parameters of an error are the level of the part of the sentence or text affected by the error, the role of the affected part in the sentence, and the significance of the affected part in the communication as a whole. A simple orthographic error, e.g. in the form of another word, can affect all three parameters. A lexical item may be a connecting element, i.e. may have a major syntactic function, a secondary function, e.g. as a modifier, or be a grammatical element which is redundant as far as content is concerned. In its syntactic function an error may disturb the relation between two equal elements, or unequal elements, e.g. subject-verb, adverb-verb. The gravity of the error is further dependent on the importance the erroneous element has in the document. It may affect the central argument of a paragraph, or a supporting argument which widens or narrows the main statement. Less serious are errors in sentences or phrases which serve only as an expansion, explanation, definition, or exemplification of an argument. Errors in modality may have a significant pragmatic effect and thereby distort or falsify the intention of a message. Finally there are errors which only affect phatic elements of a text and these are unimportant from a communicative point of view. A final assessment of the importance of the error can be made in the degree of disturbance suffered by the communication with regard to its information content, its intention, or its effect.

To sum up, it can be said that in professional practice, there are two perspectives of error evaluation. An absolute evaluation assesses an individual translator's precision and can serve a didactic function because a major omission is obviously more serious than a spelling error. A relative evaluation assesses the translation product and decides what, if any, amendments have to be carried out. At the same time, in professional translation, as distinct from translation exercises as part of language learning, it is accepted that it is the effect of the error and not the error itself which decides the gravity of the professional negligence.

These refinements of the methods of quality evaluation are, on the one hand, too complex to be developed into a practical tool for quality control, and on the other, still not sufficiently practical, because they do not consider time and cost factors which strongly influence the degree of quality that can be obtained in any form of document production.

Much simpler methods can be applied when economic considerations are the reason for evaluation. The amount of time spent on re-reading and revision, by the translator or a revisor, is an indication both of the volume and of the gravity of errors. Alternatively, counting the words corrected in relation to the total number of words of a document can be performed automatically and give an indication of the additional time required in the final stage of the translation process. It is, of course, a well known fact that revisors have different perceptions of what they want to correct and that they tend to over-correct when they know that their work is being measured in some way.

8.9 Presentation

The final stage of the industrial process, the presentation of the final document, is often overlooked in theoretical descriptions. Among translators, however, a great deal of attention is paid to the finishing aspects of the task. With the availability of a great diversity of text editing and processing facilities, clients can, and do, demand a high quality of presentation, and translators can now include in their offer of services varying grades of quality of the endproduct which are adjusted to the ultimate format in which the commissioner of the translation wants to reach one or several types of end users.

A specification may thus include several forms of endproduct. For example, a publisher may require camera-ready copy on 'art' or other special paper and, at the same time, a diskette in ASCII format for the archive and for possible later revision and new editions. Alternatively, especially in the case of work done by different translators, the result may be required in a particular word-processing format for editorial processing by a publisher, so that full uniformity of the text can be assured. Translation departments of large organisations also recognise grades of quality of presentation which are identified by such labels as 'printer's copy', 'fair copy', 'draft' and 'rough copy'. Translation companies, and especially freelance translators, usually work to the client's format and layout, and often even use paper specified or supplied by the client for the final version.

Chapter Five

The Automated Dimension of Translation

9 Human and Machine Translation

As soon as alternative methods of translation, i.e. by humans and by machines are available, the consequences of a choice between human and machine translation and the stages in the process at which this choice can be exercised become relevant for the industrial environment of translation. This section attempts to compare human and machine translation from several points of view in order to establish the completely different nature of the tasks and consequently the different translation products. These possibilities are indicated in Figure 9.1.

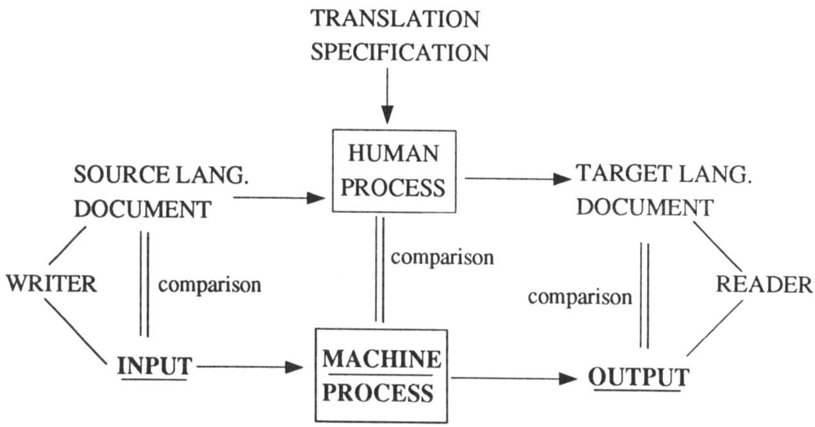

Figure 9.1 *Modes of comparing the human and the MT process*

In any comparison of human and machine translation it is also important to remember that there are several types of human translation techniques and consequently also several types of translation products. These are based on different specifications and theoretical positions; it is therefore reasonable to assume that a theory of machine translation should also make provision for such a diversity and postulate the existence of several models for different MT translation techniques and final products which may or may not match human products. These alternatives, which are, in fact, already an industrial reality, lead to a more complex model of translation and hence of translation evaluation.

9.1 Modes of comparison

Several modes of comparison can be considered, only some of which are productive of greater insights into translation or significant for a general theory of translation. In order to make sensible comparisons, the basis of comparison must be methodologically useful and pragmatically substantive.

(a) Firstly, the human and machine processes of translation can be examined for their potential comparative value. Such a comparison is only useful if we believe that machines can be constructed in imitation of or in analogy to human processes, which, on present evidence, is not likely to be the case. However, by breaking down the human process into modules, an attempt can be made to resolve the hermeticism of the process and so identify the separate steps that in some way or other have to be accomplished by machines. Some small benefit may conceivably also be derived from attempting to model parts of the human process on the computer in order to gain greater insights into how human translators work.

Knowledge about the respective stages of the two processes and their intersections is also necessary for making effective decisions about choices of alternative methods and, indeed, about the design of new, and especially mixed, often called 'interactive', methods of translation. In Figure 9.2 the known stages of a conventional model of a machine translation system are related to the steps and stages of the human process, described in sections six to eight; the corresponding steps of a general MT model are developed more fully in section 10.

(b) Secondly, there is the comparison of products. Since the end-user wants a usable translation, irrespective of the process by which it is achieved, a comparison of products would appear to be justified so that the two types of products can be assessed by the independent criterion of 'appropriateness for the intended communicative purpose'. By combining such an evaluation with time and cost considerations, it should then be possible to decide on optimal methods for different jobs. From a practical point of view, therefore, a comparison of products is important so that, by relating the various measurements of quality to cost and effort, a reasoned

Human →		← Machine
Sequence of process	*Stage*	*Process*
SL TEXT		
IDENTIFICATION OF TEXT TYPE IDENTIFICATION OF INTENTION INTERPRETATION OF SPECIFIC. →	OUTLINE OF TASK	
CURSORY READING OF TEXT →	OUTLINE OF ARGUMENT	PRELIMINARY TEXT PROCESSING POSSIBLE
CHOICE OF TL TEXT TYPE →	IMAGE OF TL TEXT TYPE	← START OF MT
CHOICE OF TRANSLATION TECHNIQUE →	WORKPLAN	
		CHOICE OF SYSTEM
READING COMPREHENSION →	SEMANTIC REPRESENT.	PRELIMINARY DICT. LOOK-UP MORPHOL. ANALYSIS
LOOK-UP AS NEEDED →	id.	SYNTACTIC ANALYSIS
MATCHING EQUIVALENTS →	TL PHRASES & CLAUSES	DICTIONARIES
COMPENSATION OF EQUIVALENTS →	id.	
TEXT PRODUCTION →	TL DRAFT TEXT	TRANSFER SYNTAC. GENERATION MORPH. GENERATION
EVALUATION OF CONTENT →	id.	
		WORD ORDER RAW OUTPUT
REVISION OF FORM →	TL TEXT/ MESSAGE ←	POST-EDITING

Figure 9.2 *The sequences of the human and machine processes*

decision becomes possible about the most efficient method by which a text should be made accessible in another language.

In order to be able to compare on a basis of equality, it must be assumed that the MT product is usable in exactly the same way as the human product. It must, therefore, be accepted that, regardless of its method of production, the MT product can have the same functional, i.e. communicative, potential and a similar place in a chain of communication as a humanly produced translation. This condition means that it can either be given directly to an end user, just like a human translation; or be further modified, in the same way as a human translation can be edited and modified to suit a different readership or function; the nature of the modifications will, of course, differ in each case. In order to characterise the distinctive nature of the human modification process of MT-produced texts, the term 'post-editing' has been created. This process is not to be confused with 'revision', as discussed in section 8.8.

(c) The third theoretical possibility is to compare human and machine translation via the input texts in the SL. This approach seems less a separate possibility than a result of the outcome of the two previous approaches, because for any practical comparison of products, the SL text must remain as a constant. If different human end products are to be compared with output from different machines, separate descriptions have to be made for the types of input texts to be used. As a result of a systematic sequence of comparisons it should be possible to establish types of SL texts which are more efficiently handled by machines and to distinguish them from types of texts that are better handled by human labour. Such comparisons can lead to the formulation of guidelines for direct users and translators detailing the optimal use of systems and methods for different types of texts.

The following sections compare and contrast the processes (9.2) and then the products (9.3), to arrive finally at criteria for comparative evaluation (9.4).

9.2 Comparison of the translation processes

For a close comparison of the processes two approaches suggest themselves, one modelled on human activities, the other on the pattern of expert systems developed for computers.

9.2.1 *Translation as problem solving*

While the core of the translation activity is undoubtedly the determination of translation equivalents, this is not a simple semantic linguistic substitution process but can be described as a complex problem-solving exercise in which a problem is defined, analysed with reference to a knowledge base, alternative solutions sought and finally a single choice from among possible solutions put forward as the most satisfactory. The problem is first expressed globally by the translation task as given in the specifications, and then separately for each unit of translation within a document. This part of the process can be explained as occurring in stages of:

(a) SL linguistic de-composition;
(b) problem identification at the SL linguistic and cognitive level;
(c) problem solution at the cognitive and TL linguistic level with reference to a knowledge base;
(d) TL linguistic re-composition.

In such a model the knowledge of the specification affects both the problem-identification and the problem-solving levels. It is supplemented in each case by appropriate additional local knowledge which assists in the solution of the problem. (See also the model by Vernay, presented in section 6.1.1). Figure 9.3 attempts to illustrate such a model.

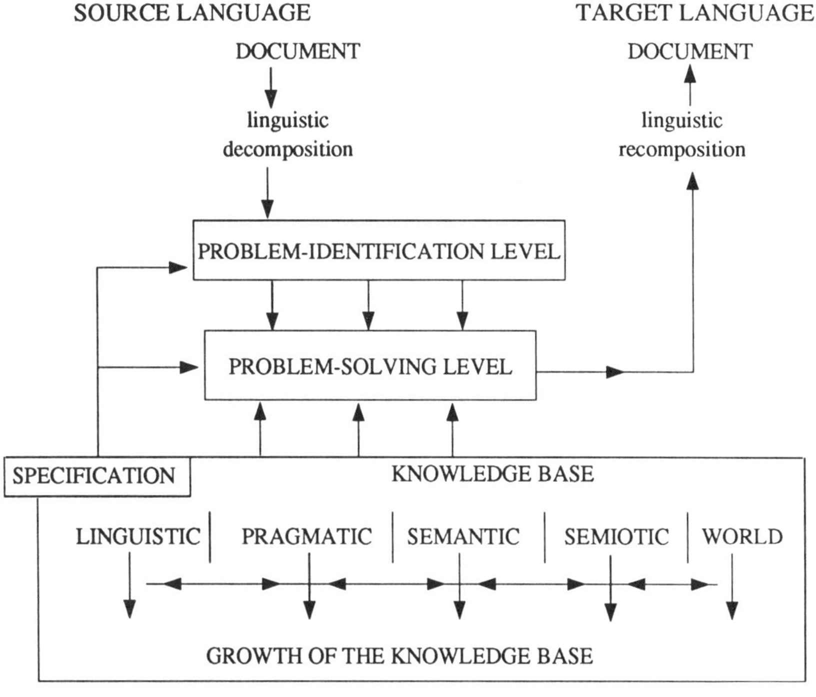

Figure 9.3 *The problem-solving model of human translation*

The human knowledge base is flexible and not strictly compartmentalised. Translators can transfer problems they cannot solve by reference to one form of knowledge to another or re-express a problem in terms of another part of the knowledge base. In fact, a great deal of the human translation process is considered to be intuitive and few translators are capable of rationalising their working methods.

The other characteristic of the translator's knowledge base is that it is constantly expanding as a result of the experience derived from the task of the translation itself. Problem solving therefore becomes easier with greater knowledge (i) as translators advance in a task because previous solutions provide patterns for subsequent ones, (ii) as translators increase their professional experience. There is also the possibility of the fortuitous discovery of a solution by serendipity.

The corresponding MT process in this model is illustrated in Figure 9.4.

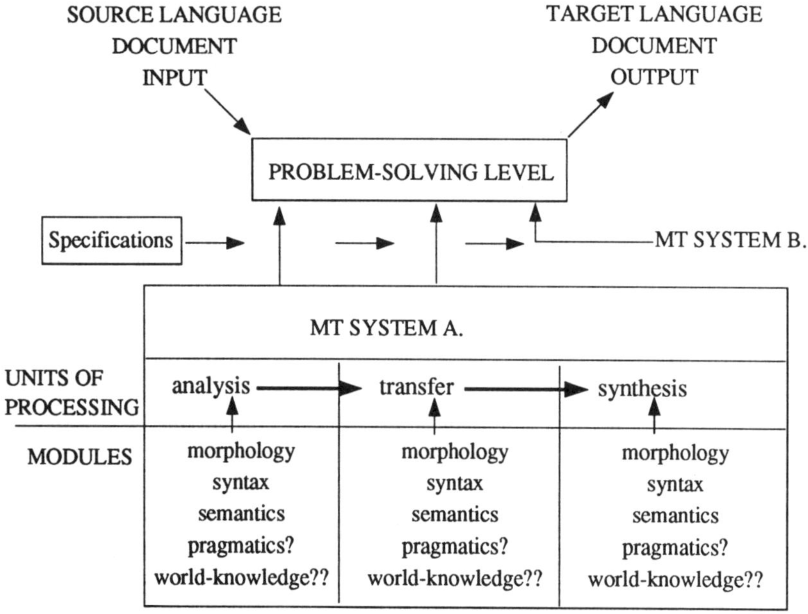

Figure 9.4 *Example of an MT model of problem solving*

The computer, by contrast with the structure of human knowledge, has a relatively limited, rigid and compartmentalised knowledge base with fixed, pre-established connections. Its expansion or modification has to be undertaken as a separate process, either after a translation, or interrupting the translation. The computer has separate parts or modules which perform operations on a text sequentially in such units as Analysis—Transfer—Synthesis, and within these in a prescribed order which may vary from system to system. (A fuller description of the MT process is given in 10.3) There is only a limited possibility of transferring problems to other parts and levels or modules of the knowledge base, the limits being set by the possibility of representation at several levels of analysis, transfer and synthesis.

It must be noted that at present the ability to construct modules for MT systems is unevenly developed. There is a wide-ranging experience at the morphological and syntactic levels, there is less at the semantic level, and very little of what is required and possible for human translation at the pragmatic level and that of essential world knowledge.

Furthermore, in existing MT systems the role of the specifications is not yet fully recognised and there is, therefore, hardly any allowance made for introducing pragmatic variables. The specifications can act as a filter controlling the results of the three stages or may indeed be used to decide on the type of MT systems to be called upon to perform the process. In existing MT applications specifications are only recognised to the extent that they can be invoked as a pre-selector of the MT system to be used or, in interactive systems, as an activator of particular modules; they cannot play the flexible role they do in the human process.

9.2.2 *The expert system view*

Another way of seeing the machine translation process is to consider it as an expert system developed for particular applications. Figure 9.5 is an attempt to illustrate this model.

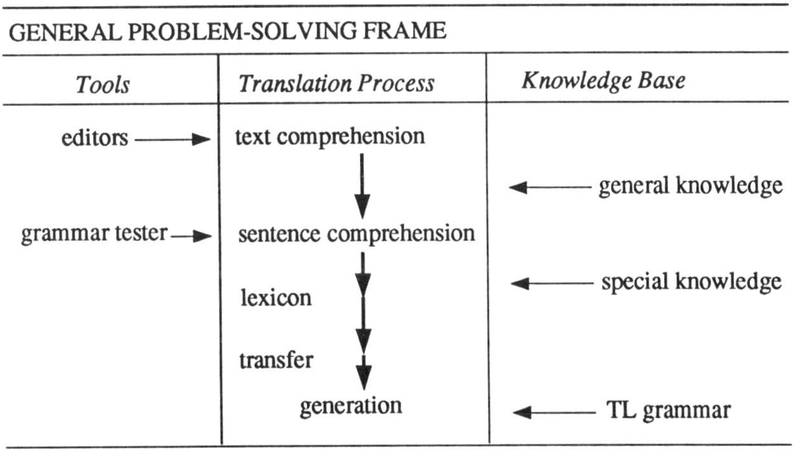

Figure 9.5 *The structure of an expert system for translation*

Compared with human resourcefulness, expert systems can only deal with very limited areas of knowledge. If translation tasks and documents to be processed can be specified to a sufficient degree of detail, there is no reason why an expert system should not produce comparable results to human products. On the basis of detailed analyses of objectives and texts, knowledge engineers would have to build up a knowledge base of equivalents at the pragmatic and textual levels. For the translation module itself, knowledge engineers would have to get bilingual equivalents from dictionaries as far as general linguistic equivalents are concerned and specific examples of textual equivalents from translators. With this knowledge they could then define textual equivalence as the situation that applies when two texts talk about the same thing in as similar way as possible.

Texts which exhibit a certain repetitiveness of features may lend themselves best for modelling as expert systems. In this way it would be possible to define the Canadian METEO System, which automatically translates weather reports from and into English and French, as an expert system.

9.2.2.1 *The type and nature of knowledge bases*

In order to make these comparisons more meaningful it is useful to outline briefly the nature of the knowledge bases humans and machine can resort to in order to solve translation problems. For this purpose, Figure 9.6 uses the model developed in Figure 9.2 and specifies the respective types of databases involved in each step.

9.2.3 *The nature of the modules in the MT process*

MT systems are usually considered to be constituted of three major consecutive modules: analysis—transfer—synthesis or generation. For particular tasks these modules are supported by separate dictionaries and grammars in order to increase the efficiency and simplicity of the processes. The gain in precision obtained by these detailed steps has to be measured against the greater inflexibility of the system which results from a rigid categorisation of linguistic phenomena. It is, for example, convenient to have a separate terminological dictionary to deal with complex terms; but once a complex nominal group has been identified as a term, it may later be impossible to decompose it into constituents in order to create a terminological translation equivalent in the target language.

While it is customary to divide the machine process into modules, this is not the case for human translation. Nevertheless, in order to highlight the differences between the two processes it is useful to consider the stages of translation identified in earlier sections as the modules of the human process. In this way a certain parallelism can be established between the core activities. Initially we can define MT as a text analysis system combined with a text generation/synthesis or production system. The problem lies in how the two parts are linked.

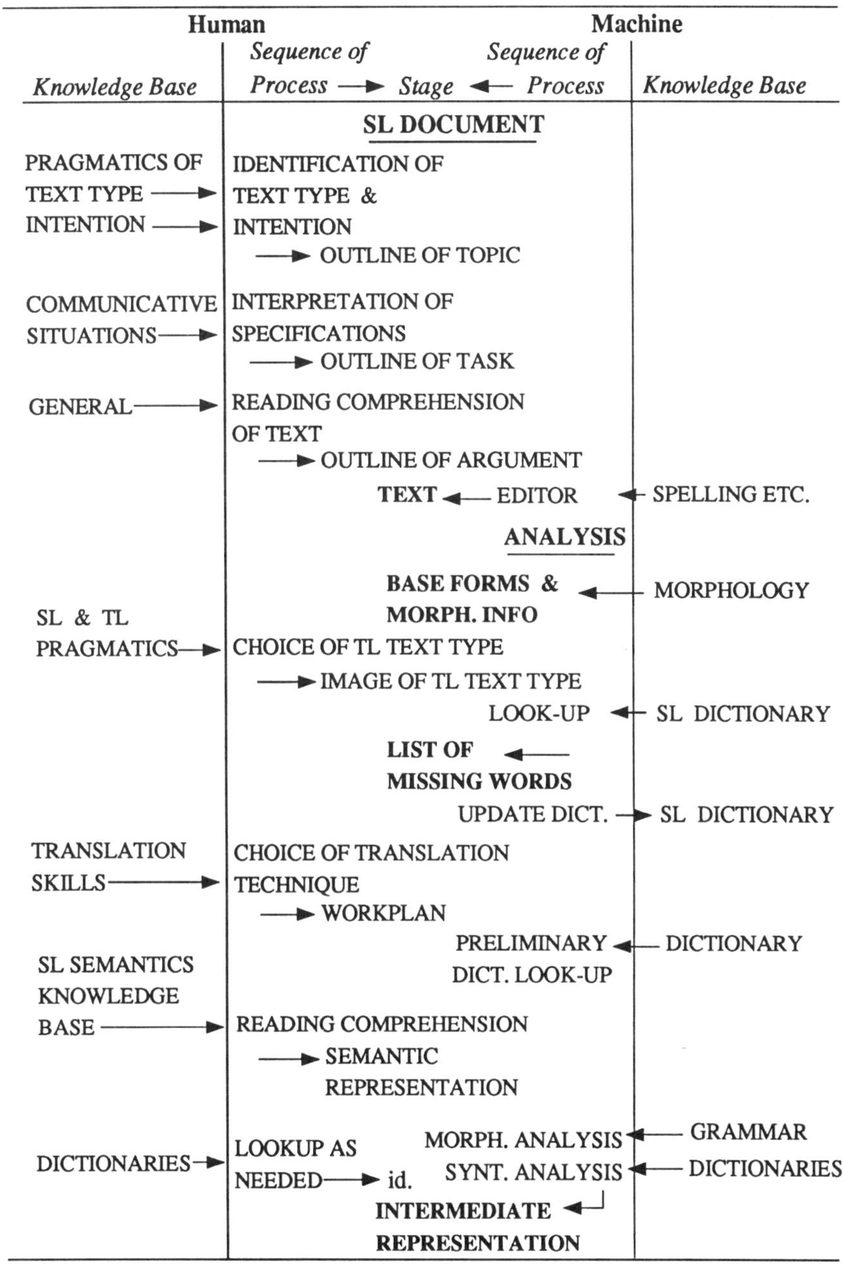

Figure 9.6 *The reference to knowledge bases in the human and machine translation processes*

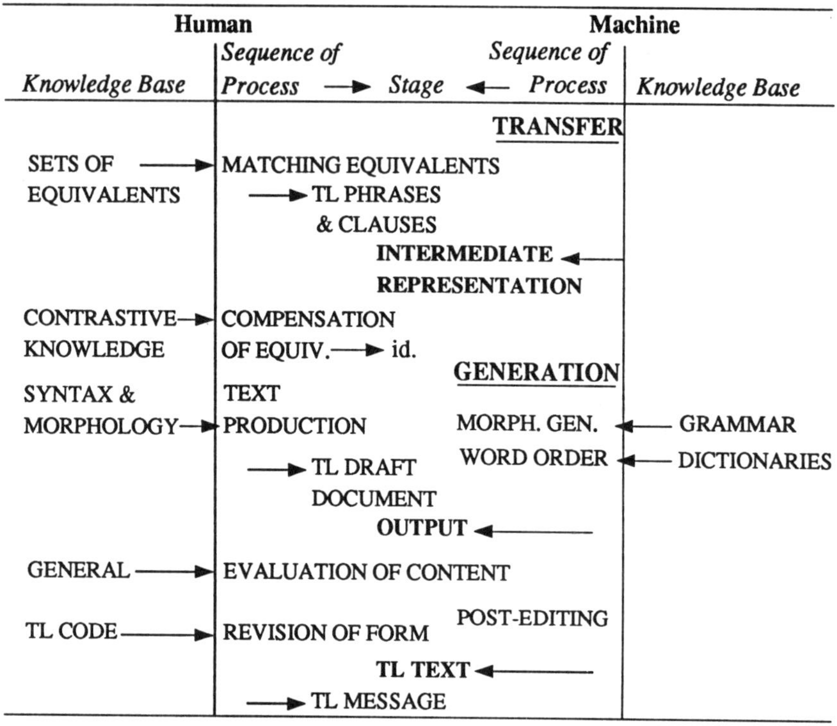

Figure 9.6 (cont'd) *The reference to knowledge bases in the human and machine translation processes*

MT systems differ not only in the sophistication of the analysis, and corresponding synthesis modules, but also in the nature of the link established between the two parts. Since experience has shown that the word-for-word technique, based on dictionary equivalents, of the early MT systems was totally inadequate, it is, for instance, crucial to determine the units as well as the levels of analysis at which the units are to be linked to other units in the target language (Bennett 1993). The human modules can be contrasted with the machine modules:

Human modules	*Machine modules*
comprehension	analysis
matching	transfer
writing	generation/synthesis

9.2.3.1 *Comprehension vs. analysis*

While human comprehension readily adapts to innovations in knowledge and linguistic expression, the analysis module of an MT system can only work retrospectively, i.e. it analyses an existing occurrence of language with reference to those previous occurrences of that language which have been systematised in the dictionaries and the grammars of the MT analysis module. The system can process the text only to the extent that its grammar and dictionaries can account for the forms it encounters in a particular text. In so far as languages are systematic, the rules derived from these observations then also have a certain predictive value which should allow them a limited amount of interpretative capacity for unforeseen patterns and expressions through 'inferencing', which the more advanced MT systems are trying to incorporate.

9.2.3.2 *Matching vs. transfer*

The human process of matching allows translators to compensate for items they cannot match in conventional ways, including the creation of so-called 'provisional' or translation equivalents which are substitute lexical items or expressions in a target language for source language lexical units for which no matching concepts and hence no lexical units can be established in the target language culture. Since such equivalents arise out of the context of a translation situation, they cannot be pre-planned and incorporated into MT dictionaries. The MT process, being based on a dictionary with pre-established units of equivalence, can only transfer those SL units to TL units it has stored in its TL dictionaries. Also, the intermediate representation of the SL text that is used for the transfer has a predetermined level of depth of analysis which does not permit syntactic shifting, semantic substitution and recombination of units, techniques which are available to the human translator.

9.2.3.3 *Writing vs. generation*

The synthesis or generation module of an MT system works prospectively, i.e. it produces sentences — of texts — in a target language which are new to the language. The production grammar required for this module must account for all the possible acceptable manifestations of language over a limited timespan in future, but can do so only on the basis of the codified knowledge of the past. The human translator, unlike the MT program, can respond to syntactic and lexical innovation and deviation from the systems of norms in the SL text and can either create equivalences by the substitution of conventional expressions in the TL or indeed attempt to re-create corresponding innovations and deviations from the norm of the TL.

9.2.4 *Current limitations of MT*

Beside the fundamental differences which characterise MT-generated texts, the greatest limitation of MT consists in the small range of possible equivalences an MT system has available and at the same time its inability to compensate. It is therefore possible to predict that texts are less suitable for MT treatment if, in human terms, they would require substantial amounts of compensation. Compensation is possible only if there is a considerable degree of understanding which leads to the processes of transposition, modulation, adaptation, explanation and allusion described in section 8.4. None of these techniques are available to MT systems unless potential cases of transposition etc. can be codified beforehand as regular patterns of linguistic differences between two languages or as regular patterns between matching text types of two languages.

Compensation may also require consideration of text units that are larger than those handled by the machine at any one time; in order to recognise the capability of MT systems in this respect, it is necessary to define the inferencing capability of MT systems. Commercially available MT systems cannot yet analyse text in the knowledge dimension, cannot yet interpret purpose and cannot yet understand text-type and larger textual units. There is consequently no transfer of information possible between these dimensions and lower levels. This makes a sentence the basic unit and all sentences are considered separate entities to be analysed in the same way, unless documents are subdivided by text type prior to input and special machine modules have been designed for different text types.

The current limitation of MT systems can also be explained as the lack of an underlying theory of equivalents. In order to supply such a theory, it has first to be decided at what level of communication equivalents are to be established. At the pragmatic level it requires a prior classification of intentions. It may, for example, be more efficient for MT systems to be restricted to one or two clearly identifiable functions such as the informative and the directive intentions which can usually be differentiated by linguistic analysis. Another gain in efficiency will arise from a restriction of MT systems to the translation of texts of certain subject fields whose dictionaries can concentrate on the denotation of lexical items within a given knowledge structure.

Design specifications for more sophisticated MT systems must therefore include definitions of the underlying model of language comprehension, the underlying model of language production and the model of matches between the two models. They must also allow for unexpected side effects which may have their own impact on the end user, or mediator.

The machine process, as it is developed at the moment, can be illustrated by the model presented in Figure 9.7.

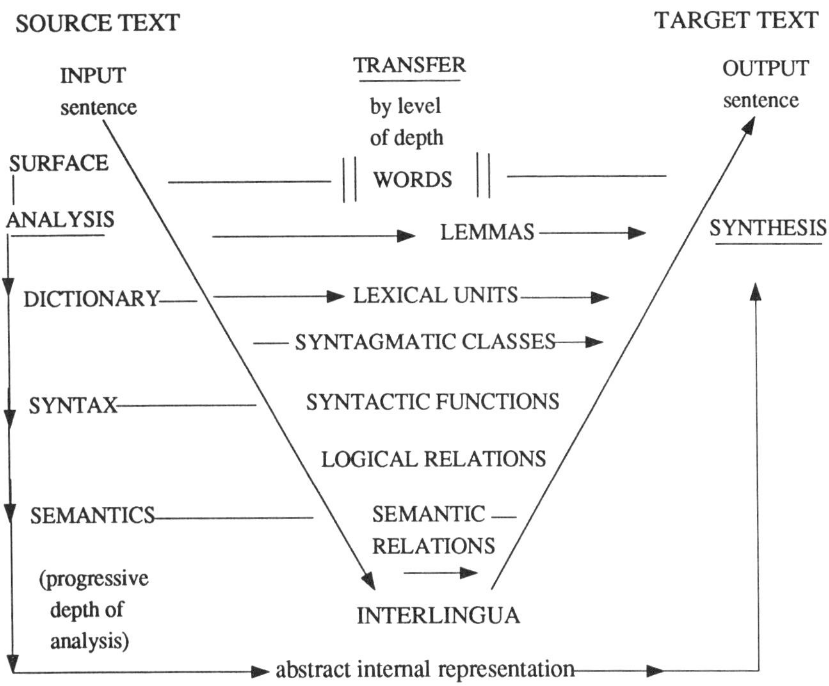

Figure 9.7 *A model of analysis, transfer and synthesis*

This model shows, vertically, the progressive depth of analysis, which can go as far down as the semantic level of analysis and transfer, in order to achieve a progressively more abstract, i.e. language-independent, internal representation. When a complete match between SL analysis and TL generation can be achieved, this can be expressed as an interlingua, i.e. an instrument in which both language systems under consideration meet on equal terms. In practice this occurs in a small number of sublanguages of restricted scope which can be exhaustively described, e.g. military commands in joint services, instructions for the use of machines, or diagnostic reports on scientific and technical processes. Because of their complexity in form and functions other languages are too complex to be treated in this way. Horizontally it shows the types of transfer that can be effected at each level of an analysis stage.

The most significant limitation of the model is its restriction to the unit of analysis of the sentence and its constituents. The absence of a text grammar, of text types and hence any possibility of considering pragmatic phenomena of texts in current MT systems are principally due to the fact that research in these areas is insufficiently advanced to have permitted a formal description of their regularities which can be incorporated into programs. For example, the model cannot account for sentence meanings because these can only be specified in relation to the whole text and by text type. The current state of the art is therefore restricted to seeing the prime objective of an MT system as the production of well-formed sentences, i.e. sentences which correspond to a native speaker's intuition of what constitutes a well-formed sentence. This criterion of success is far removed from the notion of semantic equivalence or the message value of a text and consequently the product of machine translation must differ markedly from human translation. Global similarity with the natural language of a human translation is therefore not a very useful criterion for relative assessment of MT products. Piecemeal comparison at the level of equivalents, at the level of content and at the level of the message intention/expectation are more promising alternatives. These three criteria are all directly translation-related.

Since MT is limited to sentence-level transfer, rhetorical and logical structures are not specifically considered by the analysis modules. Any continuity between sentences in a target language MT output is therefore purely coincidental. Since this is not the case with SL texts, there is a powerful justification of speaking of the MT product as MT-produced sentences and not as MT-produced texts. Alternatively, an MT-produced text can be defined as a sequence of sentences in the same order and with largely the same internal structure as the source text from which they are derived. Since sentence-level translation is an almost unique feature of MT, it might be more appropriate to admit that MT produces a separate, translation-specific, category of texts which in some way mirror the text type of the input document.

9.3 Comparison of human and machine translation products

The comparison of the two translation processes carried out in the previous section can be complemented by a comparison of the products resulting from the processes. This is made here first with respect to the nature of the output language (9.3.1) and then with respect to the types and varieties of text produced (9.3.2).

9.3.1 *Human vs. machine-produced texts*

The involvement of computers in the translation process introduces a fundamental change in communication. The use of MT systems signifies also that for the first time in human experience computational linguists have constructed a machine which produces genuinely new sentences of a language, albeit as a result of a particular method of prompting.

This computer-produced new language is the result of the conscious human design that has created the generation or synthesis modules of the translation system in question. Generically speaking, the output languages of all MT systems are artificial because they conform to the definition established in section two, namely that the rules and the lexicon of an artificial language must be established prior to its use. The computer can, indeed, only produce the sentences permitted by the systems' humanly constructed grammars and dictionaries. Such new grammars and dictionaries are conceived in terms of a particular target language which is modelled on a designers' command of a section of a natural language or the perception of what are relevant sublanguage elements for the system in question. Consequently each machine translation system only produces sentences which correspond to the designers' perceptions of the source and target languages. The grammar has a limited productive capacity which is, incidentally, also designed to prevent overgeneration. The dictionaries can only have the meanings specifically listed and there is therefore a vast difference between the dynamic lexicon of natural language on which human translators draw and the limited and fixed representation of the lexicon in the static dictionary of MT systems. Consequently the new language cannot have any of the creative potential of natural language which is the motivation behind the constant evolution and change of natural language. These MT output languages therefore also ignore the difference between linguistic rules and social norms and any deviation from their rule systems is an error. The most distinctive feature of these languages is, however, a characteristic they share with other artificial languages: though they have a pragmatic dimension, which is given by the fact that they are used in parallel and sometimes as substitutes for the production of human translations, they have no text grammar, indeed there is, on the whole, no provision for structures larger than the sentence. It follows that each MT system in existence produces its own language. In order to identify this language we can and should add the system's name to that of the natural language which has served as a model and speak of "Weidner" English beside "Atlas" English, "Logos" German and "Meteo" French etc.

Another way of capturing this particular limitation is to define MT systems as one-way converters of natural language into artificial language. From a certain perspective, they can be said to have similar functions to documentation thesauri which convert, or rather separate, the words of natural language into descriptors, i.e. words that are recognised by the system and therefore belong to the documentation language, and non-descriptors of the documentation language. A bilingual thesaurus performs the additional function of converting the descriptors of one language into those of another, according to a pre-established pattern of equivalences, and at the same time creating two sets of non-descriptors which refer to descriptors. The secret of success of a documentation thesaurus, just as that of an MT system, lies in the resemblance that the user of either system perceives as existing between the lexical items produced by the system, be they descriptors or MT dictionary words, and the words of the documents they permit the user to read. The input is written in natural language; the output is written in an artificial language that bears strong resemblances to another natural language. The success of the operation can be and is frequently expressed in terms of the closeness and resemblance of the artificial language to the desired natural language. These differences are expressed in Figure 9.8.

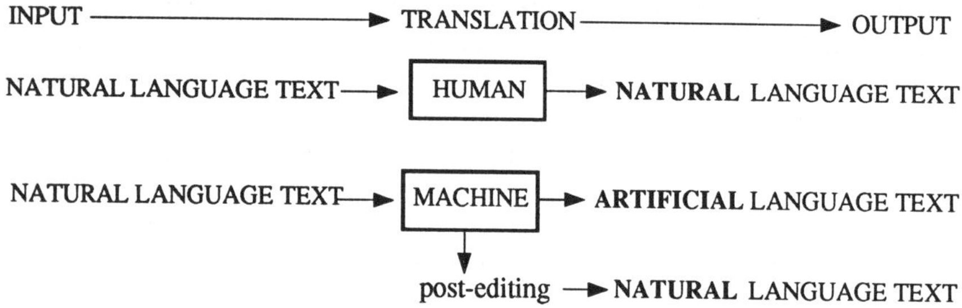

Figure 9.8 *Language difference between human and MT*

The output of an MT system is a product which is utilised by either end users who can read the artificial language or by post-editors who convert the output into a natural language text. It does not, therefore, differ from so many other texts which can have a double function: they are either drafts for further processing by mediators or finished products accepted as messages by a communication agent or end user.

To conclude: the basic premise of a theory of MT must be that a machine-translated text is never comparable to a human product of writing or text modification. It has to be considered a product in its own right with its own characteristics. It is the result of a particular automated process chosen deliberately by a writer, an end user, a communication agent or a mediator. One must assume that any of these originators are fully aware of their choice and capable of making the distinction.

9.3.1.1 *The nature of machine-generated (MT) language*

We briefly restate here the nature of artificial languages defined in section two. Artificial languages are products of human design, based on and derived from natural languages, which do not have the flexibility and multifunctionality of natural languages. Such languages are usually functionally restricted to the conveyance of information and therefore exclude connotative, emotive, aesthetic and other meanings. Artificial languages are regularly used in restricted environments for efficient communication among specialists, e.g. airline pilots, surgeons in the operating theatre, chemists, taxonomists, who understand the particular rule system of the language.

An artificial language designed for MT output is restricted by the fact that the designers proceed on the assumption that the new language will be appropriate for a specific purpose, possibly at the expense of, and thereby excluding suitability for, other purposes. In terms of machine translation, designers of the generation modules can only have a limited perception of the functions the system is to perform. Any conversion of natural language to artificial language, such as it occurs in machine translation of natural language texts, therefore implies a reduction in function and pragmatic scope. This restriction may not be apparent or significant to an individual reader of such output text but it is real nevertheless, because it excludes potential alternative interpretations of the text which were not intended by the designer.

An MT-produced document is, therefore, another translation-specific text type. It also has its subtypes according to the MT system that produces it. We could, therefore, also speak of a Systran-document, instead of 'a document written in Systran English', a Weidner-document, a Logos-document, etc. and even, where there are several languages in a system, distinguish between a Metal-English document, a Metal-French-document, etc.

If we were to accept that the machine can produce another natural language text we would have to make a number of assumptions with reference to the analysis of a text by machine, namely:

(a) that everything that is to be known about the text is linguistically expressed;
(b) that we can relate all these observed linguistic phenomena to existing grammars and dictionaries in MT systems;
(c) that we can represent the data of analysis in such a way that they are fully retrievable for the generation process.

Since these conditions are not given, except in highly restricted languages which come close to artificial languages, we maintain that the machine produces an artificial language. The challenge for MT is therefore:

(a) to construct user-friendly artificial languages;
(b) to ensure an optimum transfer of information between the natural source language and the artificial target language;
(c) to convince users that the new artificial language is as efficient for its purpose, if not more so, than the alternative natural language.

9.3.2 *Flexibility vs. rigidity in text types*

All computer-produced language is controlled through the fact that it is the result of deliberate human design. Since the artificial languages of MT systems are usually conceived at the sentence level only, it follows that they are inefficient in making distinctions at the level of larger structures or text types. This difference was not perceived by the designers of the very first generation of systems whose aim was universal under the motto "try-everything", i.e. they did not take into account that translation types and methods differ with the source document. It has always been known that human translators cannot translate all documents equally well. Human translators can, however, given time, make a reasonable job of an unfamiliar subject area or text type by learning about the subject and acquiring the necessary writing skills, i.e. by a variety of efforts generally described as 'research' or 'learning'.

If we assume a certain correlation between domain and text type we can represent the difference between the capabilities of humans and machines in the diagrams of Figure 9.9.

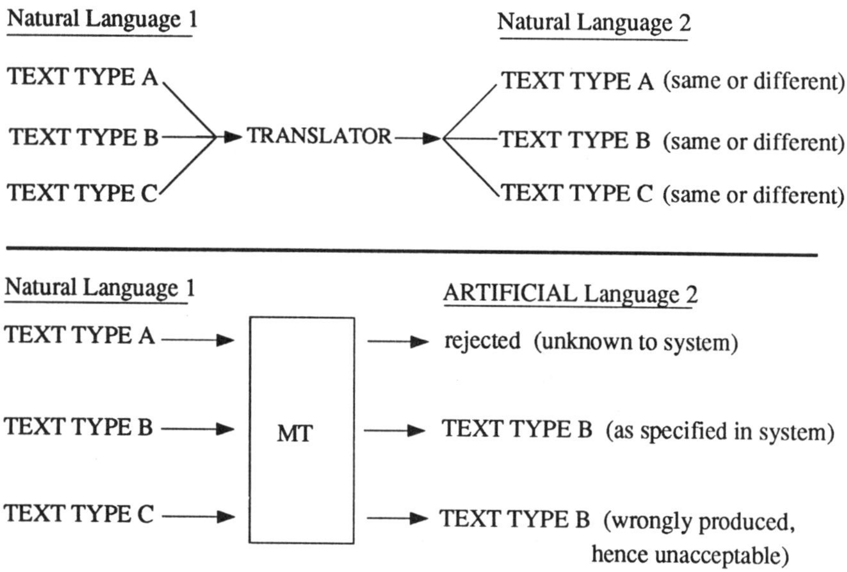

Figure 9.9 *Ranges of human and machine translation*

A human translator can efficiently handle several text types and adjust to unfamiliar types; the machine can only handle the types it has been programmed for. If it receives an unfamiliar type it may reject it, if it has been programmed to recognise unsuitable types; otherwise it will process it as if it were an acceptable type and therefore produce unacceptable output. Currently it is recognised that MT systems can be optimised for particular text types allied to subject fields and for particular functions. MT systems can be instructed to operate in a certain manner, but these instructions require prior research into characteristics of text types which are programmable. The MT text type output is therefore part of an artificial or controlled language. In science and technology artificial or controlled languages are normally created with the purpose of improving the efficiency of technical communication. It is therefore, or should be, possible to design the grammar for computer translation output in such a way that it represents an improved and controlled language, in the interest of the greater efficiency of natural language processing and communication in general. The MT translation process would then have to be preceded by a phase of text-editing which would filter out any extraneous meanings, ambiguous syntax etc..

9.4 Uses of MT

Centuries of tradition of human translation have created conventional patterns of translation products for a specific range and a limited number of users. This balance has been upset by the arrival of MT and its many products.

While in many circles machine translation is still considered a poor substitute to human translation, it can be justified because there is (i) insufficient human capacity available to translate the considerable volume of currently untranslated documents which need nevertheless to be made available in other languages, and (ii) a very large demand for immediate, very low cost translation which cannot be produced by human translators. As a secondary effect of the introduction of machines into the translation process, it was furthermore expected that the unit cost of translation in general would be reduced and that this move in turn, would stimulate further growth in demand. Consequently the nature and quality of machine translation was initially defined only in relation to human translation and by the degree of closeness they achieved to human translation. Such assessments are inherently fallacious because they are based on an erroneous conception of translation. Whether human or otherwise, translation is a mediating activity, the particular form of which is determined both by the text to be mediated and the communicative circumstances which call for this mediation.

In matters of use of translation, we must also accept that there is no single situation which can serve as a point of comparison for human and machine translation, and that there may, indeed, be no single situation in which either human or machine would be equally suitable. Having established the nature of machine produced languages, the point would have to be argued that machine translation can, under certain conditions and in certain circumstances, be an acceptable substitute for human translation.

The situation is quite different if we postulate a diversity of communicative objectives that can be associated with a text to be transmitted across a linguistic barrier and measure a translation by the success with which particular objectives have been achieved. If the coexistence of various translations of equal value and appropriateness for the situation for which they were intended and commissioned is accepted as a matter of principle, then machine translation can simply be identified as a new type of translation for which appropriate objectives have been or have yet to be determined. As there are different types of machine translation systems with varying quality and claims to adequacy of their product, there is therefore a need to identify the situations in which certain types of machine translation systems can perform optimally, or vice versa. It then also becomes desirable to identify other communicative situations for which machine translation systems might be conveniently devised.

Machine translation therefore has a proper place beside human translation as an alternative technique for achieving different communicative objectives.

9.5 Comparative evaluation of MT produced texts

The quality of human translation is subject to the variations of any industrial activity. The relevant quality indices are variable according to the quality of the source document, the time permitted for the mediation and the proficiency of the translator. There is, therefore, no single model of human translation which could be set as a standard for machine translation and there is not even a minimum standard of human translation which could be set as a target for machines.

An MT-produced document is an instance of an artificial language with a limited set of rules that are derived from the social norms governing the usage of that language and adopted by the designers of the MT system in question. This system language is related to a natural language from which its simplified grammar has been derived. It is also related to the semantic world of a particular natural language and the speech community that uses it because the MT system contains a subset of the lexicon of that natural language in its lexicon.

It has been argued that the quality of MT-produced documents should be assessed in terms of their identity with human products. Another way of approaching the issue of evaluation would be to assess MT-produced documents in relation to their conformity to the conventional rules and norms of usage of comparable target language documents. In both types of assessment the underlying assumption is that on the level of the linguistic expression form a human translation or document should be comparable to a machine-produced document. Such a comparison is academic and based on the confusion of assessing two products on the basis of their constituent elements rather than on the basis of their functions.

On a functional basis two translations can, however, be compared as to whether and to what extent they satisfy the end user's expectation. MT-produced translations, being a text type of their own, have a limited range of possible functions. It is therefore inappropriate to submit to a machine process documents that have functions the machine cannot recognise and therefore cannot process. It is equally clear that existing MT machines cannot handle the type of transformation required by a change of intention performed by human information mediators, e.g. interlingual abstracting or summarising, or other conversions of intentions, as e.g. informative translation of a directive text, directive translation of an evaluative text. By postulating MT products as text types in their own right, it is also possible to list separate functions for these text types and particular intentions and expectations that can be associated with such a product.

Once it is accepted that there are two different products with similar but distinct functions it is possible to concentrate on the value of a product to the communication market. While a general goal may be to emulate certain properties of the human product, this has to be balanced against other advantages of the product of MT, viz. immediate, regular and continuous availability at the request of the end user, lower cost, reliability of lexical equivalents, even quality, etc.

The MT-produced document is related to one or several source languages in two distinct ways. The language generation mechanism is first of all related to the text type, grammar and lexicon of at least one other natural language, i.e. the language of the source language texts that have served as a basis for its construction. This relation is seen most directly in the dictionary which matches equivalents in the source and the target languages; according to the system it is also prominent in other parts. In a multilingual system, there may be more than one language involved — a unique feature of machines; because human polyglots may suffer from interference during language production. Secondly, each output document is directly related to the SL input document which triggers off the choice of the particular equivalent at the appropriate level of grammar and dictionary in order to produce the TL document.

On one level it is possible to compare the language potential of an MT system to that of a human translator. If it is true that two human translators will always produce different versions of the same source document, the same can be said of two MT systems. The MT system that is gradually being enlarged by a human operator might eventually even be said to contain most of the grammar and the lexicon of the individual who has been adding to its repertoire. The peculiar advantage of the machine lies both in its greater reliability of performance—in the same state of development, the machine will always translate the same text in exactly the same way—and its lack of intuition—it will not produce variants in style or lexis without prompting. Its major drawback is that it cannot deal with 'new' linguistic phenomena in the same way as the human translator. In this sense the machine has no potential for language, which is built on the creative human ability to produce 'new' linguistic forms.

The view presented here of MT is not concerned with the relative merits of human as compared to machine translation, nor does it accept that comparative evaluations are appropriate for anything other than user acceptance of machine produced documents. It must also be noted that the theory presented here does not purport to express value judgements on the quality of MT in general. At a time of constantly new developments in MT, evaluation can only be carried out for particular systems at a particular state of their development.

9.5.1 *Methods of MT evaluation*

MT evaluation is carried out at two levels and for two main purposes. Macro-evaluations serve the purpose of assessing the relative merits of one system compared with another. Micro-evaluations serve for the assessment of the performance of individual systems (see Lehrberger & Bourbeau 1988).

Macro-evaluations have to judge output of competing systems with respect to the usefulness for the intended purpose for each type of application, be this post-editing, direct use, pre-translation etc. Macro-evaluations are also the first step for comparing time and cost factors between human and machine translation. Potential purchasers of a system usually submit a test piece and measure one or several of the following parameters:

(a) The number of dictionary entries that have to be added to the system to enable it to cope with the test piece and the time it takes to produce a single entry are indicators of the range of documents a system can deal with.

(b) In 'pre-translation' systems the time required to pre-edit and the types of adjustments that have to be made for efficient processing give an indication of the potential usefulness of a system.

(c) Alternatively the post-editing effort, and thereby indirectly cost and time saving can be measured in comparison with other systems. For example, this can be done by a simple count of words corrected, words shifted to another part of a document, words eliminated, words replaced by others, words added to the dictionary before transfer or in the process of post-editing.

In some systems potential purchasers perform interactions with the system in order to assess the complexity of learning the necessary editing or dictionary-making procedures.

Micro-evaluation can have several functions. It can be diagnostic, i.e. examine the cause of output error, or prognostic, i.e. assess errors for their potential solutions and future avoidance. Such evaluations are regularly carried out during the testing of a new system. Designers who customise systems to clients' requirements also need a battery of tests to ensure that the adjustments do not produce unwanted side effects. Evaluation is wrongly oriented if every instance where the MT output deviates from anticipated forms of human translation is considered an error simply because in certain processes it would be corrected by a post-editor. Instead, what should be measured is the speed with which the entire process—including human intervention—is performed with the assistance of such tools, and the ease with which human editors or translators can produce an acceptable end product. It has also been noted that re-writing part of a program in order to correct an error in one part of a system may have unsuspected secondary effects in other parts which are not immediately detectable.

As is the case with all machines, such evaluations will then have to be carried out regularly in order to test whether minor corrections to the systems really have the effect of avoiding certain errors. Since it is undesirable to have such tests vitiated by outside factors, such as the unexpected occurrence of a homonym or other unknown words or meanings, systems designers construct special test sentences which contain the type of constructions which are suspected of causing errors.

10 The Pragmatic Circumstances of Automation in Translation

This section outlines the various methods of machine translation currently in use. The main attention is, however, devoted to the known applications of MT systems. In this way the variety of tools currently coming into use will be located in their communicative settings.

10.1 Methods of MT

What follows is a simplified view of the operation of MT systems, which is considered sufficient for the purpose of this book. For fuller descriptions the reader is referred to the many good introductions to MT which have been produced in recent years (Hutchins & Somers 1991; Nirenburg 1987; Slocum 1985).

In the description of the design of MT systems, linguistic approaches are fundamentally distinguished from semantic approaches, because they are reflected in the methods of handling analysis and generation.

10.1.1 *Linguistic approaches*

So far there are three strategies using a linguistic approach. Though they differ in detail, the process can always be perceived as consisting of the three phases introduced in the previous chapter, namely analysis of the source text, some mode of transfer and finally generation or synthesis of a target text.

The analysis segments and annotates the source text with regard to lexicon and structure, thereby identifying the relationships between words. As a first step of analysis the text is matched against a machine-readable monolingual dictionary. For every 'word', i.e. every lexical unit the analysis dictionary recognises as such, the available morphological information is noted. The dictionary also proposes the possible syntactic functions of words and even firm collocations in which they can occur. The analysis then attributes the words of the sentence to such entities as nominal, prepositional or verb groups and a parser segments the sentence into its structural components.

Transfer is the intermediate phase which looks both back to the source text and forward to the target text realisation. In its simplest form it can consist of an operation which looks up a bilingual dictionary to find the matching lexical units for the source 'words', taking account of the information established during the analysis. The result of transfer is a sequence of annotated words or larger units and a description of their syntactic function and order, in the form of an intermediate representation which corresponds neither to the syntax of the source nor of the target language.

This interim product is passed to a synthesis module which orders and adjusts the words or larger units into a syntactic and morphological structure appropriate to the target language. This phase is also controlled by a dictionary and a rule system for the target language.

Within this general pattern there are three main subtypes:

(a) Language-pair-specific 'direct' systems.

This is the earliest type of system and reflects the design philosophy of the 1950s and 1960s, which exploited direct correspondences between two languages. Lexicon and syntax of the SL are analysed only as far as necessary to resolve problems of ambiguity, word order and the correct match with TL expressions. The 'directness' consists in the attempt to replace the longest possible sequences of words in a source language text by acceptable matching sequences of words of the target language wherever possible and so avoid lengthy analysis.

Initially these systems produced only word-for-word translations, but later some syntactic analysis of the source text was gradually added. These systems did not make a clear distinction between analysis and synthesis but worked on a sequential substitution basis with some transposition rules. The idea of a modular structure for systems arrived much later.

(b) Interlingual systems.

The design philosophy of these systems presupposes that a SL text can be transformed into a semantic and syntactic representation, the equivalent of the transfer phase, which is common to at least two languages, and that texts in another language can be generated from this representation (see Figure 9.7). This idea was expressed in the early phases of MT by Cherry (1966:117) as "transform from a source language A into a target language B, using rules expressed in a third language C". The interlingual representation is meant to capture the entire meaning of the text and to be accessible equally well from both source and target languages. This method has only two separate phases, the transfer being merged in the interlingua. In the first, TL texts are analysed in terms of the interlingual representation; in the second, TL sentences are produced from this representation. This approach is very economical in a multilingual environment where a single representation is intended to cover several target languages, but is notoriously more difficult the more languages have to be reduced to a common representation. Systems differ in that varying emphasis is placed on semantic and syntactic representation and further variation exists according to the choice of interlingua.

Interlinguas can in theory be based on natural or artificial languages, e.g. Esperanto, which is currently used in an experimental MT project in the Netherlands. Different projects have placed different emphasis on interlingual dictionaries or interlingual syntax.

(c) Transfer systems.
This type of system is more complex than both the others. The greater complexity is explained by the recognition that in interlingual systems a single abstract representation does not contain sufficient information relevant for all items inside the text, e.g the question whether an item is 'focus' or 'topic' of a sentence. In the analysis phase the SL text is processed to the depth required by the rules of its grammar and the result is expressed in a notation suitable for the transfer phase. In the transfer phase this representation, based on the SL analysis, is transformed into a representation suitable for the generation of a target language text. Whereas the analysis phase does not taken into account any features of the target language, the transfer phase can make adjustments to the results of the analysis with regard to the generation requirements for the target language. In the generation phase the transfer representation is then transformed into a text in the TL without any further back-reference to the results of analysis.

Transfer systems are differentiated by the depth of analysis and the degree of abstractness of the transfer representation. Early systems only worked with a superficial analysis of sentence structures (surface structure). Gradually, with advances in computational linguistics, a syntactically and semantically deeper analysis and consequently more abstract transfer representation and transfer rules were introduced.

The following areas are known to cause difficulties in analysis and hence can be responsible for the introduction of errors.

(a) Lack of or dubious agreement between subject and verb, especially in case of collectives: e.g.'this group of students wish/wishes'; 'either A or B is/are'.
(b) syntactic and semantic ambiguity: e.g. 'any' can mean 'a little', 'a few', 'none', 'no matter which', etc..
(c) different possibilities of interpreting a sentence: e.g. 'sanction', 'play' which can be either verb or noun.
(d) synonymy, super- and subordination of concepts: e.g. 'brass' for 'brass instruments'; 'wood' as superordinate for timber and '(fire) wood', or as synonym for 'wood instruments' in 'wood section'.
(e) Omissions of syntactically significant elements:
    — Omission of an article which can produce a homograph: e.g. 'Paint surface between lines'.
    — Omission of a preposition before a verb: e.g. 'to produce reports' vs. 'produce reports'.
    — Omission of relative pronouns: e.g. 'the woman the man saw'.
    — Omission of discourse markers which are anaphoric across sentence boundaries, such as pronominalisation and topicalisation: e.g. 'his father was a baker, so is his son'. 'His father was cruel, so is his son'.

(f) Ellipsis of one element of a compound: e.g. 'Close the back and front door'.

(g) Prepositional verbs which provoke overlap and conflict of rules of interpretation: e.g. 'the system manager can go on to delete several entries'.

(h) Complex nominal groups which are not lexicalised which lead to misinterpretations: e.g. 'the site level troubleshooting tasks are essentially performed...'.

(i) Abbreviations and acronyms, because they can be read as any word class: e.g. 'WHO'.

Since only some of these problems can be described formally and the machine has no intuition, such errors can be foreseen for specific cases but not completely avoided.

10.1.2 *The semantic approach*

While in linguistics-based systems the syntactic analysis is the chief component, new approaches emphasize semantic features in combination with syntactic structures. Semantic processes, however, only operate after the identification of syntactic structures. The semantic approach can also, to a certain extent, transcend the level of the sentence and take account of such important elements as pronominalisation and topicalisation.

The chief components of such systems are semantic parsing, i.e. analysis of semantic features instead of, or in addition to, grammatical categories; lexical structuring into semantic networks according to such models as, for examples Schank's conceptual dependencies; and the resolution of ambiguities with reference to an extralinguistic knowledge base. Thus, the system does in some way "understand" the SL text, before translation begins. Initially this approach was considered as an alternative to the linguistic approaches. Currently it is understood that the semantic approach is best combined with linguistic analysis techniques.

Some natural language understanding programmes are also of interest to MT, but do not provide all the information required for translation. For example, understanding an English text does not include the detailed information about the status of interlocutors needed for translation into Japanese. The semantic approach is still at the level of research. Variations can be expected according to degrees of interaction with linguistic approaches.

10.2 Users of MT systems

Since the new MT industry is just establishing itself, it must be accepted that the situation is currently in full development. It is nevertheless useful to identify some of the consequences of the introduction of MT with respect to the various groups of people involved in the industry.

10.2.1 *The translator as producer*

Traditional producers of translation look to the machine to provide cheaper, faster and a larger volume of production, without significant loss of quality, of what is, in this case, clearly seen as an industrial product. This is a natural aspiration which accompanies every industrial development. It is, in fact, essential, because it provides the motivation for the substantial investment required to develop MT software. The normal experience of industrial development then leads translation producers to aspire to more advanced systems in the direction of ultimately achieving a fully automatic tool; in the meantime, they accept machines which speed up the process and assist in various ways. At the same time, translators are examining and defining the scope of the material that is likely to be processed in future without reference to translators, in order to analyse and define their own role in the translation production industry.

10.2.2 *The writer as translation producer*

As soon as there is an industrial or machine alternative to the human process, writers gain a certain degree of independence from translators, who, until now, exclusively determined the form and the quality of the end product. Writers may now want to develop bi- or multilingual texts directly, by themselves, in parallel rather than write a text for subsequent translation. Technical authors may want assistance with writing their texts in a second language, thereby by-passing the conventional process of human translation. Writers are therefore likely to look towards translators not so much as an independent operator, but an advisor or partner in text production.

10.2.3 *Readers of translations*

Readers will want to be able to by-pass the time-consuming and costly human translation circuit, and instead obtain instant translations produced by an MT system. This is particularly relevant for the increasing amount of technical and scientific information which is becoming available in machine-readable form. For example, electronic journals may contain articles in other languages, which scholars or scientists may want to be able to browse through in their own language, without having to wait for a human translation, or to undertake the laborious process of ordering such a translation. There may indeed be two modes of accessing literature in a foreign language: one would be for publishers to provide machine-translated alternatives as a permanent choice in accessing an electronic journals; the other would be for end users to have articles machine-translated by a system directly available to them.

If, as in most industrial products, there are differences in the quality of the product which influence the price of the work, readers may also want to be able to choose and vary the quality of the translation they obtain from a machine.

10.2.4 *The information supplier*

With an ever-increasing volume of information in machine-readable form, it is natural for publishers to examine the possibilities of providing translated versions automatically as part of the general information supply, e.g. multilingual versions of electronic journals or databases. This is particularly important for the growing number of specialist databases which hitherto offer information in monolingual form via monolingual front ends only. If suppliers of databases want to offer multilingual versions of their data, they must also provide multilingual access to them. If there is insufficient demand for a particular language version to justify storing multiple language copies, there is the alternative of supplying on-call translation facilities which readers themselves can intercalate at will. Which of these modalities will be chosen will probably depend on the demand for any one type of output.

The common element among these different points of view is a greater sophistication of attitude towards the processes of writing, understanding, reading and consequently translating, and a greater awareness of the availability of differentiated products for diverse uses.

10.3 Brief description of MT systems

Since in the next section reference will be made to individual MT systems, it is necessary to give a minimal identification of those which are used as examples. This is done in alphabetical order and only to the extent necessary for their identification in the examples. For full descriptions the reader is referred to a number of standard books on this subject, especially Hutchins & Somers (1992).

ALPS: A multi-stage interactive system, developed by members of Brigham Young University, consisting of an automatic dictionary look-up facility, and, at a second stage, of some form of simple, largely dictionary-based translation module for pre-translation. The system is no longer available but is used by the firm's own translation services.

ATLAS: A Japanese system, developed by Fujitsu, based on structural transfer, for the translation of specialised technical texts from Japanese into English.
CULT: A interactive system, designed on the principle of direct translation by the Chinese University of Hongkong, for on-line translation of texts in the field of mathematics from Chinese into English.
EUROTRA: The research and development programme, sponsored by the European Community 1982-1992, for the design of a transfer-based multilingual modular system, for use with post-editing in the nine languages of the European Community Member States. It exists in form of a pre-industrial prototype and is being developed further.
LOGOS: A transfer system, developed by Logos Corp., for the translation of special subject documents requiring post-editing. Various language pairs exist and are under further development.
METAL: A transfer system, developed by Siemens AG, for the translation of special subject documents requiring post-editing. Various language versions exist and are under regular extension and development.
METEO: The Canadian Federal Government system for the production of bilingual French-English weather reports.
NTRAN: A system design of the Centre of Computational Linguistics of the University of Manchester Institute of Science and Technology for the translation of technical manuals from English into Japanese in interactive mode. The prototype was not developed further for industrial use. Its principles are incorporated into other design currently being developed.
SYSTRAN: The oldest commercially available MT system, developed in California, currently owned by Gachot SA, France. It has been used for the production of un-edited output, for post-editing use, for restricted-language document input, and for general use in the French Minitel system. This systems has the largest number of language pairs, all official EC languages, with varying sizes of dictionaries and states of quality of performance.
TITUS: An interlingua-based system, developed by the Institut Textile de France, for the translation of abstracts in the field of textiles from and into English, French, German and Spanish. Input requires documents to be written in a heavily restricted language, specially designed for abstracts in this field.
WEIDNER: A general purpose system, developed by Weidner Communications Corporation, which has been used for pre-translation, for restricted language document input and for post-editing use. Most users have substantially added to the system in the form of special dictionaries, and this way customised it to their needs.

10.4 Functional types of machine translation

Faced with the impossibility of machines to understand a text in the way a translator must understand it, and the fact that computers cannot produce natural language comparable to the expectations associated with human translation of natural language texts, there are two possible modes of viewing automatic translation. One is to see the computer as an aid to human translation; the other is to accept that the computer provides a translation service sui generis which is not really comparable to the human variety. Both views are represented as an underlying philosophy of MT design, but no system explicitly states its position in this respect.

The specific arguments for the use of MT as an industrial product for specialised areas of communication can be summarised as follows:

(a) In the interest of improved translation, restrictions on natural language usage are desirable and beneficial for certain types of documents. Technical sublanguages, in particular, which are the most common fields of applications of machine translation, already use various restricted forms of natural language.
Any restriction of natural language is a move towards adopting some of the characteristics of artificial languages which lie at the basis of all computer output.

(b) In technical sublanguages, meanings tend to be restricted and the range of grammatical structures is limited. While it is easy to read such restricted language, writers usually have some difficulty, mainly of a psychological nature, in observing the rules of writing in restricted languages.
The computer offers facilities for controlling restrictions in writing. Computer assistance in writing restricted language can at the same time be directed towards increasing both the efficacy of communication and the translatability of documents.

(c) MT can only produce artificial language. The artificial language produced by the computer can have a close formal similarity to the already restricted input language; it may therefore fulfil the same objectives of increased efficacy of communication that motivated the introduction of the restricted language in the particular domain and situation of use.
The computer control over restricted languages provides a useful start for the analysis of documents that are to be translated automatically.

(d) The MT process can be designed in such a manner that it maximises the benefits to be derived from restrictions on natural languages. A theory of MT can therefore with benefit be based on the principle of artificial language design and yield highly efficient and completely novel modes of communication.

In order to implement these principles in new machine translation systems, the restrictions imposed by the nature of natural language processing have to be developed in the direction of restrictions for improved communication. In this way, MT can be given a completely new role in the communication process.

These observations motivate the survey of the field of application of MT in the following sections and lead to the formulation of some general system specifications which will both explain the functional diversity of existing and potential systems and at the same time place these developments inside an extended theory of translation.

The following abbreviations are used in Figures 10.1 —10:

NL1	=	Natural language 1 (source).
NL2	=	Natural language 2 (target).
RL	=	Restricted language (human-designed & produced).
AL	=	Artificial language (human-designed, machine-produced).
MT	=	any process of automatic conversion of L1 language elements into L2 language elements.
|T|	=	a time interval interrupting the normal document flow.
[ ]	=	a process.

— Texts are assumed to be written in the first instance by humans in either natural (NL) or restricted language (RL). The term 'text' is here used instead of 'document' because for MT systems, not being able to interpret intention, all input is text.

— Artificial languages (AL) are either designed to be parallel to natural languages, in which case we speak of AL1, AL2, etc, or designed to be supra-natural language, e.g. like Botanical Latin or Lisp.

— Machines produce output in an artificial language which may, through a process of post-editing, be re-converted into text of a restricted or a natural language.

10.4.1 *MT as human translation aid*

The best known application of MT is commonly called machine-assisted human translation. This approach to machine translation covers generically all machine aids and can be subdivided by the various working methods involved. This application fully recognises the current limitations of MT design and provides whatever linguistic analysis and other assistance it can to translators. In this function the computer carries out a number of limited tasks which can consist of dictionary lookup, vocabulary control, pre-translation of phrases and sentences, etc., requiring the usual post-editing.

These systems are from the outset conceived as aids to translators and are intended to accelerate the human process of translation. The end product of such systems is usually measured in relation to its similarity to human products and consequently to the ease with which it can be post-edited to resemble human translation; in many cases the machine assistance is deliberately hidden from the user of the translation. From the point of view of its quality the MT output of such systems is frequently considered faulty or artificial to the extent that it does not conform to certain expectations, requiring human intervention to make it acceptable to a predefined user type. Where post-editing is not applied, it is normally considered that the end user still wants a human product, but is prepared to accept a product which by conventional standards is inferior, as long as it is either cheaper, or produced more quickly, or both.

It is generally accepted that these systems are greatly improved by concentrating on particular text types and ranges of vocabulary. Alternatively such systems increasingly have or offer subject-specific modules of vocabulary and phraseology that can be switched into the process once the human operator has recognised a particular subject orientation in the text.

The process is modelled in Figures 10.1 –5, according to stages of progressively increased machine assistance or human-machine interaction.

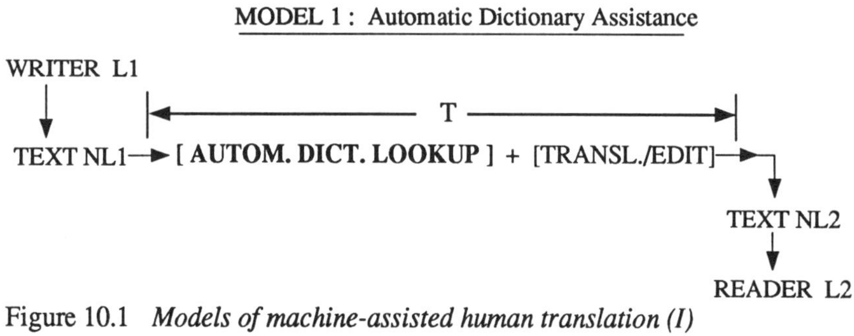

Figure 10.1 *Models of machine-assisted human translation (I)*

PROCESS:

A text is checked against an automated dictionary in order to assist the translator in consistency of word and expression matching, and to speed up the process. The aid operates by means of a program which ignores common words and function words and looks up translation equivalents for special vocabulary items which a translator would otherwise have to look up in a conventional dictionary.

This model does not involve machine translation as such, but some systems offer this facility as a first or separate stage leading to building up the dictionary. In such a case translators have to make a dictionary record for missing items.

MODEL 2: One-stage machine assistance
(Automatic pre-translation)

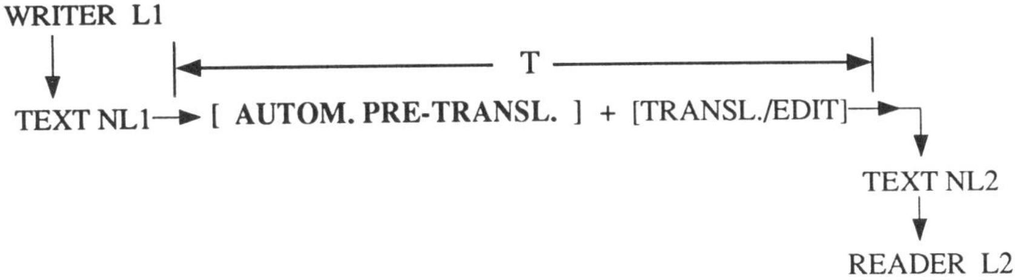

Figure 10.2 *Models of machine-assisted human translation (II)*

PROCESS:

A text is pre-translated automatically but the output is not adequate for either direct use or post-editing. The automated module offers translators words and expressions in the target language, possibly with some morphological adjustment and changed word order. In this way translators can reduce the time for dictionary look-up and also save the time of actually typing the found translation equivalents.

This model may exist by default or by design; i.e. the process of a more complex machine translation operation may be abandoned because its result is considered insufficient; or a system may be limited in its design to providing dictionary look-up and some phrasal substitution in the order in which they occur in the text.

MODEL 3: Two-stage machine assistance
(Automatic translation & human conversion)

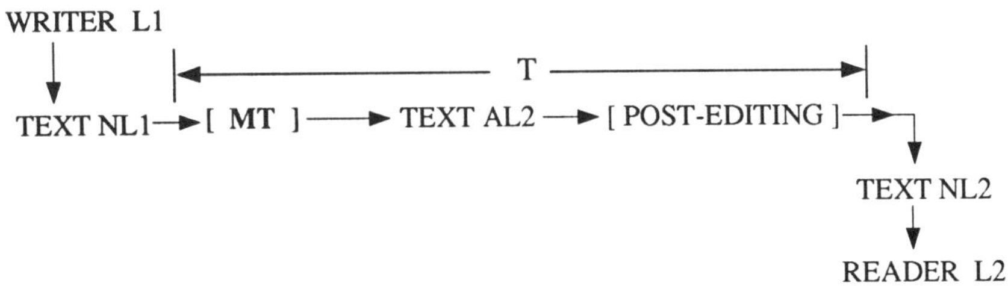

Figure 10.3 *Models of machine-assisted human translation (III)*

PROCESS:

A text written in NL1, destined for L1 readers, is subsequently selected for translation into NL2. It is decided that machine translation offers an economic solution despite the fact that the client expects a NL text. Regardless of the quality of the MT output in AL2, the document is post-edited so that the artificial language characteristics produced by the computer are obliterated. For the use of an MT system to be economically viable, the post-editing effort must be less than that required for a full human translation since otherwise there would be no point in seeking machine assistance.

MODEL 4: Three-stage machine assistance
(Pre-editing - MT - Post-editing)

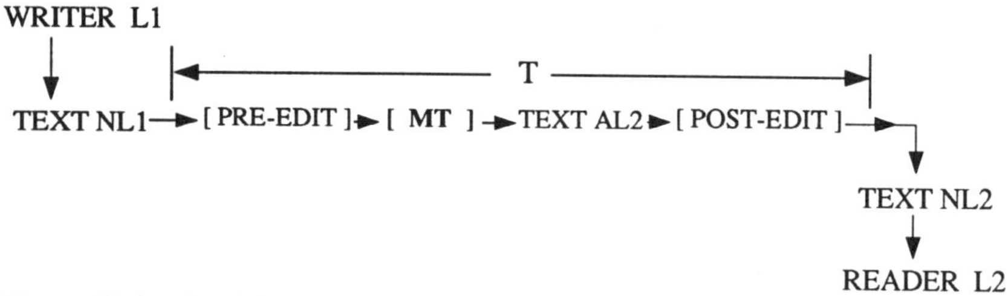

Figure 10.4 *Models of machine-assisted human translation (IV)*

PROCESS:

A text is selected and prepared for machine processing by human pre-editing. This can consist of simplifying text passages which in a translator's experience regularly cause difficulties, or of adding to the machine dictionary words the translators knows not to be there. The system produces output in AL2 which post-editors can convert into a NL2 document. The final document is not distinguishable from a human translation.

These four models of MT hide the true nature of MT and they are therefore an aid rather than an alternative to human translation. Their application is limited to the extent that the output must be acceptable to human translators for the purpose of their own post-editing efforts.

Models 2-4 are the simplest and at the same time most difficult types of MT system to design: they can be extremely simple, because they may consist of no more than a dictionary, some morphology and rearranging rules for word order—anything which speeds up the translator's work and reduces more routine tasks in the process is acceptable; they are difficult to design because they have no proper specification of objectives. If they are to assist human translators in a variety of tasks, these systems should be extremely flexible. Besides, in the design of these systems it is impossible to state what is an acceptable quality of output, other than that a post-editor must be able to produce a translation faster than by conventional means.

Examples of such systems are the so-called 'machine-assisted' translation systems ALPS, ATLAS, LOGOS and WEIDNER but also the large batch-processing SYSTRAN system. The specifications for EUROTRA also foresee its use as a post-editing system. As proof of the practical usefulness of these systems a recent article on an application of the Weidner MicroCAT system can be cited. The authors of this paper (Pym 1991:9) claim that the translation costs have been cut by 50-70% by a combination of a restricted input language (PACE) and the use of this system. The same author also reports post-editing volumes of MT output from this system of between 7000-9000 words per day.

10.4.2 *Translation by reference to existing models*

A new approach to machine-assisted human translation is based on the recognition that documents are repetitive and that the writing process frequently consists of utilising pre-existing text segments. A system design can be further specialised for use in instances where documents occur in multiple editions and versions, reflecting different stages of product documentation or revision.

Such a translation aid scans existing documents by a text-deconstruction method of text comparison, identifies similar passages and offer these to the translator as models for the new task. Current experience at the CEC with the translation of tenders offers practical evidence of the usefulness of this approach. Research currently being undertaken in the Netherlands also points in this direction. Further experience exists from research of the translation of regularly up-dated and modified computer manuals. Since only relatively small sections of new versions of such manuals require new translation at any one time and the text modifications of the SL document, while vitally important for the good functioning of the software, are linguistically relatively minor, a comparison of existing and new source document and existing translations not only saves re-translation of unmodified existing parts of the document but also provides control over the new translation of the document. In this way the machine assists in keeping product documentation precise and up-to-date.

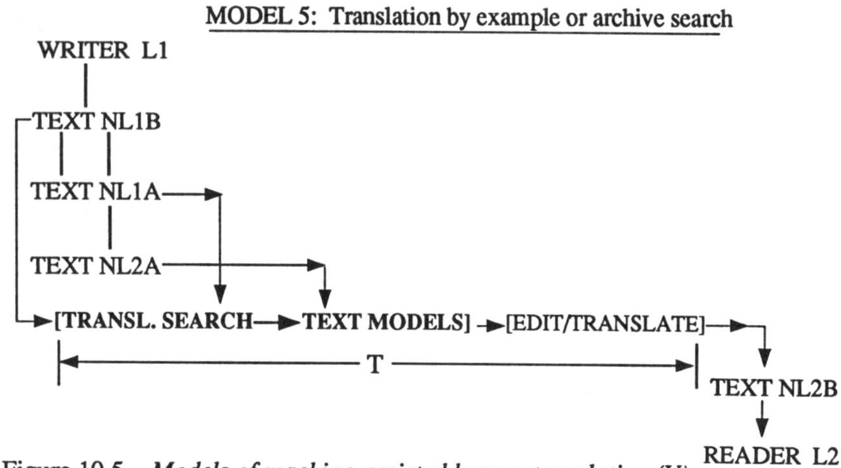

Figure 10.5 *Models of machine-assisted human translation (V)*

PROCESS:

A second version/edition of a NL1 document, say NL1B, is matched first with its precursor, e.g. a previous edition existing in machine-readable form, called here NL1A, in order to identify text passages in which the two texts differ. Then the translation of this precursor, say NL2A, will be called up from the archive and marked where its text segments coincide with the matches between the two previously contrasted texts, i.e. NL1A and NL1B. The translator therefore has three text versions on the screen, namely NL1A, NL2B and NL2A. In order to obtain the new edition, i.e. NL2B, the existing NL2A version is modified only to the extent that the NL1B differs from NL1A.

This method of translation confirms the principle of text modification explained in chapter four.

10.4.3 *MT as text-type specific independent systems*

This is the first type that can properly be called 'automatic', in the sense that human intervention is not required between input and output. The setting for this process is schematised in Figure 10.6.

In this application MT is used (i) without the intervention of a human translator, and (ii) as a text-production system for previously edited, i.e. restricted, input. The MT output is written in an artificial language, which has to be designed in such a way that it becomes usable for either or all the three forms of output indicated in Figure 10.6, i.e.:

(a) raw translation in AL2 suitable for post-editing and possible conversion to NL2;

(b) a final AL2 version which can be used almost in the same way as natural language texts because it has been pre-edited;

(c) an unedited final translation, i .e. an artificial language, which is acceptable to readers. This language will resemble one of the readers' sublanguages, and in many cases, if properly constructed, it should be as easy to read as other functional sublanguages. Readers have to learn to read this language in the same way as they have learnt to read chemical formulae, biological Latin, or musical scores, i.e. like a second language.

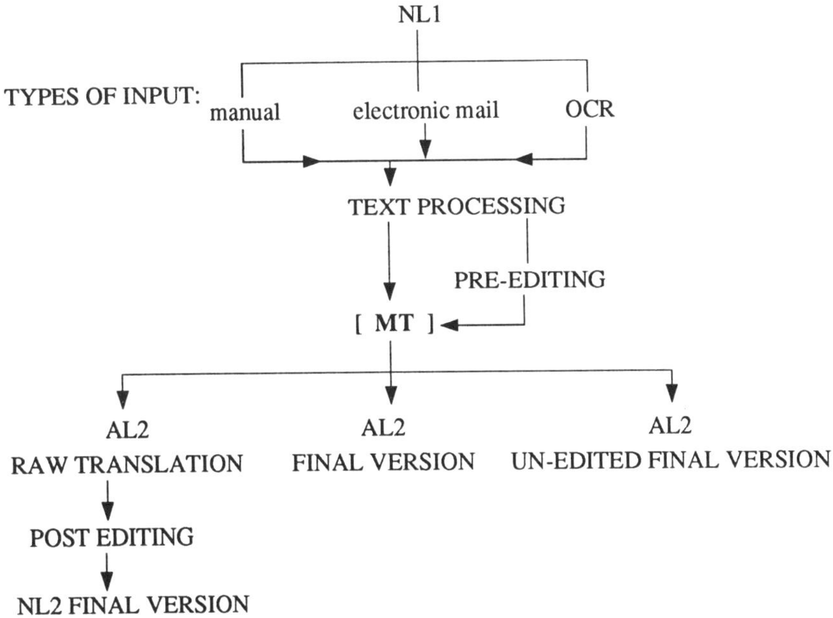

Figure 10.6 *The setting of automatic translation*

Within this setting, there can then be two separate sub-types, according to whether the process is reader or writer-oriented.

10.4.3.1 *Reader-oriented MT*

Tests have shown that readers are prepared to accept 'difficult-to-read' texts, if they can be got cheap and above all fast. This would produce a translation type as indicated in Figure 10.7.

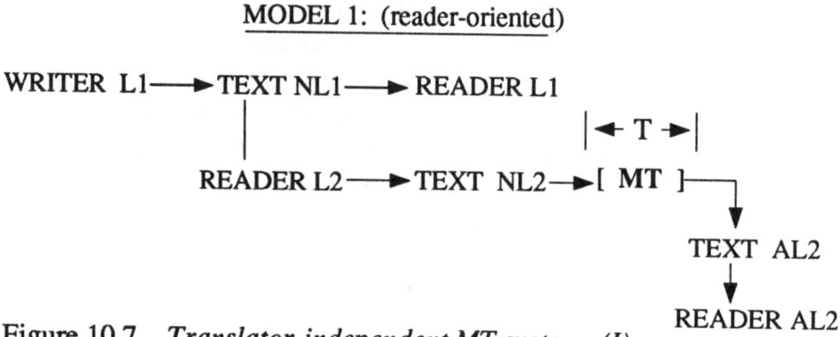

Figure 10.7 *Translator-independent MT systems (I)*

PROCESS:

L2 readers receive texts in L1 they cannot read. They submit the text to machine translation in the full knowledge that what they will receive is a machine-translated text, i.e. a product in which a document written in NL1 has been converted into the AL2 of the system.

This type of translation produces what is conventionally described as 'raw output'. This expression illustrates the mistaken focus of much writing about MT. The output is machine-produced and therefore by definition an artificial product which may be easier or more difficult to understand than a NL text; it is certainly not comparable to a human translation nor should it be confused with such.

The text to be produced is intended for a new form of reading in an environment which neither has the resources in time, talent and money for producing full-scale human translation. This does not mean that the new product must be worse than that previously produced by human translation. It will be different, may require more reading effort, but is in principle available immediately and probably with fewer risks of lexical or terminological error than hitherto. After some practice, such languages can be read with a high degree of precision of understanding and a speed that is not significantly inferior to that of reading natural language texts.

With the improvement of OCR machines and the greater number of texts available in machine-readable form, this type of translation, designed for the translation of large quantities of text, has a great future attraction for the rapid dissemination of current information to a large readership in the habit of scanning documents. Such a quick information service works on the basis of the immediate availability of documents to highly motivated readers who, with time, develop a particular ability to read the artificial language produced by the machine.

This fact can be taken into account in its design, which can maximise the concentration of information (e.g. omission of function words, contraction of words and expressions). As a consequence new reading habits will be developed in the same way as people have learnt to read databases.

The historical example of this type and use of system is SYSTRAN which has been in continuous use by the United States Air Force in this function since the 1970s (Bostad 1982). The acceptability of an artificial language for specific purposes, in this case, the scanning of scientific and technical literature, is therefore proven and is a strong indicator of the need for this type of service.

10.4.3.2 *Writer-oriented MT*

This type of system can be seen as an evolution of monolingual text editing systems in the direction of dealing with style-sensitive texts in specific subject fields. It is based on the assumption that writers know better than anybody else what they wants to say and that, therefore, any interaction the machine requires should be carried out with writers directly and not with translators who would first have to interpret what writers have said. A fully automatic and directly usable translation of a particular text type can be produced, if writers first edit their text with the aid of the computer as an editing-control device. In this case writers must consider their text a draft which is modified by interaction with the machine. The interaction would consist of a dialogue in which the machine asks questions about elements which it cannot analyse i.e., about everything which it does not have in its dictionaries or grammar or anything which permits multiple interpretations. Such an editing device may, however, hypercorrect a text, e.g. insist on the insertion of all relative pronouns, point out ambivalent references etc., deal with all questions which make texts depend on the imaginative interpretation of readers. Complex instruction manuals, for example, would be much improved if the computer prevented bored technical writers from making leaps of fancy which can cause confusion among users of the manual. In order to translate, such an editing device will then also be target language-sensitive and anticipate translation difficulties. In a second analysis stage the editing tool will then prompt writers to annotate their texts e.g. to resolve any ambiguity that can be foreseen as likely to arise in the target language. To do this writers need not necessarily be able to understand the target language. Questions can be phrased in such a way that explanations are given which the computer can work on.

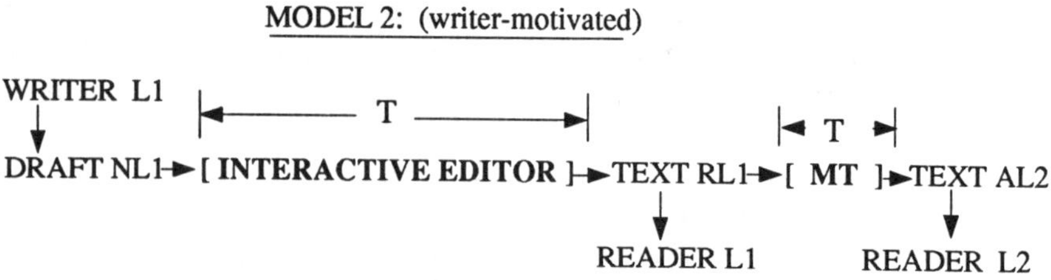

Figure 10.8 *Translator-independent MT systems (II)*

PROCESS:

A technical writer uses a computer to edit the text to give it a form which can readily be translated automatically. This restricted language text is separately usable as an improved NL1 version. In order to produce a translation, the RL1 text is translated into a matching artificial language version that meets the target language readers' expectation.

In this type there is control over the writer during the production of the L1 document. It is assumed that the NL1 text is not sufficiently restricted to be directly processable by machine, without considerable uncertainty of interpretation. It is therefore necessary to edit the text in such a way that it becomes more restricted and so suitable for MT processing. The restrictions cannot normally be produced by the machine on its own; so, human intervention is required in order to resolve ambiguities of interpretation. The RL1 product may either only serve as input to MT, in which case it is directly usable as in TITUS, or it is a product in its own right which can be used as a more efficient L1 text, as in Ntran.

It is then possible to divide the process into two phases:

— interactive editing in order to produce an efficient RL1 document;

— further editing and automatic translating in interaction with the writer, if required, in order to produce a clear and directly usable AL2 output.

The textbook example of this approach is the Canadian Meteorological Office's METEO system, which automatically translates weather reports written in a restricted form of English into French reports which appear side by side the English text on television screens all over the country. The same principle underlies the production of the periodical publications of CULT and TITUS. In addition, Systran has been used by Rank Xerox to translate what they call 'Customized English'. Weidner has also been used in this way. The design for the UMIST English-Japanese system, Ntran, represented a further development of these systems in that it provided for the writer to interact with the analysis module of the MT system in order to formulate a more effective L1 text which can then be automatically translated.

This type of system can be designed for highly specialised applications in which a writer's skill can be exploited fully for the production of acceptable source language text.

10.4.3.3 *Writer-oriented editing of pre-translated text*

Recognising the fact that many texts contain fixed and repetitive elements, subtypes of writer-oriented systems have been constructed. They offer menus of existing SL text segments into which new information has to be inserted; text segments can then be combined in a variety of ways to produce complete new messages. The existing text segments are pre-translated, and the choice of new input is easily translatable because it is heavily restricted. The best example of an application of this type of system is that of business letters. Writers are given a choice of types of letter and within these types separate menus of components by user type.

By steering writers in such a way that they do not feel constrained by the manipulation, the system can produce natural looking and fully-acceptable messages, when in reality a highly restricted language has been employed which has appropriate equivalents in other languages. For such a system to succeed, the designers have to work from sentence segments to whole sentences, and from sentences to texts. At every stage univocity has to be tested and equivalence in the desired target languages secured.

10.4.4 *MT of machine-readable restricted language texts*

There is a third major category of machine translation which currently lies outside the scope of human translation altogether, namely MT of documents already written in a restricted or artificial language.

If the previous applications were appropriate for already existing text types, it is equally possible to design systems that translate newly created text types, such as the information frames offered by databases, expert systems etc. In such a case there is greater flexibility of design, because the prior design of the new text type constituted by the database units of information can take MT requirements into account, and this can lead to MT systems that can produce fully multilingual parallel documents. The design of the text type, grammar and lexicon for the database units will in these cases also consider the control of human input so that the writing of the original database entry or document is performed with a minimum of error and a maximum of precision, economy and speed. In the many cases where a translation can be foreseen, it can be shown that a control on the human input of text also guarantees a smooth and unproblematic translation.

MODEL 3: MT of restricted language databases

[DATABASE INPUT]
↓
(a) [**INTERACTIVE L1 EDITOR**] → TEXT RL1 → L1 DATABASE USER
↓
(b) [**ADDITIONAL INTERACTIVE EDITING**]
↓
AL1
↓
(c) [**MT**] → AL2 → L2 DATABASE USER

Figure 10.9 *Translator-independent MT systems (III)*

PROCESS:

(a) Editors, or other persons feeding or updating the database, record new text, usually by filling in data into fields with some control over the input process (e.g. spelling check, completion check, etc.). In this process they convert the material into a restricted language; the machine analyses the text and asks questions concerning areas of uncertainty of interpretation. The editor then adjusts the input in the light of suggestions made by the machine. Initially questions are asked which tend to ensure conformity of the input with existing material in the database.

(b) In a second phase questions can be asked to elicit information required for the production of the target language version of the data. Writers will not necessarily understand the nature of these questions, but they can nevertheless provide the information more reliably than translators.

(c) The machine translates once it is sure that it can provide sentences which conform to its grammar, i.e. the machine is not instructed to produce some foreign language output at all costs. In this way the computer is used to produce an artificial language which can then be translated into another linguistic version of the same artificial language, whenever there is a need for it. Texts can therefore be stored monolingually, and translated automatically every time there is a query in another target language. In the case of METEO, the Canadian weather report system, readers are unaware of a translation, or, at least, cannot distinguish between source and target language text; but this does not alter the fact that they are reading an MT-produced AL text.

10.4.5 *MT of machine-readable artificial language text*

Translation systems can also deal with database information already automatically selected and stored. In this case the model would look much simpler, as in Figure 10.10.

MODEL 4: Artificial language database MT

```
[DATABASE TEXT INPUT]
    |
    └──────────────► AL1 ─────────────────► L1  DATABASE USER
                      |
                  [ MT ] ──────► AL2 ─────► L2  DATABASE USER
                  [ MT ] ──────► AL3 ─────► L3  DATABASE USER
```

Figure 10.10 *Translator-indpendent MT systems (IV)*

PROCESS:

A strictly controlled database entry is created either by human editing of the input information into the artificial language of the database, or, alternatively, the input is automatically selected, and possibly undergoes automatic control with some human interaction. In either case the database entry text is usually in a form that can be reliably translated into an artificial language format of any foreign language that has the necessary level of technology, and hence the terminology and syntax required, to process the content of the database.

This type of translation can only be applied to databases which are already designed for an artificial language, or are the product of computer processing, in which case they are already artificial. In either case, it is only possible to produce an artificial language, and the question is simply whether the L1-based artificial language has the characteristics of a language suitable for MT processing or whether such editing has yet to be performed automatically or with human interaction.

In existing monolingual databases, the artificial language is usually not controlled as to its consistency and needs further editing and restriction before it can be used as direct input to MT. In the process of preparing the database contents for effective MT processing, the input rules must be controlled more tightly and made more efficient even for monolingual use. According to the nature of the database, the content to be translated may consist of words only, expressions (e.g.'previous owner', 'appointment of a new treasurer'), phrases (e.g. 'not yet registered', 'no details given', 'date of the previous announcement in the register') and complete sentences.

Database MT is relatively new and in practice largely untested. Experimental work indicates that this type of translation will be much in demand and can be produced with a high degree of efficiency. In many cases, e.g. where the speed and volume of addition and change to the database would exceed any form of human translation, MT is, in fact, the only possible form of providing the information contained in the database in another language.

10.4.6 *Outlook*

Machine translation is wrongly seen as an alternative to human translation. Machines can only produce an artificial form of language. This fact can be exploited to the benefit of translation if this is defined as an interpretation and reproduction process with the objective of improving communication. Restricted languages in the domain of science and technology—the chief areas of intended applications of MT—serve the purpose of improving precision, economy and appropriateness of communication. Machine translation systems can be designed with the objective of maximising the advantage of restricted language interpretation and production. Functional types of MT systems can be developed on these principles.

10.5 Other Applications of MT technology

The integration of the translation component into a wider text handling environment, including wordprocessors, on-line dictionaries, automatic indexing, etc. marks a clear trend in the development of fully commercial machine translation systems or translation aids; it is, arguably, the integration of such facilities within packages which enhances the productivity of translators as much as the actual translation facility.

Existing models of translation aids are uni-directional and sequential; i.e. a user wishing to produce a text in two languages, must first compose in one (the source language) and then submit this text to the translation system for translation into the target language. This conventional type of translation is, however, only one form of multilingual composition which occurs in a greater diversity of environments than suggested by conventional models of translation. Machine aids can be developed for other approaches to multilingual text production, which might be called 'Parallel Multi-lingual Text Production System'.

Professional practice indicates at least two alternative ways of envisaging translation:

(a) A source text can be constructed with the clear purpose of translation. In such a case a text editor can assist the writer of the source text to produce a text optimally suitable for (human or machine) translation. This situation is anticipated in the Ntran system, described above in section 10.2.3, which combines text production with translation on the level of text or sentence; but it is still directional.

(b) A writer with a good command of more than one language may want to produce parallel texts more or less simultaneously, as e.g. in multilingual commercial correspondence, contracts, legal documents and even legislation. Parallel document production would also find application in the numerous cases of bilingual instructions which are produced to stand side by side. The associated text production situations cannot be directional, because writers must have freedom to start in any one language. They cannot be sequential, because writers must be able to switch back and forth in order to produce truly parallel texts.

The present state of the art permits the design and development of multilingual text production systems which offer the facilities required for parallel text production. Such a system would offer rapid on-line translation in both directions for each language pair. It could be realised in the form of a split screen facility for simultaneous editing on either window and translation from either into the other. Writers would compose a sentence on one window with a translation appearing in the other. They would then be able to edit the translated version. The newly edited version would then be translated back into the first language window. These operations would be repeated until a satisfactory parallel version had been produced.

The clear advantage of such a system lies in the fact that the combination of functions of writer and translator is being recognised, that a single software combines all the writing and translating support needed in these situations and that writers and translators have the support they directly and immediately need for their work.

10.6 Other ways of classifying MT systems

There are other ways of classifying MT systems, namely by the text-type they can handle and by degree of automation. A brief, useful survey is given in Meli (1989). These two modes are briefly outlined here in order to provide another perspective on this part of language engineering.

10.6.1 *Typology of MT systems by text types*

By text type, two modes of distinction are common; one is based on the scope of the subject field, the other on degrees of restriction of input. Regarding scope, a difference can be made between (i) systems based on a single fixed textual corpus, (practical only for research purposes and very limited applications);

(ii) systems limited to a narrow subject field,(as, e.g., the case of METEO or TITUS); (iii) systems of limited scope which envisage extendability through the addition of new dictionaries; and (iv) unrestricted systems.

Regarding restrictions, a distinction is often made between systems that require to pre-edit input and systems which input texts written in a language designed for ease of application of MT, e.g. Multinational Customized English (MCE); Perkins Approved Clear English (PACE); International Language for Service and Maintenance (ILSAM).

10.6.2 *Typology of MT systems by degree of automation*

It is also common to classify systems by degrees of automation:

— machine-assisted human translation systems
— human-assisted machine translation systems
— fully automatic translation systems.

The first group is characterised by tools which assist the translators, namely:

(a) Wordprocessor + dictionary
    — Selective dictionary look-up
    — Automatic dictionary look-up

(b) Term-bank access

(c) KWIC indexes for the avoidance of homonyms

(d) Grammatical information

(e) Morphological analysis

(f) Access to translated-text files

(g) Automatic correction of spelling and typing errors

The second group is characterised by the form and degree of human intervention:

(a) pre-editing on screen

(b) interaction during translation

(c) post-editing

Fully automatic systems are defined as operating without human intervention between input and output.

10.7 Criteria for the use of MT

When previously translators would speak of faithfulness of translations and comprehensibility of target language texts, the general property of 'user-friendliness' has been proclaimed as the chief virtue of the most popular or most widely used systems. This commercial slogan hides a number of quite different elements. Translators who have the opportunity to select a MT systems reach their decisions after consideration of criteria of cost benefit and the suitability of the system for the range of documents they have to translate. It must be recognised, however, that different user types pursue different aims, and have different requirements concerning quality, speed, subject matter and cost.

10.7.1 *Cost factors*

From an industrial point of view, users are, firstly, concerned with the cost of the new MT technology. Beyond the cost of software and hardware, other cost factors which have to be considered are maintenance and depreciation of the system. Frequently overlooked cost factors are training, infrastructure and the creation and maintenance of dictionaries. Only after training and a reasonable period of practice can translators genuinely estimate the time required and hence the cost of their own involvement in the use of the system in the form of inputting text, pre-editing, post-editing and final formatting.

In the current climate of rapid evolution of systems and electronic support, translators also look for: (i) the possibility of adding improvements without having to change the system or modify the dictionaries; (ii) the scope for system expansion with respect to range of texts to be processed; (iii) new language pairs that can be added without other changes to a system.

10.7.2 *Document selection for MT processing*

For practical purposes, the main concern of translators is to have reliable selection criteria for documents suitable for machine processing. A number of general criteria are here presented, the order and importance of which varies with the design of the system.

(a) There must be a sufficient volume of regularly occurring homogeneous documents requiring translation in order to justify the adaptation and installation of a system.

(b) The format of documents must be suitable or, at least, adaptable for processing; e.g. tables, graphics, formats, columns etc. must be separable from the running text so as not interfere with the regular process of translation.

(c) The terminology of the documents to be processed must be contained in the dictionaries of the system; alternatively the time required for building up appropriate dictionaries must be commensurate with the volume of work to be handled. The new vocabulary to be input must not create conflicts with information contained in existing dictionaries regarding such cases as (i) un-recorded meanings, and (ii) items unmarked for separate meanings in different subject fields.

(d) Input documents should be stylistically straightforward, a property normally associated with technical, scientific, and to a lesser extent, documents of an administrative nature which have an informative intention.

(e) Input documents should be free of typing errors which can introduce false homography, failure to recognize agreement between parts of speech and other elements which have a negative effect on dictionaries or complicate or falsify analysis.

(f) Input documents should be as complete as possible, because the omissions of relative pronouns or other connectives, for example, cause difficulties of interpretation.

The ideal characteristics for texts suitable for MT have been identified by Jean Gordon (1990) as "machine-readable, suitably formatted, limited and stable terminology, without polysemy, of a narrow special subject; no ambiguity, respectful of usage, no typographical or other errors, short sentences, without omissions or ellipsis, no complex idioms etc." She recognises that for such an ideal corpus the problem will be one of volume and confirms that decisions about the use of MT should be made strictly on a cost-benefit basis.

Chapter Six

Industrialisation of Translation

11 Translation in an Information Technology Environment

This final section deals with two complementary topics. It shows that translation, as practised today, is increasingly integrated in the language industry and how the technology that supports this environment is increasingly responding to the needs of the translation market.

11.1 Industrial aspects of translation

Translating is not a natural activity, like speaking and writing; it is a highly complex alternative to a widely practised but very limited bilingualism. Because they constitute an interruption or a delay in a communication process, translations are commissioned only when direct communication does not or is anticipated not to succeed. The circumstances and conditions of this need form the foundation of an extended and diversified theory of translation. At the same time translations, when they occur in industrial settings, are now becoming integrated into the technology for text processing and transmission which supports information and documentation. The definition of translation, given in previous sections, could therefore be complemented to stress this aspect, by specifying that translation is an externally motivated industrial activity, supported by information technology, which is diversified in response to the particular needs of this form of communication.

Viewed as part of a process of communication, translation is integrated into the chain of document processing in several ways. In the relatively narrow confines of technical documentation, for example, in major electronic firms or engineering enterprises which have to produce large volumes of documents to accompany industrial products, integration begins at the level of the design offices with CAD, and then shadows CAM or computer-aided integrated construction. Technical writers work in close collaboration with all staff in order to provide the firm-internal documentation and then the manuals and other literature which accompany the product. In order to serve a multilingual market translation has to be simultaneous with, or at least follow closely behind, the production of monolingual documentation if it is not to delay the marketing of the product. The translation of the documentation for a major aircraft has been reported as requiring some 80,000 hours work of translation, i.e. 39 man years, at a cost of 8 million French francs. (Yanez 1990). Such a time delay would clearly be most damaging if marketing a product would have to wait so long for translated documentation. In such circumstances it is imperative for translators and terminologists (i) to follow closely the work of designers and technical writers and (ii) to work from the beginning with computer-readable text, remaining within the electronic medium until the final print-out. Facilities for achieving this objective are provided by the use of OCR for data input, if it is not already in electronic form, the standardisation procedures provided by SGML (standard generalised mark-up language) in such environments as CALS (computer-aided acquisition and logistic support initiative) — a programme developed in the US, and imposed as a standard by the US Department of Defense — which is already being followed by a number of European countries in the form of Eurocals.

To support translators' research, information is now available on-line in forms acceptable to the user, and no longer in the single fixed, pre-determined presentation formats in which information is received from a paper source. In this way information is easier to handle and to update directly, and also easier to integrate into documents translators are producing.

It is obvious that translators can achieve substantial savings by having access at any one moment to full information on the design and production process which allows them to complete or regularly update translations in the main languages of their clients, so that they are available in final printed form at the same time as the product is ready for marketing.

Text analyzers and other linguistic tools used for MT are equally useful for interfaces such as interrogation of multilingual databases, gateways for accessing them, expert systems and associated knowledge bases and other applications of language processing such as skimming and document delivery. In the cases where language processing is taken as the focal point, dictionaries, wordprocessing, computer-assisted text composition, electronic publishing and indexation can all be coordinated in order to provide optimal assistance to translators.

11.1.1 *The cost and value of translation*

Of the approximately 3,000 languages in the world today, only a few hundred are currently relevant for the language industry, because only this number has a written tradition and is supported by a culture in which modern technology has a place. Even among these languages, their importance for translation is very unevenly distributed if measured by the number of literate speakers and potential translation users. It has been estimated that, in Europe alone, total costs for documentation production and management for all economic sectors amount to some 508 billion ECUs per year, of which some 8 billion ECUs are directly spent on translation (Bossard 1992).

Yet another picture of the relative importance of certain languages arises when they are considered from the point of view of the volume of scientific and technical publication likely to be translated into or out of them. It is generally agreed that English is the language of some 50% of all current technical and scientific publication, and that French, German, Japanese and Russian occupy another 40%, leaving only 10% for all other languages (Large 1983, Kunicki 1980). On this account the demand for translation from English is overwhelming. A different picture emerges when the translation demands of large international organisations are considered. In the European Community institutions, where there is absolute parity between its nine official languages, there is, in principle, as much demand for translation into English as there is for translation into Greek or any other official language, though it is obvious that the amount of documentation originated in any one of the nine languages bears some relation to the size of the representation of a country, its state of technological progress, its economic importance and, of course, the working languages of the staff employed in Brussels, Luxemburg and Strassburg. For example, the translation services of the Commission of the EC in Brussels reported for the year 1976 that 58% of translation were from French, 19% from English and only 11% from German. As expected the distribution of translation into the official languages of the EC member states was much more balanced, namely, 20% into English, 20% into German, 15% each into French, Italian, Dutch and Danish. With an increase of staff from the new member states, Greece, Spain and Portugal, the distribution of source languages has changed considerably.

In an industrial perspective, translations are documents which have a production cost and a commercial value. Because of the extremely variable and varied social and professional status of text producers, there is no direct correlation between production cost and the value of a source language document. The price charged for translation is in most cases equally unrelated to the commercial value of either the source or target language document. Nor is there a direct correlation between the production cost of translation and the value of a translated document. This is seen in the relatively high price paid for the translation or adaptation of an advertising slogan or for the translation of official documents, e.g. birth certificates, as well as in the variation in price of translation between language pairs, and the varying prices paid for the same translation in different parts of the world.

The great diversity of pricing translations is reflected in the different ways of calculating volume of work. Many countries seem to cost translations by page of TL text, but then there are great variations in the size of pages. For example, the following divergencies in numbers of words per page have been recorded by FIT, the International Translator Federation: (Argentina 500, Belgium & Spain 300, Korea 250). When expressed in lines, there are differences in length between 50 and 60 characters per line, and lines per page also differ from between 25 lines in Italy to 30 lines in France. More reliable is costing by 1000 words of source text as usually practised in Canada, the USA, the UK, or target text as is customary in the Netherlands. Another method now available as a result of word-processing is costing by printed characters, as currently practised in Russia (FIT 1992:35).

Overall, the price charged for a translation does, however, appear to relate more closely to actual production costs than that of other documents. This fact is a reflection on the status of translators in society who are seen as routine performers and not as creators. In this respect the appreciation of translators' work is similar to that of technical writers and information scientists, all of whom provide a service in the communications industry, but whose creative value is seldom recognised.

In the current market situation, the cost of translation is much more dependent on language pairs than on content or value of the document. In the 1960s Russian-English translation was highly priced, but as more translators were trained and the interest in Soviet technical literature declined, so did the price for this language pair. High-cost language pairs also vary with the part of the globe in which the translation is demanded. This in turn is a reflection on the supply and demand for translators in a changing market, which cannot readily produce fully qualified translators overnight to deal with a change in demand. Because of the ease and speed of international communication which permits the commissioning of translation over great distances at no loss of time, some of these price differentials are currently being levelled out.

The development of the machine translation industry is founded on the recognition that translations are commercial products in a document production and transformation industry. This implies that it is accepted that people are willing to pay for a translated document on a regular basis. The translated document is then seen either as a new source of information which has an additional cost or as an addition to the value of a source language document.

Since diverse documents lead to diverse translation types via diverse techniques, we must expect the design of industrial translation tools to replicate this diversification of techniques and end products. A distribution by subject areas, and implicitly text types, gives the following major fields of translation activities: commercial 35%, industrial 21%, scientific 20%, legislative 9%, press and current affairs 3.5%, audio-visual 2%, educational 1.5%, literary 0.3%, miscellaneous 6.7% (van Slype et al. 1983).

Different machines produce different products but, as with all industrial processes, a sizable volume of demand for any one type of product must have been identified before it is worthwhile investing in the design and later the purchase of a machine. This recognition has already led to a diversification of developments.

(a) MT designers have started to conduct market analyses for their products and are adjusting their products to the need of particular clients. There is also a trend towards greater modularisation of design and towards the production of specialist dictionaries adaptable to the needs of customers.

(b) Major users of translations are seeking to standardise their specifications in the direction of what machines can do, so that more of their translation demand can be met by a single machine and a single process.

(c) Translation producers are grouping together to get a large volume of demand which justifies the purchase of a particular type of machine. The steadily growing number of large, even international translation companies is evidence of this development. The ease of electronic data transmission now also makes it possible to get translation-related work such as editing or dictionary preparation carried out over great distances without transport delay.

11.1.2 *Growth in demand*

From other industrialisation processes we know that the arrival of machines, which diversify the products on offer, also stimulates demand. There is in any case a steady growth in translation needs, because:

(a) There are a growing number of official national languages which require full documentation in that language and hence translation into and out of the major vehicular languages of the world. For example, in Europe alone the status of the languages of the Baltic republics and those of the former Yugoslavia has changed to that of official languages to be represented at all international levels.

(b) There are more international contacts now being carried out in national languages; the use of the international vehicular languages, like English and French, is in decline even in international organisations. The prime example for this development is the nine-language regime of the EC in contrast to the small number of official languages of the United Nations established in 1945, a regime which has undergone very few adjustments since.

(c) There is growth in international business and commerce between a larger number of countries and hence a larger number of languages; this leads to a diversification of languages in international use. For example, the United Kingdom used to trade mainly in English because its commercial contacts were principally with its former colonies; today the trade has shifted to European partners in the EC and with it a need arose for multilingual communication.
(d) There is greater sophistication in industrial products which require a greater volume of documentation in national or even regional languages. A small computer program may be accompanied by hundreds of pages of explanation and operating instructions, some of which also occur on the computer screen where they also have to appear in the language of the user.
(e) There is an unprecedented demand for the translation of fiction, plays and other forms of literature; this can be seen as a simple growth in consumption of international products which is stimulated by subsidies, prizes etc. by exporting countries. For example, the CEC has introduced a programme of financial support for literary translation from the lesser used language to other European language. Equally, Brazil has instituted subsidies for the translation of its literature, which in turn produces royalties for Brazilian authors. Other countries pursue similar policies of stimulation for spreading their literature and cultural products through organisations like the British Council, the Alliance Française, the Goethe Institut, etc.
(f) Even Bible translation shows a remarkable increase in activity in recent decades. By 1900 translation of parts or the whole of the Bible existed in 515 languages. By 1950 this number had grown to over a thousand, but by 1991 that number had grown to 1,946 languages (Bible Society 1991).

The industrialisation of the translation profession itself is also discernible on a number of indicators:

(a) There is a trend from small translation enterprises to the formation of large, international translation and document processing companies. In recent years a number of small and medium-sized companies have amalgamated into much larger groups.
(b) When until recently companies acted mainly as agencies for free-lance translators, the trend is towards full document production requiring more in-house staff all of which favours automation.
(c) Free-lance translators are grouping themselves into cooperatives in order to compete with translation companies and in order to maximise the utilisation of the increasingly complex information technology infrastructure their operations are based on.

(d) Firms with limited translation requirements reduce their internal translation services and contract out their translation requirements to competitive bidding; electronic media and speed of data transmission now make it possible to have translations carried out with the same speed as if they were produced in-house.
(e) Translators diversify into document design, editing, and printing so that translation becomes only one aspect of document production.
(f) Translation jobs get bigger so that individuals cannot handle them on their own within reasonable time limits and have to resort to team work or machine assistance. Jobs now also usually involve some other process, such a dictionary production, editing and printing.
(g) The overall penetration of information technology is progressing so that translators receive more texts in machine-readable form and are required to present their work in the form of diskettes or send it electronically to the client.

Demand for translation occurs at the level of the state, at the level of large organisations (UN, Unesco etc), international corporations and industry, at the level of small firms, and finally, for private use.

In 1989 the world market estimate for the total volume of translation was for between 150 and 200 million pages, at a value of 3 milliard dollars and employing some 175,000 people. Other estimates (Hammond, 1990) put world expenditure on translation at $US 20 billion. Demand is expected to grow by 50% in 5 years. MT is expected to rise to between 5-15% of this market. These figures are always surrounded by a number of reservations because (i) there is uncertainty about how "translation" and "page" are defined, and (ii) the number of part-time translators and other professionals who translate occasionally is impossible to measure.

There are also some partial estimates and some hard figures of actual translations produced which can be used in support of these estimates. For 1986 the Japan Electronics Industry Development Association reported a translation volume of 18-23 million pages a year in Japan, at a cost of 5.5 Billion US$, mainly between Japanese and English. Another survey in 1986 reports more than 100 million pages translated in Western Europe.

In 1982 it was reported that the volume of translation for the EC institutions had grown from some 600,000 pages in 1977 to over a million in 1979 (Nyborg 1982). It must be noted that these figures reflect the position before Greece, Portugal and Spain joined the EC. The same report gives 'language costs' for the EC institutions in 1979 of 331.8 million ECU, which represent, according to institution, between 33% and 60% of the total budget. The Joint Interpreting and Conference Services in Luxembourg and Brussels reported 9,720 meetings in 1989, the equivalent of 110,000 interpreter days. Another large translation service, the Translation Bureau of the Canadian Secretary of State is reported to have an annual translation volume of approx. 120,000 pages. For 1984 the United Nations New York offices were reported as handling approx. 180 million words annually, a figure which had risen from 80 million words reported for the year 1978, and was expected to rise by 2% in 1985.

It is difficult to obtain any figures for the volume of particular types of translation. A calculation by Simpkin (1982) gives the following distribution for demand for diverse types seen from an English perspective: literary translation 5%; publication and legal translation 15%; information translation 20%; selective translation 25%; gist translation 35%. The vagueness of these categories is matched by another survey for the bilingual situation of Belgium: commercial 41%, scientific and technical 31%, administrative 21% legal 4%, other 3% (van Hoof 1971).

Demand for translation can arise suddenly for political or economic reasons and be of such magnitude that only MT appears a viable solution. For example, the implementation of the bilingual policy in Canada required the translation into French of some 100 years of laws and statutes. The return of Hongkong to China will create a large demand of translation into Chinese. The creation of autonomous regions in Spain requires large-scale translation into Basque and Catalan and possibly other languages as well. The same will occur with the expansion of the European Communities, in the former Soviet Union and the former Yugoslavia.

11.1.3 *The market for MT*

Within this expanding translation market there is a growing opportunity for MT because of the inability of the conventional market to meet the rising demand and the consequent rise in the cost of translation. Figures for actual turnover and demand for machine translation must be taken very cautiously because of the rapid changes in the design of systems and the highly ambivalent interpretations of what is meant by MT. In 1983 a survey anticipated that MT would occupy a market share of 5-15% of Human translation within 5 years (van Slype et al. 1983). This estimate proved over-optimistic. Another survey in 1986 expressed this demand in Europe as being of US$ 500 million, though in 1986 it was only US$ 45 million (Abbou et al. 1986).

Since MT cannot be applied to any text or circumstance, it is necessary to define the place of MT in this market and to examine the circumstances for possible applications of MT systems. Generally it can be stated that MT is applicable in all situations where large quantities of texts of a few, almost stereotype text types on largely constant subject matter have to be provided regularly in more than one language. The experience of Systran on Minitel in France also indicates that there is a demand for MT for private use.

A substantial new application for MT can be found as the result of new reading habits by professionals. Most commercial, financial, technical and scientific documents are no longer read cover to cover or from beginning to end, but selectively. Translation companies find that an increasing volume of their work is concerned with requests for looking through such documents as patent declarations and trade publications to find matter of relevance to a customer, for example, checking for announcement of invitations to tender or even selectively translating specifications accompanying tenders. Such a demand relates translation to automated techniques of information gathering and may lead to the connection of automatic scanners to MT systems and a close collaboration among information providers and translators. Source documents can be scanned automatically before selective human or machine translation.

Equally, information scientists processing foreign language information may now get un-edited machine translation output in their own language, i.e. without reference to human translators which traditionally slowed down the process of information provision. They can then commission human or post-edited machine translations of specially selected text with much greater confidence. MT, as shown on the examples of the use of Systran (see section 10.4.3), may indeed completely replace the costly technique of foreign language information provision, practised in many research laboratories, where the translator sits with the researcher and orally translates titles and captions to permit the researcher to gain current awareness and to home in on items of interest.

There is a particular case for MT in the many circumstances in which texts are in machine-readable form, such as databases, and in which communication is expected to be fast. The on-line information market which though currently concentrated on a very small number of languages and countries, is likely to multiply through machine translation. For the United States, which at present is reported as constituting 70% of the world market, the value of this market was estimated as being of 4-7 Milliard US$ in 1990. For the rest of the world the figures are given as 1-1.5 Milliard US$ (18%) in Europe, 0,5 Milliard US$ in Japan (10%), and about 1% in the rest of the world. In 1990 the Commission of the EC surveyed the field and recorded 2,063 databases in the US, as against 949 in the EC (Information Market 1990). About 20% of database production of the EC is exported. So far 87% of databases are monolingual. About half the databases in the EC can be accessed in English, 18% in French, 21% in German and 27% in another Community language, the overlap in the percentages indicating a small number of databases with multilingual access. Germany produces 45% of the multilingual databases in existence, followed by Denmark with 16%, Belgium and the CEC with 13% each. For the potential translation market it is interesting to note that the US has over 800 full-text databases against only approximately 15 in the EC. As these databases develop and seek expansion into wider markets the availability of MT will be a crucial element in achieving this goal. With MT there are the alternative options of (i) a priori translation of bibliographical and other databases, and (ii) on-demand translation of individual queries to and responses from databases. For example, Japanese patents can be accessed through a search of bibliographical databases, though publication has only been foreseen in a single language. The information about the existence and the content of documents published in Japanese, is available for users in other languages, by such means as the introduction of a multilingual thesaurus, as in the case of the Pascal File of INIST which is indexed in three languages and thus accessible when questions are posed in French, English, or Spanish; or when the server has added a software which permits this transposition of one language towards another, even if the text has not been previously indexed by key-words (Yanez 1990, Sigurdson & Greatrex 1987). This transposition can be integral or partial, accompanied by the revelation of the basic content of the message, focusing on a particular aspect, according to user interest. In this way it is possible to find useful information in a single operation and in a much more selective manner than by the simple application of logical operators between two words, passing through useful text analyzers, or through question understanding and finally a dialogue with the user. These processes can all be simplified with the introduction of task-specific MT modules.

MT is also increasingly becoming attractive in the paper-less environment of electronic network communication. At a time when anyone connected to a network can communicate in seconds with any partner anywhere, the desirability of full instant MT is vastly enhanced. The immediacy provided by electronic mail contact will stimulate interest in writer-oriented MT systems.

Applications-oriented MT research must start with a study of the pragmatic environment of existing forms of multilingual communication and examine its suitability for some form of automation of the linguistic transfer process. The various modules of MT systems will also find applications as a whole or in parts in such uses as aids for handicapped people, assistance for operators, electronic games, pocket translators, language teaching, telephonic information, spoken e-mail, work control, spoken alarm systems, voice keyboards, spoken announcements of weather and shipping reports, timetables for trains and plains, traffic synthesizers, etc..

The market for translated books is also steadily expanding. The 1992 annual report of the Syndicat national de l'édition reviewed the volume of translation as part of the total book production for the period 1985-1989. In France and Germany translated books represent a significant 15% of total book production.

In other countries the figures are even higher, 25% for Italy and Spain and 70% for Sweden. In the English-speaking world the volume is as low 2.5% in the UK and the USA, but for the UK these represented a respectable 1689 translated titles for the year 1991. While there is no suggestion that MT could be used for the translation of novels, plays or poetry, technical literature representing a sizable proportion of translated books, is likely to be supported by MT in the near future. Publishers will also benefit from the integration of MT into the publishing circuit.

11.2 A pragmatic view of the development of MT

The originally stipulated goal of machine translation, formulated in the 1960s and represented by the unwieldy acronym FAHQT, namely 'Fully Automated High-Quality Translation' was not only overambitious but itself unrealistic. Now that more is known about the capabilities of the computer and there is a better understanding of what is involved in translation, it is evident that the goal was wrongly expressed. This goal should always have been 'Maximum Assistance in Text Processing, Understanding and Translating' or, to create another improbable acronym, MATPUT. This goal is open-ended and current developments are moving towards it.

In retrospect, it can be seen that since the early days of MT research in the 1950s there has been a remarkable change away from the climate of euphoria and ignorance to realism and critical assessment. The early enthusiasm was necessary because without it, the new developments would not have been sustained; the ignorance is gradually disappearing as greater insights are gained into the complex processes involved in translation.

11.2.1 *MT system designers and producers*

MT system developers and manufacturers had to learn how to sell their products. The initial hard-sell techniques of inferior systems had an alienating effect on users and, in Europe at least, created a hostile climate which it has taken years to overcome. Excessive claims by manufacturers made the less informed translators fearful about their workplace. Manufacturers tried to sell over the heads of translators, as if they did not need them to implement the systems. By the 1990s manufacturers have moderated their early claims of performance and applicability of MT systems in favour of more realistic assessments of benefits. As a result the original hostility and later scepticism have been replaced by the knowledge of the limitations of MT and a sober appreciation of the real benefits to be derived from the new information technology in general. Potential users can now get more reliable information about systems, rather than publicity material only, through various conferences and journals, e.g. the annual Aslib conferences on 'Translation and the Computer' and such journals as 'Language International', 'Computers and Translation', and the late 'Electronic Word'.

By 1990 it was also established who should be involved in the design and construction of MT systems. In 1978 it was said that translators had a key role to play; yet, few translators joined the ranks of computational linguists. Direct translator involvement was not the solution hoped for. Instead, MT designers started reading about theories of translation and communications and listening to translators. In the process they discovered that translation is a more complex activity than they had thought. The fact that translation systems have to be based on models of translation which themselves require a sound theoretical foundation is now widely accepted. It will take a few more years before this realisation is fully reflected in operational systems.

11.2.2 *Translators as users of information technology and MT*

The relative slowness of translators to adopt the new technology is a result of the complexity of operating existing systems and the inability of designers to adjust to the working reality of translators. In 1986, a survey of the advances of information technology reported that, while 53% of translators used word processors, only 47% were satisfied with the existing equipment (Smith 1986). The same survey established that only a small number of translators had any actual experience of machine translation, but a relatively high 26% had a negative attitude to this type of translation aid. This can be partly explained, for example, by the fact that it is extremely difficult for translators to test systems. Short demonstrations are quite useless; translators need to test systems over a period of time and only large firms have been able to insist on these conditions in their negotiations with manufacturers. The batch processing mode of the early systems also proved too remote and slow and the facilities of the first on-line access systems proved too cumbersome.

The simultaneous introductions of wordprocessing and simple lexical database systems have, paradoxically, also had an initially adverse effect on the acceptance of MT. These two developments mark the beginning of a translator's workstation: translators can now edit text and build dictionaries for particular applications. All these facilities contribute to the qualitative improvement of both the content and the presentation of work and to a greater economy of production, while at the same time considerably increasing translators' productivity.

The paradox lies in the fact that the introduction of these tools of information technology delayed rather than advanced the introduction of machine translation, because human nature has at any one time only a limited capacity for absorbing new ideas and techniques. To put it in other words, translation as a craft is intrinsically linked to its conventional tools and most translators are traditionalists by nature, preservers of balances, accuracies and niceties. Some very successful professional translators, after all, still insist on using only pen and paper or dictation. It takes a long time and probably a full generation before the profession will widely accept the new tools. The younger generation of translators, who start their career already relying on the everyday use of wordprocessors, have more readily accepted experimentation with MT. The Translator's Handbook (Picken 1989) gives a good impression of the current state of MT acceptance among professionals.

11.2.3 *Survey of the evolution of MT*

Progress in MT design is always dependent on a felicitous conjuncture of theory, practical know-how and experience between computational linguistics, contrastive linguistics, cognitive science, ergonomics, psychology and translation theory. The history of machine translation is characterised by the happy convergence of some of these fields of study in a particular combination of theory and applications. We can speak of decades or generations of MT design according to the nature of this combination at any one time.

The first generation of MT design consisted of computer scientists who had a conservative and in many cases naive outlook on linguistics and translation. The linguistic design of the MT systems of the fifties was structuralist and concentrated on simple models of morphology and a little morphosyntax. Translation was attempted without much syntactical description by a simple dictionary matching mechanism. Where the conventional dictionary did not provide simple answers, longer phrases were used in the manner of the conventional phrase book.

The second generation, identifiable also with the period 1955-65, recognised the need for a linguistic foundation. Syntactic analysis was considered the key to the translation process. Some 'semantic' features were also incorporated in order to reduce lexical ambiguity. On the other hand there was little progress in computational techniques. Programs were still written in low level languages designed for numeric computing involving opaque techniques on slow machines which had to be shared with numerically-based computing tasks.

It is perhaps not surprising that this period did not produce much of lasting impact and led to a temporary stop in funding, especially in the United States of America and the United Kingdom. This period saw the creation of the first research groups exclusively dedicated to MT in France and Germany.

In the seventies MT re-started with a new generation both in terms of linguistic and computational innovation. The first simple theories of MT were developed and there was a diversification of strategies into transfer-based and interlingua-based design. The three phase transfer model consisting of analysis, transfer and synthesis or generation, was the first step in the direction of modular design and opened the possibility of considering multilingual translation. The interlingua-based design proved useful in only a very limited range of applications. The separation of linguistic information from algorithmic computational aspects accelerated the independent development of parsers.

Once the computational advantages had been fully absorbed, it became, however, evident that the strong reliance on syntactic rules did not yield the expected major breakthrough. Computationally, the separation of grammatical rules from performance algorithms and other instructions allowed MT research to follow two lines relatively independently, viz. software development and linguistic or translation theory-based developments. This innovation made programs more transparent and permitted linguists with limited computing skills to make meaningful contributions. Greater programming sophistication also was the first practical reaction to the shortage of multifaceted researchers and opened up the possibility of including linguisticians, lexicographers and others in the design teams. Computational progress was made possible through the availability of more suitable programming languages and better computer facilities for NL processing.

In 1977 the Commission of the European Communities conducted its first practical experiments with MT. At the same time an advisory committee of the Commission made the momentous recommendation to develop a European research capability in MT under the project name of EUROTRA.

During the 1980s research started to turn away from an overemphasis on syntax. Its distinctive nature can also be seen in the composition of the research teams, the recognition of a great variety of translation tasks and specialisation of tasks by subject field, sublanguage and text types.

By the end of the decade, the field of computational linguistics had grown to the extent that it divided into two major branches: natural language processing, which includes MT; and Speech Analysis and Synthesis. While speech analysis and synthesis is pursued in departments of electronics, computation, cognitive science and artificial intelligence, natural language processing and especially MT is now more often situated in departments of linguistics or specially created computational linguistics research units. These new units are interdisciplinary and open to external influences from cognitive science, artificial intelligence, pragmatics, psychology and, of course, computing.

In this environment, research now covers the whole range of linguistic and pragmatic phenomena that constitute texts. New syntactic theories and models of parsing are incorporated into the analysis of sentence structures. Deeper representation of source texts should allow translation to be less dependent on the surface structure of the source text and so make the target language syntax less 'artificial' and stilted. More semantic representations are incorporated in order to deal with those lexical disambiguations which are not adequately resolved by previous syntactic intermediate structures. New structural analyses are developed to incorporate suprasentential semantic and pragmatic relationships. The basic principle now is one of flexibility of analysis, i.e. that analysis should only be as deep as necessary and that various depths of analyses may co-exist for the translation of a single sentence. A further major recognition has come from less rigidity in the division between the grammar and the lexicon.

System design now examines the advantages of specialisation in subject domains and text types. For the selection of translation equivalents text-type-specific criteria are now applied at the syntactic, semantic and pragmatic levels. This work has given new stimulus to the very old field of contrastive linguistics; in this way, contrastive linguistics has discovered a new practical outlet and now creates such artefacts as transfer dictionaries and semantic representation systems which may find their way into new systems.

New impulses from cognitive psychology and AI may prove significant for the modelling of the translation process. Fundamental to this new mode of thinking is that understanding the content and the function of the source text is given a major importance. Subject specific knowledge representation may therefore come to play an important role in MT and may assist in dealing with suprasentential meaning and information that is not linguistically expressed. Content and function of texts find their expression in the text type, an as yet inadequately defined concept as far as computational processing is concerned. The textual characteristics of documents, especially in the more limited range that undergo translation, are important elements in any analysis and must be considered in translation. A greater understanding of text types will also contribute to the refinement of sentence by sentence translation systems which are likely to prove quite effective for many types of texts.

We can conclude that the situation in the 1990s is one of pluralism of research orientations which are more indicative of the true complexity of translation. This pluralism is reflected in practice where simple word by word and sentence by sentence translation system coexist with bold new designs that take into account the communicative intention and the external form of a text. At the same time, existing systems based on old designs are discovered as having more life in them than originally anticipated, and with various modifications they are made into quite sensible tools of immediate application. The outlook for MT is very promising.

11.2.4 *Practical achievements of MT*

To understand the achievements and potential of MT in the current translation world, we must consider the state of technology in the workplace outlined in the previous section. Translation support systems have proved successful if they were conceived as stand-alone facilities, working independently from electronic data transmission. Only few very large translation producers can afford the large-scale facilities required to operate a system like Systran, used by the CEC in Luxembourg, for example. Even there the implantation of the system has gone through untold difficulties of protocols etc., which have nothing to do with the quality of MT. The recent experience with Systran on Minitel in France, on the other hand, is not fully documented and therefore cannot be considered with respect to advances in implementation techniques.

Smaller-scale MT systems, by necessity limited in the range of vocabulary and syntax they can handle, are now in general commercial use, though the volume of utilization is still small when compared to the potential of these machines. There are several reasons for this:

(a) Users have not been able to identify sufficient amounts and types of documents for these systems to process because translators have yet to learn to categorise translation according to their suitability for a particular system. It requires considerable re-thinking of traditional patterns of organisation to deal with the basic question of whether a text should be processed by machine or by human translators (Schneider 1990).

(b) On the other hand, systems are not yet constructed with attention to the specific nature of texts. Most system design is still based on a general theoretical description of a language and not on a coherent theory of sublanguages. The topical dictionaries or domain-specific lexica, advertised in some systems, only deal with some lexical aspects of sublanguages. Users currently operate a compromise whereby the translator adequates the system to the texts through particular dictionary routines and through the incorporation of complete equivalent phrasal entries of texts to be translated. This is rather a council of despair and besides is only of limited scope.

The greatest user satisfaction occurs where users have recognised the full limitation of MT—of any kind—and have turned this into a benefit. It is, of course, quite another question whether these restricted forms of computer-processable English, French or Spanish are acceptable to the normal user and some research may be required into discovering what is required to make them more acceptable. Some users have developed their own form of restricted language, e.g. Rank Xerox's Customized English is no more than their version of

Systran English, and PACE English is no more than Perkins' version of Weidner English and French.

In systems with a more user-friendly design, it should not be necessary for a translator to adjust to a particular form of MT output language which has been designed as a general compromise. The present knowledge of linguistic programming already permits responding to specific requirements of major users and construct systems that deal with particular types of documents such as product descriptions or instructions for use.

One of the cornerstones of success of future MT systems is, of course, the dictionary. Dictionary making is now a major area of research and it is here where MT and conventional translator tools can benefit from joint development (Zampolli 1986). In their use of MT systems translators have already enthusiastically accepted the usefulness of specialised dictionaries for subject fields, text types and particular house styles.

There are, however, still no commercially usable tools for dealing with the multilingual side of computer-assisted electronic communication. Most text processing systems, whether readers or editors, scanners or advisory systems are strictly monolingual and cannot cope with text segments in other languages. There is considerable scope for the development of computer aids for understanding and writing texts in a second language because electronic mail, factual databases, electronic books and journals will never be translated by conventional means; all these forms of communication and text types offer new challenges to machine translation.

To sum up the effect of present achievements, we observe that translators now have a realistic view of present achievements of MT systems and increasingly a greater familiarity with IT tools in general. They also have a better understanding of the future potential of new tools and systems. Some suppliers, on the other hand, still have some difficulties with (i) cooperating with users and with each other about compatibility and (ii) being imaginative about new support for translation which exploits the positive side of the restrictions on natural language imposed upon document production by computer.

11.3 Future prospects for the language industry

Translation can no longer be considered an isolated activity at the margin of text production but is increasingly being integrated with technical writing. Text processing is becoming more sophisticated every day and electronic data transmission will soon overtake conventional mail so that professional text handling and communication will become entirely paperless. In such an environment the delays caused by full human translation, despite the speed-up of electronic processing, will only be acceptable in special cases of communicative situations. Wherever possible and appropriate in industry, commerce and administration, conventional human translation will simply be rejected because of its disruptive influence on the benefit in speed and directness created by electronic methods of communication; it is uncertain to what extent the cost factor will also contribute to the preference for the use of MT.

The demand for MT systems will increase with the growth of machine-held texts, but since automated communication is still evolving, specific MT developments will be delayed. Research is moving into applications and is now more solid because it is more interdisciplinary. There is also more supporting research in automated dictionaries, etc.

In parallel, there are research and development efforts which will bypass translation by developing multilingual document and information systems in limited domains and text types. A fair number of newly sponsored projects have implications for MT. A new generation of computer users is likely to demand facilities which are today considered to lie at the periphery of MT. Translators will eventually use translation machines like they use wordprocessors today and used dictating machines yesterday. Many translators are already working exclusively with machine-readable input and output and are thus participating in the revolution of the paperless communications, itself growing at considerable speed.

But there are a number of obstacles yet to be overcome.

(a) At the moment translation is still seen as a loop, an undesirable delay in an otherwise smooth document flow. Greater flexibility and developments in reader- and writer-oriented translation can eliminate time gaps or ease some of the delays.

(b) Translation and in particular MT needs a pragmatic theory so that its place in the normal communication process can be established with ease. Such a theory needs to explain that texts that require translation occur in a particular communicative environment which to some extent influences the linguistic forms chosen; the motivation of these linguistic choices also has to be identified since they differ from language to language.

(c) It must be taken into account that not all information contained in a text is linguistically expressed; therefore means must be provided for identifying and understanding this information in the source language and conveying it in the target language.

(d) Advances in electronic communications now provide us with international data transmission protocols and document architecture standards which greatly facilitate communication across linguistic barriers, except, of course, for the vexed problem of language. Communications engineers and planners of office systems are already providing standardised facilities into which machine translation can be fitted. These standards require the active intervention of translators in order to make them safe for their work.

(e) Increasingly a clear distinction will be required between the different types of MT systems identified in section 10: (i) MT as tools for translators; (ii) MT for monolingual writers of texts; (iii) MT for readers of scientific and technical papers; and (iv) MT for databases. Developers of MT systems do not as yet necessarily make this distinction.

The full development of machine aids to translation is limited by two factors.

The first is external and in a way closely related to the very success of the language industry. Modern communications are themselves in a state of rapid transformation and these changes affect the role and nature of human as well as machine translation. In such a climate MT research and development are seriously hampered because they cannot rely on a stable situation, but have to adjust constantly to external and internal influences. As new forms of communication evolve, e.g. e-mail, factual database and expert system information, new forms of translation will be demanded to meet the requirements of new textforms and new communicative situations.

Another limitation on the potential of MT design is more difficult to explain since it arises from the very nature of the translatability postulated for texts submitted to MT systems. Since the MT process converts a natural language text into an artificially controlled language text, i.e. the language conceived by the system designer, a new pragmatic theory of MT must recognise the particular nature of what the MT process can achieve. In particular, it must be recognised that, because of the very nature of the language produced by machines, MT can only be applied to forms of communication that are well-established and consolidated; system designers need a solid corpus of text as models and source material for writing their grammars and dictionaries. This is not the case of many texts dealing with advances in science and technology, especially in the field of electronic communication. For example, one cannot automatically translate the menu of a data retrieval system into a language where the concept of menus for choices of paths in databases is unknown. Such circumstances still require human translators and terminologists because this is not a matter of words but of cognition, i.e. the creation of new concepts, their designations and possibly new text types into which these new terms have to be fitted. Any form of human translation, therefore, inevitably depends on prior innovations in concepts and text forms and either has to wait till someone creates new concepts and their expression forms in a target language or engages in the creation of 'translation equivalents'. Since term formation is beyond the scope of any

NLP system, machine translation will by necessity depend on human text type development, terminology creation and the conversion of this work into suitable MT modules.

At a time of secondary term formation and text type innovation, however, which is claiming to be international, there is a role for translators, terminologists and translation theorists to be in the forefront and assist in the creation of multilingual designations and textforms, rather than wait for the evolution of forms which have then to be translated. This observation applies particularly to MT design. This work can also be described as providing MT system developers regularly with new types of translation specifications to which systems have to be adjusted or for which new modules of systems have to be designed. The inclusion of pragmatics in reflections on computational linguistic research is just beginning; it will take some time before it can influence system design.

Bibliography

Abbou, A., Lefaucheur, I., & Meyer, T. 1987. *Les industries de la langue: Applications industrielles du traitement de la langue par les machines.* Paris: DAICADIF

Agard. 1990. *Benefits of Computer-assisted Translation to Information Managers and End-Users* (= *Agard Lecture Series No. 171*). Neuilly sur Seine: AGARD.

Alonso, J.A. & Schneider, T. 1987. "Machine Translation Technology: on the way to market introduction". *Siemens Review* 54.6.

Baker, M. 1992. *In other words.* London: Routledge.

Barnwell, K.G.L. 1980. *Introduction to Semantics and Translation.* Horsley Green: WTB/SIL.

Bathgate, R.H. 1980. "A communicative model of translation". *Incorporated Linguist* 19 (4) & 20 (1).

Beaugrande, R. de & Dressler, W. 1986. *Introduction to Text Linguistics.* London: Longman.

Beekman, J., Callow, J., & Kopesec, M. 1981. *The semantic structure of written communication.* 5th revision. Texas: SIL.

Bennett, P. 1993. *The translation unit in humans and machines.* Manchester: CCL/UMIST.

Bell, R.T. 1991. *Translation and translating, theory and practice.* London: Longman.

Bible Society. 1991. *Bible facts: translation and language count.* Swindon: Bible Society

Bossard Consultants, Paris. 1992. *Bossard Report on the language industry.* Luxembourg: Commission of the EC.

Bostad, B. 1982. ''Quality control procedures in modification of the Air Force Russian-English MT system''. Lawson, ed. 1982.

Brinkmann, K-H. 1980. ''Present and Future Technical Aids to Easier Communication in Foreign Languages''*BABEL* 26 (2).

Brower, R.A., ed. 1966. *On translation.* Oxford: Oxford U.P.

BS 3669. 1963. *Recommendations for the selection, formation and definition of technical terms.* London: British Standards Institute.

BS 5408. 1976. *Glossary of Documentation Terms.* London: British Standards Institute.

Bühler, K. 1934/65. *Sprachtheorie. Die Darstellungsfunktion der Sprache.* Stuttgart: Fischer.

Bunge, M. 1962. *Intuition and Science.* Westport, Conn.

Bureau Marcel van Dijk. 1988. *Etude des stratégies, de financement et de commercialisation de la traduction automatique.* Luxembourg: CEC.

Cherry, C. 1966. *On Human Communication.* Cambridge, Mass.: MIT Press.

Commission of the EC. 1990. *XXIIIrd Report on the Activities of the European Communities 1989.* Brussels and Luxembourg: CEC.

Coseriu, E. 1981. ''Falsche und richtige Fragestellungen in der Übersetzungstheorie''. Wilss, ed. 1981.

Davidson, D. 1984. *Inquiries into truth and interpretation.* Oxford: Oxford UP.

Dewey, J. 1910. *How we think.* Boston: D.C Heath & Co.

Fillmore, C.J. 1977. ''Scenes-and-frames semantics''. *Linguistic Structure Processing* ed. by A. Zampolli. Amsterdam: Mouton.

FIT. 1992. *FIT Report.* Annexe XII, page 35. Montreal

Flamand, J. 1983. *Ecrire et traduire: sur la voie de la création.* Ottawa: Editions du Vermillion.

Frawley, W. 1984. ''Prologomena to a theory of translation''. *Translation* ed. by W. Frawley. London: Associated University Presses.

Grice, P. 1975. ''Implicature''. *Speech Acts* (= *Syntax and Semantics* 3.) ed. by Cole & Morgan. London: Academic Press.

Gordon, J. 1990. "Essai de typologie des textes sources, dans le cadre de la traduction assistée par ordinateur". Agard 1990.

Gouadec, D. 1981. "Paramètres de l'évaluation des traductions". *META* 26 (2).

Gouadec, D. 1982. "Méthodologie de l'évaluation de la traduction". *Multilingua*1 (2).

Gouadec, D. 1990. "Traduction signalétique". *META* 35 (2).

Gutt, E.A. 1991. *Translation and Relevance: Cognition and context.* Oxford: Blackwell.

Halliday, M.A.K. 1973. *Explorations in the functions of language.* London: Arnold.

Hammond, D.L. 1990. "The Translation Profession in the United States today". *Annals of the American Academy of Political and Social Science* 511. September 1990.

Hatim, B. & Mason, I. 1990. *Discourse and the translator.* London: Longman.

Haugen, E. 1966. "Dialect, language, nation". *American Anthropologist* 68.

Hoffman, E. 1983. "Stages in the Life Cycle of LEXIS". Snell, ed. 1983.

House, J. 1977. *A model for translation quality assessment.* Tübingen: Narr.

House, J. & Blum-Kulka, S., eds. 1987. *Interlingual and Intercultural Communication* (= *Discourse and Cognition in Translation and Second Language acquisition studies*). Tübingen: Narr.

Hutchins, W.J. & Somers, H. 1992. *An Introduction to Machine Translation.* London: Academic Press.

Information Market 62. 1990. Commission of the European Communities: Directorate General XIII.

Jakobson, R. 1960. "Linguistics and Poetics". *Style in Language* ed. by T. Sebeok. Cambridge, Mass.: MIT press.

Jakobson, R. 1966. "On linguistic aspects of translation". R.A. Brower, ed. 1966.

Jahrbuch für Internationale Germanistik XXI (1989) 2. Bern: Peter Lang.

Joos, M. 1967. *The five clocks.* New York: Harcourt, Brace & World Inc.

Jumpelt, R.W. 1961. *Die Übersetzung naturwissenschaftlicher und technischer Literatur*. Berlin: Langenscheidt

Kapp, V., ed. 1984. *Übersetzer und Dolmetscher*. München: Francke

Katz, J. 1978. "Effability and Translation". *Meaning and Translation* ed. by F. Guenthner & M. Guenthner-Reutter. New York: N.Y.U. Press

Keenan, C.E. 1978. "Some logical Problems in Translation". *Meaning and Translation* ed. by F. Guenthner & M. Guenthner-Reutter. New York: N.Y.U. Press

Kingscott, G. 1989. *Applications of Machine Translation*. (Study for the Commission of the Euroean Communities). Luxembourg: CEC.

Koller, W. 1983. "Übersetzungswissenschaft". *UTB* 810. Heidelberg: Quelle & Meyer.

Krollmann, F. 1981. "Hilft der Computer dem Übersetzer oder vernichtet er seinen Arbeitsplatz". *Festschrift Langenscheidt* 1981. München: Langenscheidt.

Krollmann, F. 1981. "Computer aids to translation". *META* 26 (1981) 1.

Kunicki, M. 1980. "La Barrière Linguistique: son importance et son évaluation". *Documentaliste* 17.4-5.

Kussmaul, P. 1986. "Übersetzen als Entscheidungsprozess". Snell-Hornby, ed. 1986.

Automatic Language Processing Advisory Committee. 1986. *Language and Machines: computers in translation and linguistics*. Report. National Academy of Sciences, USA: Automatic Language Processing Advisory Committee, Division of Behavioral Sciences.

Large, J.B. 1983. *The Foreign Language Barrier*. London: Deutsch.

Larose, R. 1989. *Théories contemporaines de la traduction*. Québèc: Presses de l'Université du Québèc.

Larson, M.L. 1984. *Meaning-based translation*. Lanham, MD & London: University Press of America.

Lawson, V., ed. 1982. *Practical Experience of Machine Translation*. Amsterdam: North Holland.

Lehrberger, J. & Bourbeau, L. 1988. *Machine translation, linguistic characteristics of MT systems and general methodology of evaluation.* Amsterdam: John Benjamins.

Levy, J. 1967. "Translation as a decision process". *To Honor Roman Jakobson. essays on the occasion of his 70th birthday.* Volume 2. den Haag: Mouton.

Loerscher, W. 1991. *Translation performance, translation process, and translation strategies.* Tübingen: Narr.

Lyons, J. 1977. *Semantics.* Cambridge University Press.

Malinowski, B. 1966. "The problem of meaning in primitive languages". *The meaning of meaning* ed. by C.K. Ogden & I.A. Richards. New York: Harcourt Brace Jovanovich, Inc.

Manning, A. 1988. "The pedagogy of thème spécialisé". *META* 33 (3).

Mareschal, G. 1988. "Le rôle de la terminologie et de la documentation dans l'enseignement de la traduction spécialisée". *META* 33 (2).

Mayoral, R., Kelly, D. & Gallardo, N. 1988. "Concept of constrained translation". *META* 33 (3).

Meli, S. 1989. "Informationsmarkt der maschinellen Uebersetzung". *Terminologie et Traduction* (3).

Miller, G.A. 1968. *The psychology of Communication.* London: Penguin Books.

Morain, J.-C. 1984. "Le traducteur à l'INRS". *Traduire* 134 (4).

Mossmann, Y. 1984. "Produktivitäts- und Qualitätssteigerung im Sprachendienst durch Einsatz der Textverarbeitung". *Lebende Sprachen* 29 (4).

Mounin, G. 1963. *Les problèmes théoriques de la traduction.* Paris: Gallimard.

Neubert, A. 1985. *Text and Translation.* Leipzig: Verlag Enzyklopädie.

Neubert, A. 1991. "Models of Translation". *Empirical Research in Translation and Intercultural Studies* ed. by S. Tirkkonen-Condit. Tübingen: Narr.

Newmark, P. 1981. *Approaches to Translation.* Oxford: Pergamon.

Newmark, P. 1988. *A textbook on translation.* London: Prentice Hall.

Nida, E.A. 1959. "Principles of translation exemplified by Bible translation". Brower, ed. 1966.

Nida, E.A. 1976. "A Framework for the Analysis and Evaluation of Theories of Translation". *Translation. Applications and Research* ed. by R.W. Brislin. New York: Gardner Press

Nida, E.A. 1964. *Toward a Science of Translating*. Leiden: Brill.

Nida, E.A. 1982. *Translating Meaning*. San Dimas, Cal.:

Nida, E.A. & Taber, C.R. 1969 & 1982. *The theory and practice of translation*. Leiden: Brill.

Nirenburg, S., ed. 1987. *Machine Translation, theoretical and methodological issues*. Cambridge: Cambridge UP.

Nyborg, K. 1982. *Report on the Multilingualism of the European Community*. Document 1-306/82. Brussels: European Parliament.

Picken, C. (ed) 1983 & 1989. *The Translator's Handbook*. 1st & 2nd edition. London: Aslib.

Picken, C., ed. 1983 onwards. *Translating and the Computer* Volume 4 onwards. London: Aslib.

Pym, P.J. 1991. "Simplified English and machine translation". *Professional Translator and Interpreter* 2 (2).

Quine, W.V.O. 1960. *Word and Object*. Cambridge, Mass.: MIT Press.

Reiss, K. 1981. "Textbestimmung und Uebersetzungsmethode". Wilss, ed. 1981.

Reiss, K. 1990. "Das Missverständnis vom eigentlichen Übersetzen". *Übersetzungswissenschaft: Ergebnisse und Perspektiven* ed. by R. Arntz & G. Thome. Tübingen: Narr.

Reiss, K. & Vermeer, H. J. 1984. *Grundlegung einer allgemeinen Translationstheorie*. Tübingen: Niemeyer.

Roberts, R. 1988. "Eight principles of translation". *META* 33 (2).

Sager, J.C., Dungworth, D. & McDonald, P.F. 1980. *English Special Languages, Principles and Practice in Science and Technology*. Wiesbaden: Brandstetter.

Sapir, E. 1921. *Language, an introduction to the study of speech*. New York: Harcourt Brace & World, Inc.

Savory, T.H. 1957. *The art of translation*. London: Cape.

Schneider, T. 1990. End Users" Needs, in: Agard (1990).

Sebeok, T.A., ed. 1960. *Style in Language*. Cambridge, Mass.: MIT press.

Sigurdson, J. & Greatrex, R. 1987. *Machine Translation of on-line searches in Japanese databases*. Lund: Lund University.

Simpkin, R. 1980. ''What the customer wants'' *Translators' Guild Newsletter* 5 (4). London.

Simpkin, R. 1983. ''Translation specifications''. *The Translator's Handbook* ed. by C. Picken. London: Aslib.

Smith, D. 1986. *Translation Practices Report*. London: Digital Equipment Corporation.

Snell, B., ed. 1983. *Term banks for tomorrow's world*. London: Aslib.

Snell-Hornby, M., ed. 1986. *Uebersetzungswissenschaft — Eine Neuorientierung*. Tübingen: Francke.

Sperber, D. & Wilson D. 1986. *Relevance: communication and cognition*. Oxford: Blackwell.

Slocum, J., ed. 1985. *Machine translation systems*. Cambridge: Cambridge UP.

Steiner, G. 1975. *After Babel*. London: Oxford University Press.

Truebridge, J.C. 1991. *Machine-assisted analysis of Biblical texts as part of Bible traslation procedure*. PhD-Thesis. University of Manchester.

Turk, H. 1990. ''Probleme der Uebersetzungsanalyse und der Uebersetzungstheorie''. *Jahrbuch für internationale Germanistik*.

van Hoof, H. 1971. ''Le marché de la traduction en Belgique''. *Le linguiste/De taalkundige* 1-2.

van Slype et al. 1983. *Better Translation for Better Communication*. Oxford: Pergamon Press.

van Slype, G. 1982. *Etude et mise au point de critères d'évaluation technico-économique d'un procedé de traduction automatique*. PhD Dissertation. Université Libre de Bruxelles.

Vermeer, H. 1974. ''Zur Beschreibung des Übersetzungsvorgangs''. Wilss, ed. 1981. & Kapp, ed. 1984.

Vermeer, H. 1986. *Voraussetzungen fuer eine translationstheorie- einige kapitel kultur- und sprachtheorie*. Heidelberg: Vermeer.

Vernay, H. 1974. ''Elemente einer Übersetzungswissenschaft''. Wilss, ed. 1981.

Vinay, J.P. & Darbelnet, J. 1958. *Stylistique comparée du français et de l'anglais*. Paris: Didier.

Wilss, W. 1975. ''Übersetzen''. *Handbuch der Linguistik. Allgemeine und angewandte Sprachwissenchaft* ed. by H. Stammerjohann. München: Nymphenburger Verlagshandlung.

Wilss, W., ed. 1981. *Uebersetzungswissenschaft*. Darmstadt: Wissenschaftliche Buchgesellschaft.

Wilss, W. 1982. *The Science of Translation*. Tübingen: Narr.

Wilss, W. 1989. ''Towards a Multi-facet Concept of Translation Behaviour''. *Target* 1 (2).

Wilss, W. 1988. *Kognition und Uebersetzen*. Tübingen: Niemeyer.

Wilss, W. 1992. *Übersetzungsfertigkeit*. Tübingen: Narr.

Yanez, A. 1990. ''L'environnement technique de la traduction assisteé par ordinateur''. Agard 1990.

Zampolli, A. 1986. ''Multifunctional lexical databases''. *Encrages* 16 (= *Les industries de la langue: actes du colloque de Tours*). Paris: Université Paris VIII.

Zierer, E. 1979. *Algunos conceptos básicos de la ciencia de la traducción*. Trujillo: Universidad Nacional de Trujillo.

Glossary

Terms are defined with respect to communication, translation and information and documentation. Terms exclusively defined with respect to Machine Translation and Information Technology are identified by MT and IT respectively.

Abstract = (1) a reduced version of a text to a fixed length.
= (2) a derived text reduced to a fixed length independent of the original.

Advisory system = see: **Expert system**

Affectivity = the textual property of expressing a writer's personal emotional involvement in the document.

Agent = in translation, the person who is in an intermediary position between a translator and an end user of a translation.

Ambiguity = the property of a sentence or expression which carries more than one meaning or admits of more than one interpretation.

Analysis = in MT, the stage in the machine translation process in which a source text is converted into an annotated intermediate representation.

Artificial Intelligence (AI) = the study concerned with replicating on a computer the functions and operations of the human brain.

Artificial language = a language whose rules and lexicon are explicitly designed by identifiable individuals before they are used.

Aspect = the point of view from which a topic is dealt with; in translation it is useful to distinguish such aspects as administrative, legal, commercial, economic/financial, educational, personal, publicity, social.

Assumptions = the projections a writer or speaker makes about the reader's or listener's ability to interpret intentional signals whether expressed linguistically, para-linguistically or extra-linguistically.

Background = the invariable elements surrounding a speech act, such as the characteristics of education and social status of the participants, the available means of communication etc.

Batch Processing = in IT, a method for processing data in which material to be processed is collected and input for processing at the same time.

Bible translation = the complex activities concerned with producing contemporary language versions of the sacred writings of Christianity.

Browsing = a technique of rapid acquisition of information by either random reading of small sections of text or by searching through peripheral areas of text concerning a topic.

Casual = the mode of expression used in communication between friends and members of a family group of the same age; it is located between 'consultative' and 'intimate' on a scale of five points.

CD-ROM, Compact Disc Read-only memory = in IT, a magnetic medium for the storage of linguistic data which cannot be modified or erased, but read only.

Close translation = a method of translation concerned with observing the highest possible degree of formal equivalences between source and target language.

Common language = the language shared by the largest part of a speech community. See also: general language.

Communication = (1) the exchange of information or knowledge by means of dialogue, writing, etc.

= (2) the transmission of information from a source or sender to a recipient.

Compensation = in translation, the expression of meaning in a target language by different means than those used in the source language.

Computational Linguistics = the study of linguistic issues by means of computational techniques.

Constructed language = see: **Artificial language**.

Consultative = the mode of expression used in communication in neutral situations which is located between 'formal' and 'casual' on a scale of five points.

Content = (1) the semantic substance of a text, consisting of a topic and an aspect, which can be expressed in various text types and forms.

= (2) the sum of ideas notions, qualities, etc. contained in a piece of writing or a document.

Cooperation = a principle of communication, established by Grice (1975), which stipulates a certain behaviour of the participants in a speech act.

Corpus = a body of texts, a collection of linguistic data.

Correspondence = in translation, a relation between the source and the target language text which may be applied both to form and content (Turk 1990).

Cursory reading = a technique of knowledge acquisition by which a text is read very rapidly and selectively in order to capture its main line of argument or its main elements of information.

Dependent text = a text which has a content relation with another.

Derived text = a type of dependent text which is produced by extracting content from a text and presenting it in another form, possibly for another purpose.

Dialect = a regionally or socially distinctive variety of language.

Discipline = see: **Subject field**

Document = (1) a generic term for both message and text.
= (2) a written text considered a unit for the purpose of translation, processing, storage and other forms of information management.

Domain = see: **Subject field**

Editing = the process of preparing a text for publication by means of correcting or re-writing.

Encoding = the process by which a writer converts an abstract conception into a linguistic form.

Environment = the temporal and spatial circumstances of a particular culture in which speech acts occur.

Ellipsis = in writing, the omission of structural elements which does not hinder the understanding of the text.

Equivalence = in translation, a semiotic value of the semantic similarity achievable between two units of language.

Equivalent = in translation, a linguistic unit in a target language which is considered to be an adequate substitute for a source language unit, both semantically and formally.

Essay = (1) a broad class of text type representing the writer's personal interpretation of a subject, the writer's view of reality.
Examples: newspaper columns, leading articles, theses, dissertations.
= (2) a short literary composition on any particular subject.

Expectation = the disposition of a reader to receive a message of a particular text type and intention.

Expert system = in IT, a tool that accepts questions in a natural language on a particular topic and can offer intelligent advice or make intelligent decisions using rule-based programs. *Synonym*: advisory system

Expression = (1) a string of lexical elements considered as a syntagmatic unit.
= (2) the level of organisation of linguistic substance, e.g. expression form.

Facsimile Transmission (FAX) = the photo-electronic reproduction of documents over distance, usually via the telephone network.

Form = (1) the physical manifestation of the linguistic expression of a document or discourse.

= (2) the expressions of a language in which a particular content is formulated, e.g. sign language English, spoken French, The form of a text consists of the text type (class & layout etc), syntax and lexical items.

= (3) a structure representing a complete unit of linguistic meaning, containing gaps or slots for variable instantiations. The form/frame is meaningless, unless correct instantiation has occurred. *Synonym*: Frame.

Formal = the mode of expression used in communication between social unequals and situations governed by the social and professional roles of the participants. It is located between 'frozen' and 'consultative' on a scale of five points and less rigid than 'frozen' but more restricted than 'consultative'.

Formality = a degree of mode of expression, which ranges from frozen to intimate.

Free translation = a method of translation which concentrates on conveying the content of the text in such a way that it becomes easier for the reader to understand, to the extent of the translator disregarding source language structures that cannot readily be reproduced in the target language.

Frozen = the mode of expression used for the communication of rigidly regulated documents or highly controlled speech situations. It is located at the extremity on a scale of five degrees of formality and is characterised by preformulated expression forms, not admitting any degree of individuality.

Full parallel text = a dependent text in which the target language text has exactly the same function, purpose, status and legal value as the source text.

General language = the language used for every day non-specialist communication among a speech community.

Generation = see: **Synthesis**

Gist = the summary presentation of the essence of a message.

Human-assisted machine translation = in MT, a technique of translation using the computer for certain aspects of the process and human participation/intervention before, during or after the computerised translation phase.

Idiolect = the linguistic system of an individual speaker.

Index = an alphabetical listing of words occurring or referring to instances of text.

Information = knowledge communicated and acquired, relating to a specific fact, subject or concept.

Inferencing = the process of using logic or world knowledge to draw conclusions from linguistic messages in order to extract information not explicitly expressed by linguistic means.

Information technology = the devices and techniques supported by computational means for conveying, analysing, storing, transmitting and retrieving information.

Information only', 'for = a product specification for translation resulting in a translation-specific text type, characterised by being un-edited and destined for internal use within an organisation.

Input = in MT, the source or first language text entering the machine process.

Intention = the motivation that makes a writer consider the combination of content, form and text type into a message. Intentions relevant to industrial translation are: informative, directive, evaluative, discursive.

Interface = in natural language processing, the connection between phases of a process, usually the connection which enables human instructions to be converted to computer instructions.

Interlingual system = in MT, a type of system whose approach assumes that it is possible to convert source text into semantic representations common to more than one language. Translation is thus possible in both or multiple directions.

Intimate = the mode of expression used in communication between close friends or members of a family for private and emotive speech acts. It is located at the extremity on a scale of five degrees of formality and is characterised by private language, non-standard and ungrammatical expression forms revealing a high degree of individuality of expression.

Key-phrase recognition = an analytic operation whereby a text is scanned for syntagmatic units stated by the user.

Key word = a word or expression used to characterise a document.

Key-word recognition = an analytic operation whereby a text is scanned for key words characteristic of a document stated by a user.

Language engineering = the techniques and practices concerned with adjusting the instrument of language to a number of specified uses, usually by the development of subject or situation-specific sublanguages.

Language industry = the totality of tools, instruments and services which exploit language for the purpose of providing assistance in those functions of language susceptible to mechanical or electronic mediation or other forms of processing.

Level = the dimension of an expression in a special language which permits the sender to adjust the choice of the lexical items and grammar to the degree of knowledge the recipient has of the content of a message.

Literal = (1) in translation, a technique which aims at the closest possible parallel between structural items of source and target language.
= (2) in semantics, those meanings which are derived from the denotation of lexical items.
= (3) in pragmatics, a tradition of language preservation based on written documents; in contrast to oral.

Literary Translation = the translation of works of creative imagination such as novels, plays, poetry, filmscripts, dialogues, etc.

Machine Translation (MT) = any process in which there is an element of automatic analysis of a source language text, transformation of this text and production of a target language text in another language.

Machine-assisted human translation = a translation strategy whereby translators use computer programs to perform part of the process of translation.

Matching = in translation, the activity of comparing linguistic expression forms in order to determine their suitability as translation equivalents.

Mediator = a person who facilitates the transmission of messages, e.g. a translator, interpreter, information scientist.

Memo = in text typology, a generic class of texts characterised by the balanced emphasis it places on sender, addressee and content (Sager et al. 1980). *Examples*: textbooks, contracts, correspondence.

Message = (1) a text endowed with a purpose (intention & expectation).
= (2) a type of communication conveyed from one person to another.

Modification = the alteration of a document for the purpose of improving its suitability for its intended purpose by means of addition, deletion or substitution.

Module = in MT, the structurally independent unit of a translation system.

Natural language = a language which has evolved gradually as the principal means of communication and expression of a community; the type of language normally used for human communication without restriction of semantic scope and syntax.

Natural language processing (NLP) = the human manipulation of written texts by means of computational techniques.

Neologism = a newly created expression, word or term to represent a new concept or to re-name an existing concept.

Nomenclature = the systematic terminology of the taxonomic sciences such as anatomy, biology, chemistry, geology, etc.

Norm = a pattern of behaviour elevated to the status of a regular occurrence which is a model for others.

Occupational role = the position from which writers or readers produce or receive a message. This role determines the range of topics and aspects an individual can use in communication.

On-line dictionary = a dictionary stored on a computer and accessible by direct interrogation.

Optical Character Reader (OCR) = a reading device which converts print into computer-readable data.

Optical Character Recognition (OCR) = A computer technique which identifies diverse print fonts and converts this information into data a computer can operate on.

Orality = the tradition of preserving a language by means of memory and transmission of the spoken word.

Output = in MT, the target or second language text resulting from the MT process.

Parallel document = a document in a second language which is identical in function, applicability and effect to one in the first language.

Paraphrase = (1) the alternative expression of a meaningful linguistic unit without changing its denotational meaning.

= (2) in translation, the alternative expression of a lexical or terminological unit in the source language by means of a longer phrasal expression in the target language.

Participant = a role player in a communicative situation.

Periphrasis = (1) the expression of an inflected element by means of separate lexical items.

= (2) a circumvoluted way of expression.

Personal factors = in speech acts, the variables of the participants' education, ideological orientation, social class etc which influence production and reception of messages.

Position = in speech acts, the role an individual adopts in communication, i.e. the position of writer, reader, speaker, listener. Positions are reversible in the same speech act.

Post-editing = in MT, the adaptation and revision of output of a machine translation system either to eliminate errors which impede comprehension or to make the output read like a natural language text.

Pragmatic = concerning the situation of the speech act, the participants and its environment.

Pre-editing = in MT, the annotation (by means of flags) and modification of the input text before, or during (interactive) the automatic process, in order to facilitate the automated translation process and optimise system performance.

Presupposition = the projections a writer or speaker makes about the reader's or listener's knowledge in planning a speech act.

Primary reader = the person(s) directly addressed by a message.

Production = the act of producing a linguistic form to express an abstract conception.

Purpose = (1) the combination of a writer's intention and consideration of a reader's expectation.

= (2) The intention of a writer or speaker converted into the action of selecting an existing text or creating a new text for transmission to a recipient. Providing a text with an intention means that the writer has made certain presuppositions and assumptions about the reader's expectation.

Reception = the act of interpreting a linguistic form in order to understand its content and the sender's intention.

Reduced text = a text whose volume is less than a text from which it has been derived.

Redundancy = the repetition of information in a message for reasons of linguistic necessity or deliberate intention.

Referential meaning = the type of meaning that attaches to words and terms which represents abstractions of naturally occurring phenomena of the real world.

Relevance = a concept developed by Sperber and Wilson (1990) for determining the functionality of a text.

Report = a broad class of texts, characterised by the fact that they refer to events or situations prior to the act of writing and that they are commissioned pieces of writing.

Examples: book reviews, accident reports, minutes of meetings.

Restricted language = a language created by deliberate restriction of the forms and functions of a natural language to a more efficient, though functionally limited, instrument by means of the selection of a limited set of grammatical structures, lexical items and meanings.

Role = the social position adopted by a participant in a speech act. A role shifts with a change in rank.

Scanning = a technique of knowledge acquisition by which a text is read cursorily in order to capture its main line of argument or its main elements of information.

Schedule = a generic class of text type characterised by the listing of items in chronological, alphabetical or other pre-established order with a minimum of syntactic means.
Examples: indexes, timetables, part lists.

Secondary reader = the person(s) not addressed by a writer's intention, but who nevertheless reads the message addressed to a primary reader.

Situation = in communication theory, the conjunction of a speaker/writer, listener/reader around a topic of communication with their appropriate temporal and spatial circumstances.

Situational factors = in industrial translation, a type of variable, external specification influencing the translation method.

Source language (SL) = the language of the text to be translated. See also: target language.

Specifications = the written or unwritten instructions accompanying a translation task indicating a set of requirements to be satisfied by the product, together with the information necessary for carrying out the instructions. Specifications must indicate the target language, the text type and the intention of the new document.

Speech act = intelligible human interaction performed by means of speech signals.

Speech analysis = in computational linguistics, the computational process of breaking down units of spoken language for the purpose of their description, conversion or understanding.

Spelling checker = in IT, a program that scans a document and notifies words that do not match the list of acceptable spellings stored on the verification program.

Status = (1) the position of superiority, equality or inferiority adopted in the occupational role on a permanent or a temporary basis for the purpose of communication.
= (2) the relation between source and target language document regarding functional completeness.

Stimulus = the psychological trigger that motivates the deliberate and conscious use of linguistic means for meaningful ideation or communication.

Style checker = in IT, a tool that scans a document and notifies any aspects of the style of a text that could be improved by bringing it into line with an image of an adequate text for the desired purpose, stored in the computer.

Subject field = a homogenous area of knowledge, characterised by a closely integrated conceptual structure. *Synonym*: domain, discipline.

Sublanguage = (1) all the linguistic elements (grammar, lexicon, phonology, pragmatics) that constitute the means of ideation, classification and communication of a particular social or professional community.
= (2) an area of language usage characterised by cohesiveness of topic and conformity to established knowledge structures.

Summary = a derived text consisting of a reduction of an original to a fixed percentage of the original length.

Synthesis = in MT, the module of the process concerned with the production of a target language text, based on the information provided by the analysis and transfer modules.

Target language (TL) = the language into which a source language text is translated.

Term bank = in IT, a tool in the form of an on-line linguistic database specially designed for information concerning terms.

Text = (1) any segment of spoken or written form and content united in a particular text type which is usually highly conventionalised.
= (2) a pretheoretical concept characterising any stretch of written or spoken language considered for analysis or other handling at any one time.

Text critiquing = in IT, the analytic operation whereby a text is assessed for such features as general legibility or more particularly, consistency, coherence, structure or sequence of ideas.

Text editing = an analytic operation whereby a text is modified to make it conform to the canons of expression chosen by the editor.

Text type = a combination of historically and socially evolved macrostructures of form, physical presentation and layout of linguistic units, usually associated with speech acts.

Textual factors = in industrial translation, a type of variable, text-conditioned specification, such as the initial status of the source language text, the relationship between the source and target language texts or the new status of the target language text.

Textuality = the property which characterises the unit of a written message.

Thesaurus = a listing of lexical units according to semantic principles.

Topic = (1) the primary area of knowledge or experience from which the concepts are chosen for expression in linguistic form.
= (2) the subject of what is being talked or written about.

Transfer = (1) in MT, the phase in the process which connects analysis and generation and in which a representation of content and form in the source language is changed into a representation of content and form in the target language.

= (2) a process of dealing contrastively with lexical and structural equivalents.

Transfer system = in MT, a type of system operating in three stages of monolingual analysis, bilingual or multilingual transfer and monolingual synthesis.

Transformation = the process of modifying a text as a result of redefining the intention of a message.

Translatability = the condition of a textual unit of having a pragmatic, semantic and linguistic equivalent in a target language.

Translation = an externally motivated linguistic process, occasioned by a particular barrier in communication, consisting of the re-expression of units of discourse, written in a sublanguage of a natural (source) language, in a suitable sublanguage of a second (target) language, so that they become appropriate to a new communicative situation.

Subject Index

(Reference is to sections of the text)

R

S

T

Author Index

In the BENJAMINS TRANSLATION LIBRARY the following titles have been published thus far or are scheduled to appear in the course of 1994:

1. SAGER, Juan C: *Language Engineering and Translation: Consequences of automation*, 1994.
2. SNELL-HORNBY, Mary, Franz POCHHACKER and Klaus KAINDL (eds): *Translation Studies: An interdiscipline*. Selected papers from the Translation Congress, Vienna, 9-12 September 1992. 1994.
3. LAMBERT, Sylvie and Barbara MOSER-MERCER (eds): *Bridging the Gap: Empirical research on simultaneous interpretation*. 1994.
4. TOURY, Gideon: *Descriptive Translation Studies — and beyond*. 1994.
5. DOLLERUP, Cay and Annette LINDEGAARD (eds): *Teaching Translation and Interpreting 2: Insights, aims, visions*. Selected papers from the Second *Language International* Conference, Elsinore, 4-6 June 1993. 1994.